CHINA POP!

CHINA POP!

POP CULTURE, PROPAGANDA, PACIFIC POP-UPS

Sheng-mei Ma

THE OHIO STATE UNIVERSITY PRESS
COLUMBUS

Copyright © 2024 by The Ohio State University.
All rights reserved.

Library of Congress Cataloging-in-Publication Data
Names: Ma, Sheng-mei, author.
Title: China pop! : pop culture, propaganda, Pacific pop-ups / Sheng-mei Ma.
Description: Columbus : The Ohio State University Press, [2024] | Includes bibliographical references and index. | Summary: "Takes an autotheoretical approach to critiquing the propaganda embedded in millennial Chinese pop culture, particularly TV dramas, films, and web novels, from both within and outside China"—Provided by publisher.
Identifiers: LCCN 2024030302 | ISBN 9780814215760 (hardback) | ISBN 0814215769 (hardback) | ISBN 9780814283783 (ebook) | ISBN 0814283780 (ebook)
Subjects: LCSH: Popular culture—China. | Propaganda, Chinese—History. | China—Social life and customs.
Classification: LCC DS727 .M3 2024 | DDC 306.0951—dc23/eng/20240806
LC record available at https://lccn.loc.gov/2024030302

Other identifiers: ISBN 9780814259306 (paperback) | ISBN 0814259308 (paperback)

Cover design by Brock Book Design Co.
Text design by Juliet Williams
Type set in Adobe Minion Pro

♾ The paper used in this publication meets the minimum requirements of the American National Standard for Information Sciences—Permanence of Paper for Printed Library Materials. ANSI Z39.48-1992.

CONTENTS

List of Illustrations   vii

Acknowledgments   xi

INTRODUCTION   1

PART 1	CHINESE POP CULTURE AND PROPAGANDA	
CHAPTER 1	The Art of Propaganda: Some TV Series circa the Chinese Communist Party Centennial	9
CHAPTER 2	Triangulating TV Series of Melodramatic Dialectic "with Chinese Characteristics": Gamblin' Professionals in Cities; Goth and Darwin in the Wild West	29
CHAPTER 3	The Ghost of *Guimi* from Imperial to Millennial China	52

PART 2	ON THE CULTURAL REVOLUTION	
CHAPTER 4	Six Million Jews and How Many Chinese: "Ten-Year Holocaust" of the Cultural Revolution	77
CHAPTER 5	The Subtitle Wagging the Screen: The Untranslated and *One Second*	94
CHAPTER 6	*Laosanjie* Peers Back at the Red Sun: Zhang Yimou of the "Chain Gang"	101

PART 3	WHITE POP-UPS	
CHAPTER 7	Brechtian AlienAsian: Socialist Ex Machina from *The Good Woman of Setzuan* and David Hare's *Fanshen*	119
CHAPTER 8	Love in a Falling City: David Hare's *Saigon* and the Musical *Miss Saigon*	137
CHAPTER 9	Eastern Witch from the West: Xianniang in Niki Caro's *Mulan*	152
PART 4	OFF-WHITE POP-UPS	
CHAPTER 10	Chinatown Comedy unto Itself	165
CHAPTER 11	Southern Woe, Minority Lens: Ride with Woodrell–Schamus–Ang Lee	191
CHAPTER 12	Bipolar America: The Anti-Asian versus *Minari*	204
CODA	Refugees with Guns, *Laobing* with Phallus: Ghost of Taiwan circa 1949	216

Works Cited		239
Index		253

ILLUSTRATIONS

FIGURE 1.1	*Minning Town*'s opening credits dedicated to the CCP Centennial	13
FIGURE 1.2	Qin Chi's rare toothy grin in *Reborn*	15
FIGURE 1.3	Qin Chi guesses Chen Rui's identity in *Reborn*	16
FIGURE 1.4	Qin Chi wrests the blood-stained knife out of Chen Rui's hand in *Reborn*	17
FIGURE 1.5	Chen Rui's bare feet under the pink bathrobe in *Reborn*	18
FIGURE 1.6	The propaganda intertitle in the closing moments of *Reborn*'s episode 28	20
FIGURE 1.7	The propaganda poster displayed on the wall of the police station in *To Be with You*	21
FIGURE 1.8	Rayzha Alimjan gives a resigned farewell to her lover in *Minning Town*	24
FIGURE 1.9	The son holds on to the shoe raised against him in *Minning Town*	26
FIGURE 1.10	Ma Defu repaints the old village name, Springing Well Village, in *Minning Town*	27
FIGURE 2.1	Xia Ming shields Su Xiao's innocent eyes from the scuffle in *The Ideal City*	35

FIGURE 2.2	Su Xiao appeals to the board in *The Ideal City*	37
FIGURE 2.3	Wu Hongmei sobs in the company restroom in *The Ideal City*	38
FIGURE 2.4	The montage of Su Xiao's surprised face and her mental screens in *The Ideal City*	40
FIGURE 2.5	Wu Hongmei climbs the stairs of her dilapidated *nongtang* in *The Ideal City*	42
FIGURE 2.6	The montage of 2020 and 1939 in *Rattan*	45
FIGURE 2.7	A long shot establishing the motif of doubleness in *Rattan*	45
FIGURE 2.8	Qin Fang tying Siteng's boots in *Rattan*	48
FIGURE 3.1	Episode 9 of *Thirty* and episode 41 of *Twenty* reprise the same scene where the *guimi* of the latter series chance upon the *guimi* of the former series	71
FIGURE 3.2	*Thirty*'s start menu for episode 1, where the character Wang Manni hugs herself	71
FIGURE 6.1	One of Little Bun's pet chicks held up from their nest in the empty trunk that once contained shadow puppets in *To Live*	109
FIGURE 6.2	A Nationalist soldier's bayonet rips the puppetry screen in *To Live*	110
FIGURE 6.3	The newlyweds and the parents are photographed between the wall painting of Mao and a cardboard ship christened "The East Is Red" in *To Live*	113
FIGURE 6.4	The "reactionary" Dr. Wang being marched to the hospital in *To Live*	114
FIGURE 8.1	Bob's gifts for Nhieu and the girl in *Saigon: The Year of the Cat*	143
FIGURE 8.2	The US ambassador dreams of securing military aid and a satisfactory conclusion to the armed conflict in *Saigon*	144
FIGURE 8.3	Dame Judi Dench's Barbara Dean looks off-frame instead of at the camera as she exits scene 32 in *Saigon*	146
FIGURE 8.4	The Vietnamese crouch by the embassy gate as the helicopter roars off in *Miss Saigon*	149
FIGURE 8.5	Ellen comforts Chris as Kim solos downstage in *Miss Saigon*	149
FIGURE 8.6	John sings of the misery of mixed-race Bui-Doi in *Miss Saigon*	150

FIGURE 9.1	The shaman or "Great Wizard" in *Matchless Mulan*	154
FIGURE 9.2	Hawk urges Mulan to join forces in Niki Caro's *Mulan*	158
FIGURE 9.3	Hawk dives down to take the arrow in order to save Mulan	160
FIGURE 9.4	The phoenix rises with wings extending from Mulan's shoulders	161
FIGURE 11.1	A Southern wedding at the Chiles estate in *Ride with the Devil*	197
FIGURE 11.2	Ang Lee's extreme close-up of Jake's bloody hand in *Ride with the Devil*	198
FIGURE 12.1	Jay Baker's Facebook post with the image of a Sinophobic T-shirt	207
FIGURE 12.2	David and his father, Jacob, squat to gather water celery in *Minari*	214
FIGURE 13.1	The *laobing* janitor Uncle Gao's facial disfigurement in the horror film *Detention*	235

ACKNOWLEDGMENTS

The birth of *China Pop!* hinged on generous HARP grants from Michigan State University, for which I am grateful. Early drafts of several chapters appeared in *Rising Asia Journal, Journal of Comparative Literature and Aesthetics, Comparative Drama, Americana, Neo-Disneyism, Mississippi Quarterly,* and *Media in Asia.* I am thankful to the journal and book editors.

INTRODUCTION

Should I open this Anglophone intellectual feast on Chineseness according to the Western routine of an hors d'oeuvre or to the Chinese routine of the entrée itself? Just as topsy-turvy, the Chinese pop culture that initiates this feast is as crowd-pleasing as a Western dessert or Cantonese sugar water at the end rather than the beginning of a meal. East-West comparative studies countenance such delightful (con)fusion. Seen from the other side, table manners and dining etiquette are all awry, even upside down. All awry is all right, given the cross-cultural, interdisciplinary, and transgeneric project, much preferable to the fixation on, even ossification of, order in any given, graven system. Unabashedly, if you please, *China Pop!* runs its tongue over millennial Chinese pop culture, particularly TV dramas, films, and web novels, images streamed or words uploaded online like complimentary sweet popsicles for over one billion Sinophone consumers in China and in diaspora—even beyond with the additive of English subtitles and translations. Just as thrilling as the brain freeze fed by the hand, so does the screen tantalize, even addict. Periodic ads notwithstanding, Chinese visual culture airs almost in real time across the globe, tantamount to "free lunch," free nightcap or daily fix, rather, for afterwork nonstop bingeing of multiple-episode TV series.

This manna fallen from the Fatherland, this opiate from the largesse of the sugar daddy, turns viewers into lotus-eaters insensate to, à la Morpheus's clue to Neo, the "silk" pulled over their eyes. As a riposte, *China Pop!* pops Pop's poppies; it detonates Our Heavenly Baba's seductive art of propaganda, His mesmerizing digital light show on the screens. The propaganda machinery has churned out countless TV series circa the Chinese Communist Party Centennial in 2021, yet with amazing flashes of aesthetic sensibility. The official organ of China Central Television (CCTV) energizes series celebrating past policies as well as present triumphalism, including COVID-19. Serendipitously, CCTV puns with closed-circuit television for surveillance. Watching the shows, the viewers are washed over by sentiments, explicit or subliminal, remote controlled by Beijing.

Manifesting its drive in the "Chinese Century," the national frenzy over being the alpha wolf culminates in "gamblin'" professionals in popular culture "with Chinese Characteristics" and a drivenness befitting survival of the fittest. Dialectically opposite to, and spatially west of, the secular, realist setting in urban China, *yao* or monsters populate the gothic genre of web novels and period dramas. Likewise, naturalist struggles unfold in China's Wild West in the vein of Hollywood westerns. Both gothic and naturalist TV series present escapist reveries from the shackles of ideology. Yet both suggest escape artists Sinologizing not only China's exotic Orient of westernmost minority cultures but also Western theories of gothic supernaturalism and Darwinian naturalism. In the land where "women hold up half the sky," TV series also grace us with a womance of *guimi* (boudoir confidantes), a close-knit network in life's struggle in a promised land of mammonism and masculinism.

This China blowup, this sound licking, ricochets in time and space, in China and elsewhere. The Chinese Communist Party propaganda extends backward, from part 1's millennial TV series to part 2's narrative revisionism over the "Ten-Year Holocaust" of the Cultural Revolution, contrary to the testimonial, documentary nature of its namesake, Holocaust literature. Starkly contrasted are two survivors'—Yang Jiang and Elie Wiesel—gazes at the respective historical abysses. Yang's backward glance is fleeting, self-censored to avoid becoming, once again, the hunted; the haunted Wiesel, on the other hand, sustains a lifelong ritual of remembrance. Likewise, China's collective memory of decades of Maoist extremism peeks through the fifth-generation and *laosanjie* ("old three years") filmmaker Zhang Yimou of the "chain gang," as it were, who has revisited political campaigns in some films widely distributed and officially sanctioned, and some other films banned.

This popped China extends as much backward diachronically as it spreads synchronically like a spatial enlargement in part 3, "White Pop-Ups." The millennial explosion of Chineseness has flung pieces of molten "otherness" worldwide, not only across the Pacific Ocean to splash over and "yellow" the promised land but also in Europe. "Pacific Pop-Ups" is no abstract alliteration or space filler; it signals concrete reifications of cultural and psychic currents. It is, after all, the title's "last word." For instance, given Marxist privileging of systemic class struggle, *China Pop!* has long spewed beyond China proper among white radicals on their quest for alternatives globally. Amid cities falling to communist insurgency, from Shanghai to Hong Kong to Saigon, universal love of romance between white(-ish) man and Asian(-ish) woman accentuates itself against mass destruction. The rage of revolutionary zeal across the globe predates armed conflicts, taking the form of an ideological tug of war. A dramaturgical iconoclast, Bertolt Brecht's alienation-effect seeks to modernize the stage and compel social action, his muse a Peking Opera female impersonator. The theory of A-effect displaces the playwright's sense of distance from Asian stylization. What is taken for granted in traditional Chinese performativity looks so novel and defamiliarizing that Brecht projects therein his epoch-making apocalyptic vision of epic theater. This progressive, left-leaning Orientalism is inherited by the socialist David Hare in his early agitprop and populist plays. Its commercial interests parallel to the German auteur's activism, Disney remakes *Mulan* as live-action mass entertainment, replenishing the new bottle from the West with the same old banalities of a mystical Orient.

"Jumping" to America, *China Pop!* in part 4, "Off-White Pop-Ups," traces one particular strain, namely, trans-Pacific pop-ups of Asian immigrant characters in the hands of mainstream white as well as "off-white," honorary-white Asian American artists. No longer just a spatial multiplication, white America and off-white Asian America internalize the amorphous Chineseness to advance their respective artistic visions reminiscent of erstwhile Orientalism. Hence, Asian immigrant straw man and woman materialize and vanish in the service of ethnic identity. Earlier still, the ancient virus for New America's pop-ups traveled across the Atlantic from Old Europe, carrying strains of Yellow Peril and celestial fetish, as in Brecht and Hare. Strewn across continents and seas are the detritus of blasted stereotypes old and new, and of patriarchal ideologies communist and capitalist. For Asian America in particular, Asianness is subconsciously fetishized, both lost in Americanization and found in romanticized ethnicity, both shunned in the image of alien (grand) parents and shining as Brechtian-ethnic creative roots. The genre of Chinatown comedies of Louis Chu, Wayne Wang, Alice Wu, and Lulu Wang comes to hinge on the paradox of roots/ruse. Language being the cultural taproot, Anglophone writers and filmmakers ventriloquize in English an Asian fictitious universe. Readers and viewers are all in on this representational dissembling. Among the rarest of success by immigrant artists, such as Ang Lee, they speak not so much for themselves as channel collective energy, as potent as

Hollywood, through adaptations and artistry. In this new millennium, both white and off-white pop-ups arise in a bipolar America, half of which lashes out in anti-Asian hate crimes, and the other half compensates by favoring transplants like *Minari* (2021), named after Chinese water celery deemed an invasive species to native plants and nativists.

Mixed metaphors from China's art of propaganda to America's minari are the Manifest Destiny of a book on East-West (con)fusion. The opening figure of speech of an apparently red, white, and off-white (yellow-ish) popsicle being consumed cross-dissolves hereby into a tricolored balloon being popped: an incremental attrition of one lick at a time gone puff, Buddhist gradual illuminations (*jianwu*) obliterated in one singular Zen epiphany (*dunwu*). Gone in one conceptual burst are the red of Communist China's self-inflation; the white of Orientalist, chinoiserie fallacy; and the off-white Asian American self-fetishization. *China Pop!* cancels a triptych construct: the fade-in of the "Chinese Century"; the fade-out of American exceptionalism; and the ethnic enigma of Asian America. In concert with my labor of love over the span of several decades, here is one last book unbecoming to purists and traditionalists, the runt—not just the "last-born" but perhaps the most unseemly to fellow academics—of a brood of over a dozen boundary-crossing, species-defying *Sibuxiang* (四不像), or Four-Unlikes, hybrid unheimlich with mixed blood.

Indulge me to "get personal," literally, in these last words from my professional litter: *China Pop!* is a thinly veiled transference of my own history of mainland Chinese parents fleeing—in the perpetual present tense—a popped China in 1949, of coming of age in Taiwan, and of diasporic half-lives in the US as neither an "authentic" Sinologist from China, nor a "natural" Asian Americanist birthed and PhD-ed, preferably, in California and the Ivy League, nor even a "genuine" Taiwanese able to speak the Taiwanese dialect. Overarching tensions among the book's four parts, within each chapter—each paragraph or sentence, for that matter, like this one—split between opposites, and textual open-endedness reveal a state of cultural and personal precariousness, existentially unresolved "honest doubt," in Tennyson's words, more truthful than some experts' good fakes, tactical feints.

Out of my dozen-strong litter, each Four-Unlike evokes the half-human, half-swine Pigsy of *Journey to the West* fame, as the Chinese folk saying goes: "Pigsy looks into the mirror, neither a human inside nor outside the reflection"—a likeness that no one likes, for it looks like no one. Why such untrammeled incongruity, muse purists, when the popsicle tastes like neither apples nor oranges, and the balloon looks like an eyesore of a crazy quilt? Why juxtapose at all China's pop culture versus Anglo-America's versus Asian

America's, notwithstanding the through line of "Pop!"—Eastern and Western Pops' popsicles of pop culture and agitprop, all psychological props, all narcotic poppies now popped? Why that exclamation mark to signal Action rather than State, dynamics rather than stasis? Why not focus solely on, per the book title, Chinese pop culture, a readily recognizable area of academic pursuit? Why not cut off, quip land creatures without sea legs, one of the book's legs straddling, bonded to, either shore of the Pacific?

Because that is the one world whence *China Pop!* came, within which it exists, and to which it will (d)evolve, bomb debris and all. Seemingly in pieces, the world remains still in one piece, hopefully in peace. Straight up like a tombstone for the dead or a monument for the living, the titular exclamation point hints at the double entendre of, on the one hand, the cleaving, splitting of Chineseness and, on the other, the world's cleaving, clinging onto itself, a oneness in a better future opened up by the exclamation. An exclamation is not a full stop to spell the end; rather, it cries out in limbo, awaiting sentence or judgment as well as the next sentence, such as this book's subtitle. Indeed, what pops up in China is blown elsewhere; pop-ups elsewhere in the name of China blow right back. Any simplistic compartmentalization favored by traditionalists would be a true monstrosity, an anemic dud from the transnational perspective lodged among and nurtured by cultures, languages, and fields of study. Therefore, to critique *China Pop!* for not focusing exclusively on China is to be blind to, among other things, the fact that this construct of China comes to us in English, heading a swarm of academic English that sounds like plain gibberish to ordinary Chinese, or Americans, for that matter. To insist on a symmetry between the geopolitical entity of China and the discursive afterlife of Chineseness in the Anglophone world is regressive.

Neither an Old China Hand nor a New Americanist, let alone an Asian Americanist, more than any single China Hand or (Asian) Americanist, I pass on this bare thread once tied to a colorful balloon, this sticky stick left by triple sugar highs, to the one who smiles back, reading this line, if not here and now, then somewhere someday. No Buddha's silent sermon holding an unnamed flower: this is a paper folding of an imitation flower crawling with English words on Chineseness, the Sinitic Anglicized, the Anglo Sinologized, the two morphing uneasily back and forth. A certain beauty over nothingness lingers in wokeness, drained of dreams, which gave so much pleasure while they lasted.

Balancing on the East-West cultural tightrope, *China Pop!* consists of four parts, each part with three to four chapters. Part 1 demonstrates in interconnected chapters the splicing of Chinese pop culture and propaganda. Part 2 zooms in on one motif that recurs due to its traumatic shock: the Cultural

Revolution. Part 3 jumps the Pacific to parse white pop-ups of revolutionary and commercial zeal inspired, allegedly, by China. Part 4 concludes with off-white, Asian American pop-ups of ethnic comedies and survival strategies. The coda resuscitates one particular group in flight from a China that popped in 1949: *laobing* (old soldiers) retreated en masse to Taiwan, often demonized as sexual predators in their dotage. *China Pop!* decomposes in hope of reconstitution. To subvert constructed realities, *China Pop!* conjures up their shadows wisping, whispering through Chinese popular culture, propaganda, Cultural Revolution discourse, and white and off-white Pacific pop-ups. Even China's "ghost island" of Taiwan is haunted by its own revenant of laobing. In return, a Taiwanese American immigrant's "ghost continent" of China flits across these pages like a good old spook. "Boo!" to vanity of both Chinese and American supremacy from this subaltern Four-Unlike, particularly when boo's homonymic doppelganger *bu* (no, un-) lives within si*bu*xiang.

PART 1

CHINESE POP CULTURE AND PROPAGANDA

CHAPTER 1

The Art of Propaganda

Some TV Series circa the Chinese Communist Party Centennial

Founded in 1921, the Chinese Communist Party (CCP) has had a hundred years to perfect its propaganda apparatus. Dictated by Chairman Mao Zedong's 1942 "Talks at the Yan'an Conference on Literature and Art" and the slogan "Serve the People," propaganda and art are the conjoint Sino-ese twins: art serving at the pleasure of the State, or "a culture army" in support of the "armed front" in national liberation (McDougall [1980] 57). Propaganda has been the ball and chain to art in its century-long incarceration. Mao's "Yan'an Talks" stipulated that art exists to advance politics, a dictum crystallized in *Quotations from Chairman Mao Zedong* or *The Little Red Book*, the Great Proletarian Cultural Revolution Bible that was all the "rage": "A revolution is an insurrection, a violent action by one class of people to overthrow another class," namely, the proletariat of workers, peasants, and soldiers—plus gullible Red Guards—taking over control in a perpetual bloodletting called revolution. The power elite to be toppled consists of counterrevolutionaries, among other stigmatized categories at any given moment of the "dictatorship of the proletariat." Revolution Incarnate was how the founding father Mao envisaged the People's Republic of China. Mao's Revolution, however, is Artless, or R-less, lapsing into mere Evolution, even corrupted into Devolution. Despite its genetic predisposition for degeneration, that Maoist ideology continues to hold sway posthumously. On June 4, 1989, Deng Xiaoping justified the crackdown against demonstrators labeled "counterrevolutionaries" at the

Tiananmen Square. Among other surveillance and repressive measures in the new millennium, Xi Jinping rationalized Xinjiang concentration camps in the name of a benevolent healing of errant Uighur minds and poverty-stricken lands.

R-Less Revolution: The Art of Heeling
Shanzhai, China's Outlawry

This so-called healing is but heeling, bringing to heel Beijing protesters and Uighur Muslims, if not to decimate any dissent and minority cultures. The self-proclaimed revolutions by Mao, Deng, and Xi constitute not so much eternal Marxist class struggle for the communist utopia. Instead, they amount to Revolution decapitated, with its capital R off, descending into evolution. Worse still, they reverse the course of history into devolution, devolving into Lu Xun's[1] social Darwinism of "man-eat-man" ("Madman's Diary" 1918).[2] The historic convulsion of the PRC in theory belies a gradual adaptation, even sclerotic ossification, of China's imperial and feudal tradition. Revolution is worn by various emperors as their new clothes, a raw prevarication by potentates orchestrating the "Chinese Century." Mao's revolutionary China evolves, rather than departs, from the past; it devolves into the past, including chronically heeling insurgent hero(ine)s in the name of healing them. Ostensibly an absolute, scorched-earth break, Mao's revolution is at best a flash in the revolving door of history.

Rather than demolishing history to remake China, the Mao Inc. taps into, flush with foreign investment from Marxism-Leninism, the *laozihao* (老字號 centuries-old brands) of *shanzhai* (山寨), China's outlawry. Shanzhai literally means mountain fortress and hideout of imperial-era bandits in opposition to the established government and its law. In contemporary usage, shanzhai has come to denote counterfeit products or any practice that imitates and parodies the real, creating an alternate reality. Classical Chinese novels are rife with such shanzhai-style heroes, rebellious and destructive at first, eventually

---

1. Chinese names in this book comply with the Chinese order of last name followed by first name, except in cases where authors or artists have Anglicized their names.

2. Deemed the father of modern Chinese literature, Lu Xun turns endocannibalism into a metaphor to critique Chinese tradition in "A Madman's Diary." The madman believes that not only the villagers but his own family members have acquired the physiognomy of typical Chinese demons, looking "Green-faced, long-toothed," eating human "heart and liver" (9). Far from delusion, the protagonist is struck by visions of a mad prophet, as the title "Kuangren" (madman) suggests. "Kuang" implies as much the ecstatic and the visionary as the crazed. Lu Xun could have entitled it "Fengzi," which would point more unambiguously to mental instability or madness.

returning to serve the royal court. Wu Cheng'en's sixteenth-century *Journey to the West* (*Monkey*) opens with the Monkey King's path of rambunctiousness until the Buddha subjugates him and tasks him to safeguard the monk Tripitaka in the pilgrimage to India. Likewise, the Boy God Nezha from Lu Xixing and Xu Zhonglin's sixteenth-century *Creation of the Gods* experiences a symbolic death to be reborn into a good, tamed retainer of the authority. One of Mao's favorite classics, Shi Nai'an's fourteenth-century *The Outlaws of the Marsh* sings of anti-establishment exploits of one hundred and eight outlaws, yet Shi's seventy-one chapters were subsequently edited by Luo Guanzhong and possibly expanded to one hundred chapters. In Luo's hands, the outlaws undergo *piaobai*, a Chinese buzzword for having been bleached clean or whitewashed (yellowwashed?). The strays of outlaws return to the imperial fold in the fight against invading Liao "barbarians" from the north and the domestic rebel Fang La in the south. These classics exemplify the conundrum of revolution, either rise-and-fall, or fall-and-rise, depending on one's perspective. Seen from the haves at the center and in the mainstream, shanzhai renegades wreak havoc for self-aggrandizing, subsequently mellowing into and healed as self-sacrificing heroes. Seen from the have-nots at the bottom and in the fringes, heroes ascend to smash the chains of enslavement, only to be heeled by the master.

In his self-promotional life story shared with Edgar Snow in *Red Star over China* (1938), Mao signals a turning point toward revolution by recalling a case of shanzhai in his younger days. A secret society, "Ge Lao Hui" (Elder Brother Society), is said to have "rebelled against the landlord and the government and withdrawn to a local mountain called Liu Shan, where they built a stronghold" (120). Mao reprised a Ke Lao Hui–style retreat in the Long March of 1934–35 from Jiangxi in the south to Shaanxi in the north. The destination of the Long March, Yan'an, epitomizes shanzhai, an inaccessible mountain sanctuary full of caves, a natural defense against Chiang Kai-shek's overwhelming Nationalist forces. Theoretically, Mao's genius lies in requisitioning half the topos of shanzhai—the early rebel, forever young and passionate—while relinquishing the late servant to the crown. His ultimate sleight of hand turns himself into the crown for all rebels, certainly the Red Guards doing his bidding of "Demolishing Four Olds" or struggling against "Ox Ghost Snake Spirit," those deemed a threat to Mao's supremacy.[3]

The communist valorizing of shanzhai with the prominent gene of Artless Revolution reaches across gender lines in millennial Chinese TV period dramas where heroines of swordswoman, doctress (as in *The Imperial Doctress*

---

3. The Maoist revolution is certainly not restricted to China proper. It radiates to the third world with great zeal, chronicled in Julia Lovell's *Maoism: A Global History* (2019).

2016), coroner (*Miss Truth* 2020), and scholar (*The Chang'an Youth* 2020) flash in cross-dressing glamor like a magic lantern before settling into traditional feminine roles, akin to their male counterparts in historical and fantasy novels. These shows' initial episodes of transitory transvestism crystallize in *Weaving a Tale of Love* (2021), where the protagonist, played by the Caucasian-looking Gülnezer Bextiyar of Uighur extraction, triples as a doctor, coroner, and seamster, all in male attire. Gülnezer is one of a host of ethnic female performers for the eye of the majority Han population. On the one hand, "feral" Uighur males are locked up and some female detainees tortured and gang-raped, as reported by Hill et al. in the BBC's "'Their Goal Is to Destroy Everyone'" on February 3, 2021. On the other, Uighur beauties like Gülnezer, all speaking perfect Beijingnese, for they were trained at the Beijing Film Academy or the Central Academy of Drama, substitute for whites in China's neurosis of idolizing and subjugating, loving and hating, the West, a West that is tonic and toxic at once. The fair-skinned, Western-looking body of Gülnezer speaks like and belongs to the Chinese public. Uighur prisoners versus Uighur beauties form one of the many split screens of China: the young firebrand Mao versus "Emperor" Mao; communist state surveillance versus capitalist free market; fantasy and hyperreal escapism in TV series versus social realism in independent filmmaking. Even in the quintessential Chinese director Zhang Yimou, his career straddles red films of *Red Sorghum* (1988), *Ju Dou* (1990), *Raise the Red Lantern* (1991), the opening and closing ceremonies of the 2008 Olympics, *The Great Wall* (2016), and other commercial, self-Orientalizing works as well as, paradoxically, such politically sensitive films on the Cultural Revolution teetering on being censored as *Coming Home* (2014) and *One Second* (2020, banned initially).

Psychological complexity of Gülnezer's fair complexion aside, this Taming of the Chinese Shrew feigns gender equity at the outset as the heroines not only impersonate but also surpass their male peers. Invariably, though, they take up socially endorsed, even state- or male-assigned positions. Devoid of religion amid Marxist materialism, these heroines function as the heroin of the masses, taking viewers on a hallucinogenic trip out of the status quo to a wish-fulfilling, time-killing circus, food to numb the mind, only to land them right back for another day in the Darwinian China.

Reborn, *Minning Town*, and *To Be with You*

Contrary to the dreamscape of period dramas by Gülnezer et al., two recent TV series of relative social realism, the 28-episode *Reborn* (*Chongsheng* 重生 2020) and the 23-episode *Minning Town* (閩寧鎮 changed in Chinese to *Shanhai Qing* 山海情 2021), come to epitomize the art of propaganda, where the Sino-ese twins are far from Oriental freaks, where state policies are transubstantiated into gold by the touch of art. A Johnny-come-lately is the 36-episode TV series *To Be with You* (約定 2021), joining the party of Party-exalting under the auspices of the national campaign *Gongfu Xiaokang* (Striving Together for Moderate Prosperity). A dual gesture, *xiaokang*—modest or relative wealth—beckons the poor rural communities to move economically in situ to the well-off middle class instead of indiscriminate migrating en masse to the coastal metropolis.

In theory, *Reborn* eulogizes China's *gong'an* (Public Security or the Police), and *Minning Town* has opening credits dedicated to the CCP Centennial. Figure 1.1 captures practically the very first frame of *Minning Town* that anchors the series in the national festivity of the centennial. The bottom of figure 1.1 lays out the dates 1921 and 2021, which flank the pan-communist symbol as well as the CCP emblem of the hammer and sickle. *Minning Town* commemorates by way of a chronicle of the 1990s national campaign of *Fupin* (扶貧 Support the Poor or Poverty Alleviation). To be exact, that campaign involves the affluent coastal province of Fujian exporting agricultural expertise and financial aid to the desolate Ningxia province nearly 1,300 miles away on the edge of Inner Mongolia's desert, while importing Ningxia peasants to work in Fujian electronics and apparel factories. The revised Chinese title *Shanhai Qing* (山海情 Mountain-Sea Love) plays on the alliance between the mountainous interior and the seaboard province. This is a massive internal migration between the coastal labor market and the impoverished hinterland. One hastens to add that the campaign was partly engineered by none other than Fujian's then deputy Party secretary Xi Jinping, China's Red Sun or president for life.

FIGURE 1.1. *Minning Town*'s opening credits dedicated to the CCP Centennial.

In practice, though, these TV series manage to probe into individual psychology—repression and taboo—despite political messaging. They embrace the "brand" of propaganda, which is the reality they inhabit, in order to "branch" out from that reality, if not to "breach" it altogether. *Reborn* opens in medias res with a police officer, Qin Chi, suffering from multiple gunshot wounds and PTSD over having lost all his team in a firefight. His survivor guilt is compounded by his amnesia over whether or not his careerist opportunism resulted in the armed confrontation. Worse still, he suspects that he was the underworld's mole who betrayed his fallen comrades. In this scenario, he hypothesizes that his near-death injury was subsequently inflicted by a rivaling gang's assassin, whose execution-style bullets differed from the ballistics of all other shots. Zhang Yi's tour de force performance as Qin Chi renders the protagonist an "undead," with no memory yet with a suicidal wish so deep that he welcomes a teenage girl's avenging knife. (Zhang Yi excels again playing an escapee from a Cultural Revolution labor camp in search of a prefilm propaganda newsreel where his deceased daughter cameoed for a split second in *One Second*.[4]) The young girl turns out to be Chen Rui, the sister of the villain whom Qin Chi slayed. An ambiguous, pseudo-Electra attachment develops between the father figure and his destroyer, who later evolves into his charge suspected at one point by Qin's ex-wife to be his young lover.[5] Rui is a pun for the young "bud," in the third tone Ruǐ, of love poised to bloom and for the "sharp," in the fourth tone Ruì, tip of the knife finding its way into Qin's abdomen.

A sepulchral walking dead throughout the series, Qin smiles but once, an almost grotesque grin of a skull in episode 25 when he promises a speedy return to his assassin-ward. He departs only to complete his death wish. Figure 1.2 captures Qin's rare toothy grin, feigning a hilarity heretofore unseen. On the heels of that singular sighting, Qin follows up with a lie: "Don't forget I want a new life too." The subtitle roughly approximates the line *biewangji woyeyao huanyizhong fangshihuo* (Don't forget I also want to change to another way of living). Technically, not living is indeed "another way" of, an alternative to, living. Ending life belongs to the many choices one makes in life, the choice

---

4. The split screen of China splits the actor Zhang Yi, who doubles as a Korean War hero in *Sacrifice* and as a Cultural Revolution labor camp convict in *One Second,* both premiered in 2020. The former film contributes to the nationalist fervor under President Xi; the latter is banned.

5. In reality, such May–December romance is shared by West and East: Woody Allen and Soon-Yi Previn; Bill Clinton and the White House intern with whom he "did not have sex"; the eighty-two-year-old Nobel laureate Chen Ning Yang and the twenty-eight-year-old Weng Fan, whom the former married in 2004. More recently, New York governor Andrew Cuomo, in his sixties, was accused of propositioning multiple female aides in their twenties.

FIGURE 1.2. Qin Chi's rare toothy grin in *Reborn*.

that ends all choices. It suggests more self-agency than dying of natural causes, yet the Freudian Thanatos, the death drive, goes far beyond, even against, Marxist materialism. The undertone of Maoist martyrdom in memory of his team members serves to veil Qin's "postmortem," a brief afterlife whose sole goal is the self-autopsy of lost memory.

More forbidden by Marxist orthodoxy than the death drive, which is almost a prerequisite in communist martyrdom anyway, the Freudian eros troubles the two leads in repressed, transferred forms. Chen Rui's vengeance commences with the knife thrust into Qin's stomach. The attempted killing ends as soon as it begins, inherent in the pun of commencement for the academic ceremony concluding years of study as well as turning to a new chapter in life. In a top-down totalitarian system, stabbing a police officer "breaks water" from the insufferable weight of politics, stealthily lets flow a bottom-up, bottled-up subconscious urge. The CCP, pregnant for a century, finally gives birth to the "monstrosity" of the Freudian eros, even more monstrous when it is delivered by a young girl's phallic scalpel. Having been robbed of her big brother, Chen finds instead a substitute for big daddy. Should it come from Qin, such impulse would be deemed reprehensible pedophilia. Yet the series generates the entanglement of revenge and dependency from the unstable psyche of the teenage-looking Chen, softening the taboo. Not that Chen's perspective makes the pseudo-incestuous relationship acceptable, but the series teases with moral boundaries while staying safe since the innocent Chen, not the experienced Qin, gives vent to such a trespass, psychologically.

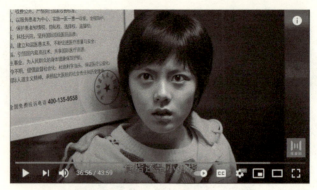

FIGURE 1.3. Qin Chi guesses Chen Rui's identity, warning her that she may lose either her forefinger or pinkie wielding the knife in *Reborn*.

The series of Chen's bungled attempts on Qin's life begins in episode 1 in the underground parking lot at the police station. Tailing and entering the elevator with Qin in episode 2, Chen pretends to be a youngster all wrapped up in her own sonic world of earbuds and iPhone. Qin guesses her identity as the unknown attacker, warning her in figure 1.3 that she may lose either her forefinger or pinkie next time, wielding that knife so amateurishly. Holding the blade with the tip pointing up, Qin deadpans, would result in the severance of the index finger, pointing down that of the pinkie. This quizzical concern for Chen's well-being rather than his own has to be taken within the context of Qin's voice-over. Adrift without memory and self-identity, unable to read the other's reactions, Qin muses to his masochistic self that the assassin's unadulterated hate offers "a sense of security," the raison d'être for his posthumous existence. Not so much vengeance as justice, the girl's knife metes out what he deserves in his own mind.

Quite a match for Qin's performance of death-in-life, Chen is played superbly by Zhao Jinmai, whose facial expressions and body language before and after figure 1.3 undulate, gradationally, between shock and horror of being caught "red-handed" in the elevator and bewilderment over Qin's avuncular lack of hostility. The pimples between the brows accentuate her adolescence. When she does succeed in drawing blood toward the end of episode 2, it ends with Qin wresting the bloodstained weapon from her hand, cutting his rather than her palm. Figure 1.4 culminates her complex performance of a hateful assault and utter helplessness, the contorted face betraying vulnerability and, ultimately, guilt.

The perverse symbiosis of predator and prey continues to unfold outside Qin's apartment. Chen hides in the stairwell day and night for the chance to

FIGURE 1.4. Qin Chi wrests the bloodstained knife out of Chen Rui's hand in *Reborn*.

complete her mission, despite the fact that Qin sustains his "stalker" by purveying her with food, drink, pillow, and blanket, eventually inviting her into his apartment. Apparently haunting her victim, Chen is also haunted by her own conscience over the victim. Chen's vigil to avenge her brother masks the gnawing pain over the psychological void. Both suffer from loss, of memory and of loved ones. Chen's antagonism mellows into transference into a desired patron, if not love for a desired partner. The pseudo-incestuous undercurrent flares up in episode 5 when Qin's ex-wife, drawn close to the amnesiac Qin cleansed of his former sycophantic, deceitful self, brings key evidence to the apartment of her old flame. In spite of her rekindled affection, Qin behaves like a nonresponsive automaton. Her suspicion is aroused when she spies two breakfasts, which is then confirmed when a young Chen steps out of the bedroom with the ex-wife's pink bathrobe neatly folded. One wonders if the slippers Qin later provides also belong to the ex-wife. The ex-wife storms out in jealousy.

By sheer luck, she has missed the scene/sin the night before when Chen, soaking wet after a shower, wore only the pink bathrobe, under which bared a pair of rather ugly feet (figure 1.5). The podiatric uncomeliness in tracking close-ups intimates a potentially unseemly human relationship under the boots of the series' politics. In an authoritarian state, showing a young woman's breasts or thighs in a dubious situation tempts fate. The compromise arrives at pointing the lens downward at the feet, a female organ with such erotic associations accrued from imperial bound feet to modern stilettos that they substitute for the pudenda. Even without the loaded symbolism, the bared feet are undeniably there, in episode 5, if not before. Those feet, albeit henceforth unseen, continue to tread lightly, figuratively throughout the series, leaving traces and hints of repressed emotions.

FIGURE 1.5. Chen Rui's bare feet under the pink bathrobe in *Reborn*.

Episode 6 further flirts with the transgressive motif as Chen stammers out her assumption that Qin "has been out all night" in order to clear up his ex-wife's misunderstanding. Chen does not say this in so many words; she falls silent out of embarrassment over having been (mis)taken for the lover. In the same way Chen stutters and stops, the viewer fills in the blank, inferring from the filmic tease of an eroticism that has transpired imagistically, imaginatively. The art of propaganda lies precisely in its duality, its power of dissembling: it intimates ethical lapses while retaining plausible deniability; it embraces express political messages while trafficking in aesthetic asides. The tracking close-ups of flat feet with crooked toes serve as a case in point. *Reborn*'s production team and actors would no doubt aver that they are mere cinematic formality leading to full-body shots. To rephrase the Michelangelo-riffing ladies in T. S. Eliot's "The Love Song of J. Alfred Prufrock" (1915), the crew of *Reborn* would surely demur: "That is not it [foot fetish] at all, / That is not what I meant, at all." The foot fetish comes into being, so the Chinese claim, as a result of the West's dirty mind in the likes, pun intended, of Freud's "Fetishism" (1927) and Georges Bataille's "The Big Toe" (1929).[6]

---

6. Freud argues in "Fetishism" (1927) that "the fetish is a substitute for the woman's (the mother's) penis that the little boy once believed in and—for reasons familiar to us—does not want to give up." The father of psychoanalysis follows up by associating the foot fetish with Chinese bound feet: "A parallel to fetishism in social psychology, might be seen in the Chinese custom of mutilating the female foot and then revering it like a fetish after it has been mutilated. It seems as though the Chinese male wants to thank the woman for having submitted to being castrated" (198). Bataille in "The Big Toe" sees the big toe as "the most *human* part of the human body, in the sense that no other element of this body is as differentiated from the corresponding element of the anthropoid ape" (20). The toe no longer serves the prehensile function of clinging to tree branches. Yet Bataille proceeds to argue that the human's "light head" disdains the foot and the big toe "as spit, on the pretext that he has his foot in the mud" (20).

Not to mince (Chinese) words, *Reborn* constitutes a case of *Gōngān*'s *Gōngàn* (公安之公案). With the first, level tone of *ān*, *Gōngān* means Public Security. Yet this police procedural presents a *Gōngàn* with the falling, fourth tone of *àn* or case. *Gōngàn* is known in the West as Koan. This *Gōngàn*, meaning "Public Case" à la Zen Buddhism, revolves around, dialectically, the private psychosis of a self-destructive police officer and a girl who loves the man she hates. Both are rather unpalatable characters by the gold (red?) standard of communist propaganda.

In its inception, *Minning Town* appears to be even more jingoistic than *Reborn*. But the drama's execution is so meticulous on human psychology, and peasant psychology in particular, that toeing the party line, even praising the CCP obsequiously, becomes a front for thinly veiled critique of bureaucracy. That peasant psychology comes through conspicuously in the local dialect that characters playing Ningxia residents speak, complemented by the Fukienese accent of Fujian officials, academics, and factory owners. This dialect drama version with dialogues recorded live on location is shown alongside a *Putonghua* or Beijingnese version that is subsequently dubbed in the studio. The parallel soundtracks supposedly satisfy different needs of regional authenticity and of official endorsement. Why the need for a Putonghua version where the disembodied voice is often out of sync with the actor's lips? The bulk of over one billion domestic viewers is so familiar with the actual voices of *Minning Town*'s stars that the Putonghua postproduction rerecording causes a near-Brechtian alienation effect.[7] To translate the German playwright's "A-effect" of distancing into video-game-inspired Chinese slang *A-diao* (A掉), what is being attacked, annihilated, or A-ed (ate?) is the official authority itself. Which numbskull official would fail to see the implication of the Standard Chinese that comes through as doublespeak? On the other hand, it does not take a Ningxia or Fujian native to detect performers' slips of the tongue in the dialect version's polyphonic heteroglossia. The protagonist Ma Defu, played by Huang Xuan, loses his Ningxia accent on occasion, lapsing into Beijingnese inflections. Be that as it may, the illusion of local dialects is adeptly maintained overall, a dramaturgical accomplishment beyond the usual suspects of stereotypical country bumpkins who fail to speak properly, associated with northeastern clownish characters in Zhao Benshan's long-running *Rural Love Story* (2006–21). After all, Putonghua means the average, normal, and standard

---

7. Struck by the wonders of Beijing Opera stylization performed by Mei Lanfang in Moscow in 1935, Bertolt Brecht in "Alienation Effects in Chinese Acting" theorizes the foundation of the epic theater, whereby the audience is hindered from identifying with the performers. As a consequence, Brecht believes that acceptance or rejection of the characters must take place on a conscious rather than subconscious level. See chapter 8 herein.

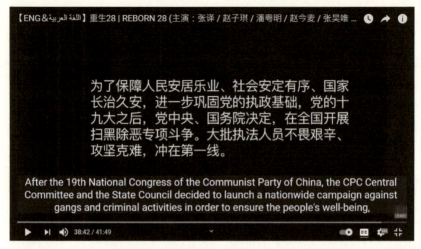

FIGURE 1.6. The propaganda intertitle in the closing moments of *Reborn*'s episode 28.

speech. Dialects that deviate from it are, by corollary, below average, abnormal, and substandard. Jin Liu in "Ambivalent Laughter" seeks to complicate Zhao and other dialect performances through the lens of the carnivalesque from Bakhtin; it remains unclear as to how "woke" Chinese audiences are when it comes to Western literary theories.

Presenting these series for the celebration of the CCP Centennial or for the glory of the Party in general is taken for granted. For instance, *Minning Town*'s opening credits already cited in figure 1.1 demonstrate overt "bracketing" by politics. *Reborn* is no exception. While the audience may still be in shock over Qin Chi's demise, the closing moments of episode 28 display an intertitle translated as "After the 19th National Congress of the Communist Party of China . . . launch a nationwide campaign against gangs and criminal activities in order to ensure the people's well-being" (figure 1.6). Its unctuous tone notwithstanding, the English subtitle has already streamlined the bombastic Chinese officialese. Qin and Chen's private neuroses are the bitter pill sugarcoated by sloganeering. The artistic, cathartic healing with Thanatos and Eros all but wedded remains, so to speak, under the State's heel. In fact, the collective State serves the people, as the saying goes, by (un)veiling the people's psychological, even pathological, taboo that is otherwise unspeakable.

This approach of political packaging, befitting the artistic content or not, is a universal style. Yet another centennial-inspired TV anthology series of six stories, *To Be with You* (2021, henceforth *To Be*) opens with the first 6-episode story, "New Year's Eve Banquet," on two police officers. The camera pans up to capture the poster displayed high up on the wall of the police station

FIGURE 1.7. The propaganda poster displayed on the wall of the police station in *To Be with You*.

(figure 1.7). The poster consists of four four-character maxims on police loyalty and justice, signed by Xi Jinping on May 19, 2017, the day Xi announced the policy. Not only did the CCP 19th National Congress occur in October of 2017, but *To Be* deliberately alludes to that year—both indications of President Xi tightening his grip on the CCP.

Coinciding with the CCP Centennial in 2021, both *Minning Town* and the anthology series *To Be* reprise the thematic double entendre of healing and heeling. These series honor the Party leadership for lifting China from the proverbial "century of national shame" spanning the mid-nineteenth and the mid-twentieth century to the "Chinese Century" of the twenty-first. Such "national shame" consists of Western and Japanese imperialist partitioning of the subcolony China as well as abject poverty, ignorance, provincialism, and backwardness. These negatives in socioeconomic conditions amount to a national, collective disability, embodied in a wide spectrum of characters' physical and mental challenges, personality traits, and moral failings. Loss of memory from trauma plagues *Reborn*'s protagonist. The ping-pong player in the second story, "Youth Forever," in *To Be* collapses during a match and loses her memory for the next two decades. Old-age dementia incapacitates a retired college professor in the fifth story, "An Unusual Summer," in *To Be*. Instead of being the breadwinners of the family, two fathers are wheelchair-bound in *Minning Town* and the fourth story, "Longing," in *To Be*. The wheelchair is a figure of speech. The amputee in *Minning Town*, for instance, pushes himself around in a wooden box inches above the ground.

Not to be outdone, the aging eatery owner of "A Bowl of Duck Blood Vermicelli Soup," the sixth and final story of *To Be*, has a severe speech defect. The restaurateur runs an old shop bound for the dustbin under the city of Nanjing's gentrification project, desperate to pass on, before he passes, trade secrets of the soup recipe, bamboo-cutting knife and sieve, spices including dried bamboo slices, and whatnot. From his royal splendor as the First Emperor of Qin in Chen Kaige's *The Emperor and the Assassin* (1998), Li Xuejian has "fallen" to an elderly noodle-shop vendor fading away in a city always called by its ancient name, Jinling. Strategically, its modern name is used but once, in the last episode, when a tour guide corrals a group of red-capped tourists into the new—not the old—duck blood restaurant for "a taste of Nanjing."

On an old city street with towering cranes and wrecking balls over the rooftops, Li's speech act is so garbled that Chinese subtitles are required for even a native speaker to follow. His elocution verges on an extreme sport robbing himself of the power of speech, which ironically encapsulates art as much out of the propaganda of *To Be* as out of the dispensing of his own vocal virtuosity. Resorting to prelingual body language and gestures, groans and grunts, snorting and wailing, Li's consummate artistry reminds one of the anatomically challenged John Hurt's first sound or lisp, "My name is John Merrick," in *The Elephant Man* (1980) and the deaf performer Marlee Matlin in *Children of a Lesser God* (1986). The inexpressible runs through these memorable feats onscreen. Like a fugue, "Duck Blood" repeats the leitmotif of the ineffable through an old city to be redeveloped, an old man to be replaced, and an old taste to be reconstituted.[8] At the climactic end on the eve of his shop's demolition, political exigency necessitates Li's character to mouth "Without the Party, we won't have our today"—awkward-sounding English that is idiomatic Chinese. This closing flattery is like *Minning Town*'s opening tribute to the Party Centennial and other propaganda moments. To argue whether it is a small price to pay for art or too dear a price is an academic exercise totally oblivious to the conditions under which these TV series negotiate their existence. One should not, however, exclude the possibility that the crew and the actors mean what they parrot, that they believe what they preach. Finally, the favorite plot twist of traffic accidents in Asian soap operas, particularly the Korean Wave, as a device to cut short romance is strewn across these series as well. The worst-case scenario of accidents is another father in "Longing" who perishes driving a tractor during the construction of a dam.

Not only physical handicap but emotional bereavement and psychic hurt also buoy these series' ratings atop the infinite, tumultuous mass of TV and

---

8. In a Darwinian China, even acting involves one-upmanship whereby more and more extreme roles are taken on to demonstrate actors' virtuosity. Li's speech defect belongs to the kind of disabilities shared by the mentally challenged public bathroom employee played by Jiang Wu in *Shower* (1999) and Jet Li's autistic son, played by Wen Zhang, in *Ocean Heaven* (2010).

web series, a virtual ocean into which most shows sink without a trace. As national poverty comes embodied in individual disabilities of ignorance, superstition, and wild passion, the CCP is credited with healing China via policies of economic development as well as individual martyrdom. Nonetheless, this doctor-esque healing of the nation secretes a doctrinarian heeling of nationals. The "a" in healing mutates, unawares, into the "e" in heeling, consolidating consensus, rallying public opinion, the will of the people subsumed into that of the politician. One strategy lies in the infusing of wealth and progress from coastal elites and metropolis to the rural interior. *Minning Town* accomplishes this on a continental scale. Microcosmically, *To Be* threads this motif throughout. "An Unusual Summer" chronicles how a Shanghai engineer–urban planner originally from the countryside sponsors a young man following his footsteps from mountain impecuniosity to metropolitan self-sufficiency. "Longing" details a college graduate from the city doing her service teaching in the remote southwest highlands. Despite the stunning natural beauty, the mountain villages have no jobs, no web connection, and no hope other than venturing to the city of Guangzhou as migrant workers. The teacher introduces online marketing for local farm products and delicacies, packaged to cater to online shoppers, whereas the area secretariat expedites the government campaign of cell phone towers, broadband connectivity, and express parcel delivery. "Longing" closes with a "happy ending" as the teacher's developer mother visits the mountain village with an eye toward investment in this tourist-heaven Shangri-la. The village is engaged to sell its produce as well as itself *as* produce—its scenery, clean water and air, rustic ways and people.

In the words of Deng Xiaoping as he opened the post-Mao China to market economy since the late 1970s, the capitalist drive to "get rich quick" is relentless throughout and beyond these centennial series. Making money has become a national campaign, an obsession reaching an absolute fever pitch no less than the Red Guards' Mao cult. Call this national craze the Renminbi cult, or even the *Meidao* (美刀 Beautiful Blade) cult, since the US dollar is the preferred currency of the rich and famous! "Beautiful" translates "America" by cherry-picking and tweaking its second syllable into "mei," which means beautiful; dao (blade) approximates the British, round "o" sound of *do*llar. America, from its currency to its culture, is beautified as well as razor-sharp. Xi Jinping's "socialism with Chinese characteristics" ought to be, as Confucius cautioned thousands of years ago, "correctly named/branded" (正名 *zhengming*) as "consumerism with the CCP imprimatur," an ideological and capitalist vise crushing the skull of culture and humanities, except artistic propaganda, or propagandist art, in such shows as *Minning Town*.

FIGURE 1.8. Rayzha Alimjan gives a resigned farewell to her lover in *Minning Town*.

To be sure, righteous and diligent Party secretaries always ride to the rescue of the people under the yoke of corrupt and incompetent local leaders. The protagonist Ma Defu, after all, is the town's Party secretary. Political conformity aside, *Minning Town* exposes public crimes and private misdemeanors, faulty governmental policies and wayward individual emotions. It does not shy away from searing moments of children running away from the deprivation of the mountain villages, of a lover's resigned farewell as she is "sold" to another village (figure 1.8), of the younger brother's rage over having been forfeited for the older brother Ma Defu's education, of a son's revolt against his father's punishment (figure 1.9), and of the protagonist repainting the village name on the eve of its relocation and abandonment (figure 1.10). These and other figures are screenshots that punctuate the national healing from poverty, but they also go beyond political messaging in artistic expression. Granted, these freeze frames fail miserably in transmitting the essence of motion pictures and television, i.e., the movement of images and sounds. Yet each of them does capture a split second, admittedly the thinnest of slices, in hours-long narratives. In addition, these screenshots in print would pale into black-and-white reproductions, losing the shows' colors, such as the pinkness of Chen Rui's bathrobe hem in figure 1.5, which segues into the flushed face of Qin Chi's jealous ex-wife.

Like Gülnezer of Uighur descent, Rayzha Alimjan in figure 1.8 is a Chinese actress and model of Kazakh ethnicity. This single shot does little justice to her flowing expressions that culminate in that teary smile. The camera angle is entirely justified in shooting from behind her lover Ma Defu's back since Huang Xuan, who plays Ma, is, to put it euphemistically, minimalist in facial expressiveness, in keeping with his cadre dignity. Rayzha's exceptionally high-ridged, non-Han nose is not visible in the frontal shot, nor is her charisma showing through the unkempt hair and the shabby peasant attire. One only needs to check her out in *The Longest Day in Chang'an* (2019) to see her statuesque beauty, which is entirely shrouded by misery in *Minning Town*. The sadness of her countenance as she looks to Ma, whom she still loves, epitomizes the villagers' fate out of their control. She is traded by her aging, drunken father for a mule and other commodities, reminiscent of the plot of Zhang Yimou's *Red Sorghum* (1988). Her future husband in another village happens to adore her, but their happiness comes crashing down, literally, when the well he is digging collapses and cripples him.

Note the bottom right-hand corner of figure 1.8 that advertises, in three lines literally translated: "Macao Suncity [Sun City] VIP Club," "One Hundred Family Happy Interaction with Real Adult Film Actress," and "Reputable Recommendation: 1802.com." Against a woman's pain is advertised the pleasure of at least one hundred families' fathers, husbands, and sons partaking in online gambling. *Baijiale,* One Hundred Families' Happiness, is a common saying for general well-being, now applied to card games hosted by adult film starlets. The websites of dramasq.com and others that stream *Minning Town* and other TV dramas free of charge insert not only "corner ads" but also periodic commercials of 1802.com, whereby a young woman in low-cut dress deals cards most invitingly. Once the card players log on to the website, they join the Macao Sun City VIP Club. *Minning Town*'s explicit political intent excludes neither Rayzha's exquisite acting on the screen nor porn starlets' erotic gaming off-screen, at least off this screen on *Minning Town*. Some other corner ads are more explicit, referring to, in salty Cantonese slang, *dabo nüyou,* which can only be appropriately rendered in the vulgarity of "'big tits' adult film stars," presumably, hosting the game. The split screens of China are as variegated as a kaleidoscope. The National Radio and Television Administration–sponsored series *Minning Town* comes to sport a sleazy corner badge in nearly every frame. The model song and dance of revolutionary China comes at no cost to viewers, courtesy of the largesse of a Macao casino, which purchases, monetarily and through a graphic fingerhold, a tiny corner of each frame, the tip of another China submerged. To see the leftist propaganda show means to be blind cognitively to its bottom right-hand corner, a duality inherent in the forked-tongued Putonghua dubbing.

Figure 1.9 focuses on an untraditional clash between father and son. The father character personifies villagers' regressiveness, fleeing from the hardships of the government-directed resettlement, mocking the campaign of

FIGURE 1.9. The son, in a gesture of defiance, holds on to the shoe raised against him in *Minning Town*.

growing Fujian mushrooms as a cash crop in Ningxia's adobe huts, saddling his son with mounting debts, and many more reactionary activities. One of his worst sins is lording over his son, who rebels by leaving home for Fujian factories. Father and son grappling with each other, the son holds on to the shoe raised against him, warning: "You will not hit my face with the sole of your shoe," which so shocks the father in his routine public shaming of what he deemed unfilial pious behavior that he stops. The son proceeds to shove him aside before leaving for the south. Symbolically, to slap someone with the sole of the shoe is the ultimate humiliation, as though squashing the face like a worm into the mud. From the most abject position, prostrate on the ground, as it were, he used to be subjected to in public, the son now stands erect and elbows out his father to rise up in the world.

As Ma Defu succeeds at long last in persuading all the village elders and, subsequently, the entire town to relocate to the new government-designated site, figure 1.10 shows him retracing the old village name, Springing Well Village, in paint so thick that it drips down, as though from the eponymous spring. The new coat of paint is a belated coming to pass of the village boast that it is "where water is the sweetest." If the place had truly been blessed by such bountiful wells, the wholesale move would have been moot. Ma's fresh lie of Springing Well Village is followed by a line in "fine print," added by a village son, Duoduo, to inform his father who absconded decades ago: "Ba, [we've] moved to Minning Town." Duoduo's mother suffers from delirium ever since her spouse's desertion, and fears that he, upon return, would not be able to find them. To assuage the mother, the son fakes a message. The divorcing of words and reality in *Minning Town*'s finale is heart-wrenching. Despite the drippy scripts, Springing Well Village is anything but, soon to be a ghost

FIGURE 1.10. Ma Defu repaints the old village name, Springing Well Village, in *Minning Town*.

town in ruins. Duoduo's direction, likewise, is to a father who has long ceased to exist, if not deceased.

Reborn's last smile in figure 1.2, *Minning Town*'s teary smile in figure 1.8, and the last (painted) words in figure 1.10 bid adieus to a vanishing world from which performing arts are born, to a mummified Mao(ism) from which viewers' eyes cannot but well up. In the (kindred) spirit of Ralph McTell's "Streets of London" (1969), we have walked through a gallery of snapshots illustrating three TV series' Chinese art out of propaganda, "something to make you change your mind." Far more torturous than the London balladeer's lyrical nostalgia, though, a political irony looms over Beijing.

Shanzhai, mountain stronghold for rebels, grounds Maoism before the launch of military and ideological insurrections that eventually overran China. The CCP continues to romanticize shanzhai as the core of its iconoclastic, populist identity. In the Chinese Century, the Party engages in revisionism of the image of isolated mountainous hinterland, one to be catapulted into modernity with urban amenities. The tactical change comes because the headquarters of Maoist shanzhai has been transplanted to Beijing. The CCP Centennial TV series thus repaint China's arid interior in fresh colors, even as the symbolic mobilization entails commercialization and fetishization of the old traditional ways of life. Just as Springing Well Village has dried up, despite flourishes of the local Party secretary's paintbrush, the Old China of the past and the poor is remembered as it is dismembered from the New China under the CCP. Thus, the sphere of Beijing shanzhai's influence reaches all extremities of the land, not just the inland backwater but also Xinjiang, Tibet, Macao, Hong Kong, and, last but not least, "China Taiwan," a term favored in official documents, daily parlance, and even opening credits to films and TV series with Taiwanese actors.[9] That is perhaps the hidden cause for Chinese media to cast, so frequently and so generously in a nation chock-full of young thespians, token Taiwanese from the democratic island nation, sucking beautiful faces and bodies across the Taiwan Strait before it does the Beautiful Island, "Ilha Formosa," as Portuguese sailors called it in 1544. Secure in this "Greater" China, the CCP shanzhai executes its Manifest Destiny of global merger, healing and heeling foreign lands and foreign subjects. Next in line after the 2020 Hong Kong national security law over the Fragrant Harbor: Taiwan, to which the CCP propaganda with a full head of serpentine art has turned its Gorgon's gaze. Flee where this time—another Taiwan, like 1949?

---

9. How much does Mainland China love "China Taiwan" actors? Let me count some of the names, in the order of appearance on my mental screen: Wallace Huo, Jimmy Lin, Mark Chao, Ethan Juan, Show Lo, Jay Chou, Guan Hong, Fu Mengbo, Darren Wang (his first name in Chinese, *dalu*, literally translating into "Mainland"), Roy Chiu, Chun-Ning Chang, and Nita Lei. The gender imbalance is striking. In this random listing, all the Taiwanese exports except the last two are male. Why does the Mainland Chinese audience find male Taiwanese performers more to their liking? Nevertheless, most of them agree to silencing themselves, subjecting to postproduction Beijingnese dubbing to mask their Taiwanese accent. Whereas Gülnezer and Rayzha speak Beijingness while sporting "white" faces, Taiwanese actors embody Taiwaneseness while speaking like Beijingers. The split screen of Taiwanese actors and their dubbed Beijingnese sends a subliminal message of the island nation's unification with the "mother" tongue of the motherland.

CHAPTER 2

Triangulating TV Series of Melodramatic Dialectic "with Chinese Characteristics"

Gamblin' Professionals in Cities;
Goth and Darwin in the Wild West

Propaganda of another sort, Chinese TV series couple the genre of conservative melodrama with the political ideology of Marxist dialectic to perpetuate traditional family values, as much directed by the Chinese Communist Party (CCP) top-down as oozing from the people's, the "partygoer's," mind bottom-up. Let us count the title's inconsistency between the plural "Characteristics" and the singular "Dialectic" as but one of President Xi Jinping's "Chinese Characteristics" since the Chinese language, apparently, has no "s" to make countable nouns.[1] For that matter, let us discount the inconsistency of numbers altogether: the title's triangle meets the subtitle's multiplicity—three in Chinese symbolizes many, as it does universally in the "magic of three." Insofar as the first half of the argument is concerned, while Chinese wagerers run rampant in TV series, one well-wrought show, *The Ideal City* (2021), soars above others on gamblin' professionals, eclipsing fellow "comrades." To borrow from Christophe Den Tandt's *The Urban Sublime in American Literary Naturalism* (1998), *The Ideal City*'s "oceanic sublime" of "urban markets of speculation" and Darwinian survival in China's coastal cities parallel naturalism in its Wild West in such 2021 TV series as *Rattan* and *Hunter* (9). The struggles shared by the continental coast and the interior point to porous boundaries

---

1. As I indicated earlier in the first note to chapter 1, all Chinese names comply with the Chinese order of the last name first, followed by the first name, except in cases where the author and artist have Anglicized their names.

and fluid (symbolic) capital, flowing from the financial capital of Wall Street in Den Tandt and from the political capital of Beijing in TV series. Despite the buzzwords promulgated from the very top, the "Chinese Characteristics" are not unique; they are shared by the Burkean sublime, the American metropolis, literary naturalism, and Chinese TV series of melodramatic dialectic.

Given China's "casino economy," white-collar professionals of business-(wo)men, attorneys, public relations specialists, fashion or interior designers, celebrity scouts, restaurateurs, and even law enforcement officers from contemporary TV dramas are all serial gamblers betting compulsively on stocks, business investments and contracts, court cases, company mergers or downsizings, criminal and forensic investigations, national security conspiracies, and, last but not least, romances in a zero-sum game. The breathless litany of melodramatic formulas notwithstanding, the last ingredient of love provides the "pixie dust" of magic to spice up whichever genre the series finds itself in. Unequivocally upholding heteronormativity and phallocentric patriarchy by way of romance, these series perpetrate conservatism. The root word "conserve" conjures up "conservation," part of the rationale for harmony- and consensus-building TV dramas preserving order and stability under the CCP. These shows thus aim to maintain the status quo, the here and now, as the CCP theorizes that a messianic revolution has already been effected in 1949. No other demolition of the known old in favor of the unknown new is to be countenanced.[2] Faced with such conservatism, this critical triaging of gamblers, goths, and Darwins seeks to initiate a cognitive reassessment.

These TV series' professionals excel in their respective calling as well as in their shared impulse to take risks, to live on the razor's edge. The attempt to cheat death, individual or company-wise, builds up toward the dramatic climax through Aristotelian conflict and narrative obstruction. In late capitalist-socialist China, gamblin' professionals are professional gamblers writ large, a new breed of Marxist Messianism Sinologized, with the new clothes of old patriarchal conservatism. This game of Russian roulette of win-all, lose-all seems so irresistibly addictive to Chinese melodramas that its spinning has never stopped, spinning out series after series "with Chinese characteristics," where traditional morality, family bonding, and State supremacy invariably prevail. Beyond "Russian" and "Chinese," the preceding sentence also secretes "Anglo-American" up its sleeve, since the freewheeling, predatory "casino capitalism," in Susan Strange's coinage, is synonymous with the US. With King Midas–President Xi's touch of "Chinese characteristics," cannibalistic practices

---

2. Shaohua Guo in *The Evolution of the Chinese Internet* (2021) agrees: "The history of modern China is a history of revolution—or the potential to bring about drastic change" (1). However, that putative "revolution" resembles "rotation."

of Wall Street capitalism are alchemized as wolfishly and communistically red, as in cultural franchises of *Wolf Totem* (2004, 2015) and *Wolf Warrior* (2015, 2017), let alone wolf diplomats like Zhao Lijian, spokesperson for the Ministry of Foreign Affairs, spearheading the "Chinese Century" abroad.

Subconsciously, China walks the tightrope stretched taut between the title's two ends: the American slang à la "gamblin' man" versus the "Chinese characteristics" à la Xi. China's drive to reverse its colonial "century of national shame" by beating the lone superpower in its own game of capitalism suggests a jealousy, the paradox of hating what it loves, or "mock[ing] the meat it feeds on," in Iago's punchline to Othello. The double helix of desire interlaces as much in body politic as in individual romance. Whereas the game implicating money with love, not to mention the duplicitous gaming of the genre of TV melodramas by politics, animates almost all TV series, the first half of this essay elects to focus on a single and singular show, *The Ideal City*, lest it be reduced to plot summaries of the minutiae of business enterprise in *Sweet Life*, talent agents and hoteliers in *Vacation of Love*, national security agents in *The Eye of the Storm*, Public Security officers about to retire in *Trident*, drug interdiction in *Never Say Goodbye*, and many more. From *The Eye of the Storm*'s Dalian, Liaoning, in the north to *Vacation of Love*'s Sanya at the nation's southernmost tip, these series dot across coastal cities, many of them international ports, particularly the one in the middle, Shanghai, to which all shows gravitate, even if not set squarely along the storied Bund and Pudong. *The Ideal City*, for one, reprises the establishing shots along the Huangpu River, with the Oriental Pearl Tower and Shanghai's cityscape framing its forty episodes.

Exorcized from these series of social(ist) realism set in first-tier cities are not only new repressions of Communism but also old ones of Confucianism. In the name of rationalist moralism, Confucius railed against *guaililuanshen* (literally: demon, violence, monstrosity, God/numen). Chairman Mao disdained not only Confucius's "unlikes" but Confucianism itself, deemed part of feudalism to be expunged. Millennial TV series, however, triangulate Chinese subconsciousness betwixt the maritime cosmopolis and the hinterland of China's Wild West. Not so much *Frontier Gothic* in David Mogen et al.'s collection title as the Chinese psyche's posterior or shadow, these gothic and naturalist tales of *Rattan* and *Hunter* comprise, in the western edges of China, the atavistic tails to family dramas and urban corporate cultures of coastal cities. The doppelgangers of cities and wilderness, the twins of human and nonhuman, map out popular culture on the cusp of a self-proclaimed Chinese Century.

This discourse within the Sinosphere evinces little ripple beyond itself, though, far from upending the Anglophone cultural hegemony. The power to speak to, if not for, over one billion Sinophone speakers is severely restricted by the fact that these shows are rarely, if ever, translated, subtitled, and distributed via Anglophone global media. As a cognitive reassessment, this present task encounters difficulty in venturing beyond an intellectual niche. Chinese speakers are not keen to wade through critical analysis in English on TV series that constitute, for most and at best, after-work nighttime entertainment rather than primary materials to pore over in hope of subverting Sinocentric positionality, possibly the viewers' own positionality.[3] On the other hand, non-Chinese-speakers are, by default, denied access to these shows without subtitles. As tantalizing as it sounds, E. M. Forster's "Only connect!" remains a tall order.

The Ideal City

Based on Ruohua Ranran's (若花燃燃 "Like Flower Blooming Blooming," literally) web novel *Su Xiao's War* (2021), this 40-episode series chronicles the rise and fall of the construction project comptroller Su Xiao (Sun Li, a renowned TV actress ever since *Empresses in the Palace* [2011]) through Shanghai's corporate world. A brilliant, imaginative comptroller with a photographic memory of numbers, Su Xiao's direct, bold approach steps on many toes and is repeatedly sabotaged by her superiors and colleagues, until she lands in the company run by the appreciative president Wang Yang (played by veteran Chen Minghao), pitted against a fellow yet rivaling company managed by her eventual love interest Xia Ming, played by Zhao Youting (Mark Chao), hailing from, to translate the parenthesis after his name in the opening credits, "(China['s] Taiwan)." Not only does Zhao Youting perform *in* China, but his Taiwaneseness performs *for* China by way of the implied possessive apostrophe "s" in the interest of the Fatherland's "inseparable" territorial claim over the autonomous island nation. What role, if any, does that parenthesis play in the large number of relaunches of Taiwanese actors' careers across the Taiwan Strait, in the far bigger and more lucrative Chinese market? Why the gender imbalance of many Taiwanese males and few Taiwanese females blooming in a second spring in China? Given Taiwanese males' supporting roles, their first

---

3. Dennis Broe in *Birth of the Binge* (2019) sees potential for emancipation as well as for servitude in bingeing. Broe posits: "In its purposely addictive nature, seriality is a mode of digital engineering . . . pointing toward liberatory viewing" (1). But he follows it with the possibility that serial bingeing opens up "portals to forms of addiction and unseen kinds of toxicity," likened to a "morphine drip" (3–4). Ultimately, the paradox of bingeing betokens a "substance that is both poison and cure" (4).

billing notwithstanding, the spotlight remains on Chinese actresses and China silhouetted by "guests" in its employ, either speaking in a Taiwanese accent or altogether muted and redubbed in Beijingnese. Zhao Youting, in that regard, is a happy exception, who mimics Putonghua or Standard Chinese with a Beijing flare, a striking improvement over his flat monotone in *Chronicles of the Ghostly Tribe* (2015).

Both Wang Yang and Xia Ming belong to the parent company Yinghai (Win Ocean) under the stewardship of Chairman Zhao Xiankun, with actor Yu Hewei's commanding presence and perfectly pitched elocution. Chairman Zhao spots Su Xiao's talent and promotes her to Yinghai's economic vice president, upending vested interests of Yinghai's ruling elite, depriving Wang Yang of the lifeline of Su's daredevil strategies, and imperiling Xia Ming's Machiavellian plots. This, after all, is Chairman Zhao's intention: to shake up the entire system. Company intrigues and countermeasures are myriad, charting the swing of melodramatic dialectic between climactic win and loss, between winning at the expense of one's soul and lover, on the one hand, and, on the other, win-win for all involved, demonstrated by Su Xiao's deft proposals time and time again. To stamp out corruption, Su counsels a proportionate split of savings from material costs between contractors and Wang Yang's company, to the great delight of both parties. To ease company debts to Yinghai, Su advances the notion of transferring debts into loans, albeit thwarted by company politics. To redistribute wealth equitably, Su proposes that all employees be eligible to purchase company stock. All such win-win strategies militate against, however, the corporate upper crust, beneficiaries of a system rampant with kickbacks, bribes, and perks.

Su's win-win tactic adheres to China's *gongying* (both/all win) slogan as it expands through the Belt and Road Initiative; into China's Second Continent, Africa;[4] across the South China Sea, the Pacific Islands, South America, the Arctic Circle, and even outer space. Through this feel-good rosy lens of win-win, the capitalist, Darwinian struggle waged by both Su and China is sentimentalized with melodramatic happy endings, where good companies and people prevail over evil. Indeed, Su Xiao's beautiful face articulates somewhat ugly Party doctrines in episode 39 in comforting her erstwhile employer Wang Yang, fallen amid internal power struggles. Punning on the company name Yinghai or Win Ocean, Su likens the corporation to a ship under the helmsman Chairman Zhao for "you and I" to follow. The Great Helmsman Chairman Mao casts his shadow still, half a century after his death. The centralized hegemony empowers Su Xiao, first channeled by Wang Yang and subsequently

---

4. See Howard French's *China's Second Continent* (2014).

by Chairman Zhao. Without these authority figures, Su Xiao would have been ousted long ago, as feared by the far more astute and calculating Xia Ming.

Chairman Zhao's enlightened leadership is attributed, as early as episode 1, to his previous government service to the ultimate authority in *The Ideal City*, the district official He Shengli, his Christian (communist?) name Shengli meaning "Victory," on the heels of the surname He for "Congratulate." Amid other urban planning projects, He Shengli is tasked with granting construction licenses. In the first episode, He Shengli is injured in an accident during one of Yinghai's opening ceremonies, crushed under a cement wall of poor quality, destabilized by too much cost-cutting sand. Apologizing to He in person, Chairman Zhao is practically kicked out of the hospital ward after having been excoriated for pursuing profits over social obligation in such housing projects for the people, contrary to He's mentorship in the government agency prior to Zhao's switch to the private sector.

Forty episodes later, Chairman Zhao throws his weight behind Su's daring proposition for employees-*cum*-shareholders. That Zhao privileges people over profits is long foreshadowed by the communist ideology embodied in He Shengli, his namesake "Victory" for all except profiteers on the company board, local as well as overseas from the capitalist Singapore speaking English and accented Chinese. Such foreign ruse deconstructs itself in the Singaporean character David Lee's (Beijingnese Ren Zhong) atrocious English and standard Beijingnese slips in supposedly bad Chinese. As incredulous as David Lee's instinctive retroflexes—the slippery slurring "er" endings, the sleazy personal and public dealings of Li Xue, executive assistant to He Shengli, never touch He himself. The red line of censorship over official corruption is never crossed. Su Xiao's ex-boyfriend latches on to Li Xue, whose jealousy prompts her to deny Su her newly acquired comptroller license. This personal vendetta is only one of Li's wrongdoings, which culminate in her fall after the scandal of her insidious transactions with an unscrupulous businessman. The turmoil never taints He Shengli's stature, despite the fact that Li works for him and under his supervision.

Good riddance to Su's traitorous ex-boyfriend, to be replaced by a worthier lover—Xia Ming (Summer Bright, literally). If Su gambles within the system to balance public and private good, Xia games the system to maximize profits, even to the detriment of Su, having her scapegoated despite his own sense of guilt. If Su is accompanied by her namesake Xiao or "thin bamboo," as she wears on her necklace that symbolizes integrity and perseverance, Xia is a lonely soul talking to his AI companion (escort?) nightly. Put another way, Su is the bamboo; Xia the owner of a robotic female voice. If Su is an adventurous yet righteous gambler, Xia is her crooked counterpart, with certain

FIGURE 2.1. Xia Ming shields Su Xiao's innocent eyes from the scuffle in episode 17 of *The Ideal City*

saving grace, nonetheless, that makes possible the lovers' union in the closing moments. Contrary to Su the idealistic, straightforward gambler, Xia is a pragmatic, even shady, gambler manipulating power dynamics. Xia Ming is anything but "Summer Bright," "Wintry Dark," rather. Xia, however, epitomizes melodramatic dialectic to a T, i.e., Taiwan, now that even a man from Taiwan, a sovereign state, comes to execute the CCP mandate of sugarcoating with pathos Marxist dialectic to make it go down smoothly in the people's mind, if not shoving it down their throat.

Xia Ming's game plan, not to mince words, follows closely the Marxist-Maoist dictum of *jihua maodun* ("fomenting/sharpening conflicts"). Marx and Mao seek to bring about proletarian revolutions by not only enlightening the oppressed of their historical enslavement but also by legitimizing violence and bloodshed. "Insurrection is justified; revolution is no crime," Mao has championed indefatigably. In episode 17, finding his car blocked by a bully parked illegally in a narrow yet busy lane, Xia leisurely inquires after Su Xiao's preference and wanders off to purchase meat-filled steamed buns called *baozi* around the street corner. Upon his return, as expected, a long line of stranded cars has formed, numerous drivers embroiled in a war of words, soon escalating into a fistfight. Figure 2.1 shows the mastermind Xia shielding Su Xiao's innocent eyes from the scuffle he himself has orchestrated. As the police clear the scene and Xia pulls off effortlessly along yet another illegally parked vehicle, Su finally realizes what Xia has been up to. Xia has initiated the naïve mathematical genius Su to the art of business war: faced with a formidable enemy, one induces a crisis, surreptitiously, to gain leverage.

Although a comptroller's expenditure chart lists materials and costs, it secretes a *guanxi* (human relationship) genealogy. Against relatively fixed prices and specific numbers, as volatile as the market may be, the human heart is truly elusive and mercurial, the final deciding factor. That Su subconsciously orders meat rather than vegetable baozi suggests that she is about to scale the food chain from the prey to the predator, "learned" by Xia to read the human mind. Look again at her expression of wonderment about to break into a barely suppressed grin, her vision blinded by Xia's protective palm! Her progress comes at the expense of accepting, even treasuring, Xia's patronizing gesture, the Buddha's palm from which even *Journey to the West*'s Monkey fails to escape.[5] In addition to teaching a lesson in Marxist dialectic of conflict producing rather than conflict resolving, Xia instructs as well in the melodramatic joy of submitting passively to patriarchal tutorage. Su's greatness hinges on "great" men who adore her while putting her to good use—Wang Yang, Chairman Zhao, and, of course, Xia Ming. Heroine worship presupposes hero worship.

Judging from his mental stratagem and physical carriage, Xia Ming is a consummate gambler, a man of few words with a blank poker face, even when threatened by an underworld loan shark as Xia's company crumbles under mounting debts. Reminiscent of the traffic gridlock, such debts are deliberately incurred by Xia to force Yinghai's hand in a sell-off. This severance would then free Xia to market a plot of barren agricultural farmland, unbeknownst to all, about to rise exponentially in value because of the imminent extension into the outskirts of Shanghai's subway lines. The saving grace for Xia's apparent shenanigan lies in, discovers Su Xiao in her visit to the farmland, the fact that Xia has for years sheltered company retirees toiling all their lives to build Yinghai's high-rises without having ever owned a speck of city property. These retirees belong to the disenfranchised multitude Yu Hua chronicles in *China in Ten Words* (2011): "huge swathes of old housing razed in no time at all and replaced in short order by high-rise buildings. These large-scale demolitions can make Chinese cities look as though they have been targets of a bombing raid" (126). Yu's native perspective informs Anna Greenspan's observation of *Chai* (拆 tearing down) in Chinese cities: "the Chinese, who take a notorious delight in puns, now refer to [China] as 'Chai-Na'" (*Shanghai Future* [2014] 148). Faced with the inexorable onslaught of modernity and urbanization, Xia anticipates that the rise in property value would save his company, employees, and the homeless elderly accommodated on the farmland. Xia's charitable

---

5. See Wu Cheng'en's sixteenth-century classic *Journey to the West,* where the Buddha dares the rebellious Monkey to fly from his hand, which transforms into Five Finger Mountain trapping Monkey for five hundred years, until the monk Tripitaka arrives on his journey to the West—India—to acquire Buddhist sutras.

FIGURE 2.2. Su Xiao appeals to the board in episode 39 of *The Ideal City*

scheme in conjunction with Su's proposal of employees-*cum*-shareholders convinces Chairman Zhao to take the moral high ground on behalf of all company staff and the public, while forfeiting immediate business interests that are the sole concern for board members.

Figure 2.2 captures the pivotal moment in episode 39 when Su appeals to the board's and the company leadership team's emotions in front of the blowup of one of those retirees under Xia's wing, a Master Niu or "Ox," which signifies bullishness and supreme expertise. "Master Niu," Chairman Zhao recalls in private earlier, "is not named Niu at all, but he is so skilled in laying bricks that we all called him Master Niu." This wistful, nostalgic tone rubs off on the fifty-six-year-old chief engineer looking down shamefacedly in figure 2.2 as well as other members of the senior leadership team at the table, having worked alongside Master Niu in their youth at the construction site. Arguably, mourning for Master Niu, who has been cared for not by themselves but by an unknown company upstart Xia Ming, is tantamount to self-mourning for all the board members nearing retirement. Sixty used to be the official retirement age for male workers in China. Originally, the leadership team is poised to dethrone Chairman Zhao, yet Su's affective presentation, coupled with Xia's chameleonic yet ultimately benevolent sleight of hand, swings the votes dialectically. Melodrama for individual plight serves to preserve the hegemony of centralized power. Chairman Zhao survives the no-confidence vote, despite framed charges in government investigations euphemistically known as "invited for tea," to implement Su's and Xia's power-sharing plan. Whether all onboard the ship *Win Ocean* would come to own the ship remains to be

FIGURE 2.3. Wu Hongmei sobs in the company restroom in episode 7 of *The Ideal City*.

seen, if there is a sequel to *The Ideal City,* tentatively titled, shall we say, *The Real City.*

What we do witness in reality, however, is fierce, cutthroat competition in respective professions like crowded lanes of a swimming meet for one billion strong contenders, starting from preschool screening through college entrance examinations and job markets. The TV industry, for instance, countenances a handful of such "gold medalists" as Sun Li over the past decade, where many flail in "Male/Female No. 2 and No. 3"—actual terminologies in use—and more forgettable roles before drowning. Ranking from top to bottom comes naturally to the Chinese, from exam results to job applications, culminating in Su Xiao's winning bids for construction contracts, which spell Xia Ming's and other bidders' losses. Also serving as a counterexample to Su's win-win triumphalism is the Chinese conglomerate Evergrande (恆大 "permanent" and "grand") on the brink of collapse in 2021, saddled with over $300 billion in debt, sending panic and jolts throughout global stock markets. Contrary to its namesake, the property developer is neither forever nor all that epochal.

In his minimalist performance, well-nigh nonperformance, Zhao Youting subverts his earlier action hero persona from *Black & White Episode 1: The Dawn of Assault* (2012), *Black & White: The Dawn of Justice* (2014), and *Chronicles of the Ghostly Tribe*. Cast against type, all the supporting cast scintillate with similar tour de force performances. These "lesser" roles prove to be "more," exceeding all expectations. Zhao Youting's quiet conniving in the company versus his Thoreauvian "quiet desperation" home alone shines alongside other stars as "minor" characters. A case in point: Su Xiao's *guimi* or confidante is Wu Hongmei, the timid, mousy HR employee played by Gao Ye, whose reputation thrives on Pan Jinlian–style, temptress sexiness in *Absurd Accident* (2017), *If There Is No Tomorrow* (2020), the 12-episode TV series *Detective Chinatown* (2020), and *Vacation of Love* (2021). The erstwhile "loose" woman has become so "tight" that she sobs throughout the series, repeatedly humiliated by her HR boss, Maria, parachuted in from abroad and smattering her conversations and commands with English. Figure 2.3 seizes one of these moments in episode 7 when Wu retreats to the company restroom to cry yet again, her lipstick smeared across her face like a clown. She sniffles as well in the dingy shared bathroom of her *nongtang* (decrepit, turn-of-the-last-century row housing) tenement, always a high-angle shot looming over her stooped body, whimpering uncontrollably until a stall opens to reveal a curious neighbor finishing his business.[6] Miserable at work, Wu is largely ignored at home by her penny-pinching, video-game-addicted partner, played by Dai Xu, who used to be the impeccably dressed and coiffed defense attorney Mai Fei in *The Best Partner* (2019–20).

Wu Hongmei wagers on a Cinderella transformation with Chairman Zhao, which comes to fruition toward the concluding episodes when her thick glasses are off, with alluring hairdo and dress, awaiting the arrival of Zhao. Conservative patriarchy consolidates itself not only in offices serviced by young, beautiful secretaries but also after work by a mistress bending down at the door to help him change into slippers, serving a bowl of noodles with homemade sauces, watching, with a grateful smile, the master savor her noodles. That Chairman Zhao is as soft-spoken as Xia Ming exemplifies a soft masculinity rather than a softie, one that rules over all in the guise of caring, fatherly—loverly—gentleness, reflecting the rhetoric of China's "soft power." Whereas the manly Wang Yang wines and dines clients, Chairman Zhao, the strong(est) man, has no need for such formality.

This difference comes through in the dramatic turn of episode 25. Learning of her promotion to the post of economic vice president at the Yinghai headquarters, Su professes her intention to decline and stick with Wang Yang. Wang joyously drives her to Yinghai, waiting by the curbside to take her back. Yet in the chairman's office, without even raising his head or addressing anyone in particular, Zhao asks casually: "If we sign with Baogang [state-owned Baowu Steel Group], what price should steel be?" Caught off guard, indeed,

---

6. *Nongtang,* or *"lilong"* in Anna Greenspan's *Shanghai Future* (2014), "recalls British row housing, which was designed for the efficient mass-housing of urban workers. With the *shikumen* structure, this was conjoined with the traditional patterns of Chinese courtyard dwellings" (117).

FIGURE 2.4. The montage of Su Xiao's surprised face and her mental screens in episode 25 of *The Ideal City*

not knowing that the question is directed at her, actress Sun Li's big, slightly bulging eyes almost pop out, followed by superimposed rapid-fire images of mental calculations of stocks and market shares (figure 2.4), which would shape the landscape of the national construction business. The montage of Su's face and her mental screens resonates with Burkean and Den Tandt's "oceanic sublime." Chairman Zhao reminds one of the patient, seemingly disinterested, snake offering an apple that Su cannot refuse. Coming downstairs, a dazed Su repeats Zhao's question to Wang Yang, who seizes, turns, and walks back to his car, crushed. All his muscular vitality resembles but sound and fury, nullified by the temptation from the tree of knowledge and power. Raided by the parent company, voided of any fighting chance in a fast-evolving market, Wang Yang lapses into a prolonged incommunicado hangover in the name of entertaining nonexistent clients. Melodramatic dialectic, by definition, shies away from those fallen through the cracks, the disenfranchised losers in a nominally win-win contest. The possibly alcoholic Wang offers a fleeting glimpse of the dark side of melodramatic dialectic. Although the TV series elects a homonym of Yang, the name Wang Yang does pun with "ocean," one to be sailed across or ridden roughshod over by Chairman Zhao's company, Win Ocean.

Yet even the supreme leader Chairman Zhao has to be re-educated by Xia and Su. Receiving Su Xiao's proposal of "All Employees Become Stakeholders," Zhao bursts out: "I told you to merge companies, not to cut board members' life," or more idiomatically, "not to revolt against the board." In this rare flare-up, his voice raised, Zhao subconsciously splits *geming* (革命 revolution) into its two components: "cut" and "life." To stage a revolution is to cut short the life of antirevolutionaries. The subsequent two times when Chairman Zhao reiterates his initial objection, he presents it in a slightly revised way: "I didn't ask you to cut my life," replacing "board members' life" with "my life." One possibility is that the board and he are synonymous in his mind. But since the board lends its support to Zhao's second-in-command Wang Mingyu, who has sworn to defend the board's interest and stocks, including, needless to say, Wang Mingyu's own 15 percent, against Su's proposal, Chairman Zhao's shifting rhetoric may be a tactical move to personalize his sacrifice. As Yinghai's largest shareholder, Zhao stands to lose the most in endorsing Su's populist, anti-elitist idea. Zhao's change of heart from his initial outburst has been preempted in episode 1, of course, through his brief hospital audience with Director He, the Party conscience and the infallible leader.

A wonderful supporting cast indeed forms the backbone on which *The Ideal City* rises. Akin to Hollywood's Lon Chaney, "Man of a Thousand Faces," Gao Ye, Chen Minghao, and Yu Hewei merit critical accolades. Characters, however, blossom in sets, which are ingeniously designed in a TV series on urban architecture. Lighting appears to be a perennial problem in scenes within Wang Yang's crappy, cluttered company, as though the TV director angles for noirlike silhouette and chiaroscuro. Progressively, Su moves to Xia Ming's midsized company with natural lighting and finally to Yinghai's skyscraper with the stunning panorama of the Huangpu River, the Bund, and Pudong's Oriental Pearl Tower and World Financial Center. The wide-open space bathed in sunlight liberates Su, only to trap her in cliquish politics and commercial greed.

Home life follows the same trajectory. The upscale apartment with a grandiose cityscape finds Xia Ming talking to his virtual assistant named "Xiao Du, Xiao Du," "du" a double entendre for both a common surname and "ferrying across," implying a more purposeful life with Su than with a computer-generated female voice. Xiao is "little" for intimacy. Xiao Du is the Chinese version of Apple's Siri or Russian-made Alice. That Xia always summons twice points to his intuitive grasp of the doubleness, the duplicity of virtual reality in simulation of the real. From Xia's top penthouse, the show drops, figuratively, to Su's modest rental, with memorable backlit shots of calls to her father or jumping rope as Su gropes in the dark of company politics, and finally crashes at Wu's dilapidated nongtang (figure 2.5 from episode 22). As Wu and her partner bend down to negotiate the narrow stairs, a slapdash disrepair surrounds them. The red banner and lanterns at the bottom of the frame wish all residents a Happy Lunar New Year, as though mocking Wu's conditions: parasitic rural parents to whom any New Year homecoming is inconceivable; a self-absorbed partner in whose companionship Wu is to spend the remainder

FIGURE 2.5. Wu Hongmei climbs the stairs of her dilapidated *nongtang* in episode 22 of *The Ideal City*.

of her life; and a job as much a dead end as the nongtang itself. Su's and China's soaring is shadowed by Wu's sore life, to be salved as Chairman Zhao's "kept woman" or as his true love.[7] But that is a future as hypothetical as all employees owning company stock. To own oneself, one owes it to the captain of the ship. Gratitude comes before being granted capitalist privileges disguised as communist rights.

Gothic *Rattan* and Naturalist *Hunter*

Ideal or otherwise, the city's shadow or ghost is banished en masse to China's Wild West. Dialectically opposite to, and spatially west of, the secular, realist setting of the majority of urban Chinese TV series, *yao* or monsters come to populate the Chinese gothic genre of web novels and period dramas. Likewise, naturalist struggles unfold in China's Wild West in the vein of Hollywood

---

7. The juxtaposition of Su Xiao's soaring and Wu Hongmei's soreness validates a fundamental difference between Western and Eastern thought. Tracing modern skyscrapers to Gothic cathedrals of vaulted arches and flying buttresses, Rem Koolhaas maintains in *Delirious New York* (1997) that "the greater the distance from the earth, the closer the communication with what remains of nature (that is, light and air)" (82). Or, alternately, worshippers move closer to God in the Middle Ages. Yet Zhang Yang's 1999 film *Shower* presents Beijing's crickets living in high-rises as emaciated because they are removed from *diqi* (earth air), no longer virile in chirping and traditional cricket dueling. The air in Chinese reckoning exists not only above but also below, within soil. Air comes as much in the form of physical existence of oxygen as in spiritual energy or vitalism pregnant in the earth.

westerns. Both gothic and naturalist TV dramas present escapist reveries from ideological bondage. Yet both suggest escape artists Sinologizing not only China's exotic Orient of westernmost minority cultures but also Western theories of gothic supernaturalism and Darwinian naturalism.

Yet urban TV series' relative realism, including "politically correct" jingoism, and the supernatural, primitive wild are not mutually exclusive. Given that the American West is one of the pivots for American exceptionalism, Western scholars have long explored the shared root of romanticism in seemingly disparate genres of realism, naturalism, and gothicism, particularly that which unfolds in the frontier wilderness of the turn-of-the-last-century West in Jack London, Frank Norris, and Bret Harte. Eric Sundquist, among others, has identified "gothic intensification of detail" within naturalism ("The Country of the Blue" [1982] 13). A critical consensus converges around the characteristic of "naturalist gothic" in Christophe Den Tandt's *The Urban Sublime* and in Eric Carl Link's *The Vast and Terrible Drama* (2004). Charles L. Crow's *American Gothic* (2009) and David S. Gross's "No Place to Hide" (1993), likewise, concur as to the prevalence of "Gothic Naturalism" in the context of American literature. American realism, repressed phantasmagoria, and Darwinian survival of the fittest blend together in the American West as these Western writers and their capitalist nation expand, while plagued by anxiety over its success and by conscience over those trampled along the way. The higher the climb, the riskier the fall, and the more bodies one squashes. Just as America projects unknown danger and repressed guilt onto the estranging frontier, the strangers in the frontier and beyond bear the brunt of London et al.'s xenophobia, Sinophobia in particular over "perennial aliens" from the other side of the ocean.[8] Young America's physical multiplication and psychic regression in the nineteenth century lay out a "déjà vu" scenario for Old China's "China Dream" in the twenty-first. What America has done to its West, China reprises "with Chinese characteristics." The West, as James K. Folsom notes, "is a country of the mind" (40).

All three TV series aired in 2021; available around the world through various online platforms, *The Ideal City, Rattan,* and *Hunter* triangulate unwittingly China's present condition. As though evicted from Shanghai's skyscrapers and nongtang, the eponymous gothic monster *Siteng* (literally, "Control/Govern Rattan," translated simply as the series' English title *Rattan*) fuses extraterrestrial intelligence from outer space with forest rattan. Put another way, the protagonist Siteng weds the aliens' AI with a primordial organism's

---

8. See chapter 1, "Sinophobia/Sinophilia, circa 1870–2020, Harte-Trump," in my *Tao of S* (2022).

instinct. The traditional Chinese moniker *yao* or monster, laden with ambiguity, bifurcates Siteng into a spectrum of evil alterity and benevolent spirit. The female lead, Jing Tian, splendidly dramatizes the character's ethereal beauty and mysterious power, with a dazzling wardrobe of modernized *qipao* (women's traditional long gowns) and accessories. By contrast, the ex–police officer Wei Jiang in *Hunter,* played by Qin Hao, lapses into self-abject survivor guilt after a bloody confrontation with poachers of the endangered Tibetan antelopes, only to find his partner executed. Siteng's regal feminine beauty and Wei Jiang's broken, traumatized masculinity polarize Chinese viewers' wanderlust for the non-Han, exotic, and even Orientalized Other. Siteng materializes out of traditional Chinese female ghost stories, with the added cachet of the natural world of the borderland, even the planetary beyond. With lawlessness projected from China proper onto the Wild West, Wei Jiang, a pun on "defend territory," battles Chinese and Indigenous poachers and other riffraff. Far from a solo fight, Wei's is a communal/communist endeavor, assisted by fellow police officers and locals. Despite the different contexts, what David Mogen et al. describe in *Frontier Gothic* is quite apt: "the dark, gothic underside of American frontier literature ironically symbolizes the desolation wrought by progress, the psychological deprivation of alienation, and the threatening but revolutionary possibilities that appear when civilized conventions are left behind" (23). Displaced westward from cities, gothic and naturalist Chinese TV series pitch an angelic-demonic female and a Chinese hero in location shooting to entertain the Sinophone spectators globally. China's frontier and its inhabitants function as props in the psychodrama of, by, and for China, just as the West Coast has done for America.

Author Wei Yu (尾魚 "Tail Fish" in Chinese) opens her web novel *Banyao Siteng* (*Half-Monster Rattan*) squarely in Tibet, whereas the TV adaptation only hints at Tibetan dresses, speech patterns, foodstuffs, and lifestyle. Conspicuous symbols of Tibetan religion and culture, however, are elided on TV. The shooting location shifts among Shangri-la, Yunnan, adjacent to the province of Tibet; Wuxi, a famed city in Jiangnan or south of the Yangtze River; and the colossal movie studio at Hengdian, Zhejiang. Be it the physical western China, Western Orientalism of Shangri-la, or Jiangnan's legendary water-towns, i.e., the classical, painterly towns with waterways and exquisite gardens and estates, the sets of *Rattan* eschew altogether contemporary China reflected in *The Ideal City*'s Shanghai. With its golden age of traditional drama and culture from the turn of the last century, Wuxi and Jiangnan at large are chosen to evoke the past nostalgically, as the split screen of figure 2.6 illustrates.

The montage of the 2020 image of an automobile in color and a horse-drawn carriage in 1939 in black and white from episode 2 encapsulates the trending genre of *chuanyuewen* (穿越文 literature of temporal and spatial

FIGURE 2.6. The montage of 2020 and 1939 in episode 2 of *Rattan*.

FIGURE 2.7. A long shot establishing the motif of doubleness in the reflection of sky in water in episode 2 of *Rattan*.

crossing) that fuses imperial and millennial, old and new China. This contrast implies further descent downward into prehistoric, old-growth forest and rattan, as well as ascent upward into the futuristic, Sino-fi extraterrestrial existence.[9] Both the automobile and the carriage are bound for Dana, a minority town out of China's "left field," so to speak, where the supernatural abounds. Also from episode 2, figure 2.7 is a long shot, establishing the motif of

---

9. For Sino-fi, see chapter 8, "Online Bingeing of Free Chinese TV Bound to Soft Power: Entrance Exam Series and Sino-Fi," in *The Tao of S*.

doubleness in the reflection of sky in the water, as if the vehicle skirts the sliver of space between worlds. That proximity of mountain and water already surfaces at the lower right-hand corner of figure 2.6's upper half. Doppelgangers of past and present, human and ghost, master and slave, Jiangnan and Shangri-la, man and woman recur throughout. Yet this motif is manifested as much in the Wild West as it is in Shanghai. *The Ideal City*'s logo in the web novel's cover as well as in each TV episode's opener evinces a cityscape reflected in the sky upside down, a mirage in a body of water, as it were. Realism in the city advertises itself by way of a dreamscape.

The halfness pregnant in these images bespeaks Tzvetan Todorov's definition of the uncanny in *The Fantastic* (1973), dangling between the rational and the mystical. It acquires unique salience in light of not only the tongue-and-groove, yin-yang circle of Taoism but also the tradition of yao, often female ghosts with long black hair and white silky dress exacting revenge against patriarchy. Outlawry par excellence, yao's standing is further burnished for its kinship to the insurrectionist CCP. Inhabiting the limbo state between light and darkness, yao manifests fluid duality throughout popular culture, crystallized in the feminine trope of lush, cascading hair. Taiwan–Hong Kong actress Brigitte Lin's *The Bride with White Hair I* and *II* (*Baifa Monüzhuan*, both in 1993) pivot on the climax when love metastasizes into hate, the protagonist's long black hair graying instantly into snowy white. The Chinese title's *mo* (demon) is synonymous with yao. The hair color denotes desirable youth and beauty versus devilry and wrath. During Mao's reign, the revolutionary model Peking opera *The White-Haired Girl* (1951) instigates antifeudal revolt through the suffering of the eponymous woman whose hair turns white after having been violated by the landlord, to be avenged by the Communist Eighth Route Army. The ghostly long hair flows further afield, across J-horror *Ringu* (1998) and its millennial international brood, dripping wet as they climb up the killing well, in addition to the Taiwanese–Hong Kong–Chinese franchise of *Painted Skin* (1992, 2008, 2012), which winds up morphing via computer-generated images the protagonist's hair color tones rather than skin tones.

The flipping of black and white hair exemplifies a narrative of masquerade and encryption. Starting from its title, all key names in this web novel occlude as much as they clarify. The story opens in medias res when a tourist to Dana in western China, Qin Fang, is pierced through the heart by a tree stump when he is drugged, his car pushed over a cliff. Qin's blood magically revives Siteng, buried underneath, courtesy of special effects and CGI. Such cinematic gadgetry plays a far greater role than *The Ideal City*'s secular storyline. Siteng, the manifest or yang half of her, was stabbed in the back four score and one years ago by the evil half, Bai Ying, split from the host body after having been denied the hand of an undeserved lover. Bai Ying's lover serves at the direction of Qiu Shan, a fiendish "witch hunter." Bai Ying's name approximates the dark half of yin in a Taoist circle. The homicide or suicide of a schizophrenic sprite enacts the black/white dichotomy in that Bai Ying, true to her namesake, wears black, her face hidden under a black hood. Siteng, by contrast, is in a white gossamer robe. In episode 27 of *Rattan*, as Siteng lays dying after Bai Ying's second ambush decades later, Siteng's hair slowly grays. By contrast, Qiu Shan's hair is shockingly white to symbolize his deviousness—representational ageism in a people of black hair, natural or dyed. Both Siteng and Bai Ying belong to *Yizu* (苅族 Yi Tribe) since time immemorial, sired by extraterrestrial meteors and forest rattan in the case of Siteng, the hardness of rocks wedded to the clinging of rattan. An archaic word rarely seen, yi (苅) puns with "foreign" (異) and "barbarian" (夷). Yi shuns the two historically fraught terms while secretly gesturing to its homonyms. By uttering the sound of the first word, the speaker winks, knowingly or involuntarily, at the latter two in Fredric Jameson's *The Prison-House of Language* (1975).

The shamans, such as Qiu Shan, pitted against Yizu constellate into *Xuanmen* (懸門). Meaning hanging or suspended, xuan is a double entendre of 玄 for the occult, or sects of mysticism. Anathema to each other, Yizu "witches"—none of them is male—and Xuanmen witch hunters—all males except one who is a disguised witch—are most alike with their names encoded. The division of female witchcraft and male exorcism is unabashedly sexist and ageist. The esotericism of exorcising rituals would have been deepened by Tibetan Buddhism and native Lamaism, had the director Li Muge tapped into local symbolism. Instead, Li settles with cartoonish scenes and props for the witch-hunting wizards, himself included with a miniature folding fan and an array of fashionable hats, like formulaic comic relief to the main story of Siteng and Qin Fang's romance.

That romance is winningly hilarious, between the "dominatrix" of a divine being and her lowly serf, who is commanded in the first episode to tie her boots in figure 2.8—*his* boots, rather, given up to shod her bare feet on the forest floor from which both are resurrected: Siteng by Qin's blood, and Qin by Siteng's magic power. Gazing into the distance, Siteng strikes a stylized, regal pose over the squatting Qin. The affectation of her body language and elocution, although dubbed in the studio, join to effect a haughtiness far above humanity. Siteng thus catwalks through thirty episodes as if she were a fashion model totally oblivious to the eyes below. The only exception of Siteng being out of character is in episode 25 when she impersonates a man impersonating her. This sounds torturous, but Jing Tian's comic skits are far more side-splitting than all the comic sidekicks' acts put together.

FIGURE 2.8. Qin Fang tying Siteng's boots in episode 1 of *Rattan*, underlining the master-slave relationship.

After protracted dialectical struggles against a fellow witch, Scarlet Umbrella, her bad "twin" Bai Ying, and Qiu Shan, who created and abused a young Siteng, the series ends by merging romance with environmental concerns, deviating from the phallocentric and human-oriented Anthropocene. Back into the forest where they originated, a reincarnated Siteng pushes the comatose Qin Fang, who gave up his sentience in exchange for Siteng's second coming. (The plot twists prove far more elaborate and convoluted than this synopsis, in keeping with the genre of melodrama's rounds of teary farewells and reunions as well as gothic deaths and rebirths.) Qin turns out to be the *Qingtian* (propping up the sky) Tree on which Siteng used to cling, until Qiu Shan forcibly divorced the rattan from the tree. As Qin and Siteng enter the forest and etherealize into light, the human drama comes to an end, to be continued by life and death beyond human senses and cognition. With development and progress spreading like cancer from *The Ideal City* and the coast, *Rattan* registers its demurral, if not dissent, in the metaphor of Govern Rattan, which remains governed and exploited by humans.

This ecological angle permeates *Hunter* as well, mediated through Darwinian naturalism, Hollywood westerns, and action thrillers. With breathtaking cinematography, *Hunter* erupts in an adrenaline rush, with explosions and firefights galore, interspersed with tense stillness. The Chinese title *Lielangzhe* (*One Who Hunts Wolves*) is not to be taken literally, as no physical wolf graces the series. Rather, poachers are nicknamed *langzi* (wolves), an ambiguous symbol in today's China. The wolf is idolized as the top predator amid social Darwinism, while betokening uncontrollable ferocity and precarity. Poaching of endangered animals has long been a favorite motif set in the western hinterland away from coastal cities and central plains and, theoretically, away from the sphere of influence emanating from Beijing. Tian Zhuangzhuang's *The Horse Thief* (1986) and Lu Chuan's *Mountain Patrol* (*Kekexili* 2004) feature as two prominent examples out of a myriad of films and TV series located in or near Tibet. While Beijing reaches its tentacles into corners of minority lands, this cultural annexation—"cultural genocide" to some natives—in Tibet, Xinjiang, and the southwest is ironically portrayed as a defense against criminal elements plundering natural resources. Beijing has its western borderland in a chokehold in the name of fending off reverse colonization by evil forces.

Déjà vu all over again: early America psyched itself up for colonization across Native American territories by means of a paranoia over reverse colonization propagated in captivity narratives, such as Mary Rowlandson's 1682 account of her "Captivity and Restoration." In denial of America holding Native Americans captives, captivity narratives justify physical and conceptual violence in American history. White fear rears its ugly Trumpian head again, propped up by contemporary conspiracy theory of the Great Replacement. Accordingly, white populations of European descent are allegedly being replaced by peoples of color.

Contemporary politics aside, *Rattan* and *Hunter* disturb like skeletons in the Chinese psychological closet. These Wild West stories manifest latent fear of individual and collective demise in a China plunging ahead with the fervor of social Darwinism and hegemonic domination. Together with *The Ideal City*, they gesture to the inevitability of companies sinking alongside the unsinkable *Win Ocean* steered by the Great Helmsman; of Siteng getting murdered by none other than herself, a yao or yin within the yang of the Chinese Century; and of the archetypal hero of *Hunter* wasting away, a drunk whose shaking hands could not even shoot straight, even with a shotgun of multiple pellets. Missing with a shotgun blast is considerably worse than doing so with a pistol, as in the case of Kirk Douglas's alcoholic Doc in *Gunfight at the O.K. Corral* (1957). However, bad shots are key to the longevity of Wei Jiang et al. as well as to the longevity of the series. Even the poachers, who show none of Wei Jiang's symptoms of alcoholism, can never find their targets, even with an AK-47, the automatic rapid-fire assault rifle. Die-hard on both sides in over-the-top duels and action sequences, the series relies on spectatorial suspension of disbelief to splice human frailty in the wilderness with heroic and demonic immortality.

The ex-cop Wei Jiang quit the police force after losing his partner to a gang of armed poachers. Years later, the gang re-emerges. Wei Jiang, aided by a young police officer in the tradition of the "buddy movie," avenges his partner as well as his own honor. Much of the action seems inspired by Hollywood with a veneer of China's Wild West. Captured most likely on Steadicams through the rugged terrain, running and shooting at each other in the forest harks back to *The Last of the Mohicans* (1992). Wei Jiang fighting his way out of a desert depot evokes innumerable precedents of heroes trapped in a ravine, saloon, sheriff's office, town, or fortress in the lawless, "Indian-infested" west. Panoramic shots of Wei Jiang and his partner riding through the bleak desert, along the ridge of a hill, in between soaring conifers are patently references to cowboy movies.

In addition to the legendary sandstorm from the Gobi Desert that envelopes the depot at the climax of the duel, one apparent Chinese characteristic may simply be that the shotgun is slung across Wei Jiang's back rather than resting in the leather case by the side of the mount. Shouldering the shotgun recalls how ancient *wuxia* (swordsman) carry the sword in novels and films of knight-errantry. Nor does Wei carry a sidearm like cowboys. On a more serious note, one distinct and perhaps "stinky" Chinese characteristic lies in the poachers' shared local accent, intimating their non-Han identity and social class, particularly the "substandard" speech pattern and intonation affected by Fifth Elder Brother, nicknamed Fox (Sui Yongliang), and the gang's hanger-on Batu (He Chen). The other gang members' elocution is only marginally better. In real life, both Sui and He are of Han descent, the former trained at Beijing's Central Academy of Drama, the cradle for the bulk of Chinese actors. These fake minorities are depicted as so feral that they prey upon native feral animals, if not one another, for profit. They constitute naturalism's "evolutionary throwbacks," who barely speak Putonghua or Standard Chinese. Cruel and vengeful, the gang help themselves to meats boiling in a hotpot while Fox at the table muffles his cry of cutting off a pinkie to make up for a botched mission. Against such Indigenous depravity, Putonghua-speaking Han police officers sacrifice their lives to, allegedly, save minorities from themselves. Through dialects and other features, the non-Han versus the Han dialectic is staged by the cultural apparatus under the CCP, a behind-the-scenes Party manipulation like Xia Ming's calculated traffic jam and company debts.

Fox's mangled Mandarin resonates with other accents prevalent in TV series on drug dealers speaking either in a nonstandard accent or in English outright. Although these drug-interdiction shows fall outside the parameters of this present triangulating, gesturing to them in closing underscores the nationalist impetus that is the common denominator of melodramatic dialectic shared by the trio of gamblers, goths, and Darwins. Bad Chinese- or English-speaking drug-trafficking villains invariably make their incursion into China from abroad, either through Southeast Asia as in *Wolf Warrior* or from the Anglophone West as in *Never Say Goodbye*. This foreign invasion taps into modern Chinese history when the Qing dynasty was "quartered," so to speak, by Western colonial powers, Japan included, in the wake of the mid-nineteenth-century Opium Wars. Drug or *du,* a loaded word, carries the odious ring of this "century of national shame" until, supposedly, the founding of the PRC (People's Republic of China) in 1949.

If there is any validity to President Xi's mantra "with Chinese characteristics," they would stem from history as much as language, or, more precisely, the inimitable traits of a tonal language. Consider the infinitude of du! Intentionally or subliminally, opium or drug of du is associated with all its sound-alikes. In tonal rather than alphabetical order, dū in the first tone of Mandarin means capital (都) as in the nation's capital of Beijing, where drug-interdiction policies originate and TV series licensing is granted. Erstwhile opium and current synthetic drugs are deemed dú (毒) in the second tone for "poison," encompassing all addictive substances. Whereas "drugs" in English have a neutral connotation for medical prescriptions, the Chinese dú points to poison and toxicity exclusively. Dǔ in the third tone means to gamble (賭) in ferrying drugs, invariably from outside China—never domestic or homemade—across customs and borders under the Public Security's surveillance, which concludes, at long last, in the fourth and last tone dù (渡 crossing, overcoming).[10] Among the many homophones not mentioned, one stands out: dú (獨) in the second tone signals the loner, either the Chinese hero in drug enforcement, as heavy-handed as Wei Jiang's name of "defend territory," or the drug cartel archvillain. Beijing TV syndicates under the National Radio and Television Administration monopolize not the sale of addictive drugs but the procurement of entertainment, the opiate of the secular masses. History and language coalesce into a quintessentially Chinese echo chamber to amplify the antipathy against drugs in these TV shows. Besides the individual "loner," dú (獨) stigmatizes ethnic and cultural independence in the midst of China. Flashing through the essentialist Sinocentric mind is the insufferable *Zangdu, Jiangdu,* and *Taidu*—the full horror of which would only come through in the Chinese original, watered down considerably in the translation of Tibetan, Xinjiang, and Taiwan Independence, although Taiwan *is* independent and has been so, de facto, since 1949. For these marginal entities to win, to gain sovereignty, it entails China's loss, geographically and ideologically. The win-win rhetoric is incompatible with the nativist sentiment. Hence, this dú or independence comes across as a dirty, hated word in a China imposing its beloved "Chinese characteristics" onto the non-Chinese.

---

10. Ironically, China has been labeled a drug-exporting country that produces large amounts of amphetamine and other illicit drugs. Recent reports of killing of Chinese drug traffickers in the Philippines also highlights the discrepancy between international perceptions vis-à-vis China's self-image. See Daphne Galvez's and Helen Flores's reporting.

CHAPTER 3

The Ghost of *Guimi* from Imperial to Millennial China

Guimi (闺蜜) is one of millennial China's favorite lexicons for boudoir confidantes, a coterie of two to four, usually three, female friends, a support network in life's struggle in a promised land of mammonism and masculinism. The use of the archaic word gui or boudoir signals that guimi stands on the shoulders of a long line of female bonding. In classical novels and costume dramas, ladies rarely appear alone, customarily attended by their maids or ladies-in-waiting. The traditional master-servant affiliation stands the ladies in good stead in court intrigues and family squabbles revolving around such men as the emperor, the patriarch, the husband, the betrothed, the intended, the philanderer, or male surrogates in the form of female matchmakers or even mothers and relatives. Although marginalized, this womance lineage forms a subtext, one overshadowed by the bromance of, for instance, the fourteenth-century classics of *Outlaws of the Marsh* and *Romance of the Three Kingdoms*.

In a "New" China where "women hold up half the sky," this womance subtext, in Chairman Mao's choice words in his Proclamation of the People's Republic of China in 1949, "has stood up," *fanshen* or flipping around from the prostrate position, manifested currently in young female protagonists in the 2020 TV series of *Twenty Your Life On* (二十不惑, literally, *Twenty No Temptation*, henceforth *Twenty*), *Nothing but Thirty* (三十而已, literally, *Barely Thirty*, henceforth *Thirty*), and *Go Ahead* (以家人之名, *In the Name of a Family*, henceforth *Family*). That the hit series do not mellow into forty- or fifty-year-old or more senior women suggests ageism despite the nominal refutation of sexism. The Chinese title of *Twenty No Temptation* flouts *The Confucian Analects*' golden rule of "Reaching forty, no more temptation" by revising the threshold downwards. Millennial youth, a time rife with temptations, is endowed, instead, with the wisdom of those twice her age in ancient China, a self-congratulatory fallacy typical of melodramas. *Twenty* revolves around four young and beautiful female roommates at the juncture of college graduation; *Thirty* focuses on three women turning thirty years old and dreading the loss of youth; *Family* features three flatmates fighting and supporting one another from their college days to the job market. Seemingly exorcising traditional sexism in their shared female focus, they exercise not only ageism but implicit sexism in women's subjugation to money, if not to men with money. This irony is foreshadowed by the communist slogan of fanshen. Taken literally, merely turning over from a prostrate to a supine position does not elevate a bottom dog; on the contrary, the reversal makes it worse, now that women are allegedly unshackled from feudalistic patriarchy by communism. Unbound from men by the Great Helmsman, females remain handmaidens to mammon in mammoth corporations headed by male CEOs, sinking under the weight of liquid assets plied by men.

Liquid assets with the connotation of cash flow conjure up yet another tradition on whose shoulders guimi also stand: imperial and neoimperial Asian female ghosts piled high over time in a mountain of jostling, mutely screeching bones where the cheerful story of guimi perches. Female ghosts from imperial, feudal, and neoimperial Asia embody males' anxiety over their own power, fearing its loss, haunted by guilt over exercising it. Exorcising female ghosts from millennial China's women-centric TV series somehow deepens repression, making the TV series even more illusory. Such collective wish-fulfillment belongs to the dreamscape of President Xi's "China Dream." Before tackling the "superstructure" of Chinese guimi, however, one must plumb the broad, inter-Asian "base" of bones stacked up from imperial and neoimperial well-being/s, beings born out of killing wells of suicides and femicides. Since precious few emerge from the mouth of the well in ghost stories and films, guimi may well be well-beings' afterlife. Guimi are modern China's ghosts prettified with long black hair and toothy grins so perfect as to be out of this world. The popularity of guimi is in and of itself symptomatic of millennial young women's repression under patriarchy and of their own beauty propped up by the ugly bones of imperial female ghosts. The practice of suicides and homicides via wells has indeed stopped, but the spirit, pardon the expression, lives on.

Asian Well-Being/s

Serendipitously, the trope of female ghosts runs through the diametrically opposed genres of Asian melodramas and horror films, particularly through the metaphor of water. These films are populated by watery ghosts perished in the river or well, retaining attributes of liquidity in their avatars across Asia, from India to Japan to China and beyond. Patriarchal misogyny assigns blame to women, preferably youthful temptresses like the biblical Eve. Christopher Marlow's Doctor Faustus eulogizes "The face that launched a thousand ships" and endless human misery. Shakespeare's Hamlet laments "Frailty, thy name is woman." Had they had Chinese-language proficiency, Faustus and Hamlet onstage would no doubt intone the age-old maxim *Hongyan huoshui* (紅顏禍水 Rougèd Cheeks, Cursèd Water). Beautiful women are historically scapegoated for bewitching emperors, causing the fall of dynasties in the figure of speech of northern China's Yellow River that periodically flooded. The gesture to the Bible, Marlow, and Shakespeare disabuses ourselves of any Orientalist demonization of the other, whose only fault lies in sharing some of the West's worst instincts.

This cursèd water begins to lap against the Asian moviegoers' mind as far back as the poignant lyrics by and on the river of Kamal Amrohi's 1949 Hindi Bollywood ghost movie *Mahal*. Not exactly a scary film to make the audience scream, *Mahal* makes them shed tears instead through the tragic, unrequited love story stretching over several lifetimes. The imposing mansion, Mahal, built with colonial power and owned by a judge's son, is haunted because of the haunting river nearby, in which Kamini and her unnamed lover drown; to which Kamini's reincarnation Asha moves while singing "The one meant to return will return" throughout, particularly in the film's closing shot; on which Asha rows a boat intoning "never reaching the shore." "The one meant to return will return" does not say "will have returned," or, better still, "has returned." Rather, the line denotes a state of perpetual returning, casting in doubt any actual arrival. The refrain of imminent revenant bespeaks a desire never consummated. The Hindi refrain resonates eerily with what Judith Zeitlin attributes, by way of "the earliest Chinese glossary, the *Erya*," to the Chinese word *gui*, a pun on ghost and return (*The Phantom Heroine* [2007] 4).[1]

Connected through the subterranean body of water and inter-Asian culture, the returnee in the Bollywood musical shape-shifts into ghosts in Masaki Kobayashi's Orientalist-expressionist-avant-gardist *Kwaidan* (1964), based in

---

1. The double entendre of gui for "ghost" and "return" manifests, in Zeitlin's view, "a favorite logic of ancient Chinese texts to define a word in terms of a homophone" (4).

part on the American writer Lafcadio Hearn's *Kwaidan: Stories and Studies of Strange Things* (1904). Kobayashi's anthology film is so fraught with specters of ancient Japan that ancient Japan becomes spectral. "Black Hair" continues to grow beyond death in the eponymous story. "The Woman of the Snow" features a snow spirit who sucks dry human blood, yet ice seems to unfreeze as she returns human blood in bearing three children. "Hoichi the Earless" is a blind monk who chants the saga of the vanquished Heike clan women jumping into the river en masse. "In a Cup of Tea" a ghost is reflected; eventually, even the writer of that ghost story looks back from the bottom of the cup. Kobayashi favors this mise-en-scène, as the maddened samurai ex-husband in "Black Hair" also stares into the stone water jar and sees his own likeness, a crazed man with disheveled hair.

From ancient to modern Japan, Hideo Nakata's J-horror *Ringu* (1998) deviates from Kobayashi's arthouse approach, upgrading ghosts with horror conventions and modern amenities. Courtesy of *Ringu*'s Sadako pushed into the well, possibly by her own father, and similar casualties in Chinese and Chinese American novels, the world gains a new definition of well-being. In the English language, well-being means the state of happiness and health, as we wish each other well or toss coins into the proverbial wishing well. As though ripping asunder the English word "well-being," Asian subconsciousness flips it into its perverse negative of killing well, which begets watery ghosts of female suicides jumped or femicides dumped into the family well. The West's gothic genre favors the family crypt and cathedral vault as the setting where the vampire is resurrected and the innocent virgin violated, where Christianity is soiled by kinship with evil. By contrast, Asian ghost stories break water from the family well, where life-sustaining water becomes the amniotic fluid to ease into the world preternatural haunting. Gothic horror intensifies, framed by Western religiosity; Asian well-beings multiply, rippling through the subterranean body of water from the body flailing in the family and patriarchal tradition.

All three Asian films of female ghosts come with foreign-sounding titles. Each hails from a foreign culture, the otherworldliness befitting alien visitants. The Hindi word *Mahal* has a Persian and Arabic root. *Kwaidan* means "Strange Tales" in Chinese. *Ringu* japonizes the telephone "ring," with the added association of rings and ripples from the well as well as the ring or clique of evil. Within each film respectively, self-splitting persists. Asha in *Mahal* veils her whole face in a ghungat throughout, until the final courtroom scene, as India's "real face" pits itself against British law. "In a Cup of Tea," one of the four shorts in *Kwaidan*, displaces the apparition onto the bottom of a medieval Japanese cup, a fate subsequently befalling a turn-of-the-last-century writer, all viewed from the safe distance of 1964. Likewise, *Ringu* projects the ghostly Japan onto prewar Western-influenced spiritualism, not to mention the West-originated modernity of telephone, television, and VCR.

Part of this broad inter-Asian base, Chinese literature has many Sadako-style well-beings, albeit those bodies once alive have rarely been so named and memorialized in a body, pun intended. Whereas only one of the following Chinese instances resembles Sadako pushed by the father or father figure into the well, all the cases wind up in the well through the invisible hand of patriarchy. In chapter 32 of the eighteenth-century classic *Dream of the Red Chamber* (紅樓夢), the maid Golden Bracelet (金釧兒) to Madame Wang, the male protagonist Jia Baoyu's mother, is slapped and expelled by Madame Wang for "leading astray" Baoyu. Shame and despair drive Golden Bracelet to jump into and drown herself in the family well. Her tragic end is foreshadowed by her last words to Baoyu as he flirtingly puts a lozenge in her mouth: "What's your hurry! 'A golden hairpin dropped in the well, what's yours will always be yours'" (chapter 30, 226). That she cites a common saying with unwitting Freudian, oral-sexual connotation does not save her when conventional wisdom collapses in the face of her master's rage. From her expulsion in chapter 30 to her suicide two chapters later, Baoyu continues to enjoy amorous relationships with various women, as if already forgotten about the golden accessory, bracelet or hairpin, out of his sight. Although the gold may still belong to the owner Baoyu, he has compensated the loss with subconscious escapism to other women, until the shock of her suicide and the punishment by his father.

Golden Bracelet is one of the *Sida lienü* (四大烈女 Four Fierce/Fiery/Righteous Women) celebrated by the readers' misogyny in *Dream of the Red Chamber*. Owing to an unworthy lover, loyalty and self-preservation, and unrequited love, the other three "fierce women" commit suicide by slitting the throat with the lover's sword, by hanging in honor of her master's death, and by cracking the head against the wall. A gang of four scapegoats sacrificed on the altar to romance and male fantasy! Yet a dark scenario unfolds in that Cao Xueqin, perhaps the greatest Chinese novelist, has touched on the collective unconscious, where handmaidens like Golden Bracelet are but expendable ornaments. Golden Bracelet's ominous words reveal that her namesake on the wrist can be erased and displaced onto the hair. She takes her own life not because she fails to return to Baoyu but because that is the only way *to* return as part of Baoyu's collection of playthings, giving the Hindi refrain "The one meant to return will return" a Sinitic, sinister spin.

Four centuries earlier than *Dream*, chapter 41 of *Romance of the Three Kingdoms* tells of Lady Mi's martyrdom. General Zhao Zilong is entrusted by the emperor Liu Bei in escorting the imperial consort Lady Mi and heir A-Dou to safety in the chaos of a battlefield. Injured and urged to mount

Zhao's steed to escape, Lady Mi replied: "What would you do without a steed? But the boy here I confide to your care. I am badly wounded and cannot hope to live. Pray take him and go your way. Do not trouble more about me" (https://www.threekingdoms.com/). She then left "the child on the ground . . . turned over and threw herself into the old well," followed by the formulaic poem in her praise:

> The warrior relies upon the strength of his charger,
> Afoot, how could he bear to safety his young prince?
> Brave mother! Who died to preserve the son of her husband's line;
> Heroine was she, bold and decisive!

Lady Mi's decision hinges on the lone horse and their sole protector. Even combining both would ensure, probably, only safe passage for the rider and no one else. Hence, she elects her child. "Seeing that Lady Mi had resolved the question by dying," Zhao decides to push "over the wall to fill the well," a makeshift grave for the lady. To protect the child, Zhao "loosened his armor, let down the heart-protecting mirror, and placed the child in his breast. This done he slung his spear and remounted." The novel does not say that the armor and the heart-protecting mirror are reinstalled because, in all likelihood, they no longer fit, now that the child occupies the space. Although exposing Zhao and the child to grave danger, this is the trade-off when a soldier takes on the role of a surrogate mother, carrying the child in the manner of suckling. Lady Mi has been replaced, akin to Golden Bracelet.

Informed of the incident in chapter 42, Liu Bei "took the child but threw it aside angrily, saying, 'To preserve that suckling I very nearly lost a great general!'" The novelist's ensuing couplet minces no words in exposing Liu Bei's chicanery: "No way to comfort a loyal subordinate / deliberately throw his own child in front of the horse." "Deliberately" aims to translate the word *gu* (故), which carries a strong undertone of affectation and ruse. Most revealing is Liu Bei's utter silence on Lady Mi's sacrifice. Her death factors into his calculus of statecraft insomuch as winning over General Zhao's allegiance by putting on an act that suggests the general outweighs his heir, and definitely one of his consorts. Ironically, the infant child A-Dou, who costs his mother's life and entails his father's playacting, is known historically as *Fubuqi de A-Dou* (扶不起的阿斗 one who is so incompetent that no amount of help will put him on his own two feet). Indeed, Liu Bei's Shu Han dynasty fell during A-Dou's reign. Despite the novelist's satiric tone regarding Liu Bei's performance, suspicion lingers that Lady Mi had already been "dead and buried" discursively with the filled-in well and the maternal swaddling afterwards. This appears to confirm what Paola Zamperini calls the "good death" as opposed to the "bad death . . . that engenders ghosts and that needs to be 'exorcised'" ("Untamed Hearts" 79). Zamperini views female suicides "not as virtuous martyrs or victims of an unjust patriarchal system, but as passionate agents of free will" (77). It begs the question, though, as to whether Lady Mi exercises agency in taking her own life or she foresees her own tragic end if she survives at the expense of the heir or even General Zhao. Among the three lives, hers is the most expendable in the eye of her husband-master-emperor and, judging from centuries of reception, in the eye of the Chinese reader.

Given the popularity of Zhang Yimou's 1991 *Raise the Red Lantern,* it is in fact based on Su Tong's novel *Qiqie chengqun* (妻妾成群 The Harem of Wives and Concubines), a story of feudal oppression of women symbolized by "the well of the dead" (死人井 *sirenjing*) under a purple wisteria arbor in the polygamous husband-master's back garden. The color of purple wisteria dilutes, oxidizes the blood spilled in the well, which the plant absorbs along with water and dirt. This "altar" secreted at the back of the compound is relocated by the Chinese filmmaker to the rooftop hanging room to exploit the heritage site of the Qiao Family Compound in Shanxi. Su Tong's novel ends with the fourth wife, Song Lian, gone mad after witnessing the third wife being thrown into the well for having cuckolded the master of the house. The mad woman's last words that conclude the novel are "Song Lian says she will not jump into the well." But she is already in the well, not drowned, but neither is she truly alive. She is a living dead, a ghost in the company of the third wife's and at least three more women's corpses. J-horror's Sadako need not be the sole sighting of well-beings. A deranged Song Lian wanders in her master's compound like a will-o'-the-wisp, a ghost light for fellow guimi weltering in a homeland or homeswamp "with Chinese characteristics."

Maxine Hong Kingston's 1976 ethnic classic *The Woman Warrior* opens by translating the trope of female suicide, yet another Asian well-being from afar: "In China your father had a sister who killed herself. She jumped into the family well. . . . I do not think she always means me well. I am telling on her, and she was a spite suicide, drowning herself in the drinking water" (3, 16). The Asian American protagonist declares independence here and now by disowning the death-oriented Chinese patriarchy and by owning a matrilineage all the way back to there and then. Kingston's ethnic identity manifests itself, ambiguously, in the duality of drinking and drowning water, of an enabling and disabling China that continues to wrap "double binds around my feet" (48). On the Orientalist trope of bound feet stands Kingston's liberated Asian American woman warrior.

Similar well-beings can be culled from Japanese culture. The 1969 film *Double Suicide,* based on a *bunraku* (puppet theater) play, chronicles lovers' twin drowning. Haruki Murakami's *The Wind-Up Bird Chronicle* (1994–95) is partly set at the bottom of a well. Such plethora of killing wells and troubled waters do not the stereotype of death-prone Orientals make, though. To argue that Oriental cultures are death-prone on account of this literary and filmic motif is like arguing Christianity is a death cult on account of the crucifixion. Both contentions blithely dismiss Asian cultures' vibrant multiplicity and Jesus's resurrection.

Note the distancing in all these cases of Asian well-beings authored by Chinese males, plus one Chinese American female. Jia Baoyu escapes into female companionship to repress any thought of Golden Bracelet's desperation. Lady Mi's death is entirely dropped from her husband's consciousness when the infant prince is presented, notwithstanding the poem's praise of Lady Mi as *nüzhangfu* (female husband, female hero). Su Tong projects female oppression to the pre-Revolution 1930s. Kingston empowers her protagonist in the 1970s by remote controlling China. Such is the sound wave rippling through and out of the turn-of-the-century *Ringu,* or waves that are quite unsound, ill tidings of more well-beings.

Also note the company these well-beings keep. Golden Bracelet is one of the four fiery women and suicides in *Dream of the Red Chamber*; Lady Mi belongs to the constellation of multiple eulogized "female husbands"; Song Lian barely survives from at least four other cases of femicides; Kingston's fictional aunt joins her subtitle's *Memoirs of a Girlhood among Ghosts,* a phantasmagoria in America and Chinatown. Intertextually, these well-beings from Asian suicides and femicides form a society, a phantom sorority, literally and figuratively underground, deep in Asian subconscious. So does *Ringu,* siring its brood of *Ringu 2* (1999) and *Ringu 0* (2000) from the J-horror well, on one side of the Pacific Ocean, and *The Ring* (2002) and *The Ring Two* (2005) in the Hollywood well, on the other side. The last is directed by *Ringu*'s filmmaker Hideo Nakata, who closes his Hollywood debut with a profanity, a most un-Japanese turn of phrase, "I'm not your fucking mommy," as Naomi Watts grimaces to seal the well with a slab of stone, damning Samara to darkness. Siring "its" brood may as well be "his" brood since all the filmmakers, even the genesis of Koji Suzuki's misogynist novel *Ring* (1991), are male, multiplying "her" brood of immaculate conceptions from the namesake Sadako or chastity.

True Horror

The paranormal tenor of these ghost stories vests a sense of uncertainty in modern readers and viewers, who hesitate to either countenance or disavow ghosts. This coheres with the very definition of "the uncanny" in Tzvetan

Todorov's *The Fantastic* (1973).² Once that gothic paradox betwixt time and beyond time vanishes in secular, social realist, and melodramatic Chinese TV series, ghosts are exorcized by default. Yet that exorcism of female ghosts in the name of women's emancipation and empowerment may well be wishful thinking, more apparitional than apparitions, more self-deluding than "seeing ghosts," given the ageism and sexism hiding in plain sight in *Twenty, Thirty, and Family*. True ghosts are those humans who turn others into phantoms, into either the erstwhile demonic bent upon avenging themselves or the modern angelic empathizing with guimi over the loss of men and, implicitly, financial security. True horror resides in the mirage of beautiful fakes taken to be real. Hyperreality trumps reality.³ Far more than ghost movies, true horror is that which is taken for granted, so normalized, even valorized, that it has become an object of desire, an object of beauty.

Asian cosmetic surgery springs to mind as women and men rush to acquire—by means of scalpel, bleaching, and other extreme measures—stylized Western facial and physical features. Among other Asian American representations, Maxine Hong Kingston notes that "Asian girls were starting to tape their [epicanthic] eyelids" (*Woman Warrior* 182). Adolescent "home remedy" has since been adultized as double eyelid surgery for women and men with disposable income and body parts of skin and flesh and bone to be disposed of. Likewise, Patricia Park in *Re Jane* (2015) exposes West-idolizing when the *honhyol* or mixed-race protagonist Jane Re is complimented by her English cram-school colleague in Seoul: "Honhyol has the white skin, big eyes, big nose, small chin, long legs" (187), reminiscent of Toni Morrison's Black protagonist dreaming of *The Bluest Eye* (1970).

Popular Chinese puns on ideal mates also enlighten: Gao Fushuai (高富帅 Tall Rich Handsome) for males and Bai Fumei (白富美 White Rich Beautiful) for females. Both Gao and Bai are perfectly legitimate last names, which come first in Chinese. The two ideals, read aloud together, flow aurally like a parallel couplet in classical poetry or, as intended, like a couple in modern China. Matching Chinese couple(t) is a merger of sound and sense, of good sound and beaucoup cents of a couple flush with cash. The tonal harmony lies in

---

2. Todorov argues that the fantastic in literature is marked by "a hesitation of the reader . . . as to the nature of an uncanny event" (157).

3. Alberto Castelli in "Perspectives on Asia: Is China Kitsch?" likens China's "Hyperreality" to kitsch, "a dense world of signs and simulation that becomes more real than the real itself. . . . Computer technology, visual media in general (TV, radio, and video games) have the capacity of obliterating space and time and recreate a digital-virtual space and time where reality is replaced by simulations (TV series)" (3). In a China where "adultized children and infantile adults" view "commercialization" as a form of "religious belief" (5–6), "kitsch is the response to the sense of spiritual vacuum left by the retreat of Maoism" (13).

the symmetrical three-character names complimented by the internal rhyme, indeed, the repetition, of the pivotal "midfielder" fu or rich that lifts the performance of both the forward shock troops of masculine height ("Tall") and feminine fair complexion ("White") and the defense of the basics of good looks ("Handsome" or "Beautiful"). In reverse, either the first or the last word would mean little without the operative word in the middle. However, all these qualities are transactional, circular in nature, for those not naturally born as such. Money pays for medical procedures for height (leg-lengthening), fair skin (skin bleaching), desirable Western features (double-folded eyelids, a higher and narrower nose ridge, shaved cheek bones, an angled, even pointy jawline, and whatnot), which in turn earn wealth through marrying or being kept by sugar daddy or sugar mommy or success in showbiz and other biz.

The male and female names resemble a Chinese *shuenkouliu* (順口溜), a mellifluous, witty type of doggerel popular among folks playing on the monosyllabic, tonal, homonym-riddled, p(f)un-filled Mandarin and other Chinese dialects. To be fair to the Chinese tradition of *shuenkouliu,* the twin names augur desirable qualities, but their likeness to childish jingles, even silly tongue-twisters, lends themselves to be mocked. The nice sound turns against itself like the punchline of a joke, divorced from its power as a magic spell. By mouthing the ideals, a Chinese talks out of both sides of the mouth, confirming the general sentiment of the society with a touch of irony, an implicit critique. Sour grapes, perhaps, since few fit the profile! But repeating these names with the discursive equivalent to a smirk, a shrug, even a grimace diverges from doing so with the mouth agape, looking up at tall idols looming above like stars.

This caveat notwithstanding, the phrasal order of the ideal male, followed by his female counterpart, signals the entrenched phallocentric culture as ancient as the Old Testament's Adam and Adam's rib—in that timeless order. Rather than Keatsian "beauty is truth, truth beauty," Asia's mantra reads "cosmetic beauty is truth, truth cosmetic beauty," or simply "horror is truth, truth horror." Rather than Alexander Pope's "The sound must seem an echo to the sense" ("Sound and Sense"), this Chinese couple(t) turns the tables into "The sense must be an echo to the sound." What sounds good to Chinese ears not only makes perfect sense but also adds its two cents' worth in the piggy bank of symbolic capital. In a dizzying tautological fashion, the good sound of the couplet Gao Fushuai and Bai Fumei makes good sense as a couple, who make good money. The form of rhythmic couplets comes to dictate content to the extent that meaning-making serves to maintain such inured cultural habits as the inalienable sound-*cum*-sense, a knee-jerk, taken-for-granted reaction that leaves little room for negotiation.

The proof is in the pudding, in the words put before you. In the traditional Chinese script, the two names, should Confucius and other straight-face sages sanction such modern coinages, used to be written from the top right-hand corner down, line by vertical line, all the way to the bottom left of the page, like this:

白 高
富 富
美 帥

Yet Chinese romanization of pinyin based on the English alphabet has long immersed generations of schoolchildren in Anglicized, horizontal, and left-to-right reading and writing practice, if not the warp and weft of thought itself. This is further consolidated by computer input through the keyboard of the English alphabet, no longer in the order of strokes for each Chinese ideogram. The new system of English typing has superseded the old system of Chinese calligraphy or handwriting. Neither romanization nor computer input predetermines the layout, though. Japan, modernized even earlier than China, maintains traditional word order in newspapers and even manga. Japanese novelist Minae Mizumura is inspired by this reordering of writing in *Shishosetsu from Left to Right* (1995), described in her essay collection *The Fall of Language* as "a fictionalized autobiographical work," both a "how-I-became-a-Japanese-writer story" and a "how-I-failed to-become-a-writer-in-the-English-language story" (63–64). "By juxtaposing the two languages [in the title and throughout the novel]," adds Mizumura, "what I hoped to convey above all was the *irreducible materiality* of the Japanese language" (65, italics mine). By contrast, the *materiality* of the Chinese language is traded for digital expediency, each straight line of its classical texts fallen sideways, simplified, with multiple words retired, merged into the one with the least number of strokes. The corporeality of Chinese words vanishes in the stream of time like well-beings and their fellow guimi in the modern flow of currency.

Had literati from imperial China traveled into the future, they would be dumbfounded by the modern Chinese language so unheimlich that it seems a foreign tongue. In fact, typing the traditional vertical script from right to left, top to bottom, requires twisting the computer's arm, so to speak. To a layperson, it involves layout manipulation and a bit of dissembling since the cursor refuses to go perpendicularly from top to bottom. It goes horizontally by default. What comes naturally to a modern Chinese at the keyboard estranges a premodern Chinese holding the ink brush, and vice versa—the estrangement of one's own past or future, thus of oneself. One comes face to face with one's own ghost. To paraphrase William Faulkner's famous adage: "The ghost is never dead; it's not even past," as in the very words one deploys on this page to string together erstwhile ghosts and modern dreamscape of guimi. Neither are Asian well-beings born out of water dead or past; they seep into guimi floundering in and ultimately rising above liquid assets to consummate happy endings.

Guimi Flailing in Liquid Assets

At first blush, to claim young ladies of TV guimi are dynastic well-beings' next of kin sounds downright preposterous. How can ghosts, as beautiful as they come in Pu Songling's archetypal *Strange Tales from a Chinese Studio* (1766), be related to jovial, exquisite guimi, other than the fact that the two initial g's alliterate? Joking aside, to trace back to their fountainhead, many Sinophone ghost movies spring from Pu's classic, which abounds with female ghosts. For instance, one of Pu's most renowned tales, "The Painted Skin," inspires a host of film adaptations revolving around a demon who wears an elegant woman's skin that requires disrobing for touch-up now and then. These ghosts leave a textual presence, apparently positivist proof of their existence. Yet the notion of ghosts as empirical evidence is, in and of itself, an oxymoron, given readerly "hesitation" over the gothic and the fantastic theorized by Todorov. Estrangement inherent in Pu and the genre of ghost stories destabilizes a spectator's hold on the world in the book, on the screen, if not the hold on the world altogether. In addition, Pu's human skin is but skin-deep, veiling the fiend underneath. As though foreshadowing "horror is beauty, beauty horror," Pu concludes "The Painted Skin" with the moral "Someone is obviously a demon, but people consider her beautiful" (qtd. in Zeitlin's *Historian of the Strange* 30). On the other hand, TV series on guimi are realist dramas in a land of Marxist materialism where such "feudal superstition" finds no quarter, resulting in the total absence of ghosts. However, the eye candy of guimi masks social injustice of ageism, sexism, social Darwinism, communist authoritarianism, and countless other isms. Whereas Pu exposes the visible horror under the painted skin, guimi's painted face and impeccable coiffure and dress countenance no trace of horror, now that horror is the invisible reality, systemically and ideologically. Well-beings and guimi differ primarily in terms of the type of scope through which one surveils the alternate universe commanded by imperial man or by millennial mammon: a ghostly telescope to scan dynastic patriarchy in the distance of time; or a guimi stethoscope to detect contemporary mammonism in deep space.

To rephrase Kurtz's deathbed confession in *The Heart of Darkness* (1899), this argument on China's "Horror Then! Horror Now!" would be much simpler if the cast of guimi were the proverbial "artificial beauty" with, verifiably, a fixed nose or chin or jaw or eyes or skin. But *Twenty, Thirty,* and *Family* feature performers much too young to require surgical intervention, including *Family*'s thirty-year-old Tang Songyun playing, convincingly, a high schooler in the initial episodes. That said, it is but a common practice to powder an Asian actor's face crystalline white, eerily like a death mask next to a neck and shoulders betraying a darker hue. Such sharp unnatural contrast has come to be the natural look on the screen. If any, artificial beauties are usually relegated to supporting roles, silicon apples to the eye next to the leads' natural apples. One of *Family*'s mothers, Chen Ting (Yang Tongshu in her midforties), a belle of long standing on TV, has been rumored to have undergone cosmetic surgery, probably the result of gossip and jealousy over her looks. Further afield from China with its own paragons of artificial beauties, the 1994 Miss Korea second runner-up, Hyeon-a Seong, used to have a round face, typically Asian, evident in the 1998 TV series *Watching It Again and Again* (看了又看). Her cheekbones were subsequently shaved off, leaving a long, slender, and stylized Western face.[4] Biographical fact turns fiction in Kim Ki-duk's *Time* (2006), where Seong stars as an obsessed woman putting herself through a complete face-off, hoping to cling to her fickle lover with a new face and body.

Generically distinct as family drama and horror, guimi and well-beings appear to be apples and oranges, yet the blood tie is not that far-fetched should both fruits be artificial, factory- or studio-manufactured, *man*-made. Filmic ghosts serve as props to prop up everlasting romance or *ressentiment* across social divides and even across several lifetimes in denial of death. Classical human-ghost heterosexual love stories sugarcoat the bitter pill of the natural course of life of aging, loss, death, as well as the blunt force of patriarchy. Perpetual retelling of revenants and reincarnations is symptomatic of traumatic repetition compulsion over thwarted desires, which readily flip into revenge. On the other hand, modern female homosocial guimi sugarcoat the millennial reality of mammonism headed by male CEOs and fetishized capital. Imperial ghosts served to displace patriarchal guilt before; millennial guimi perpetuate a feel-good sentiment now. What was once cast as alien ghosts haunting male conscience has been upgraded to dream girls pleasing to all eyes and to the modern ego. One shocks; the other sucks up.

To rephrase Marx and Engels's "Manifesto of the Communist Party" (1848), "A spectre is haunting China—the spectre of communism" as well as the specter's specter: capitalism. Inaugurated by Deng Xiaoping's open-door policies since the late 1970s, China mongrelizes capitalism-communism, or

---

4. See chapter 1, "Asian Cell and Horror," in my *Asian Diaspora and East-West Modernity.*

"socialism with Chinese characteristics." Despite the euphemistic terms, China resembles Sino-ese twins of one body with two drivers, not two heads, but a head and a phallus: the market-driven, profit-seeking business world, including media and entertainment, capped by the autocratic communist party. The wolfish Darwinian competitiveness in the marketplace jars with the socialist collective utopia in ideological orthodoxy, each plotting to lord over the other, to be the winner over the loser. Each wishes to be, in yet another favorite pairs of lingo, *ba* vanquishing, possessing *zha*.

Hero-worship in Thomas Carlyle's formulation of "totalitarian personality cult" has been Sinologized in millennial China as ba-worship.[5] Ba (霸) means hegemon, ruler, superman, and/or tyrant. Well-nigh amoral, beyond moral standards, ba goes all the way back to the Spring and Autumn (771–476 BCE) and Warring States (481/403–221 BCE) period in Chinese history, when vassal states vied for the coveted position of *bazhu* or hegemon, before the First Emperor of Qin crushed them all. By definition, ba is neutral, alluding to an evil tyrant abusing power as well as to a benevolent sovereign exercising power with discretion. Far from a political system where individual rights lie at its foundation, the Chinese feel, for lack of a better term, "at home" with ba, having lived for thousands of years at a home headed by a long line of ba, from emperors to Chairman Mao to President Xi, as long as the aphrodisiac of power had not gone to the head overmuch. Ironically, ba or hegemon is the homophone of "father" (爸), the patriarch of the family or the nation. Should ba be the master of the household, its opposite zha (渣 dregs, lees, trash) would be the runt, the pathetic, good-for-nothing loser. The ba-zha split befits the winner vs. loser, eater vs. eaten, and at-the-table vs. on-the-menu dichotomy of social Darwinism. Applicable to all walks of life, from business CEOs to top test takers in schools, ba morphs between the Burkean hologram of the sublime and its inherent terror, bastardizing the Wise King and the Dark Lord into Master-*cum*-Monster.

As the setting of the business world prevails in most Chinese TV series on guimi, the representative ba is a company CEO respectfully called by his surname, followed by *zong*, short for *zongcai* (總裁 Supreme Decider, literally, with a hint of the omnipotent Supreme Dictator). Zong also happens to be the first word in *zongtong* or president. Zong can thus be roughly translated as president or chairman. Rather than mutual exclusivity of ba versus zha, Taoist yin-yang binary complementarity joins hands with Marxist dialectical materialism in producing a precarious harmony in TV series on guimi balancing

---

5. See David R. Sorensen's introduction to *On Heroes, Hero-Worship, and the Heroic in History*, p. 1.

between super(wo)men, on the one hand, and, on the other, their intended with lesser qualities that endears them to the common folk. The former—the dream self of ba—lies beyond reach; the latter of zha reflects part of viewers themselves.

Of the three TV series on the air almost simultaneously in 2020, *Twenty* leads *Thirty* in China's overall ratings partly because the twenty-year-olds in college are relatively carefree compared with the thirty-year-old working mom and "shopgirl" juggling career and family. More of a light comedy than *Thirty*, *Twenty* appeals to TV viewers' nostalgia for, even regression to, younger days. Thus, the audience's preference for dreamscape gravitates them to one series more than the other. A youthful, if not juvenile, style marks *Twenty* from the outset. Accompanied by a fast-tempo, bouncy theme song, the opening credits consist of a series of quick cuts of symmetrical images of each lead actor in split screen, as if through a child's kaleidoscope. The opening credits end with each episode's title rendered in roundish cartoon scribbles, as if in a child's hand.

The order of billing of the four guimi reveals the show's hierarchy and, by extension, China's. Of the four women, the "tallest," most eye-catching *ba*, Guan Xiaotong (playing fashion model and social media influencer Liang Shuang), receives top billing, adjacent to the "tallest" male actor, Jin Shijia (playing Zhou Xun or the investment group CEO Zhou zong), and another male actor, Niu Junfeng (playing Zhao Youxiu). Zhou zong embodies the idealized qualities of *gaoleng* (高冷 tall and cold/cool): the actor is 6′2″ and his face is carved with a perpetual sneer. An imperious, condescending mannerism of cool idols attracts worshippers in pathological crushes, variously euphemized as *nuelian* (虐戀 abusive, sadomasochistic obsession) or *anlian* (暗戀 secret crush). The widely accepted, even venerated, masochistic fixation is a throwback to Golden Bracelet's attachment to Baoyu and to Lady Mi's self-sacrifice, except it seems to sublimate the master-slave, owner-owned relationship into the self-agency of a willing slave smitten with love. The most chilling manifestation of ba-worship lies in attributing to such ba as Zhou zong "*gao zhishang*," or high IQ (intelligence quotient), to justify dictatorial leadership in a disturbingly eugenic, fascist manner, symptomatic of hero-worship. Swept up in a national frenzy over triumphalism and innate greatness, China's media conglomerate *aiqiyi* (愛奇藝) taps into this ba-worship by making over its name as iQIYI with the website of, even more blatantly, iq.com.

Niu Junfeng's character, on the other hand, comes across initially as a zha, a slick charlatan, whose first name, Youxiu (excellence), foreshadows his subsequent redemption as an art photographer. Niu's role is decidedly not as central as the other three co-starring ladies in second billing shown in the ensuing frame. To put it bluntly, the order of billing is determined as much by the performers' roles as by their height, look, and gender. The tallest female and male appear first, flanked by a secondary male actor. Arguably, even the tallest male, Zhou zong, plays but second fiddle to the other three female leads. Despite their ample airtime and tour de force acting, the three females have their names deferred to second billing.

The three thus relegated comprise Luo Yan, nicknamed Rock, withdrawn, socially awkward, indulging herself in the fantasy world of video games. Rock can afford to do so because of financial support from her attorney mother. Rock is played by Li Gengxi, who demonstrates the breadth of her acting in taking on this escapist persona, quite a departure from the insomniac, suicidal high schooler in *A Little Reunion* (2019). The other, even wealthier, roommate is Duan Jiabao (played by Dong Siyi), girlish and burikko (cute), practically a *fuerdai*, or child of the nouveau riche since the market liberalization of the late 1970s. Duan is so generous and good-natured that she is treated as an ATM machine by friends, except for her roommates, particularly Jiang Xiaoguo (played by Pu Guanjin), who shares her own coupons with Duan to help save money. To round off the four roommates, Jiang capitalizes on her Manchurian accent to silhouette a humble origin, as Manchuria or China's northeast is reputed to export impoverished migrants to coastal metropolises. A recent college graduate and a lowly intern at Zhou zong's company, Jiang still shares with her dormitory suitemates due to limited resources, a scrapper in the cosmopolitan Shenzhen, Guangdong. The petite Jiang, shortest of the four, has a crush on Zhou zong, who, despite his haughtiness, is secretly impressed by Jiang's thick-skinned drivenness. Pu Guanjin, who plays Jiang, has undergone cosmetic surgeries after this TV series, trimming her round face, whitening her skin. Her superb comic performance as the zha in *Twenty* invariably brings tears to the eyes for those who have since witnessed one actor's and one nation's striving to be the ba—and the cost it entails, including losing one's cheek bones and natural skin color.

Such is millennial China's strategy of making ba-worship palatable. To make the bitter pill go down, Mary Poppins's spoonful of sugar is replaced by a mutual attraction of the ba Zhou zong and the zha Jiang Xiaoguo, their power differentials notwithstanding. This ba-zha magnetism plays out between Liang Shuang and Zhao Youxiu as well. Sweeter still, two ba-s compete for Jiang's love. Zhou zong finds a rival in Duan's younger brother, a fencing champion with such good looks that young women constantly ask him to exchange WeChat accounts, equivalent to Facebook accounts or email addresses. Thus, two hegemons from two ends of the marriage market vie for Jiang's affection, one mature and established, the other a young and appealing fuerdai. Caught in between, Jiang reminds one of the symbol that leads the twelve-animal Chinese zodiac: the diminutive and unpresentable rat, a survivor amid market-driven adoration of ba, a residual of traditional virtues of single-minded tenaciousness, devotion, and honesty. So hard-working is Jiang that she even boasts of qualities of the ox, the second in line in the Chinese zodiac, pivotal to plowing and long revered in agriculture. In an underhanded and circuitous way, Jiang dominates *Twenty*'s opening episode, overshadowing the female ba Liang Shuang yet to make her debut.

To rephrase an American idiom, *Twenty* has the ba and eats it, too. Liang Shuang appears belatedly, in the closing moments of episode 1, to the great shock of her three roommates. They cower under her towering shadow and defer to her as Shuangjie (elder sister Shuang), a term of respect reserved for those older, more senior, and higher-up. Seeing the pieces of luggage piled on her upper bunk, a convenient storage space, Shuangjie flings them across the floor, ordering lights-out at 10:30 p.m. sharp to commence her beauty snooze. Guan, who plays Shuangjie, may indeed be the most senior actor of the cast, having been catapulted to the big screen in Chen Kaige's *The Promise* (2005) in her cameo appearance as a beggar girl. For that matter, Pu Guanjin, who plays Jiang, has a supporting role in the 2016 indie film *Mr. Donkey*, albeit a decade behind Guan. Insofar as *Twenty* is concerned, however, Jiang is the only one holding down a steady job and deserves the title *jie* (elder sister).

Absent from the dormitory for years, Shuangjie has been staying at her own luxurious apartment, thanks to the largesse of her fuerdai lover "Golf." Her roommates so nicknamed him behind her back because their romance began when Shuangjie caddied at the golf course for the rich and famous. Jiang and other roommates reluctantly share with her that Golf is to marry another fuerdai with a degree from Columbia University, dashing her dream of marrying up. Complimented as having such "long legs," or "all legs under the neck," in Jiang's endearingly whispery, mumbling, yet crisp elocution, Shuangjie's stature as the Goddess or ba crumbles upon Golf's betrayal and the disintegration of her fan base online. She begins her climb back up in the fashion model and social media business with the support of her guimi and the art photographer. The ba of yesteryear is crushed by a bigger ba with an Ivy League diploma. But Shuangjie's renascence in showbiz, despite a vengeful Golf's obstruction, elevates her above and beyond the nouveau riche with Western cachet. China's homegrown ba beats foreign-imported ba, except Shuangjie's height, china doll skin, and other inborn endowments are as remote as Columbia University or the West's capital investment to most Chinese audiences.

Although culminating in the coming-out of the star Shuangjie, the opening episode of *Twenty* pivots on the "rat" Jiang Xiaoguo. Even the childish script of the first episode's title, "Is it wrong to love money?," describes Jiang's money problem rather than her independently wealthy roommates'. In episode 1, Jiang is ashamed to have been found with her antique Apple 5 cell phone by her ex-boyfriend, with whom Jiang purchased the phone back in their sophomore year. Not only a spurned lover, Jiang feels like a *lushe* (魯蛇 loser), having been caught "red-handed." Jiang blurts out the subterfuge that her regular phone is temporarily out of work. To impress her ex with a new cell phone at the upcoming class reunion, Jiang scrounges around for funds, exhorting a school friend to pay back the debt of 300 RMB. Rather than paying the outstanding and long-standing debt, her friend uses the scholarship stipend to buy new apparel and shoes for job interviews. Enraged, Jiang confronts her friend in a shopping mall, a confrontation that is recorded and uploaded online. Cyberbullying ensues, smearing Jiang as the bully riding her downtrodden friend. Overshadowing both passionate romance and heart-warming friendship is cold cash, along with the chilling cyberspace of disinformation. With the exception of fuerdai, every character seems to be drowning in debt. Seemingly a debtor, Jiang would owe far more had she dressed herself appropriately for her position at Zhou zong's investment company. The episode title is a rhetorical question, for it is clearly not wrong to love money, only if such money comes at the expense of friendship, love, and the true self.

This segues to Shuangjie's breaking up with Golf in the following episodes. Even this setback fails to faze Shuangjie, who finds her moral fiber in severing ties with Golf. That inner core, however, must couple with that outer look, as episode 3's title "*Yanzhi ji zhengyi?*" (顏值即正義?) illustrates. Yet another rhetorical question, the episode title equates the physical appearance with fairness, even justice. A popular saying in modern China, the title betrays a skewed value system, especially when it rolls off the tongue as a matter of course to justify an unjust system. Whatever happens, the saying suggests, it is one's own fate in accordance with one's face. The natural corollary seems inevitable: to remake one's fate, one starts by remaking one's face. If episode 1's title belongs squarely to Jiang wrestling with mammon, episode 3 befits Shuangjie, female charisma par excellence. Shuangjie lets drop remarks of unabashed entitlement: "If you are beautiful, you are halfway to triumph," or "The face is one's passport," whereas her opposite, Jiang, fumes over losing out on job interviews to taller, more attractive applicants. Translated literally, yanzhi in episode 3's title denotes "physical appearance worth," or the worth/value/ranking of physical appearance. That notion of zhi or worth is grounded in monetary value, where the easiest ranking derives from the sum total of a woman's body parts.

Man with money makes ba, from Golf to Zhou zong to *Thirty*'s Hong Kong–based Asian American millionaire Liang Zhenxian, an avowed bachelor with whom the upscale clothing store associate Wang Manni is in love. The formula of acknowledging and disavowing ba repeats itself when each ba is given up by the woman to be true to herself, with the support of her guimi. Shuangjie chooses the young art photographer over becoming Golf's mistress; Jiang moves on from both ba-s—Zhou zong and Duan's brother; Wang Manni retires to her village in Quzhou, China, rather than staying in Shanghai as a kept woman. Compared with the college setting of *Twenty*, *Thirty* with the three professional women features far more location shooting. Wang's home village in the mountains offers tourist sight-seeing and exotic customs, crossing nostalgia for the pastoral with dream of a Chinese Shangri-la. One of Wang's guimi, Gu Jia, played by Zhang Ziyi look-alike Tong Yao, reprises the homecoming motif in acquiring a tea farm in China's remote interior, a sanctuary when her marriage and pyrotechnics company collapse. Though married, Wang's guimi suffer from husbands either besotted by a young woman à la Glenn Close of *Fatal Attraction* (1987) or with zero emotional intelligence (EQ), still preoccupied with the fish in his aquarium while his wife miscarried.

All three distraught over their careers and families, they embark on a vacation together in episode 9, flying from Shanghai to Shenzhen, where the thirty-year-old guimi ride bikes leisurely across the campus of Huanan University, where they chance upon the four twenty-year-old guimi from *Twenty* at the university auditorium. This television marketing spectacle of having two top-rated TV series overlap creates an effect that is almost spectral, a fitting closure to an argument yoking apples and oranges, imperial ghosts and millennial guimi. The two sets of guimi from two TV shows cross paths like each other's shadows. Tiptoeing into the tiered auditorium on a whim, the professional women, two recent divorcees and one long-time "old maid," sit one row behind the four college students. The interlopers are the students' future; the students are the interlopers' past. The past and the future seat themselves in tandem, spatially and temporally, in the perpetual present of episode 9. Neither group comes to fully recognize the other, except a fleeting glance at, not to mince words, one's own ghost so strange yet so alike (figure 3.1). The four students turn to face those behind them because the professor, male authority figure once again, has drawn class attention to the three strangers giggling in the last row. Figure 3.1 captures the moment when the three mature women bow out of the auditorium under the students' curious stare. The exact scene with identical dialogue, mise-en-scène, and plot returns serendipitously in episode 41 of *Twenty*, before the series folds in episode 42. Not only do the two sets of guimi inhabit the same space, but they do so twice at different

THE GHOST OF *GUIMI* • 71

FIGURE 3.1. Episode 9 of *Thirty* and episode 41 of *Twenty* reprise the same scene where the *guimi* of the latter series chance upon the *guimi* of the former series.

FIGURE 3.2. *Thirty*'s start menu for episode 1, where the character Wang Manni hugs herself.

times in two separate shows, an embryonic eternal return in the fan's mind's eye.

This doubling motif is embedded in *Thirty*'s alternating film still of each episode, the arrow at the center of which must be clicked to start screening. Figure 3.2 captures the very first episode's film still. Wang Manni embracing herself in figure 3.2 will shift in subsequent episodes to her two other guimi, cuddling and commiserating with herself respectively, which subconsciously undercuts the healing, cathartic power of guimi. Why not have them hug each other? The freeze frame suggests that each woman is unto herself, conjuring up the shadow of well-beings. Whereas the phantom sorority constitutes itself after the fact of individual drowning, each death unmitigatedly solitary, episodes of millennial guimi attempt group therapy after the frozen picture of failed self-help.

Before parting ways in figure 3.1, however, the two groups talk past as well as at each other. The beauty of the thirtysomething, Wang Manni, takes note of the beauty of the twentysomething, Shuangjie, sitting in front. Wang whispers her admiration of the "post-00" generation, referring to those born after 2000, now in their late teens or early twenties. Directing her guimi's eyes to Shuangjie, Wang praises the flawless makeup that sculpts a ceramic doll of a face, while Wang's own skin is as smooth and iridescent as a ceramic doll and while the students' laptop screens an ethereal princess from imperial China. That princess from *Novoland: Eagle Flag* (2019) happens to be played by Jiang Shuying, whose next role is Wang Manni. *Thirty* plays on the metanarrative of mise en abyme. Intertextuality notwithstanding, a simultaneous dialogue continues apace. Parallel to Wang's observations under her breath on the post-00, the "rat-pack" leader Jiang Xiaoguo assuages Duan's fear over her imminent twenty-two-year birthday party: "Why worry? You're only 22. Behind you are twenty-five, thirty. How are they going to face themselves?" Literally, of course, three thirty-year-old women sit right behind them. Shuangjie picks up where Jiang left off, rubbing it in, unaware of those at her back: "Haven't you heard? The face after 25 slides down like a roller coaster." Taken aback, the thirty-year-olds exchange a hurt look, bemused as to whether they resemble "old aunts." Wang Manni, the star of the thirtysomething, closes by salvaging their self-esteem: "When I was 22, I also bought all kinds of skin care products. But when I'm 30, I realize love is the best skin lotion," although she has just fallen out of love with her Tall Rich Handsome partner. One remedy for romantic disillusionment, shared by both series and many other TV shows, is self-medication through alcohol, the sole legal "opiate of the masses" sold over the counter.

Pushed down by men with money, an imperial Chinese woman sinks to the bottom of the well, kept company by other well-beings. Imperial and neoimperial suicide and femicide have a note of finality, yet the afterlife of well-being "will return" time and again like the Bollywood tune's refrain. By contrast, pushed down by money from men, a millennial Chinese woman sinks to the bottom of the bottle, kept company by her drinking pals of guimi. Drowned imperial women rise as ghosts in ghost stories and cinematic horror; drunken millennial women sober up, more refreshed and lovely for the happy ending in melodrama and romance. Which is more uncanny: return of repressed ghosts, or magical thinking over guimi? Which sounds like ghost whispering: imperial horror distancing beautiful ghosts, or millennial melodrama idolizing guimi beauties, or the blood tie (blood that ties) of forgotten phantoms and trending phenoms?

Mi in *Guimi* (閨蜜) means honey-like sweetness based on the radical of *chong* (虫 insect or honeybee), but mi puns with "secret, veiled" (密) based on the radical of *shan* (山 mountain). Hence, the sweetness and bonding of the fad of boudoir confidantes buoys atop a secret mountain of bones of female ghosts, welling up from imperial to millennial China. True guimi or companionship enfolds imperial well-beings and millennial boudoir confidantes across time and space, although either party—and us viewers—pretends not to see the other, the mirror image floating on ancient waters or modern liquidities.

PART 2
ON THE CULTURAL REVOLUTION

CHAPTER 4

Six Million Jews and How Many Chinese

"Ten-Year Holocaust" of the Cultural Revolution

Over three decades ago, I was perhaps the first Asian to receive a US doctorate on the strength of a dissertation on the Holocaust, one entitled *The Holocaust in Anglo-American Literature: Particularism and Universalism in Relation to Documentary and Fictional Genres.* Quite a mouthful of academese, the title was the best I could manage after my prospectus on a far more concise "Contrasting the Holocaust and the Cultural Revolution" had been summarily rejected by the traditional English graduate program director at Indiana University (IU), partly because its bibliography involved too many non-English, non-Western texts. The prospectus did leave a thin trace in my 1987 article, "Contrasting Two Survival Literatures: On the Jewish Holocaust and the Chinese Cultural Revolution" in *Holocaust and Genocide Studies,* in print a decade before Vera Schwarcz published the comparative *Bridge across Broken Time: Chinese and Jewish Cultural Memory* (1998).

This project at hand returns me to the bridge broken between the two halves of my professional life, a bridge that would have spanned the two unheimlich cultural memories, so familiar yet so estranged. In "Six Million Jews and How Many Chinese," the precision of number in Jewish casualties juxtaposes with Chinese obfuscation, estimated to range from "hundreds of thousands to 20 million," an absurdly broad range that in and of itself bespeaks what Louisa Lim called *The People's Republic of Amnesia* (2014).[1] That Lim was referring to the Tiananmen Square Massacre on June 4, 1989, only underscored ongoing State repression. On the other hand, the periodization of Mao's 1966–76 fanaticism absorbs the Cultural Revolution (henceforth the CR) into millennia of Chinese history bouncing between Taoist-dialectical *fen* (severing, war) and *he* (uniting, peace), with the emphasis on the latter. *He* denotes *hexié* (with the latter word xié in the second tone), harmony, that glosses over the unseemly, a Chinese instinct and cultural habit satirized by netizens' double entendre of *hexiè* (with the latter word xiè in the fourth tone), "river crab" to be eaten, and by Kai Strittmatter's tongue-in-cheek "harmony between orders and obedience" in *We Have Been Harmonized* (2018, 20).

Whereas survivor testimonies and fictions by Elie Wiesel, Primo Levi, and the like delimit human rationality and civilization, intimating the incomprehensible abyss beyond, which is the genocide, the extirpation of an entire gene pool or a race, Yang Jiang and Feng Jicai frame dehumanization and bestiality within vestiges of communal bonding. In fine, factual and experiential specificity suggests the unfathomable horror of the Holocaust; broad and historical generalization returns the potential stray of the CR to the fold of Chinese suffering. Neither are the roles of *Endlösung* perpetrator, bystander, and victim applicable to the CR, nor are the split between survivor-witness and nonsurvivor. Whatever their experiences, the Chinese population remains interpellated by the authoritarian apparatus half a century later, including cultural memory of the Ten-Year Holocaust. The cleansing of the Chinese mind intends to reform, the state propaganda has long argued, de facto a campaign of mass education compared with the mass murder of the cleansing of European Jewry.

While Holocaust studies relies heavily on empirical, positivist evidence of Nazi pogroms, the linguistic root of Holocaust conceivably evokes the opposite metaphor of fiery conflagration incinerating historical memory. Instead of physical, material-based traces of "watermarks," the Holocaust signals erasure, leaving fragments and ashes to be pieced together. The Chinese nomenclature "Ten-Year Holocaust" (*shinian haojie* 十年浩劫) borrows from the Jewish cataclysm for an apocalyptic veneer or an international cachet; however, its formulaic stylization à la four-character maxims Sinologizes, co-opts the very notion of a unique, unspeakable affliction. What lies beyond the power of words and human understanding in Wiesel and Levi mutates in Yang and

---

1. Melissa De Witte in "China's Cultural Revolution" cited Stanford sociologist Andrew Walder, who claimed that the upheaval was "a power grab from within the government, not from without," and "led to the deaths of 1.6 million people."

Feng into a matter of course in the survivorship of eating bitterness, or *chiku* (吃苦), a centuries-old cliché for persevering despite life's adversities.

By pairing literature on the Holocaust and the CR, apples and oranges in the eye of IU's graduate program director, I pare, belatedly, the East-West traumas down to the inedible core. The Aryan rotten apple of Christendom meets the Chinese homonyms wedding orange (*ju* in Mandarin or *ji* in southern China's various accents) with its sound-alike, *ji* for luck—the deadly banality of evil coated with sweet citrus. To be precise, Nobel laureate Elie Wiesel is situated dialogically with Yang Jiang, relatively unknown globally yet renowned in the Sinophone world less for her scholar-husband Qian Zhongshu than for her own writings and translations. At one end of the bridge towers Wiesel's lifelong obsession with the West's apple, the original sin of the Holocaust; at the other, Yang avails herself of the Chinese glass half-full of citrus juice, sweet and sour memories of her family of three, including their daughter Qian Yuan.

Across linguistic, cultural, and experiential divides, we witness the explosion of the Holocaust versus the slow burn of the CR—the undead from the Nazi conflagration versus those by a thousand communist/communal cuts. An acute condition well-nigh impossible to "get over" is pitted against a chronic condition one must "get used to"—surviving a calamitous flare-up and a Gentile death blow as opposed to a way of life with low-grade fever and paralyzing seizures, or fever and chills, within China's own body politic. The posttraumatic Wiesel runs parallel to Yang's still traumatizing experiences; the apocalyptic Jewish Holocaust juxtaposes with the cyclical Cultural Revolution, with the last word "Revolution" meaning not so much irreversible change as iterative rotation. His *Night* (1960) on the nightmarish Auschwitz after having been liberated contrasts with her *Six Chapters from My Life "Downunder"* (*Cadre School Six Records* 1981) out of a never-ending serial under Mao's panopticon, posthumous Red Sun. His tightly testimonial yet biblical, apocalyptic memoir diverges from her modeling after the literati *zawen* (loosely impressionistic essay) tradition of Shen Fu's *Six Records of a Floating Life* (1877). On the one hand, Wiesel's literal, particularist style is grounded in (uprooted by?) the haunting Holocaust, which gestures, dialectically, to a cathartic healing. On the other, Yang's allegorical, universalist style flaneurs (feigns?) leisurely, which intimates, dialectically, heeling like a good dog, heeding the party "red" line. Any dialogical relationship across languages occurs via translation. Key excerpts of *Night*, reincarnated from the original Yiddish, come face to face, mid-bridge in English translation, with their doppelganger from *Six Chapters*, already translated, and the first two parts of *Us Three* (2003), the compressed dreamscape yet to be rendered in English.

Elie Wiesel's *Night*

Elie Wiesel (1928–2016) was a staunch advocate of particularism over the Holocaust, namely, the view that holds the Holocaust to be unique, incomprehensible, and marked by its obsessive hatred of the Jews. This particularism undoubtedly is derived from his personal experience in concentration camps agonizingly recorded. In *Night,* Wiesel's memoir of the dark days under Hitler, the writer is compelled to contemplate the event that totally demolished a traditionally religious universe he deeply believed in. He reflects that with the Nazi onslaught, the covenantal relationship between God and his Chosen People came to an abrupt end: God's vow to man was shattered. For Wiesel, the experience of the Holocaust is so horrendously incredible and the metaphysical implications so devastating that he begins to suspect the sufficiency of the matter-of-fact autobiographical approach by which individual experiences and, by extension, historical events are reputedly preserved.

The memoirist also believes that the Holocaust is so incomprehensible as to defy not only the autobiographical-testimonial but the fictional mode of writing. This sense of unfathomability is yet another result of the collapse of his religious faith. It is difficult, however, for any writer, including the memoirist, to sever himself entirely from a value or belief system that he used to hold dear. Elie Wiesel's apparent rejection of some basic tenets of Judaism, therefore, is fraught with contradictions and ambivalences.

Undeniably one of the major Jewish figures in the United States, if not in the world, awarded the Nobel Peace Prize in 1986, Elie Wiesel launched his writing career with the publication of his first book, *Night*. Originally written in Yiddish, the work, entitled *Un di Velt hot Geshvign* (*And the World Was Silent*), was first published in Argentina in 1956, ten long years after Wiesel was liberated from Buchenwald by American troops. It so happens that Alain Resnais's elegiac documentary *Night and Fog* debuted in 1956, providing a visual primer for the unimaginable horror Wiesel chronicled. Parts of *Night* receive graphic illustration, unwittingly, through Resnais's grainy footages of barbed wires and watchtowers, boxcars, railroad tracks leading to Auschwitz's front gate with the deceptive inscription of "Work Means Freedom," barracks and clinics, emaciated corpses bulldozed into mass graves, gas chamber cement walls scratched by victims before they expired, cloths made of women's hair, fertilizer made of human bones, soaps made of human flesh, lamp shades made of human skin, and much more unspeakable evidence of crimes against humanity. Wiesel's thin yet condensed and powerful memoir appeared in French in 1958 as *La Nuit* and in English in 1960 as *Night*. The book chronicles Wiesel's experience under the Third Reich, a core experience that would set the tone for all his later writings, which are almost exclusively on the Holocaust, either obliquely or directly.

In order to understand Elie Wiesel's response to the Holocaust, one must examine certain aspects of the Jewish tradition of commemorating historical suffering. As a result of millennia of wandering in foreign lands, of enduring and outlasting unrelenting discrimination and pogroms, the Jews have evolved a unique concept of history. It includes a history of suffering that tends to forge a Jewish sense of identity won not through rejoicing over imperial expansions and grandiose conquests, as in the case with most other ancient civilizations, but through commemorating the catastrophes that have befallen the Jewish people. As illustrated in many cultures, national disasters may well be subjected to either a politically motivated program of popular forgetfulness and transformation or an individually motivated process of dilution. Most people maintain that traumatic experiences, especially massive sufferings, are best forgotten or reduced to manageable size lest these experiences prevent the people as a whole or the individual from functioning in a normal world. However, given the Jewish history of suffering and the disposition to remember national calamities, the Holocaust is painfully absorbed into the Jewish tradition, and, as a result, alters that tradition in a most disorienting way.

Thus, when Eliezer, Wiesel's full name as used in *Night*, witnesses the deportation of Jews from his hometown, he instantly recalls "the captivity of Babylon or the Spanish Inquisition" (26). Wiesel's response is typical of the reaction of those in his and many other religious Jewish communities. His hometown, Sighet, in Transylvania, was inhabited by a sizable population of orthodox Jews devoted to a life of religious piety. Nevertheless, this resorting to tradition to interpret and understand the present event proves futile as Eliezer is transported, along with his family, to Auschwitz. Wiesel records the horrendous scene that greets him in Auschwitz in a succinct and factual style: "Not far from us, flames were leaping up from a ditch, gigantic flames. They were burning something. A lorry drew up at the pit and delivered its load—little children. Babies! Yes, I saw it—saw it with my own eyes . . . those children in the flames" (42).

The sensory perception of this reality and the memoirist's insistence on testimonial details could not be sustained because of the irreal and surreal nature of the event. The factual approach of most memoirs presupposes that words can be mimetic of external reality. Eliezer, however, finds that "none of this could be true. It was a nightmare" (42). The paradox is thus quite evident: while utilizing a factual and documentary style, Wiesel denies the efficacy of that style.

To confront this irreality, religious Jews typically are wont to take recourse to their faith, which is, unwittingly to themselves, transformed in the most radical way: they recite Kaddish, the prayer for the dead, for themselves—an experience, Wiesel suggests, that has never happened to Jews heretofore. In the desperation of seeking an appropriate response to the atrocity within their tradition, the Jewish inmates' action bespeaks the unprecedented nature of the event. Its enormity is felt to be so unique and disorienting that it lies outside of the interpretive powers of the tradition. Eliezer, therefore, rises to question or even deny the whole tradition that he inherits:

> Never shall I forget that night, the first night in camp, which has turned my life into one long night, seven times cursed and seven times sealed. Never shall I forget that smoke. Never shall I forget the little faces of the children, whose bodies I saw turned into wreaths of smoke beneath a silent blue sky.
> Never shall I forget those flames which consumed my faith forever.
> Never shall I forget that nocturnal silence which deprived me, for all eternity, of the desire to live. Never shall I forget those moments which murdered my God and my soul and turned my dreams to dust. Never shall I forget these things, even if I am condemned to live as long as God Himself. Never. (44)

Even though the narrator is saying that he has abandoned his faith after that first night in the camp, the language he uses has a distinctly biblical ring. The reiteration of "never" in a crescendo, culminating in the final condemnation of God, is a rhetorical device with strong resemblance to the Hebrew tradition of lamentation. The phrase "seven times cursed and seven times sealed" once again shows how much Wiesel is indebted to the Old Testament. More ironically, as Wiesel is saying that his faith is consumed forever, he ends his "prayer" with a confirmation of the everlastingness of God, albeit in a damning tone of voice. Wiesel's style clearly derives from the Jewish literary tradition of lamentation that commemorates historical calamities as well as those Jewish martyrs who perished in them.

Wiesel's elegiac and lamentational style often leads to a contemplation of the metaphysical and mythological nature, rather than merely the physical and historical aspects, of the cataclysm. This tendency to explore the metaphysical implications of historical traumas finds its source partly in the metaphysical outlook of life inherent in Judaism—or any religion, for that matter. Jews view life and the universe in a transcendental way, positing an Almighty God. To an orthodox Jew such as Elie Wiesel, the meaning of the universe rests ultimately with a God who is far beyond the grasp of the human senses and human comprehension. When a devastating blow shakes the centuries-old foundation of this religious view and disrupts the uniquely covenantal relationship between God and man, then this blow must be demonically unique, and must carry bewildering and inexplicable metaphysical overtones.

The metaphysical implications of the Holocaust at once demand attention and elude it. Elie Wiesel's urge to bear witness to the atrocity, for instance, becomes ultimately obsessive, as illustrated in the earlier quotation where Wiesel uses eight "nevers" to virtually make the vow of branding the horrendous scene upon his mind. The Holocaust becomes so central to his memoir that Wiesel chooses to end the book with an image that portends the haunting quality of the event:

> One day I was able to get up, after gathering all my strength. I wanted to see myself in the mirror hanging on the opposite wall. I had not seen myself since the ghetto.
> From the depths of the mirror, a corpse gazed back at me.
> The look in his eyes, as they stared into mine, has never left me. (127)

The penetrating gaze possessed Wiesel after he had been liberated and reasonably recuperated. Spiritually and psychologically, however, part of him was "dead." This preoccupation with death and the past characterizes much of Wiesel's prolific writings and evokes great compassion in the reader. Dwelling endlessly on his and his people's unique affliction has led Wiesel to literary reflections of astonishing depth. But, at the same time, Wiesel is driven into a psychological impasse: he is haunted by a past which the majority of nonsurvivors wish to forget and which he as a survivor cannot but remember.

With the exception of a number of books which project a less haunting image of the Holocaust, Elie Wiesel's writings since *Night* are marked by an obsessive quality as if that gaze of a corpse, which is his own face reflected in the mirror, has permeated his whole being and extended to the entirety of his literary output. Wiesel himself is aware of the consequences of such an uncontrollable passion:

> Those who lived through it lack objectivity: they will always take the side of man confronted with the Absolute. As for scholars and philosophers of every genre who have had the opportunity to observe the tragedy, they will—if they are capable of sincerity and humility—withdraw without daring to enter into the heart of the matter; and if they are not, well, who cares about their grandiloquent conclusions? (*Legends of Our Time* [1968] 6)

And Wiesel has consistently taken the side of the Absolute as he contemplates the significance, or the lack thereof, of the Holocaust. He believes that "perhaps some day someone will explain how, on the level of man, Auschwitz was possible; but on the level of God, it will forever remain the most disturbing of mysteries" (*Legends of Our Time* 6). In addition to the unfathomability of the event that he continuously returns to, Wiesel contemplates his traumatic experience in another more unsettling way: "It is Auschwitz that will produce Hiroshima, and if the human race should perish by the nuclear bomb, this will be the punishment for Auschwitz, where, in the ashes, the hope of man has extinguished" (*Legends of Our Time* 180). The reference to Hiroshima calls to mind Wiesel's various remarks on the atomic bomb as part of the reverberation of the Holocaust. No one will mistake this passage, as well as all the preceding ones on Hiroshima, for a rational conclusion reached by a measured thinker. Yet what Wiesel underwent under the Third Reich was far from rational, amounting to a state of mind resembling madness in the extreme. This passage echoes the dark oracles delivered by such an ancient Hebrew prophet as Isaiah or Jeremiah haunted by the massacre of his people, which they narrowly escaped.

So narrow an escape that only the thin shadow of Eliezer stumbles down from the mountain of corpses, his father left behind, the burnt offering. This ending revises the biblical Abraham whose son Isaac, the scapegoat, was spared. Wiesel himself calls Isaac "the first survivor" in his interviews with Harry James Cargas.[2] Yet the Good Book did not keep the books in mathematical accuracy. Coming down the Moriah mountain alone, "Abraham returned unto his young men [servants], and they rose up and went together to Beersheba" (Gen. 22:19). Where was Isaac? Why did he not descend the pyre with Abraham? Some unfinished business with God, like the "ram caught in a thicket by the horns" or any PTSD patient who left the soul on the killing field (Gen. 22:13)? Was the ram Isaac's soul or his fallen comrade who died in his place? In accordance with biblical accounting of one father plus one son equals one, only half of an Eliezer survived, while Eliezer's father and various father figures, including God, are incinerated on the altar to inhumanity.

Night opens with a father figure, Moché the Beadle, who initiates Eliezer into Jewish mysticism, parallel to Eliezer's secular father deeply involved in business and community affairs. Moché also embodies Jewishness in that

---

2. See Harry James Cargas's *Harry James Cargas in Conversation with Elie Wiesel*, pp. 106–7.

being a foreign Jew, he is deported before the Sighet Jewry. Sole survivor of Nazi atrocities, Moché returns from the dead to warn Jews of the genocide, which no one believes. One of a few female characters in *Night*, Madame Schächter resembles Moché in her otherness within a patriarchal narrative. Embodying Jews deemed the other to Christendom, these two are foreign by virtue of their names' diacritics, if nothing else. High-strung, even neurotic, Madame Schächter is the mad prophetess who foresees the Auschwitz conflagration awaiting the transport. For her visions that disturb fellow Jews trapped for days inside the horrible boxcar, she is gagged and beaten ruthlessly. The unlistened-to stories Moché and Madame Schächter feel compelled to share foreshadow Wiesel's and other survivors' obsessive retelling of the Holocaust from which the world has increasingly turned away.

Once the father and son find themselves in Auschwitz, they try to sustain each other throughout persecutions: Dr. Mengele's selections for the gas chamber and crematorium; hard labor and starvation; sadistic cruelty and summary execution; dysentery and other illnesses. Believing himself chosen for extermination at one point, the father passes on his knife and spoon, "the inheritance" (*Night* 86). Yet their roles of the bestower and the bestowed begin to reverse toward the end of the memoir. Eliezer must father his father, who has become "like a child, weak, timid, vulnerable" under tremendous duress (117). Eliezer teaches him to march in step and shares the meager ration. The upending of the patriarchal structure resonates with Rabbi Eliahou's son running ahead in the death march, while his father staggers behind (103). Meir's son even robs his father of pieces of bread (113). The pattern of the son becoming the father by replacing or even betraying him culminates in the death of Eliezer's father. Eliezer realizes that "in the depths of my being, in the recesses of my weakened conscience, could I have searched it, I might perhaps have found something like—free at last!" (124). The prolonged five-part confession with several phrasal deferrals, including uncertain markers of "might perhaps" and "something like," signifies an inner struggle that ends with the irony of simultaneously unburdened of the father yet loaded with the survivor guilt. The father's passing haunts the son's surviving. Likewise, to infer the death of the ultimate Father, the Jewish God, from His indifference during the Holocaust calls into question human hubris in divining the divine mystery. Wiesel's lifelong wrestle with his God's silence while Jews perished in the crematoria proves, ironically, the existence of God whose ways remain unfathomable. Elie Wiesel's Jewish father-son, God-man relationship at the heart of *Night* shifts to Yang Jiang's Chinese husband-wife, State-individual tension in *Six Chapters from My Life "Downunder."*

Yang Jiang's *Six Chapters from My Life "Downunder"*

Yang Jiang (1911–2016) left behind a spare, laconic testimony to the CR, translated by Howard Goldblatt as *Six Chapters from My Life "Downunder"* (henceforth *Six*). "Downunder" in the title unfortunately alludes to the Antipodes, as though China's CR had anything to do with Australia and New Zealand. Goldblatt's footnote to Qian Zhongshu's foreword explains that "Downunder" is chosen to render *xiafang*, "downward transfer," or simply send-down, that "applies more poignantly to the twenty million intellectuals uprooted from their academic and research institutions to live with the peasants in the countryside" in the name of re-education by the proletariat (1). "Reform" had long been Chairman Mao's ploy for mind control and political hegemony, continued down to this day in terms of Xinjiang's Uighur labor camps under President Xi Jinping. Goldblatt's comparative degree in "more poignantly" stresses the fact that, despite their two-year rural dislocation and hardships, the couple fared far better than most intellectuals without the shield of Qian's reputation. Qian, after all, belonged to the committee which translated Mao Zedong's *Selected Works* and *Poetry*, in addition to authoring other eminent publications.

Contrary to his wife's gentle style of ironic understatement and wry humor, Qian's foreword is trenchant, elaborating on the missing chapter of "A Sense of Shame," a sorely needed confession from bystanders and victimizers of the political campaign. This reckoning of personal responsibility and shame, Qian argues, far outweighs Yang Jiang's "mere adornments" of "Records of 'labor' and 'leisure,'" which happens to be Yang's chapter 2 and 3 (1). That Qian would dare raise the specter of those who sinned against their fellow countrymen suggests Qian's inimitable stature. Be that as it may, Qian launches his critique of the powers that be in the guise of critiquing his wife's memoir. Qian concludes his foreword by calling attention to the model of Yang's memoir, Shen Fu's *Six Chapters of a Floating Life*, which "only contains four extant chapters," just as Yang's book should have had a seventh chapter. Tongue-in-cheek, Qian muses: "So who can say that the day will not come when the missing chapters of these two books will surface to fill in the gaps" (3). Qian intimates that occlusion and repression mark these personal essays theoretically chronicling uneventful, leisured lives. The structural glitches reveal far more than the structure itself; the lacuna far more than the words.

Heeding Qian's summons and emboldened by Vera Schwarcz's crossing of Jewishness and Chineseness as well as the personal and the cultural, my modest effort herein tries to bridge the gaps not only within Chinese collective memory but also East-West comparative studies on traumas. That little hyphen in "East-West" begs the big question of hemispheric as well as cognitive connections. A short horizontal bar, the hyphen is as infinite as human history, the fulcrum on which history itself turns. In the US history alone, that hyphen stretches from Chinese coolies' level shoulder pole to the transcontinental railroad of sweat and blood from coast to coast to Lady Justice's scales tilted by an apparently white Goddess for whites. That she is blindfolded from Greco-Roman sculpture to this day symbolizes that either she is fair (fair-skinned?) or she is blind to non-fair-skinned people or both. Oft-elided by writers and readers, the hyphen reorders "the slovenly wilderness" of East and West, leveraging theoretical and pragmatic revision like Wallace Stevens's little round "jar in Tennessee" on a hilltop.[3] Given the historical, racial slant rather than a balanced line that is the hyphen, how to relate to one's geospatial and psychological opposite? In the face of escalating political bipolarization and personal disenfranchisement, this is a task as urgent as wedding the right half of the brain to the left, the First World to the Third, the haves to the have-nots, and one superpower to the other. Together, they constitute one brain and one world. Half of them results in either Elie Wiesel's Holocaust-centric particularism or Yang Jiang's self-censored universalism.

Without identifying any specific illness, Qian in the foreword uses *jianxiezheng* (間歇症) to imply the chronic condition with intermittent flare-ups of leftist-Maoist fanaticism in China's body politic. Habituated perhaps to the fixation on precision in the English language, Goldblatt translates it as "malaria," far too specific a malaise for the general condition deliberately unnamed, even more wrong-headed given malaria's association with tropical, Orientalist diseases. The Chinese author nods to the ailment that cannot be named; the translator names a particular medical problem that misrepresents.

Published in 1981, *Six* dwells on the couple's thought reform at "cadre schools," euphemism for poor rural villages, from 1969 to 1971, a thin two-year slice out of a centenarian's long life, and a prolific one at that. *Us Three* (*women sa* 我們仨 2003) offers an overview beyond the cadre school, immensely helpful in contextualizing *Six*. *Us Three*, however, is yet to be deemed profitable enough to merit translation, whereas Wiesel's books had all been rendered in English, many by his wife Marion Wiesel. Since cross-cultural understanding of traumas hinges on translation, the CR is bound to be unfamiliar to the West, except stylized memoirs favored by English-language publishing houses. In fact, *Six* and *Us Three* remain somewhat obscure even among contemporary Chinese-language readers, a symptom of collective amnesia over Maoist extremism. A potpourri of a book, *Us Three* comprises three parts and five

---

3. See Wallace Stevens's "Anecdote of a Jar" (1919).

appendices, concluding with Qian Yuan's sickbed scribblings and drawings of her father. It is a moving tale narrated by a self-possessed, self-restrained, and enormously admirable narrator, who has nothing to gain from publication other than committing to memory her loved ones for posterity.

Parts 1 and 2 consist of a long dreamscape of loss and melancholia in the wake of Qian Zhongshu being summoned by unidentified authorities to attend a conference: "No bag. No notebook. 9 A.M." (13, all translations of *Us Three* mine). If neither bag nor notebook is required, then the person is the subject for meetings, struggle meetings by default amid the CR. The person is not to discuss a subject, but to be discussed as the subject. This deduction from the curt command entails reading between the lines, reading into orders telegraphic and blurred by design. To argue that no textual proof supports the inference is to ignore Yang's self-censorship, not posttrauma but during the *longue durée* of the trauma, during what Qian aptly terms *jianxiezheng*, the chronic illness with unpredictable eruptions. Whereas Wiesel was liberated from Auschwitz to freely explore the inexplicable horror, Yang survives in a China haunted by the revenant of Maoism, no different from the US with the specter of Trumpism.

Plagued by anxiety under a mysterious landscape, Yang Jiang and their daughter Qian Yuan scramble to follow an "ancient post road" along a river, where an exhausted eighty-four-year-old Qian is sequestered on a ferry boat numbered 311. An ancient post road would have been traversed by multiple sojourners, but it disorients like the Freudian unheimlich, un-home-like, since the familiarity of Chinese intellectuals' persecution and exile throughout history revisits with a vengeance. The ferry number 311 encapsulates the broken trinity of the Qians foretold by the single line on the book cover under the title of *Us Three*: "I alone miss us three." Out of the trinity, which is three-as-one, Yang is the only one left, hence the loaded number for the boat doubling as a prison ship and the final ferry to the beyond.

By temperament, Yang is much too mild to countenance Kafka-esque existential angst. Yet her experience is no less phantasmagoric than that of K or Gregor Samsa,[4] particularly menacing when the innkeeper along the post road presents three warnings in print:

1. Follow the post road. Where there is no road, stop.
2. Places where you can't see, don't go.
3. Things you don't know, don't ask.

---

4. See Franz Kafka's *The Trial* (1925), *The Castle* (1926), and "Metamorphosis" (1915).

In stifling officialese with the weight of printed matter inherent in the Chinese tradition, the commandments of Dos and Don'ts resemble the rhetoric of "a gang of kidnappers, full of bureaucratic baloney," a private thought she keeps to herself, but a wink to her readers: China's officials kidnap their own people (22). With three additional rules, Yang and her daughter are instructed to impress their thumbprints on the back of the round, numbered tag that provides access to all inns and meals along the way. The ease of "in-house" service and the privilege of visitation presume agreeing to all the terms, being resigned to one's identity as a number, as an abducted complicit in one's own incarceration. Yang embeds more dreamscape within this dreamscape when her dream-self floats from the inn to Qian Yuan's bedside as she slowly dies of cancer in 1997, followed soon after by Qian's death in 1998, leaving Yang alone to reminisce.

Part 3 recalls the family's happy times on the continent in the 1930s, at Oxford and the Sorbonne respectively. Qian and Yang thoroughly enjoyed the academic freedom and the carefree lifestyle of the young, made all the happier with the birth of Qian Yuan in 1937. Turning from allusive dreams to autobiographical materials, part 3 decides to open on a high note of fairy-tale-style freedom, sweeter still for its one-off-ness, never repeated, certainly not in the formulaic closure of "happily ever after." Upon return to a war-torn China, Yang spills much ink in part 3, in the appendices, and elsewhere to describe Qian's botched employment at the prestigious Tsinghua University in Beijing, sabotaged by those envious of Qian's talents. Such extensive, detailed detective work to restore the ins-and-outs of the Tsinghua saga in the 1930s owing to Qian's *guanxi* (human relationship), or the lack thereof, contrasts starkly with the textual silence over those behind their decades of political persecution from Three-Anti and Anti-Rightist Movements of the 1950s to the CR of the 1960s and '70s.[5] The specificity unearthed regarding *one* failed academic appointment satirizes the generality of decades-long injustice endured mutely, unvindicated even after death. Although wronged, Yang cannot afford to right the wrong, which would be deemed as wrong as being a rightist. Overly rhetorical? Too much of a fanciful tongue-twister? Truth, as they say, is stranger than fiction: this torturous sentence is right-on about leftist politics on the other side of the earth, eerily akin to the alt-right's conspiracy theories about America's far left in post-Trump sound and fury.

---

5. Yang Jiang, in fact, devotes the novel *Taking a Bath* (1988) to the first campaign against intellectuals in the early 1950s, the Three-Anti Movement. *Taking a Bath* is but a euphemism for the persecution nicknamed "Pants off to cut the tail." Intellectuals are likened to animals in human clothing, yet tails are said to give them away.

Six begins with the family disintegration as the couple were sent to be reeducated separately, cast in the metaphor of the family bed disassembled for transport. Such allusions, even similes with explicit markers of "like" or "as," never cry out stridently for attention; rather, they quietly, implicitly share the story in a voice never raised. For instance, their son-in-law Deyi debuts in the family send-off for the sixty-year-old Qian somehow assigned to the "advance" team for the cadre school. The generous Deyi helps strangers with their heavy luggage at the train station. Without warning, Deyi reappears as a suicide: "Deyi had taken his own life a month earlier" (16). This abrupt shock gives a whole new meaning to the earlier matter-of-fact, unemotional association of the train station farewell to people off "on an ocean voyage" (10) with streamers stretched taut between the departed and the loved ones. Wiesel's testimonial, documentary minuteness stops at the edges of collective insanity of the genocide. By contrast, Yang leaves much unsaid. The unspeakable Holocaust lurks beyond as transcendent evil; the unspeakable CR is entirely in human terms for the sake of survival then and now. The Nietzschean-Aryan will to power defies rationality and humanity; the Maoist-Communist will to power usurps the instinct for human survival.

Never resolved is this pattern of contradiction between Deyi's death and life-affirming refrain, such as "flesh and blood are still more likely to withstand abuse than anything else" (13). Joining Deyi is "a corpse dressed in a blue uniform . . . a suicide, thirty-three years of age, a male" laid in an "earth mound that looked like a huge steamed bun," the swelling soon caved in after a snowfall as if swallowed up (47). This second chapter, "Leisure: Tending a Vegetable Garden," closes with the morbid thought of "an old man with a bag slung over his back and a cane in his hand walking step by step down a mountain path directly into his own grave" (49). The self-sufficiency of eating vegetables one plants and grows lapses into oneself being eaten by the earth, which thinly veils the system and the people behind it.

That irony is sharpened when their "teachers"—the peasants in charge of thought reform of cadre school "students"—steal from the students' vegetable garden, the building materials for the outhouse, even the excrement in the outhouse, rumored to be superior fertilizer for it comes from intellectuals.[6] The proletarians are supposed to give as instructors; they take instead from their students. A nation is supposed to protect its citizenry; it exploits them regardless. Collective guilt, nonetheless, is not solely the State's. Chapter 5,

---

6. As objectionable to polite society as feces may be, it is in fact a common, shared motif running through narratives on the Cultural Revolution and the Holocaust. Vera Schwarcz in *Bridge across Broken Time* maintains that such familiar words as "excrement" litter "the familiar terrain of Chinese history" and "the rougher terrain of Jewish terror" (44).

"Adventure: While All Ends Well," records three instances where Yang Jiang goes astray, most precariously when she follows the wrong team after a propaganda film to the wrong barracks. She has indeed been brainwashed, any thinking mind zapped, erased by the film's shrill sloganeering. A synecdoche of China gone awry under the self-serving, egomaniacal leadership, Yang projects the nation's devastating herd instinct onto herself and herself alone, playing safe with self-caricature in place of what actually transpired, namely, transgressions against her and the like-minded.

Yang's style of minimalist internalization manifests itself when she finds Qian in a pathetic state when they reunite at the cadre school. Without any probing into the physical and mental discomfort, Yang singles out, pun intended, Qian's facial carbuncle, which "had an angry, threatening look about it" (18). A sixty-year-old man with a teenager's "pimple"! Assuredly, it springs from, not a second spring, a hormonal rush, in old age, but from the coerced regression to children's vulnerability and dependency, not to mention malnutrition and distress. From books and intellectual labor, Qian and fellow students at the cadre school take up farm implements to eke out a living from the arid, rocky countryside, enacted in chapter 2, "Labor: Digging a Well."

Yang prefaces the team's hard labor of well-digging with a skit performed at the cadre school where an "entire 'troupe' push[es] the well-boring machine round and round" while intoning "Heave-ho! Heave-ho!" (22). The "troupe" in quotation marks highlights the performativity of labor at the cadre school or of the school itself, on the performance stage as well as off. A double consciousness is built into the very fabric of Chinese political campaigns, whereby one performs or double-talks to the satisfaction of the State rather than for the sake of self-satisfaction. So mechanical and robotic is the skit that an audience member blurts out "It's as if . . . as if . . . we're all so . . . so . . ." (23; ellipses in original). Without spelling out the obvious, the group's ensuing laughter cements the bond in adversity. To persevere in the tumultuous strife, an individual finds strength in the family, the coterie of trusted friends, and even the earth that yields little despite their back-breaking work. Yang used to find mud "a terribly dirty substance, full of spit, snot, feces, and urine. But the effect of having it ooze up through my toes was a feeling of intimacy with the soil" (26). Taken for granted before, even looked down upon before, dirt acquires new-found dignity when one is treated as the scum of the earth, squashed into the mud. By the same token, the attachment to loved ones intensifies owing to the severance forced upon them, the dehumanization befallen them.

To prevent being crushed by state terror, an individual internalizes injustice, evidenced by Yang's self-deprecating humor and Qian's inflammation on the cheek. A nation out of balance is displaced onto the body's own endocrine disorders, which, needless to say, derive from being uprooted, isolated from family and community, and subjected to gratuitous humiliation, if not violence. That which is "needless to say," however, is never said in Yang Jiang; it is to be intuited. To pinpoint the cause risks incensing the censors. Inflicting such discursive, psychological, and physical violence comes at the behest of Chairman Mao and the Party for the edification and reformation of the "Black Five Kinds," "Poisoned Weeds," "Ox Ghost Snake Monster" locked up in "cowsheds," and other stigmatizing labels.[7]

These undesirable intellectuals-turned-laborers are wont to express their affection less with one another, who may turn against them, than with a safe nonhuman other, a cadre school pet dog, Quickie. Yang is not alone in showering Quickie with food and warmth; all cadre school members attend to Quickie's well-being. That Quickie and other dogs feed on human feces ties them subliminally to the intellectuals fallen into the bowels of China, awaiting crumbs from Chairman Mao's table. In the haste to relocate the cadre school, Quickie is lost, becoming "either a pile of manure" or "eating manure to stay alive" (65). Quickie's ending resembles that of the vegetable garden—"a piece of empty land strewn with clods" (50)—or of the whole cadre school. Repeatedly in the closures to six chapters, an overwhelming sense of waste of their labor and lives stands as a silent accusation, a lame one at that, since neither the "J'accuse" is ever vocalized nor is it aimed against any culprit. Consistently, the indictment turns inward: "After undergoing more than ten years of reform, plus two years at the cadre school, not only had I not reached the plateau of progressive thinking that everyone sought, I was nearly as selfish now as I had been in the beginning. I was still the same old me" (98). Self-blame disguises the sense of futility and the systemic abuse by the State.

Whereas Wiesel concludes *Night* with the haunting of a schizophrenic self, Yang facetiously proclaims her own incorrigibility, despite decades-long reform. Wiesel's traditional patriarchal mindset meets Yang's maternal love for her husband and daughter. Wiesel's factual, testimonial approach to the black hole of the Holocaust frees him, paradoxically, to reflect on the limits of reason. Yang, on the other hand, resorts to literary conceits of understatement, allusions, analogues, and metaphors to deflect potential wrath from the authority. Hitler's Third Reich is dead and gone; Mao's Communist Party recently celebrated its centennial on July 1, 2021. The exocannibalistic anti-Semitism is relatively easy to finger. By contrast, to parse victims from victimizers and bystanders in the endocannibalistic class struggle among one's

---

7. Vera Schwarcz in *Bridge across Broken Time* adds to this list of epithets: "ox-devils," "snake spirits," "rotten dog's head," "evil wind," and "pests and vermin" (112).

own people proves virtually impossible. Wiesel had spoken voluminously, albeit gazing in despair into the void of the Holocaust; Yang had left largely unturned the tombstone that is the CR, one of the subterranean undercurrents coursing through the Chinese Century.

CHAPTER 5

The Subtitle Wagging the Screen

The Untranslated and *One Second*

Instead of the tail wagging the dog, the few English words at the bottom of the screen, big and small, tell the tale of Chinese-language films and TV series for the global Anglophone audience. This Americanism suggests the irony that a little, negligible thing or body part like a dog's tail has come to dominate the story itself. Practically, the subtitles speak for the foreign-language film. In the hands of amateurs, the subtitles not only wag the screen—they whack it, twisting it all out of shape like bad TV reception. This universal pitfall deepens in the case of modern China. To rephrase Chairman Mao's dictum regarding women holding up half the sky, the English subtitles apparently hold up the whole sky; they (mis)speak on behalf of the show, missing egregiously when the Red Sky over the Cultural Revolution (1966–76) and beyond does not particularly wish to be wagged, "woked." The whole sky turns out to be a big hole, a crime scene's bullet hole shot through Chinese consciousness of the *People's Republic of Amnesia*, as Louisa Lim calls the country in 2014. Such weight of political censorship compounds inherent fissures between the alphabet of written English, added extradiegetically in postproduction, and the tonal oral Chinese recorded live on location. The translatable and the Anglicizable thus clings on to the edge of the screen like a rock climber's fingerhold, suspended over the abyss of the unsayable in collective memory.[1]

---

1. This chapter is drawn from "The Subtitle Wagging the Screen: The Untranslated and *One Second*'s Cultural Revolution." Special issue on "Untranslatability: Theory, Practice and

Zhang Yimou's 2020 film *One Second* scarcely survives such layers of translation from traumatic experiences fictionalized in Yan Geling's Chinese-language novel *Prisoner Lu Yanshi* (2011) and filmscripts to filmic narratives, not just *One Second* but also its predecessor *Coming Home* (2014). Political headwinds prevented Zhang's film from its premiere in the 2019 Berlin Film Festival. Not yet approved by the Beijing authority for global release and doubtful that it ever will be, a pirated version with Chinese subtitles quietly materializes on YouTube, https://www.youtube.com/watch?v=gqcGwQhLjck, which could be taken offline even as we speak, its existence as fleeting as any subtitle. Another pirated version with atrocious English subtitles is subsequently uploaded: https://www.youtube.com/watch?v=hSwGiOsh5Y4. A similar fate may befall the English version, which is just as well.

In current Chinese lingo, these pirated versions on YouTube are *shanzhai* versions. Shanzhai, mountain strongholds for rebels throughout the history of imperial China, lie at the heart of the revolt of the insurgent, populist Chinese Communist Party (CCP) against colonialism and feudalism in the name of the proletariat of workers, peasants, and soldiers. Shanzhai has evolved to designate any counterfeit product or practice that imitates, even parodies, others, causing tremendous harm to consumers, endangering their health and finances, both domestically and internationally. Shanzhai is translated by Allan H. Barr as "Copycat" in Yu Hua's *China in Ten Words* (2011). Even in an Old China Hand like Barr's, the translation of "Copycat" elides the fact that this cat does more than copying: it is quite catty, red in tooth and claw. With *One Second*'s shanzhai versions widely available, the CCP's success as an antiestablishment renegade has come back to haunt itself: what it prohibits has been disseminated surreptitiously through social media. Despite the makeshift, even slapdash quality of the English version, it befits the very definition of shanzhai in defying the CCP authority devoted to self-preservation, even self-glorification.

The protagonist Zhang Jiusheng, played by Zhang Yi in *One Second*, escapes from a Cultural Revolution labor camp in search of a prefilm propaganda newsreel where his supposedly deceased daughter cameoed for a split second, hence the film's title. Like the father's quest for one second out of an hours-long feature, the film leaves unsaid and unseen much of the context: Where did the escaped convict come from? Which crime did he commit? What happened to his daughter, who had apparently denounced him for her own survival? Why did he seek out an image of his daughter rather than her real self? What is the real and what is the reel? Similar occlusions

---

Politics," *Journal of Comparative Literature and Aesthetics* (JCLA), vol. 45, no. 1, spring 2022, pp. 196–200.

and repressions enshroud the female lead "Liu Girl" and the supporting actor "Fan Movie." Liu Girl is played by Liu Haocun, her name in the film but a nickname because she and her brother, called "Liu Younger Brother," have grown up nameless orphans to parents who had perished during, if not due to, the fanatic and bloody political campaign. Fan Movie is played by Fan Wei, whose nickname in the film honors this touring propaganda film projectionist. His son is mentally challenged for having helped himself to his father's film solution, which damaged the young child's brain. That the actors' "real" Chinese surnames become their "reel" surnames plays into, unwittingly, the homophones in English.

The preceding exegesis has gone beyond a literal translation of the filmic universe, diving into the unspoken, the inferred within the Chinese context as well as the intercultural and cross-generic give-and-take. Hence, translation in *One Second* constitutes not only a linguistic practice from fiction to film, from Chinese dialogues to English subtitles, but also a cultural practice from lived experiences to artistic expressions and political suppressions. As such, *One Second* and other narratives of the Cultural Revolution are cliff-hangers climbing up from the valley of "the Ten-Year Holocaust," barely hanging on just like the flash of "white" light, the thin line of English subtitles, before they sink out of frame. *One Second*'s untranslatability on account of political censorship and cultural parameters is entirely different from Walter Benjamin's philosophical reveries in "The Task of the Translator" (1955). Benjamin projects his utopian vision of art for art's sake onto translation, totally unconcerned with reader reception. By contrast, the untranslated in *One Second* stems not from a ritualistic divine source but from the precarity over speaking out. Benjamin has the luxury of musing about the translator's task in theory; Zhang Yimou, as world-renowned as he is, must attend to the consequences of such musing in practice. Benjamin can afford to divorce his rumination from real life; Zhang's reality hinges on self-censorship.

Let us start from, as W. B. Yeats puts it in "The Circus Animals' Desertion," "where all the ladders start," the bottom of paltry, shoddy English subtitles. In a film that thrives on the filmic language of body gestures and dynamic movements with few spoken words, the practically first attempt at dialogue is mistranslated. After loading up the film reels on his moped, the projectionist Fan's assistant Yang He (rendered as "Yanghe") appears ready to leave at night for the next screening site. To a surprised friend, Yang He responds: "Fan film [Fan Movie] is looking for any fault. Who dare go at night?" The rhetorical question is a literal translation of *sheigan zouyelu,* which should be taken figuratively: "Who dare play hooky!" or "Who dare cut corners!" Yang's rhetorical question confirms his intention of immediate departure, contrary to the erroneous subtitle. Yang He takes to the road dutifully, nighttime notwithstanding, to deliver the film reels.

Inept, homemade translation continues unabated. After their physical, even brutal, scuffle over the film reel Liu stole from Yang He's moped, Zhang Jiusheng offers an apology: "I wouldn't beat u if I knew y r girl"; "Why you steal this, sale it?" No matter how subpar, the subtitles do fill the void left by political censorship. Availing oneself of the English version, alas, afflicts the global reception of *One Second*. Liu's vulgar rejoinder to Zhang's question, "*Guanni pishi*," is gentrified as "It isn't your business," which loses the sting of the original "It's none of your Goddamn business" or even worse with the f-word in place of the G-word. A tramp's tough talk from the gutter is softened for "ears polite" of the world. No translation is perhaps preferable to bad translation; no memory preferable to bad or planted memory. The choice between an empty glass and a poisoned chalice should be obvious. Conceivably, broadminded non-Sinophone cinephiles could watch it like a silent film without comprehending the dialogue, helped along by the plethora of universal grunts, cries, laughter, and nonlingual sounds. The cinephile's feeling of disorientation offers a visceral taste of the confusion and uncertainty that the protagonist Zhang and millions of victims like him had suffered. Perhaps it is too harsh to call the English version a poisoned chalice. A bottle of corked wine, then, where the translator's good intentions are betrayed by incompetence.

This unintentional misspeaking fails the film's minimalist representation, one that leaves much to be intuited. From the bottom subtitles, the "lowest" common denominator of film language, let us lift our eyes to study the amorphous images on the screen, transcribed onto the viewer's mental screen as synaptic (mis)firing between a little-known Chinese past and a virtual present, if not perpetual on YouTube. The known at our fingertips triggers the unknown from a strange country of a distant time. The mistranslation over Yang He's imminent night ride leads into the dark, unknown Cultural Revolution for the new millennium.

The unfathomable cataclysm uncoils through recurring, defamiliarizing motifs that are, nonetheless, familiar to every human being: families, or rather, broken families of fathers and daughters, either party dead or lost or estranged. The thematic unfolding of one of the oldest human relationships constitutes a metanarrative, a mise en abyme, each frame within the frame reflecting the others through the unspooling of films and of family relationships. On our digital devices, we in 2021 and beyond watch Zhang Yimou's film, where Fan Movie projects the propaganda film *Heroic Sons and Daughters* (1964) by way of the rotation of an obsolete analog 35mm film strip. Parallel viewings coexist within Zhang's film; they also coexist within the film and without, as you and I are shocked by the horror, moved by the anguish. Within *One Second,* villagers watch the propaganda film that is on tour, circling the countryside, whereas Zhang Jiusheng waits for that second in the prefilm newsreel. The spirit of everlasting martyrdom eulogized in *Heroic Sons and Daughters* is but a vehicle for the bereaved father's brief séance with the departed soul. The cyclical nature resides as much in the touring film reels as in Zhang Jiusheng being treated to what Fan Movie, after the public screening, has spliced together for his eyes only—the small number of frames in a loop where his daughter comes alive again and again. That one flicker illuminating the ghost of a daughter deconstructs the Chinese tradition of family. Fan Movie applies glue to reattach film stocks, the very glue that turned Fan's son dim-witted. The magic of a professional projectionist so mesmerizes Zhang that he is unaware of having been betrayed by Fan to the village authority. Witnessing the severe beating Zhang endured upon arrest, an apologetic Fan performs one last sleight of hand, sliding into Zhang's coat pocket two frames of his daughter's negative.

Negative is the word. Instead of the real daughter, Zhang keeps close to his heart her likeness, albeit overexposed. Yet even the negative keepsake is confiscated by the authority, which discards it like trash en route to the prison. His daughter's negative is soon buried under the sea of blowing sand. When Zhang is released from the labor camp two years later in an epilogue of happy ending, he searches in vain, with Liu Girl's help, for the negative in the barren desert. Sensing the futility of their effort, the father-daughter pair exchange resigned smiles, gazing into the infinite stretch of sand. They have, in the end, each other, as they gaze into the same direction of screen left. This tableau of lost-and-found segues into rather melodramatic closing credits with Liu Haocun. Now restored to a chic twentysomething, her well-groomed ponytail cascading down the back of a baseball cap, Liu sings softly, at times whispering, the theme song "One Second" into the microphone, wiping away a tear or two spontaneously.

This sensitive touch is not totally unexpected, given that the street urchin's smeared face and tattered clothes have been redeemed throughout by her pretty looks and fashionably unkempt, frizzy bouffant hairdo straight out of the "skin job" Pris's (Daryl Hannah) coiffure in *Blade Runner* (1982) or Maggie Cheung's in *Chinese Box* (1997). If Zhang Yimou ventures into China's dirty past, Liu Haocun's hair styling is already sanitized. If the epilogue's post–Cultural Revolution return to normalcy, not only personal freedom but also the possibility of a new family, intends to heal the primal wound by squatting at the heels of official narratives, the subsequent ban proves that the filmmaker has failed. If Liu's tearful singing intends to provide a closure, rounding off the sharp edges of collective memory, the subsequent ascent of Liu's stardom contrasts sharply with the nameless daughter's descent into the hourglass of history.

Singing has a way of lingering in the ear long after it is done, which presents yet another contrast. The fruitless hunt for the negative in the desert is accompanied by a high-pitched, heart-wrenching female vocal, possibly a rustic folk song in local dialect, unintelligible to the majority of Sinophone viewers. This is the only place absent of Chinese subtitles. A postproduction technical oversight? Conceivably, it could be an ingenious move to suggest the emotional intensity soaring far beyond words, rendering subtitles inoperative, redundant. Against this searing "surround sound," the new father and daughter bond over the realization of all that is lost: the past is a long roll of negatives, each frame the bleached bone of a fading present. The indecipherable soundtrack then eases, pun intended, into Liu's "One Second" of the closing credits, the only place of the film with both Chinese and English subtitles. Liu's tears and twice-translated lyrics spell the end of the nameless, faceless folk singer's no lyrics.

The film's father-daughter mise en abyme involves intertextuality. *Heroic Sons and Daughters* is based on the novelist Ba Jin's 1961 reportage, *Reunion*, on the Korean War. Dispatched by Beijing to the Korean theater in the early 1950s, Ba Jin in a first-person narrative tells the story of a Party secretary, Director Wang, spotting among the People's Volunteer Army (PVA) at the Korean War his long-lost daughter Wang Fang. (The PVA from China included Mao's eldest son Mao Anying, who was killed by American bombing in 1950.) Over a decade ago, Director Wang was forced to entrust his young daughter to a janitor in order to join the communist underground activities in Shanghai. Personal sacrifice of the father and the daughter comes to a tear-jerking happy ending as they are reunited in the Korean theater of war to entertain Chinese theatergoers. The film version juxtaposes this family reunion with a People's Liberation Army martyr's self-immolation for the sake of the collective family of China and North Korea. The martyr happens to be Wang Fang's adoptive brother, who radios the artillery what has become a catchphrase, "For victory, fire at me!" as he has inserted himself amid the phalanx of American invaders. His last words ricochet from the 1964 black-and-white footage to Zhang's 2021 film, which, in reverse shots, captures the villagers' eyes welling up. Zhang's "quotations" of an old film elicit villagers' tears and perhaps our sneers. One father finds his daughter, who in turn loses her adoptive brother, who in turn is apotheosized in the communist pantheon, who in turn is almost an object of ridicule to millennial China weaned on "socialism with Chinese characteristics," a.k.a. wolfish capitalism in good communist lamb's clothes. The early

Ba Jin found traditional families repulsive, such as in the celebrated *The Torrents Trilogy* that opened with *The Family* (1933); the late Ba Jin mellowed to sing of revolutionary families.

This play on reversals of past and present, of *ressentiment* and reform, infuses the film with an ironic gallows humor that insulates the absurd horror, the horrible absurdity, of the Cultural Revolution. Zhang and Liu put on an act of estranged father and daughter when they are picked up consecutively along a desolate road by an unwitting truck driver, each blaming the other for having abandoned the family. With the driver playing the fool, this skit in the truck cab amounts to verbal and physical commedia dell'arte. The audience laughs through tears, bracing themselves against the bleak desert landscape and ceaseless human betrayals. The funnyman Fan Wei's tour de force as Fan Movie also sustains the comic streak throughout, a harmonic relaxing to counterpoint the contraction over father-daughter relationships and of our hearts.

CHAPTER 6

Laosanjie Peers Back at the Red Sun

Zhang Yimou of the "Chain Gang"

Zhang Yimou's banned film *One Second* (2020) traces the futile quest of a Cultural Revolution (CR) labor camp convict for the split-second cameo of his deceased daughter in a propaganda newsreel. To counteract the overwhelming sense of loss and misery, Zhang closes with a happy ending of sorts when the convict is released and reunites with a substitute daughter "Two Years Later," the only intertitle in the film that would place the reunion circa 1978, two years after the twin deaths of Chairman Mao and his infamous CR. The rarity of intertitles signals that timing is of the essence for those weathering the CR. It makes sense for a *laosanjie* ("Old Three Years" for high school and middle school graduates during the period 1966–68) returnee like Zhang to see the changing of the guard from Mao's hand-picked successor Hua Guofeng to Deng Xiaoping as a turning point in the life of the nation and of the individual. Having graduated from high school in 1968, at the height of Mao's CR, Zhang was "sent down to the countryside" as one of the laosanjie, their higher education deferred and their youth wasted in China's wasteland for a decade until post-Mao reinstitution of college admissions. Along with Tian Zhuangzhuang and Chen Kaige, two fellow "chain gang" members "reeducated through labor," Zhang Yimou matriculated at the Beijing Film Academy in 1978, beginning a new life no different from his film's ex-convict. Tian, Chen, and Zhang eventually arose as fifth-generation directors compelled, albeit under State censorship, to bear witness to their trauma.

One Second is not the first time Zhang tells, with a slant, the tale of the "Ten-Year Holocaust." Also revolving around an escapee's search for his family, *Coming Home* (2014) has already ventured to peer back not so much in John Osborne's anger as in laosanjie's anguish. Earlier still, *To Live* (1994), based on Yu Hua's novel, gives a bird's-eye view of the bleakness prior to and under Mao from the 1940s to 1960s. As brief and veiled as they are, these backward peers pierce a taboo subject largely stylized in collective memory, sanitized by the panopticon Red Sun. Both *One Second* and *Coming Home* are filmic adaptations of Yan Geling's Chinese-language novel *Prisoner Lu Yanshi* (2011). *Coming Home* suggests, in Holocaust survivor Jean Améry's words, "the necessity and the impossibility" of any return, for the notion of home, if not that of homeland, has been ripped asunder.[1] Jewish Holocaust absolutism in its inimitable uniqueness juxtaposes with Chinese relativism: Mao's ceaseless revolutionary campaigns, the CR included, are deemed cyclical revolutions, i.e., rotations between *he* (union) and *fen* (separation). Neither evolution of the same old nor revolution of the brand new, *One Second*'s trope of the film reel is shared by all these filmic peers backward. The circular turning to unspool the reels for a linear story encapsulates the paradox of an apocalyptic CR that was but repetition of the same old madness, of moving forward by looking backward.

His first name meaning, literally, "Who Can Recognize" or "Who Dare Acknowledge," the protagonist Lu Yanshi (陸焉識) has been labeled an anti-Rightist since the 1950s and has languished in the labor camp near the Gobi Desert in China's northwest for twenty years. The film opens with the climax of Lu's prison break to visit his family, only to be betrayed by his daughter Dandan in an attempt to preserve her ideological purity and her ballerina role in Madame Mao or Jiang Qing's propaganda opera. Such *in media res* opening is reprised in *One Second*, excising Yan Geling's labor camp horror altogether, not to mention the trumped-up charges to send Lu to the re-education camp in the first place. Also repeated is the daughter's betrayal of her parents to curry favor from the authorities. Family is sacrificed in the name of the nation, which in fact hides personal survival and advancement.

When Lu does return, his beloved Yu suffers from dementia, finding Lu a total stranger. Resonating with the implication of his name, no one, not even Yu, recognizes Lu. Thus begins the film's slow burn in the wake of the opening's fiery climax of Lu's capture and Yu's head injury at the train station. Performativity comes to dominate the film. The revolutionary ballet performed for an audience of one, namely, Mao, morphs into Lu's various play-acting

---

1. See Jean Améry's *At the Mind's Limits* (1980), pp. 82–101.

also for an audience of one, Yu, in hope of restoring Yu's memory. Lu disguises himself in multiple roles—all to no avail. Yu has forgotten Lu, just as the motherland has put under erasure any memory trace of the historical injustice.

Diegetic role-playing is made possible by extradiegetic, authorial performativity. Neither the novelist Yan Geling nor the actors Chen Daoming (Lu) and Gong Li (Yu) belong to laosanjie; they are of the next generation and even younger. At most bystanders or latecomers to the cataclysm, non-laosanjie artists have assumed, imaginatively, the personae of victims by way of what Marianne Hirsch calls "postmemory" for those who come after.[2] In comparison to Holocaustal postmemory's leaning toward individual and familial suffering passed down viscerally, the CR discourse stretches taut between personal and political, confessional and collective, tensions. Parsing the intersection of trauma and memory studies with literary and filmic textuality, one wonders how generations to come would come to remember a past they have never experienced, and how they would recognize a China that is long gone, gone forever through bans known, such as *One Second,* and bans unknown. A "half-breed" like *Coming Home* born to a non-laosanjie mother, Yan Geling, and a laosanjie father, Zhang Yimou, comes after the relative "thoroughbreds" of *To Live,* Tian Zhuangzhuang's *The Blue Kite* (1993), based on Xiao Mao's filmscript, and Chen Kaige's *Farewell My Concubine* (1993).

Reverse Engineering from Zhang's Film to Yan's Fiction to the Cultural Revolution

Unlike the film from an omniscient perspective, the novel purports to be dictated by Lu Yanshi to his granddaughter Feng Xuefeng (馮學鋒), while the film's Dandan (Danyu in the novel) becomes the narrator's aunt in the novel. Note the change of the family name from the patriarch's Lu to the matriarch's Feng to dissociate themselves from the political prisoner Lu. The shrinking of cast and cutting of plot twists condense the sprawling story that shuttles between past and present. The film opens in the thick of action, as Lu escapes the labor camp to visit Feng Wanyu (馮婉喻 simplified as Yu in the film. Henceforth "Yu" for the character in both novel and film for the sake of clarity). The novel spans their arranged marriage, arranged by Lu's stepmother

---

2. Originally intended for post-Holocaust literature and art, Marianne Hirsch's term *postmemory* has been widely applied to trauma survivors and their descendants, the latter group implicitly and subconsciously impacted by a historic tumult that they have not viscerally experienced.

wedding him to her own niece, as well as Lu's two-decade-long saga at a labor camp in China's borderland. The family tension between the stepmother and the couple constitutes a large swathe of the novel, all skipped cinematically.

The prison camp's starvation and savagery are elaborated, at times verging on the fantastical from a non-laosanjie novelist fantasizing the nightmarish camps.[3] Several instances stand out: subconsciously, prisoners stage a mass protest in the form of sleepwalking. How is it possible that sleepwalking turns contagious, reminiscent of Fritz Lang's choreography of underground miners slouching out of the escalator in synchronized steps and body movements in *Metropolis* (1927)? Furthermore, any prisoner who changes his position in sleep must cry out first "*Baogao!*" (Report, Sir!). Conduct becoming to the notion of "chain gang," this hyperbole can only be taken as a figure of speech for the Big Brother surveilling every citizen's every move, sleeping positions included. While Yan's point is well taken, she unwittingly predicts the millennial surveillance technology of China's facial recognition and digital tracking known as *Tianyan* (Sky Eye). To push the labor camp to the extreme of human endurance, even over the edge into surrealism, Yan summons flocks of birds, en masse, defecating midair on the prisoners. The wretched of the earth are, pardon my French, "shit on" not only by their human tormentors but by wild animals.

The novel crystallizes its motifs in the metaphor of the female protagonist Feng Wanyu's or simply Yu's *jiefang jiao* (解放腳). The phrase refers to "liberated bound feet" for feet subjected to binding in accordance with the Qing dynasty custom but unbound once the Qing was overthrown and Western modernization introduced. "Unbound bound feet," so to speak, straddle past oppression and present liberation, bearing scars of bone disfigurement from early-age binding but also growing back somewhat to their natural form. Like her feet between bestial hooves and human feet, Yu is both a self-effacing, traditionally regressive woman standing by the philanderer of a husband and a romantic who remains steadfast in her devotion to the persecuted.

A brilliant scholar selected for overseas studies at the age of nineteen, Lu boasts of photographic memory and is well versed in four languages. In the labor camp, however, he feigns a stutter to elude political persecution. State oppression seals not only Lu's expressive hole of the mouth but also his ejective hole of the anus. Lu is terribly constipated, given the prison diet and pressure. The entire person, head to toe, inside and out, is under State control. Lu manages to escape from the camp only after watching the documentary

---

3. For narratives based largely on personal testimonies, see Wang Ruowang's *Hunger Trilogy* (1980). For reportage, see Liu Binyan's *People or Monster?* (1983).

on blood-sucking bugs in which his scientist daughter Danyu or Dandan appears, different from its filmic reincarnation *One Second*, where the protagonist absconds in order to watch his deceased daughter on the newsreel. While the daughter in a white lab coat demonstrates the plague of bugs, she, her family, and others are being bled dry by politics. Spinning off Dostoevsky's narrow escape from the firing squad, author Yan Geling has Lu spared at the execution ground. The reprieve comes at the expense of Yu offering her body to the official in charge.

Surrealism is not the only color-filtering lens through which the CR is imagined. Melodrama intrudes as well in that the Alzheimer's syndrome strikes at the very moment when Yu receives the official notice of post-Mao amnesty granted to Lu. Amnesty coincides with amnesia; Lu's imminent release punctuates the onset of Yu's illness. Yet the novelist elects to romanticize Alzheimer's by portraying Yu as cleansed by the onslaught of memory loss, a mind so crystal-clear, so purged of social trappings that it no longer withholds profanities and physical violence. Like her unbound bound feet, the Alzheimer's patient is free of inhibition to lash out, concluding with her strange behavior of disrobing herself, restored to the "birthday suit." The novel concludes with Lu leaving his family with Yu's ashes, back to the remote northwest camp where the ex-commandant Deng's son has taken the reins.

Zhang Yimou trims the novel considerably in *Coming Home*. The film opens with the intensity of Lu's flight after he has failed to rendezvous with his wife Yu, all thwarted by the informant of a daughter. In the chaotic capture amid shrill sirens, screeching wheels, and massive crowds at the local train station, Yu is shoved to the ground, her forehead bloodied, foreshadowing her dementia and conjuring up previous abuse in the hands of Master Fang. That Yu mistakes the post-Mao returnee Lu as Fang repeatedly arouses Lu's suspicion. Dandan confirms that Yu was hit by Fang with a ladle. But what actually transpired may have escaped a young child's powers of observation. Circumstantial evidence points to rapes by Fang in exchange for sparing Lu's life. Zhang Yimou has altered Yan Geling's rapist from an official granting a commutation to Lu on death row to a nonofficial artisan, a leader of the commune apparently with no government position. Whereas a corrupt, lecherous official on the page is permissible, one onscreen risks the whole film being condemned.

Dandan betrays Lu because the bad element of a father may prevent her from getting the lead role in *The Red Detachment of Women*, yet another propaganda play like *Heroic Sons and Daughters* in *One Second*. To perform loyal sacrifice and martyrdom onstage, Dandan scapegoats her parents, not to mention how the patriotic drama masks troupe intrigues and influence-peddling behind the scenes. Upon release and "rehabilitation" in the post-Mao China, Lu enacts multiple scenarios of homecoming in hope of jolting Yu's memory: a piano-tuner to tune the piano in preparation for Lu's return on the fifth of the month, the Groundhog Day of endless reprise for Yu; a good Samaritan delivering unsent letters to Yu; and a letter-reader who smuggles in a word or two in Dandan's favor to urge an end to the daughter's banishment from home. Tuning and playing piano nearly work when the familiar, elegiac female vocal on the soundtrack brings back the past, but also the specter of her abuser. Hence, the half-embrace with Lu abruptly halts when Yu extricates herself, mistaking Lu to be the man, possibly Master Fang, taking advantage of her yet again. The traumatic repetition compulsion has rendered Yu beyond retrieval. The arrival on the fifth, wǔ (五) in the third tone, happens to pun with its homonym of wú (無) in the second tone, which means nothingness. Nothing or no return on the fifth brings on wù (悟) in the fourth tone for "awakening" to the futility, not for Yu but for the audience.

Lu performs as a stranger to Yu when he is in fact her husband. Such performativity sums up the CR, a history that is stranger than fiction, where families and loved ones turn against one another for self-preservation and/or for protecting others, shielding them from mob violence. In point of fact, Lu assumes a series of role-playing on the counsel of a medical doctor, who recommends the Western technique of hypnotism to stage "déjà vu" occasions with an eye toward triggering her memory of the past. "Déjà vu" is delivered in English by Chen Daoming, who plays the polyglot Lu, perhaps the only nod to the West in a Chinese-language film. Yet such Western techniques prove ineffective in neutralizing a misery, in President Xi's catchphrase, "with Chinese characteristics." Zhang's Western filmmaking expertise co-opts Western pseudo-scientific practice, if only to illustrate its limitation in combating a uniquely Chinese malaise traceable less to individual psyche than to collective subconscious.

Similar to *One Second*, intertitles are utilized to pinpoint the time period, the larger context that determines the fate of the individual. "Three Years Later, the end of the Cultural Revolution" marks Lu's repatriation from the camp and the impossible journey to reach the Alzheimer's patient. The intertitle toward the end of the film begins the cinematic coda—"Many Years Later"—when an elderly Lu has apparently played along all these years, carrying Yu in a three-wheeler to await Lu at the train station on the fifth of every month, brandishing a placard calligraphed "Lu Yanshi," one written by none other than Lu Yanshi himself. Yu has long forgotten how to write.

It is worth noting that the historic pain of the CR is transmitted to us by the joint effort of laosanjie Zhang Yimou, who personally experienced the

CR, and of non-laosanjie Yan Geling. Yan was too young and her family background too well connected for her to be sent to the countryside for reform. Instead, she served in the People's Liberation Army at the height of the CR, a much-coveted position at the time. Although all the actors in *Coming Home* are one or two generations after laosanjie, they are entrusted with reanimating the CR. Like Yan the author, Zhang's cast, in a body, peers back to pierce the historical amnesia, of which Yu's ailment is but a synecdoche. Whether the backward glance to resurrect historical memory is as futile as Lu's return and cosplay, only time will tell.

To Live amid the "Chain Gang"

Over a decade before *Coming Home* and *One Second*, Zhang has stolen a brief glance at the CR in his 1994 film adaptation of Yu Hua's novel *To Live* (1993). In the wake of the Literature of the Wounded or Scar Literature in the late 1970s, Yu Hua and fifth-generation filmmakers are embroiled in a period of soul-searching over the Maoist cataclysm, largely by means of a panoramic overview of recent Chinese history and culture. Yet the epic, collective approach is in and of itself a distancing strategy. Rather than "indulging" in personal suffering and thus incurring official wrath, the author's pen favors broad strokes, and the director's camera, in a manner of speaking, long shots, evidenced by Zhang Yimou's filmic intertitles of "The Forties," "The Fifties," "The Sixties," and "Some Years Later." Likewise, Tian Zhuangzhuang's *The Blue Kite* proceeds in three sections named after the boy narrator's three "fathers": "Dad," who meets his death during the Hundred Flowers Campaign; "Uncle," who wastes away in the Great Leap Forward; and "Stepfather," who perishes during the CR. Chen Kaige's *Farewell My Concubine* is even more expansive, spanning half a century from the Nationalist Republic of China to the People's Republic of China.

Yu Hua's novel *To Live* is no exception, written in the style of a lengthy, often rambling, parable out of the folk oral tradition, woefully inadequate in psychological nuances for characters bordering on cartoonish types. Yu Hua's narrator "I" is a young folk ballad and story collector when Communist China was first founded, reminiscent of the lead in *Yellow Earth* (1984), one of the first films by fifth-generation filmmaker Chen Kaige, with cinematography by Zhang Yimou. The translator, Michael Berry, has italicized the narrator's periodic voices to distinguish from the protagonist Xu Fugui's story, contrary to Yu Hua's identical fonts for both narratives. In the typical Anglophone thinking and writing practice, Berry manages to clarify and register different voices that Yu Hua, in a Sinophone instinct for de-individualization, subliminally wishes to wed into one: the small "I" with the big "I"; the narrator with the author and the reader.

Despite the title *To Live,* both the novel and the film revolve around the string of deaths of Xu Fugui's loved ones and of massive disintegration of family, community, and culture under the weight of Maoist extremism. In the novel, Fugui is the sole survivor of his family, accompanied by an old ox named after himself, sharing his life story with the narrator–ballad collector. With Fugui and his eponymous ox, Yu Hua spins the fable's staple of talking animals into talking *to* animals, as Fugui the old man engages Fugui the old ox in a way that implicates a gallery of oxen variously called by the names of those in Fugui's bereft life. These bovine phantoms include, in the order of their "disappearance," his late son Youqing, daughter Fengxia, wife Jiazhen, son-in-law Erxi, and grandson Kugen (renamed Little Bun in the film). This human-ox correspondence implies that human beings are destined for a life of hardships like animals of burden. The choice of the ox, however, Sinologizes the children's story convention in that the ox is a revered animal in the traditionally agrarian China that has relied on the ox for ploughing and other agricultural activities. Fugui's talking not just to his ox but also to nonexistent ones piques the narrator's and the reader's interest. In a circular fashion, however, Fugui the man talking to Fugui the ox equals Fugui talking to himself, a reflection of Yu Hua writing as a nameless, almost transparent, narrator, telling a story to the Chinese who already know the story, even if repressed.

The fairy-tale tenor surfaces in Yu Hua's refrain of the Xu family fortune. "A long time ago our Xu family ancestors raised but a single chicken. When that chicken grew up it turned into a goose, the goose in turn grew into a lamb, and the lamb became an ox. This is how our family became rich" (36). Two prodigal sons, Fugui and his father have squandered the family wealth in gambling. Michael Berry points out in his translator's afterword that Zhang Yimou's film reprises this "animal tale" twice. First, Fugui's son Youqing pushes the query as to what happens after the ox. "Communism," Fugui quips, "and there'll be dumplings and meat every day" (242). But after the deaths of loved ones through famines and bureaucratic ineptitude, Fugui is left with his grandson, Little Bun, who wonders, like his deceased uncle Youqing, what comes after the ox. "Little Bun," grandparents reply, idealism having mellowed into pragmatism, "rid[ing] trains and planes. And life will get better" (243). While the earlier answer to Youqing hews closely to the Party indoctrination, the present one to Little Bun aspires to post-Mao capitalist-socialist progress, which already undercuts ideological religiosity.

FIGURE 6.1. One of Little Bun's pet chicks held up from their nest in the empty trunk that once contained shadow puppets in *To Live*.

Whereas Yu Hua ends with an old man talking to ghosts, the film's finale comes across as decidedly upbeat. As the closing credits roll in figure 6.1, Fugui is surrounded, not by spectral cows, but by a bedridden Jiazhen and his grandson Little Bun. Son-in-law Erxi is off frame preparing food. All three have long perished in Yu Hua. Although Yu Hua's oxen are anthropomorphized as a surrogate family, they remain literary tropes or props for storytelling. Such tropes are dropped altogether by Zhang Yimou, who swaps them for the prop, literally, of shadow puppets. Figure 6.1 shows one of Little Bun's pet chicks held up from their nest in the empty trunk that once contained shadow puppets, all incinerated as "Four Olds" during the conflagration of the CR. Yu Hua's prop of the ox is replaced by Zhang Yimou's prop of shadow puppets. In Zhang's closure, old puppets are themselves replaced by little chicks.

Zhang's motif of substitution via shadow puppets extends backward from this last frame captured by figure 6.1. Concurrent with the overthrow of corrupt feudalism by communist revolution, Fugui has lost his family fortune, the Xu ancestral land, to Long Er (Long'er in pinyin), the cheat with loaded dice and the shadow puppetry troupe owner. The old China dies along with Fugui's decadent past. Good riddance, the reader may applaud, since Fugui, embodying that old China, is so debauched that he rides "a fat prostitute" "like riding on the back of a horse," among other outrages (13–14). Epitomizing the depravity of feudalism, Fugui's fall is an allegory for the fall of a moribund world, so long as readers are cognizant of the communist lens through which the precommunist, premodern China is represented.

FIGURE 6.2. A Nationalist soldier's bayonet rips the puppetry screen in *To Live*.

As a final act of mercy for Fugui robbed of all belongings, Long Er bequeaths him a trunk of shadow puppets, which is useless to Long Er anyway, now that he is the new landlord. These shadow puppets have accompanied Fugui through thick and thin. Figure 6.2 illustrates the moment when a Nationalist soldier's bayonet rips the puppetry screen amid one performance. Hence, both Fugui and the puppeteer Chunsheng are forcibly conscripted—the notorious *lafu* in Chinese—by Chiang Kai-shek's army to pull cannons in the battle against the People's Liberation Army (PLA). The Nationalist Army, despite their superior weaponry such as the cannons and the US-made military trucks, crumbles in a besiegement. Their leader absconds, loaded with cash, the final straw that breaks the morale—a thinly veiled parallel to Chiang Kai-shek fleeing to Taiwan with large amounts of gold and dynastic treasures from the Forbidden City. Subsequently liberated by the PLA, Fugui and Chunsheng repay the debt by staging a shadow puppet show lit by the campfire, before being sent back home with travel funds. The stark contrast of the shock of the Nationalist bayonet and the appreciative clapping of the PLA spectators contributes to the slogan "recalling past bitterness, thinking of present sweetness." The feudal and Nationalist injustice is purged by the Communist revolution, the excesses and overzealousness of which, however, are secreted by Zhang Yimou in an underhanded manner.

During the Great Leap Forward of the 1950s, each family's pots and pans are smelted in the village commune to, theoretically, produce steel for bullets and bombs, as Chairman Mao fancies in the imminent Armageddon against Western imperialists. The grandiose vision of the Founding Father is executed by way of local superstition, through the eyes of a "town *fengshui* [geomancy] expert," a Mr. Wang. "To find the ideal spot with perfect *fengshui* to smelt iron," Wang initially favors Fugui's "thatched hut," which would spell its demolition (105–6). Only when Jiazhen, Wang's old acquaintance, makes a timely appeal does Mr. Wang turn his gaze elsewhere. The fate of China and of one single family hinges on the whims of masters in control of state affairs and of communal fengshui.

Just as the puppet trunk is being dismantled for nails and puppets for metal hooks, Fugui hastens to beseech that the antiques be preserved for shows to entertain the crew tending the fire throughout the night to melt down sundry metals. Although the shadow puppets are saved in the name of all-night performance, their son Youqing crosses into the shadowland, the cause of his death thus altered from the novel. The inspecting district chief, who turns out to be his fellow puppeteer Chunsheng, backs his car unwittingly into a dirt wall and crushes to death Youqing, dozing behind the wall. Such trade-offs transpire throughout the film. Losing his family wealth, Fugui gains the livelihood of shadow puppetry. Coming into the possession of the Xu mansion and land, Long Er loses his life, executed for being a landlord at the height of land reform in the fifties. Long Er's last words to Fugui en route to the execution ground are well taken: "Fugui, I'm dying for you!" (84). Retaining his shadow puppets, Fugui loses his son instead. Even Fengxia, a deaf-mute after a prolonged bout of fever, is given to others as a maid to put Youqing through school. Privileging the son over the daughter bespeaks a misogynist patriarchy founded on women either mutely suffering like Jiazhen or altogether deaf and mute like her daughter Fengxia.

All their kitchen utensils confiscated by the State, villagers eat at the People's Commune mess hall, much to the delight of the people. Yet drought and famine soon follow, resulting in millions starved to death. The State takes away not just their metal but also their mettle, dignity, and even lives in *The Great Leap Backward*, as Lingchei Letty Chen puts it in her 2020 monograph. Material dispossession parallels spiritual and symbolic void, as Youqing's body, along with those of millions of other Chinese, vaporizes into thin traces of memory for the living. Youqing's body turns into a shadow, or a shadow puppet in the real puppeteer Chairman Mao's trunk, laid side by side with amateur and fake puppeteer Fugui and Chunsheng. Neither his former profession as a puppet master nor his present position as the district chief matters, as Chunsheng is labeled a capitalist roader and persecuted by Red Guards to the extent that he commits suicide, despite his promise to Jiazhen. Jiazhen exhorts Chunsheng: "You've got to keep on living . . . You still owed us a life . . . Hold on to your life to repay us" (200). Taking his own life is as much an answer to political injustice as a settling of debts and personal guilt over Youqing's accident. Chunsheng, like those around and above him packed into the trunk called China, is a mere pawn in political struggles. Herein lies perhaps the hidden rationale for Zhang's conceit of shadow puppetry, which is nowhere to be found in Yu Hua's tear-jerking melodrama. Given that the puppet master animates and gives voice to the puppet, the ultimate puppeteer orchestrating recent Chinese history, Chairman Mao, is safely insulated behind the scenes, beyond scrutiny, enjoying utter impunity.

But attributing all the blame to Mao may be no less a cop-out and a diversion than the national narrative that lays the responsibility for the historic catastrophe squarely at the feet of Madame Mao, the Gang of Four, and their henchmen, particularly the fanatic Red Guards. As the mastermind of the CR, Chairman Mao remains eulogized to this day and, conceivably, into the foreseeable future. The culprits for "man's inhumanity to man" are projected elsewhere. Like Trump's "stolen" presidential election of 2020, this is the Big Lie perpetrated in plain sight of the Chinese people, some of whom go along with the official revisionism for self-preservation. Others parrot such revisionism either whole- or half-heartedly. To trace back to Mao certainly moves closer to the truth than does political propaganda. Nonetheless, it shifts focus from the Chinese people, whose mercurial roles of victims, bystanders, and victimizers await reckoning. As if in passing, Qian Zhongshu's foreword to Yang Jiang's *Six Chapters from My Life "Downunder"* (1981) calls for a seventh chapter of "A Sense of Shame," or a mea culpa from bystanders and victimizers of the CR. Such a chapter or even book of shame is yet to be authored by the Chinese themselves.

The historical and psychological blur accounts for the motif of psychic displacement. To accept the national rhetoric damning a handful of bad leaders absolves not only the Supreme Leader of Mao but also each and every Chinese who may have failed to stand up and speak truth to power in an autocracy. What they can do, as does Qian Zhongshu, is to intimate through innuendo, understatement, irony, black humor, allegory, doublespeak, historical analogue, and a myriad of circuitous avenues. The substitution between the novel's ox and the film's puppets is but one example of the overarching theme of replacement. To indirectly finger the Big Boss Mao behind the Red Guard *xiaogui* (little ghosts or little kids), Zhang deploys the fraught marriage of the deaf-mute Fengxia and a model worker, Erxi, with a crooked neck in the novel but a more "presentable" disability of lameness in the film.[4]

---

4. Jiang Wu, who plays Erxi with a bad leg, has assumed roles with disabilities before. Nostalgic for the Old Beijing, Zhang Yang's *Shower* (1999) features Jiang Wu acting as the mentally challenged son of one of Beijing's old-time public baths, fast disappearing amid modernization and urbanization.

FIGURE 6.3. The newlyweds and the parents are photographed between the wall painting of Mao and a cardboard ship christened "The East Is Red" in *To Live*.

The matchmaking of Fengxia and Erxi is conducted by the team leader, an ambiguous character who unabashedly takes advantage of Fugui's family during the famine but who comes to Fengxia's rescue, given her poor prospect of finding a mate. Never named, hence morphing into all official *lingdao* (領導 leader), the team leader in Yu Hua pockets a slice of Fengxia's sweet potato with the subterfuge of equal distribution. He also extorts a portion of the rice that Jiazhen begs from the limited resources of her own father in town. All such nefarious dealings of the team leader are cut in Zhang's film. To present a local cadre in such a negative light may doom the film of ever coming to light.

During the matchmaking meeting arranged by the team leader, Erxi and Fengxia's parents exchange neither traditional gifts nor promises of love but proof of ideological purity and correct class background, including Fugui's ripped and waterlogged discharge paper by the PLA, long framed and displayed on the wall. *The Collection of Chairman Mao's Sayings* is proffered by the prospective bridegroom under the gaze from Mao's portraits on the wall and Mao buttons on the lapels. The ritual meeting is less for the couple than for an audience of one, Chairman Mao. Since Mao is absent, his looming visages in portraits and statuettes notwithstanding, one is obliged to conclude that Mao is present everywhere, omnipresent through every single pair of Chinese eyes scrutinizing one another on behalf of Mao. Figure 6.3 culminates Mao's God-like ubiquity. The newlyweds and the parents holding the Little Red Book are photographed, flanked between the wall painting of Mao and a cardboard ship christened, in Mao's slanting, rule-defying calligraphy at the bow, *dongfang hong* (東方紅 "The East Is Red"). "The East Is Red" is a

FIGURE 6.4. The "reactionary" Dr. Wang being marched to the hospital in *To Live*.

Chinese revolutionary song and the de facto national anthem during the CR, opening with the lyrics "The East is red / The sun rises / China has birthed a Mao Zedong." Ham-handed brainwashing, the slogan and the lyric pun with *dong* for the East as well as Mao's name. Serendipitously, the direction and the leader overlap, the Orient collaging with the rising sun, the Man with His Nation.

Fengxia's happy "maiden voyage" launched by the Great Helmsman sinks when she dies of postpartum hemorrhage, so massive that the young Red Guards who double as obstetricians and nurses panic and fail miserably. These Red Guards take over the running of the hospital after having professional doctors and staff purged, locked in "cowsheds," tortured, and struggled against. Figure 6.4 encapsulates the perversity of the CR when the worried husband Erxi extracts Dr. Wang from the cowshed and marches him, still carrying the placard that denounces him as a "Reactionary Academic Authority," underscored by his name crossed out in red, to the hospital in case of emergency. (Historically, a prisoner about to be executed would have his name crossed out in red ink.) Fengxia, after all, is unable to communicate, even cry out in pain. Erxi's stealth move is justified by the authority of the People re-educating Wang, commanding him to attend the delivery of a model worker's wife. The Manichean plot backfires when out of kindness, Fugui purchases seven *mantou* (buns) for the starving Dr. Wang, who passes out from overstuffing himself. The new mother dies from excess bleeding; the old professor faints from overeating. China's old intellectual is cast out, so impotent that he cannot even save himself, let alone a patient. Only the newborn Little Bun survives, baked from Fengxia's womb. This episode is fraught with gallows humor and strident irony, crossing the farcically bloated professor with too much intake and the stomach-churning hemorrhaging with too much output.

The postpartum hemorrhaging counts as one example in Yu Hua's preferred method of dying—bleeding to death. Fengxia's brother Youqing in the novel died at a young age of blood transfusion to save County Magistrate Liu's wife. Youqing was literally leeched "white" by inexperienced doctors and nurses (150). Yu Hua's Magistrate Liu is Zhang Yimou's district chief, or Chunsheng the puppeteer-turned-Party cadre. This theme resonates with *Chronicle of a Blood Merchant* (1995), where selling blood earns the protagonist and fellow villagers a relatively good life and where the town's "blood chief" is as dubious as the team leader, unscrupulous yet helpful at times. The episodic picaresque novel of *Chronicle* is only possible because it precedes publicity over the impoverished Henan province's AIDS villages as a result of selling blood through unsanitized needles and problematic medical protocol. After which, Yu Hua's signature cavalier, folksy, and masculinist tone of *Chronicle* would sound insensitive, even heartless. Yet Yu Hua's blood "fixation" can be traced back to his childhood memory, raised by his physician parents near the hometown clinic and morgue. Blood, body parts, and even death used to be daily routines, recorded in the chapter "Reading" in *China in Ten Words* (2011). The child Yu Hua once enjoyed taking naps on the morgue's concrete slab for corpses, "refreshingly cool . . . that clean concrete bed" (60). Such macabre imaginary has germinated from the child to the artist. Despite the happy coincidence of childhood experience and artistic leitmotif, blood is a metaphor that pulses through China, be it in ten or ten thousand words. Bound together, allegedly, through one "bloodline" that is mythically and affectively rather than scientifically and rationally defined, the Chinese people have their lifeblood sucked dry during the tenure of the "chief surgeon" Mao in (mal)practice from 1949 to 1976, give or take a few years, all the while cheering their own desiccation, if not siphoning off others.

The shadow puppets in Fugui's trunk are finally torched during the CR. Only the vessel survives to house the grandson's chicks, much as the space of China remains, albeit somewhat hollowed, for the Chinese to go on living. The physical burning of traces of Four Olds is the tip of the fireberg, so to speak, consuming all those deemed old, backward, retrograde, and counterrevolutionary. Similar conflagration marks the climax of mob violence in Chen Kaige's *Farewell My Concubine,* when the protagonists, a consummate Peking Opera female impersonator and his partner, are ruthlessly manhandled, kneeling to witness their costumes, masks, and, of course, lives, go up in flames. Even without such physical bonfires, the "passionate intensity" of the

Yeatsian "worst" flares up in the crowd's frenzy at the train station in *Coming Home*, near the Gobi Desert in *One Second*, and the Red Guards' beating of the ailing cadre and his family in *The Blue Kite*.⁵ Despite the shield of Red Guards' Mao buttons, Little Red Books, and Mao's mantra "Rebellion is justified; revolution is no crime," such violence begs the question of personal and collective accountability of not only Red Guards in cahoots but also bystanders in attendance far and near. In turn, each fifth-generation laosanjie filmmaker from the chain gang peers back at the Red Sun that never sets in China's collective unconscious, having long been set in stone by Mao's lilting brushstrokes on a paper boat—and everywhere else.

---

5. See W. B. Yeats's "The Second Coming": "The best lack all conviction, while the worst / Are full of passionate intensity" (*The Collected Poems of W. B. Yeats*, 184–85).

PART 3
WHITE POP-UPS

CHAPTER 7

Brechtian AlienAsian

Socialist Ex Machina from *The Good Woman of Setzuan* and David Hare's *Fanshen*

Anchored in working-class culture and socialist belief, the German playwright Bertolt Brecht theorizes alienation-effect to advocate performers' and spectators' emotional dissociation from the stage in favor of thinking through, to borrow the title of Timothy J. Wiles's 1980 book, *The Theater Event*.[1] The A-effect intends to overhaul the modern stage for a non-Aristotelian, non-Stanislavsky alternative, partly inspired by a Peking Opera female impersonator, Mei Lanfang, whose performances, for lack of a better word, "wowed" him in Moscow in 1935. Considering the political implications of the visit, John Fuegi in *The Life and Lies of Bertolt Brecht* (1995) asserts that Brecht was invited to Moscow with the express order "to be extremely explicit in opposing the Nazis in his own writings" (327). But party affiliation aside, the theory of A-effect served to legitimize the dramatist's own sense of dis-orientation by "Oriental" theatrical stylization. That which is taken for granted within traditional Chinese dramaturgy so shocks Brecht that he finds the model for

---

1. See chapter 3, "Brecht's Epic Theater and Visionary Dialectics," in Timothy J. Wiles's *The Theater Event* (1980). Wiles also complicates the claim of Brecht as a socialist: "Most critics prefer to divide his writing into periods, finding him an existentialist in the twenties, a communist in the thirties, and, finally, a Marxist humanist in the forties" (87).

his vision of epic theater.[2] The white love for the inexplicable, mystical Orient means to love it to death, to read into the riddle of a "Chinese box" the West's own wish fulfillment. The West's enlightenment comes at the expense of occluding the East. Not to mince words, Brecht births epic theater over the dead body of Chinese theater, a collage of fragmentary impressions rather than an evolving, organic heritage. This self-centered, left-leaning Orientalism is inherited by the socialist David Hare in his early agitprop and populist plays. Critiquing Brecht's theory and practice of alienation-effect, this exploration focuses on his seminal essay "Alienation Effects in Chinese Acting" (1936), his play *The Good Woman of Setzuan* (1947, henceforth *Setzuan*), and Hare's copycat or "copychinese" *Fanshen* (1976).

Alienation, by definition, involves a split, and for Brecht, alienation in drama entailed a departure from Aristotelian-Stanislavskian conventions. Such division is constitutive of Marxism, which posits dialectical forces vying for dominance throughout human history. Contestation of opposites within oneself and one's world recurs in Brecht's dramas. But even the word "alienation" casts its own shadow. Effecting Brecht's alienation required an alien nation—a phantom one at that—to prop up the white state of being. The operative word may well be spelled with its uncanny sound-alikes: AlieNation, even AlienAsian. These two neologisms—an "alien nation" composed of "alien Asians"—dwell holographically within "alienation." The long shadow cast all the way to the other side of the earth bespeaks Brecht and Hare's quixotic quest beyond the capitalist West, chancing upon a solution in socialist ex machina. The Oriental Other provides an "out" from their Western selfhood, an escape clause from the contractual bond(age) to the West by virtue of birth and cultural upbringing. The socialist China peoples their stage, as though crowding off the Western tradition.

This replacement harks back, ironically, to Greek tragedies' deus ex machina, yet another Western legacy against which the playwrights presumably rebel. In Aeschylus's or Euripides's tragedies, deus ex machina or God from the machine, i.e., lowered with ropes or on a crane, or emerged on a riser through a trapdoor, rounds off the play with a divine, even cathartic, closure. In Brecht and Hare, the socialist China does not descend only when the curtain drops—it constitutes the whole play. Yet these early plays featuring socialist ex machina and Brechtian AlienAsian are but a mere "yellow"

---

2. Ronnie Bai notes that Brecht later renounces the term "epic theater" in favor of "dialectical drama" (398). The shift to dialectical drama allows Brecht, a Marxist, to reconcile antithetical conflicts at the heart of alienation-effect: empathy versus reason, feeling versus thinking. Timothy J. Wiles sees the same shift from "epic theater" to "dialectical drama" (*The Theater Event*, 70).

touch ("stain," some critics argue) on their largely white corpus. Whether a people's awakening to self-sufficiency in Brecht's Setzuan or Hare's communist apologia in the West's counterculture movement, this socialist ex machina is fully enacted in these early plays to intimate an Oriental utopia in the making vis-à-vis the capitalist West. Nevertheless, such dabbling in the East occupies but a minuscule portion of their corpuses, exposing the whim of young idealistic artists coming of age, a momentary flirtation with the unknown beyond the West, before they settle in for their more mature body of work. This is the irony of Brechtian and Harean AlienAsian, who had once served to liberate progressive young dramatists from the West but had since aged into an anomalous alterity, a strange-looking hors d'oeuvre to their increasingly mainstream, crowd-pleasing oeuvres. Youthful dalliance in cosplay? Given up later, for it would look so ridiculous on aging men!

Brechtian AlienAsian

Instead of a Freudian primal wound, Brecht's first impressions of the Peking Opera female impersonator Mei Lanfang's performances in Moscow were more akin to an awe-struck primal wow, or perhaps a primal womb, giving birth to a conceptualization of epic theater that had long been gestating in Brecht against the bourgeois theater of interwar Weimar Berlin and the Golden Twenties. Richard Bodek in *Proletarian Performance in Weimar Berlin* (1997) has argued that Brecht arose out of the working-class culture and its left-wing politics, tapping into "Communist agitprop theater and Socialist musical festival culture" (1–2). Bodek maintains that, in Brecht's view, Germany was split into a "bipolar public sphere: proletarian and bourgeois. The former was good; the latter was decadent or worse" (138). Seeking an exit from the Aristotelian mimetic tradition of identification and empathy as well as Stanislavsky's bourgeois theater predicated on the illusion of the fourth wall and actors' and spectators' complete conversion, Brecht felt emboldened by Mei to advance the alternate dramaturgy of A-effect to appeal to rational thinking on the conscious level rather than emotional identification on the subconscious level. In so doing, Brecht recycled and perpetuated time-honored Orientalist stereotypes inherent in Western (sub)consciousness. Allegedly speaking for the "little people," Brecht, like so many revolutionaries, speaks primarily for himself by muting others, Mei Lanfang and Chinese theater in particular.

Brecht's self-indulgent theorizing crystallizes in his pioneering "*Verfremdung* [Alienation] Effects in Chinese Acting," written shortly after his Moscow encounter with, as John Fuegi puts it in his 1995 book, Mei Lanfang and "the avant-garde novelist and theorist Viktor Schklovski [sic]. Schklovski used the Russian term 'Otchysdenie' to describe work he and Meyerhold had been doing ... rendering the strange familiar and the familiar strange," which apparently contributes to Brecht's "Verfremdung" (323–24). As early as 1987, Fuegi in *Bertolt Brecht: Chaos, According to Plan* contends that Russian formalism need not be the only source of A-effect since Verfremdung "could be seen as a one-word summation of the preface to Wordsworth and Coleridge's *Lyrical Ballads,* where it is argued that the Ballads render the strange familiar and the familiar strange.... The terms 'alienation' or 'distanciation' only capture one side of the dual formation" (83). Many scholars echo the Russian-German tie Fuegi puts forth, although not the English-German one. Min Tian, with some proviso, also traces A-effect to Viktor Shklovski's "*Priem Ostranenniya*—'the device of making strange'" (*Mei Lanfang and the Twentieth-Century International Stage* [2012] 183).

In addition to the Russian-German connection, a critical consensus has converged over Brecht's appropriation of Chinese theater for his own agenda. In *Bertolt Brecht and China* (1979), Renata Berg-Pan gives no quarter when it comes to the bullish dramatist in the china shop, i.e., Chinese theater: "Brecht was so eager to find his own ideas confirmed, that he undoubtedly misunderstood some of the gestures and mimes of the Chinese actor" (164). Berg-Pan concludes convincingly: "Brecht's own political and philosophical views [comprise] a set of rose-colored glasses. He was hoping to find something revolutionary in the acting of Mei Lan-fang" (175). Likewise, Antony Tatlow stresses the personal dimension of Brecht's analysis: Brecht "responded so strongly to Mei Lan-fang, because of a dilemma into which his own ideas had led him and for which the art of Mei Lan-fang seemed to suggest a solution" (*The Mask of Evil* [1977] 310). Ronnie Bai writes in "Dances with Mei Lan-fang" that Brecht "chose to ignore ... the irresistible empathetic power with which general audiences may also be seized" (419). Brecht's alienation-effect appears to Bai "to be a product of nothing more than his 'misunderstanding' of Chinese stage conventions. To escape his own dramatic tradition or to strengthen his anti-illusionistic stance, Brecht looked to the classical Chinese theater tradition" (421). Given the importance of these critiques, few scholars see fit to analyze the essay itself in order to expose its crude Orientalizing. Taking apart Brecht's essay for rebuttal would offer a critical purchase to parsing the dynamics of AlienAsian in *The Good Woman of Setzuan* and *Fanshen.*

In "Alienation Effects in Chinese Acting," Brecht prioritizes his quest for an alternative "*non-aristotelian*" theater "not dependent on empathy," whose precedents, Brecht believes, reside in German county fairs' clowns and the formulaic set of panoramas, among other things (176). A contrarian iconoclast by temperament, Brecht goes against the drama tradition, tying his dramaturgy to the proletarian culture, now wedded to the "found object" AlienAsian from afar. Chinese stage performances, needless to say, hail from outside the West, better still from outside the capitalist system, filling the theoretical void that has long troubled Brecht. Brecht's essay proceeds to record a series of impressions of exotica, cataloguing pennants carried on a Chinese general's shoulders, silk tatters on a Chinese beggar's silk robe, and more. Apropos of Mei Lanfang, Brecht poses the rhetorical question: "What Western actor . . . could demonstrate the elements of his art like Mei Lan-fang without special lighting and wearing a dinner jacket in an ordinary room full of specialists?" (179). Apparently having witnessed Mei's impromptu performance in a dinner jacket at a reception banquet, Brecht displaces his own quoting of Mei onto Mei "quoting the character" (179). This psychic move to externalize reprises Brecht's overall projecting onto the Chinese Other his own sense of alienation. The stylized period performance jars against the modern attire, producing the alienation effect Brecht perpetuates. As opposed to the Stanislavsky method of identifying with the character, Brecht imagines Mei "quoting the character" while remaining apart, inviolably sovereign, crystallized by his "anachronistic" dinner jacket ill-fitting, pun intended, the dynastic female role Mei impersonates.

Brecht sees in Mei an *"artist observ[ing] himself,"* who *"expresses that he knows he is being watched,"* observations so revelatory that Brecht italicizes them (177). Brecht ascribes to Mei a double consciousness: Mei's self-awareness of being watched as well as watching himself. It is true that the Stanislavsky fourth wall does not prevail in traditional Chinese dramaturgy. It is also true that many dramaturgical elements showcase themselves to the audience: the band is visible onstage, for instance, and the tableaus or poses that performers strike onstage are timed according to the accompanying music. As the music grinds to a halt, the performers freeze for dramatic effect, an expressionist and symbolist body language diametrically opposed to the Western mimetic, realist stagecraft. But such features stem from the Chinese tradition; they become contrary to the Aristotelian drama of empathy and catharsis only in Brecht's imaginary. The avant-garde, even postmodernist turn of *"artist observ[ing] himself"* is attributed to Chinese acting, so outlandish as to appear imperialist. Brecht imposes his own fixation onto Chinese performativity and claims an epiphany that solves all his theatrical problems in one fell swoop. Brecht's Orientalism is based on mystifying the Orient as the panacea for the Occident's predicament.

Brecht's observation is, on occasion, entirely wrong-headed: "Deeply excited, the performer takes a lock of hair between his lips and chews it" (178). Excitement hardly captures the climax of a wide range of emotions, including but not exclusive to: shock, fear, desperation, and resolution. Long hair queues or wispy whiskers are indeed clamped between the teeth to suggest emotional intensity. Brecht imagines, without any scintilla of proof, a "cinematic close-up," as it were, where the static biting devolves into a dynamic chewing. This betrays a Western mind conceptualizing a non-Western facial "tableau" in Western metaphors, namely, gnashing one's teeth in rage.

Ultimately, Brecht hopes through this performance to generate "thinking being[s]" (180). Yet much of Brecht's assumptions about Chinese acting arise out of his self-contradictory wishful thinking. On the one hand, Brecht claims that "the Chinese performer is not in a trance," and he sees "the Chinese actor's V-effect as a *transportable technique*." On the other hand, he claims that "we have here the artistic counterpart of a primitive technology, a rudimentary science. The Chinese performer gets his V-effect by association with magic. 'How it's done' remains hidden" (181). How to square "not in a trance" with "by association with magic," claims only one paragraph apart? Chinese actors are said to be in full possession of themselves while being possessed by some greater supernatural force. "How it's done" is rather obvious: decades of harsh, abusive apprenticeship catapult Mei Lanfang into stardom. It is not magic but the rod that lands Mei Lanfang in Moscow to "motivate" Brecht. The dramatist who urges rationality lulls himself to sleep in his Oriental La La Land.

Brecht concludes that "the V-effect was achieved in the German epic theatre not only by the actor, but also by the music (choruses, songs) and the setting (placards, film etc.). It was principally designed to *historicize* the incidents portrayed" (182). To encourage analytical, dialectical reasoning, Brecht hypothesizes an A-effect that privileges any dramaturgy that splits apart dramatic identification between drama and spectators. This goal is achieved by splintering drama itself through its various elements—dialogue, performance technique, set, prop, lighting, and music. Brecht staunchly refuses to let feeling overwhelm thinking, in hope of engendering action and social change to better the society. Ironically, Brecht's insistence on historicizing fails to extend to the history of Chinese theater, which is transported to buttress his own epic theater. Brecht is the one who is transported: not to Chinese theater, though, but to his own fantastic reverie. Rather than either Aristotelian-Stanislavsky identification or Brechtian alienation, however, why not have it both ways? Why not a third option of both-and, namely, Mei becomes the character by quoting her, or her type—*dan* or *qingyi*, young women, one of the four types of roles in Peking Opera? (The other three types are *Sheng* for the male roles, *Jing* for males with painted faces, and *Chou* for clowns.) At the reception end, why not the third option of the spectator empathizing while critically examining simultaneously?

Suggesting such a nonbinary, both-and approach is far from flippant or anachronistic, given a Chinese dramatic tradition undergirded by imitation and rote memory. Whereas the modern West has deviated from classical and medieval practice of the master-disciple legacy, Chinese performers continued to celebrate, at least in Mei Lanfang's lifetime, the emulation of the ancient ways. Long apprenticeship in Peking Opera led to mastering the performing style of a certain type of character. What Brecht calls "quoting the character" culminates theatrical perfection, valorizing both the female impersonator tradition and its heir, Mei Lanfang. Contrary to alienation, Mei was believed to embody tradition.

Ultimately, Brecht's erroneous take springs from the fundamental difference of the notion of selfhood. While Brecht's modern West prefers an autonomous, impermeable, even sacrosanct individual self that deigns to "quote" verbatim other selves, the Chinese self is comparatively malleable, prone to merging with the communal other, certainly with the alleged spirit, the *qi,* of the masters. Citing others carries more of a tone of reverence in Mei's China than plagiarism, in theory at least. Based on that difference, Chinese scholars have pointed out Brecht's China "complex" that hints at a neurosis, a subconscious remaking of the world—China in the case of A-effect—for Brecht's own purposes (Wei Zhang in *Chinese Adaptations of Brecht* [2020] 65). Min Tian maintains as well that "Chinese acting in fact does not generate anything identical with, or even similar to, the Brechtian 'A-effect'" (185). Tian further explicates: "Since Chinese spectators are expected to be familiar with the stories, the characters, the conventions, and even the leading performers of various schools of traditional Chinese theatre and their virtuosity, the object of the Chinese performer is to try his best to meet the high expectations of the spectators, not to appear strange or surprising to them" (190).

A case in point: Brecht is duly impressed by Mei's onstage routine as a fisherwoman. "Now the current is swifter," he writes, "and she is finding it harder to keep her balance, now she is in a pool and paddling more easily" (178). So refreshing as to elicit a "primal wow" from Brecht, this expressionistic act is rather familiar, if not banal, to the Chinese, who would only be taken with Mei should the execution of each movement and the elocution be flawless in accordance with the idealized prototype the female impersonator sets out to portray, to "quote." Tian even cites many distinguished performers of the Qing dynasty to prove how they claimed to identify fully with the characters they played (qtd. in Min Tian 199). Mei in his memoir underlines the same point: "not only his appearance but also his singing, reciting, movements, spirit, and feelings must become so closely identical with the status of the character that it is as if he is really that character. In the meanwhile, the spectators, spellbound by his performance, forget that he is the performer and accept him as the character" (qtd. in Min Tian 199).[3] Where Brecht sees Chinese A-effect, no alienation whatsoever is found by Chinese artists and spectators.

Brecht's essay lacks theoretical rigor as well as referential clarity, demonstrated herein:

> When Mei Lan-fang was playing a death scene, a spectator sitting next me exclaimed with astonishment at one of his gestures. One or two people sitting in front of us turned round indignantly and sshhh'd. They behaved as if they were present at the real death of a real girl. Possibly their attitude would have been all right for a European production, but for a Chinese it was unspeakably ridiculous. In their case the V-effect had misfired. (181)

Who are "they"? The one who "exclaimed with astonishment," or the ones who "turned round indignantly and sshhh'd," or both? Whoever "they" allude to, one assumes all of them are non-Chinese, since Mei's 1935 Moscow tour aimed to impress Western guests. If both the shock and the admonition are "ridiculous" to the Chinese, Brecht presumes alienation or dissociation from the death scene to be the Chinese reaction. Nothing can be further from the truth. What is deemed the "misfired" reaction of audience empathy is precisely what Mei hopes to accomplish. The quote reveals a Brecht bifurcated between onstage and off, in consonance with his A-effect theory: refusing to be emotionally immersed in the stage performance, Brecht turns half of his attention to the audience. Unwilling to be enrapt in Mei's act and unable to read the Chinese tradition, Brecht wills himself to read the audience, culminating in something tantamount to a child's daydream without an in-depth grasp of the theater event.[4] That Brecht's narcissistic musing becomes, in Wei Zhang's words, "one of the 'three great theatrical systems' in the world, the other two being Stanislavsky and Mei Lanfang" can be attributed to the fact that Brecht deployed Chinese motifs in his plays and essays. Simply because Brecht resorts to China as a trope, he is bestowed a much-coveted role in

---

3. See Mei Lanfang's *Wutai shenghuo sishi nian* (*Forty Years on Stage*).

4. Bret Harte does a similar thing, turning his puzzling gaze from Chinese stage performance to his fellow viewers in theater in "John Chinaman," a short essay from *The Luck of Roaring Camp and Other Sketches* (1929). See chapter 1, "Sinophobia/Sinophilia," in my *Tao of S* (2022).

world drama's triumvirate. Yet this reputation is undeserved, especially in light of the superficiality with which Brecht deploys these motifs. As Eric Hayot has observed, "Brecht's China skates, as it were, on the surfaces of his text," where China presents "no more than chinoiseries, vaguely participating in some very general ideology of the exotic" (*Chinese Dreams* [2004] 55–56). Chinese elevation of Brecht also betrays a nostalgia for China's good old days, when the quintessential female impersonator Mei Lanfang reigned supreme, before Chairman Mao's unrelenting, frenzied political campaigns and persecutions devastated the "Four Olds": Old Ideas, Old Culture, Old Habits, and Old Customs.

Socialist ex Machina from *Setzuan* and *Fanshen*

The socialist "father-son" pair of Brecht and Hare choose to set their plays in the imaginary community of China—imagination verging on fantasy, though. For example, John Fuegi in *The Essential Brecht* (1972) finds *Setzuan* "a very German play set in a very German milieu," only disguised as "a Chinese costume piece" (131–32). Riddled with such misrepresentations, Brecht's titular Setzuan (Sichuan in pinyin romanization) is a province rather than a locale or a city. Likewise, David Hare's northwestern Chinese village of Long Bow derives its name from a "creative" word-splitting of the original Changchuang (張莊 or Zhangzhuang in pinyin), the village of Changs, ostensibly the most common surname there. The A-effect is knowingly or unwittingly applied to their materials. Reminiscent of Brecht's primal wow over Mei Lanfang, Hare's play evinces similar subjective bent upon venturing into the AlieNation of AlienAsians.

Based on William Hinton's *Fanshen: A Documentary of Revolution in a Chinese Village* (1966), Hare inherits not only the Marxist agricultural consultant's vocabulary of Long Bow and such but also Hinton's blithe ignorance of the Chinese language and culture. Hinton's preface exposes a key problem with translating Maoism, literally, since Hinton relies on "two interpreters" throughout his China sojourn (xii). One wonders if interpreters double as handlers, as they often do. The acknowledgment and subsequent references identify them as "Ch'i Yun and Hsieh Hung" (vi, 14). In Ch'i Yun's company, Hinton is dispatched by the Communist authority to the Long Bow village to observe land reform while teaching English. The moniker of Long Bow where the Maoist revolution unfolds comes about through a bit of Ezra Pound–style gratuitous wordplay over the village name of Changchuang, explicated in the first footnote. Rather than staying faithful to the Chinese name, Hinton elects to be fanciful. Shorn of its position as an ordinary family name, the word Chang is autopsied, sliced in half:

> In written Chinese the character for *chang* is made up of 11 brush strokes. The first three comprise the radical *kung* which means bow—the hunter's bow. The last eight comprise the phonetic *chang* or *ch'ang* which means long. It is from the separate elements of the written word rather than from the meaning of the spoken word that I have extracted the designation "Long Bow." (ix)

Admittedly, those surnamed Zhangs often introduce themselves as "*gongzhang zhang*" (弓長張 bow long zhang) to distinguish from its homophone, the other surname Zhang (章), as in Zhang Ziyi of *Crouching Tiger, Hidden Dragon* (2000) fame. Whereas the Chinese self-introduction of "bow long" is the means to the end of "Zhang," the Western authors decide to treat the means *as* the end for the name of their alternate universe, a name that is catchier, more attention-grabbing than the lackluster Zhang Village. To transpose Zhang into Long Bow sounds like name-calling to Chinese ears, an offense the Chinese communists and Western theatergoers are keen to ignore, if they happen to be aware of it at all. The equivalent of Hinton's rechristening would be to nickname, with malicious intent, the author as "William Hint On," or David Hare as "David Rabbit." Divorcing the script from its sound, the word from its meaning, Hinton and then Hare execute Brechtian A-effect in imposing white designs onto the other, which has failed to strike back against such imperialist capriciousness, all in the name of constructing the anticapitalist alternative. Because foreign words—and cultures, for that matter—are illegible, one legitimizes fallacy by reading into them, so long as one controls the discourse.

Brechtian AlienAsian-effect animates Brecht's and Hare's plays. Peking Opera conventions introduced by Mei Lanfang are amply deployed. Traditional Chinese theater often opens with characters' self-introductions upon entering the stage and is interspersed with characters' appealing to the audience. Accordingly, both the German and the British dramatists have their characters address the audience directly, thus breaking the Stanislavsky illusion of the fourth wall. Brecht's mask-wearing and Hare's large cast of "thirty or so parts" played by "about nine actors," according to stage directions, all of them with nonsensical, well-nigh unpronounceable latinized first names, result in a similar Orientalist impression that the audience is beholding a symbolic fable of types rather than a realistic play of individuals (5). Renata Berg-Pan indicates that Brecht's own productions of *Setzuan* aspire for a "Chinese look" with Chinese costumes and masks of "Mongolian features," possibly the proverbial slant eyes, wispy goatees, and whatnot (191).

In tandem with Brecht's Orientalist masks, *Setzuan* is largely staged like a parable of an irreverent farce. Three Gods descend to earth in search of good people, finding only one—the prostitute Shen Te with a heart of gold. Antony Tatlow in *The Mask of Evil* considers the three Gods "more Chinese than anything else in the play" (268). Tatlow suggests that this polytheistic, pagan feature is most Chinese as opposed to Christian monotheism, quite forgetting the Holy Trinity of the Father, the Son, and the Holy Spirit. The divinity of three-in-one informs Christianity, particularly Catholicism. Brecht's three Gods are, in fact, less Chinese than parodic, a quality consistent with Brecht's style of "calculated hostility" and disdain, characterized by Timothy J. Wiles in *The Theater Event* (83). One of the trio is hard of hearing, equipped with an ear trumpet. Moreover, the Gods return to the stage several times with progressively shabbier demeanor, sustaining indifference, rejection, and even injury from nonbelievers' attack. High and low not only coexist but are subverted: just as the deities betray human frailties and flaws, the downtrodden manifest ennobling qualities under socialist circumstances.

In return for her hospitality, the Gods reward Shen Te handsomely, which allows her to open up a tobacco shop. Eric Hayot observes that she sets up "an opium den" in "an alternate script," further proof of Brecht's Orientalizing streak (*Chinese Dreams* 92). Shen Te's kindness, however, is exploited by all: the destitute from far and near latch on to her like blood-sucking parasites, reminiscent of the clientele in her former profession. To survive mounting debts and communal dependency, Shen Te cross-dresses, assuming the guise of a male cousin Shui Ta, a harsh yet pragmatic businessman, who manages with an iron fist to transform a failed venture into a thriving tobacco factory, simultaneously reforming hangers-on as self-respecting, self-reliant workers idealized in socialism. From buying and selling as an exploitative middle(wo)man, Shui Ta manufactures the product and expands the enterprise. Rising among the workers to the top post of factory manager is Shen Te's intended, the coxcomb Yang Sun, the erstwhile suicide who has so smitten Shen Te, at least her feminine and maternal side, that she plans to sell her shop to realize his dream of becoming an airplane pilot. In keeping with Brecht's socialist conviction, honest work has made an honest man out of Yang Sun, who has come down to earth from his flight of fancy. The doppelgangers Shen Te and Shui Ta epitomize the proletariat converted to their better selves at Shui Ta's communelike workshop. Critiquing "Alienation Effects in Chinese Acting," Min Tian notes that "surprisingly Brecht did not exploit the fact that Mei Lanfang was a female impersonator" (194). Seeing alienation where there is none,

Brecht fails to see the truly alienating gender-bending that is put before his eyes. The aftereffect of the female impersonator's putative A-effect, arguably, ripples from 1935 to 1947 when Shen Te morphs into a male impersonator.

The characterization of the eponymous good woman Shen Te lies at the crux of the play. John Fuegi in *Bertolt Brecht* (1987) quotes the German American star Louise Rainer, who finds Brecht "cruel, selfish, vain," with a "harem" around him (90). Out of this "harem," Fuegi contends in *The Life and Lies of Bertolt Brecht* that *Setzuan* is inextricably tied to Margarete Steffin, one of Brecht's "women" slaving for the charismatic lover-master, conceiving his children and his plays, and receiving no credit in return. "The play shouts the agony of Steffin," Fuegi bemoans, "who lived much of her life as an author wearing a male disguise. Shen Te knows her 'lover,' Sun [Yang Sun], is . . . a coldly ruthless and manipulative male figure of the type Brecht so often depicted positively" (389). This assertion, fusing Brecht's "life" with his "lies" or stage plays, points to two possibilities. On the one hand, Steffin is possibly the ghost writer, which Fuegi implies throughout. On the other, Brecht may have subconsciously slipped into Yang Sun shadows of himself taking advantage of Steffin. In the latter scenario, Brecht's guilty conscience contributes, perhaps unconsciously, to the reformation of Yang Sun through hard work. Brechtian proclivity for bad-scoundrels-turned-good-socialists may simply reflect the dramatist's feel-good self-defensiveness over his kept women. Wei Zhang adds a Freudian wrinkle to *Setzuan*: "Shen Te's story is rendered through a Brechtian dialectical representation of social and external elements and internal human nature and psychology" (*Chinese Adaptations of Brecht* 64). But the psychic dimension appears without much evidential support. A drama of cross-dressing and self-rejuvenation, the Marxist Brecht would surely refrain, in a manner of speaking, from stooping as low as Freudian psychology.

Yet Shen Te / Shui Ta does manifest Freudian slips of sorts, particularly when she professes "And I can mimic man" (35), and when he blurts out "My cousin can't be where I am" (66). Nonetheless, Shen Te's self-dividing is attributed to socioeconomic rather than psychic exigencies. By blurring the two genders, Brecht attempts no commentary on the duality of human sexuality, nor on patriarchal misogyny, which he appears to take for granted. Rather, Brecht presents the cross-dressing as part of the survival tactic in human history. The titular, explicit goodness and the latent badness cohabit characters as a fact in human nature, far from any metaphorical, existential rumination. The shift between good and bad hinges on concrete props and acting in the play. Shen Te wears the pants, if not the mask or face-painting in Brecht's original production, of Shui Ta. The water-seller Wong has a pitcher with a false bottom to hoodwink his customers. Besotted with Shen Te, the barber Shu Fu offers her, anachronistically and farcically, a "blank check" (73). But the barber happens to be the one who breaks Wong's arm with a hot curling iron. While bringing out the characters' doubleness, all such props—pants, pitcher, check, and curling iron—cultivate the Brechtian A-effect on account of their utter absurdity. Conceivably, water-sellers would starve to death in rural, impoverished China, particularly Setzuan with lakes and waterways aplenty. Blank checks and curling irons are yet to grace premodern China.

The Greek tragedy stagecraft of deus ex machina is literal in *Setzuan*'s alternate endings. Eric Bentley's 1947 canonical translation of *Setzuan* first lays out the American production where theaters often do not have "'fly-space' to lower things from on ropes" (103n1), followed by the German production with a fly loft above the stage. Hence, the German play literally executes the ascent of the three Gods-*cum*-Judges after they have absolved Shui Ta of the charge of murder against Shen Te, seeing that they are one and the same: "*the ceiling opens. A pink cloud comes down. On it the* THREE GODS *rise, very slowly*" (105, italicized stage directions). By contrast, the American performance concludes figuratively, with the Gods "*imagined to step into a cloud which rises and moves forward over the orchestra and up beyond the balcony*" (104). To imagine the Gods' movement, it entails Shen Te's choreography of craning her neck to look up and beyond, akin to Chinese theater's stylized symbolic body language. On the scale of non-Aristotelian A-effect, the American production comes much closer to what Brecht strives for. Theatrically, a lack in mimetic, realist terms yields a plenitude in imagination.

If Brecht's *Setzuan* resembles an Oriental allegory like Franz Kafka's "The Great Wall of China" (1917), Hare's *Fanshen* is, unabashedly, communist propaganda modeled after fellow apologists like Edgar Snow's *Red Star over China* (1937), or fellow imagineers like Andy Warhol's *Mao* series, 1972–74, and, decades later, Don DeLillo's *Mao II* (1991). Calling himself a "scholarship boy . . . making his rather troubled way through society by brains and not by birth," Hare has dreamed since his "secondary education" of "getting away, of traveling the impossible sixty miles to the capital city [London]," winding up nearly six thousand miles away in rural China in *Fanshen* ("Obedience, Struggle & Revolt" [2005] 16–17). Composed at the age of twenty-eight, *Fanshen* may well belong to David Hare's relative juvenilia in a long and distinguished career. The play continues Brechtian A-effect, not by splitting Shen Te into Shui Ta or by blurring good and bad in multiple characters. Instead, Hare de-individualizes characters to create types based on Marxist-Maoist categories of class: the wealthy landowners, the middle peasants, and the poor proletariat.

Translating class struggle to the theatrical stage, Hare arranges to have "*a small raised platform on which certain scenes are played. The rest of the acting area thrusts forward into the audience*" (5, italicized stage directions). Thus, Hare makes possible contrasting as well as complementary scenes simultaneously onstage, such as when "*two meetings . . . played antiphonally*" (17). Although "antiphonally" suggests linear alternating performance, as in antiphonal singing, or singing in turn by two parts of a choir, it remains, spatially and experientially, one synthetic, collective choral event. The two meetings compose one theatrical performance, each side feeding into the other. Hooked up like a cyclical series, the dialogue continues in terms of question and answer, answer and denial, denial and question—an endless intellectual pursuit some may deem a futile academic exercise. Moreover, as the stage thrusts into the spectators' space, the back and forth immerses, hypothetically, viewers, almost a stage precursor to live online viewer feedback. Act 1, section 2, where two meetings take place concurrently, exemplifies Hare's dramaturgy.

Throughout section 2, Brechtian A-effect joins forces with the Revolutionary Model Dramas' formulaic props of banners displaying slogans of propaganda at the height of the Cultural Revolution. When *Fanshen* debuted in 1975, the left-wing dramatist had assuredly availed himself of parts, if not all, of Madame Mao or Jiang Qing's pet project of Revolutionary Model Dramas that include, most prominently, *Taking Tiger Mountain by Strategy* and *The Red Lantern*. Serving as silent films' intertitles, these slogans set the scene, mark the lapse of time, punctuate breakthroughs from mental stalemates, and function in myriad other ways. Slogans are designed to win over people, either veiled subliminally in consumerist advertising or forced fed barefacedly in communist agitprop. Here, the young Hare is unapologetically didactic, advancing through a series of banners in caps, telling more than showing the movement of ideas of the Chinese Communist Party (CCP) cadres on the raised platform and that of the peasants on the general stage. As the stage spears into the audience, viewers are implicated in the ideological lesson: "*Slogan*: ASKING BASIC QUESTIONS," "*Slogan*: THE VISIT OF SECRETARY LIU," "*Slogan*: THE FORMING OF THE PEASANTS' ASSOCIATION," "*Slogan*: THEY TALKED FOR EIGHT HOURS," "*Slogan*: THEY TALKED FOR THREE DAYS," and, finally, "*Slogan*: THEY STOPPED PAYING RENT" (17–21). The CCP Big Brother's imperious moralizing buttonholes the viewer through mind-numbing capitalization.

That basic question—"Who depends upon whom for a living?"—launches the Marxist fundamental of class struggle to instigate the proletariat revolt (16). As Secretary Liu refuses to provide the answer to his cadres and urges them to think instead, one of the cadres, T'ien-ming, on the raised platform "crosses to another part of the stage" to preside over the peasants' meeting (17). The parallel dialogues begin to interweave. On one side of the stage, the Party secretary guides the two remaining cadres Man-hsi and Yu-lai in a nativizing of Karl Marx's industrial laborers. Reified and exploited in the West, workers on capitalism's shop floor are now Sinologized, Mao-ified as peasants toiling in feudalism's fields. On the other side of the stage, the Party representative T'ien-ming engages the peasants in an identical investigation. Just as one cadre gropes for an answer, a poor farmer picks up the thread in chronicling a life of bitterness and misery that leads to the present quandary. Just as a peasant is lost in the theoretical subversion of property and land ownership, Liu and other cadres plunge ahead with the messianic deliverance. From a halting Q&A start, the twin dialogues pick up speed, culminating in breathless, line-by-line switches between the two groups compartmentalized onstage, as though they were puzzling out a universal problem that only rests when they reach the conclusion of *Fanshen*.

True to its title *Fanshen*, "turning over" from a supposedly prostrate, kowtowing position and, conceivably, standing up, the communist ideology turns human history of the few controlling the bulk of the resources on its head. The masses come to share, in theory, several rounds of equitable redistributions of wealth. Contrapuntally enacted, feudalist pain and communist pleasure accentuate each other. While the young Hare saw this as communist enlightenment of the ugly economic truth, the mature Hare may have learned from the CCP's catastrophic, far uglier, economic policies from the 1950s to 1970s that he had collaborated unintentionally in communist brainwashing of the ignorant domestic poor and of idealistic foreigners. The split stage unites to push one coherent interpretation to a democratic audience with a diversity of views. The dialectic contestation of capitalism and socialism would do well to merge for a way out of the binarism, no different from the third option between Brechtian A-effect and Aristotelian-Stanislavskian empathetic identification. It would be even better if Hare owns up to the autocratic reins over the People held by Secretary Liu, T'ien-ming, and other Party standard-bearers at the behest of Chairman Mao's mantra: "Serve the People." Eerily resonating with the Father of Chinese Modernism Lu Xun's grotesque vision of "Man Eat Man," the CCP serves the People's flesh to the People from the calamitous Great Leap Forward to the Cultural Revolution, when untold millions perished in famines and persecutions.[5]

---

5. Among his other works, Lu Xun's "A Madman's Diary" (1918) features a crazed protagonist, who imagines that his family and villagers are consuming human flesh.

In the spirit of communist insurrection, of going against the grain, even the grain of communist doctrines, the spotlight in section 2 pans from the intended—the leaders—to Yu-lai, one of the two cadre members obtuse in critical thinking. Yu-lai sinks under Secretary Liu's barrage of inquiry, stammering out monosyllabic half-answers that betray incompetence in dialectical reasoning. Drifting into silence, Yu-lai sputters: "If . . . ," "I . . . ," and "Why?" (17, 19, 20; ellipses in original). But the last question initiates Yu-lai's earth-shattering awakening: "we create their wealth," "Take us [peasants] away, they'd [landlords] die. Take them away, we live" (20–21). Yu-lai's soul-searching embodies the proletarian epiphany, "We shouldn't even pay rent," immediately followed by the last "*Slogan*: THEY STOPPED PAYING RENT." Words made flesh, Yu-lai's thought materializes into action in the ensuing sections. Yu-lai's ambivalence between dullness and perspicuity intensifies in section 3, when he wards off a violent mob about to assault landlords, only to personally "hit Ch'ung-wang twice," an incorrigible town elite, to force a confession (25). Occupying the limbo state between the Party and the Ego, between good and evil, makes Yu-lai fertile soil for creativity.

Yu-lai's proclivity for violence rears its ugly head even in his debut. Whereas other characters' self-introductions close with the number of acres, livestock, farming implements he or she owns or does not own, Yu-lai stands as a glaring exception: "I am Yu-lai, an ex-bandit" (7). Hare shifts from the communist class classification based on material possession to Yu-lai's sole marker, a fraught one given the 1930s and '40s China balkanized by warlords and their bands of renegades. Yet outlawry encapsulates the CCP's early self-image that defies unjust laws and corrupt authorities in keeping with anti-heroes of the fourteenth-century *Outlaws of the Marsh* (*The Water Margin*) that Mao Zedong had openly praised. Setting Yu-lai even further apart from the rest of the cast is what precedes the declaration of his former occupation. Yu-lai holds up a book to announce "This is the book *Fanshen* by William Hinton," with a footnote that "the actor should give publisher and current price" (7). Like Brechtian AlienAsian, Yu-lai's metanarrative moment exposes not only the mirage of the fourth wall but also that of the Western author-dramatist-actor playacting pseudo-Asianness.

Yu-lai worsens from pummeling landlords to abusing and striking his daughter-in-law, a "slut" and "an idle cunt," whom he sneers at again and again (38, 40). Residual of feudal forces, Yu-lai and his henchmen enrich themselves under false pretenses of land redistribution. Yu-lai even orchestrates an attack against the CCP Work Team probing corruption. The Work Team's counterpunch is swift and harsh, incurring the charge of "left extremism" from Secretary Ch'en (74). Ch'en calls for a reset to ameliorate the Work Team's expedient approach with "support only from the poor peasants, thereby neglecting the middle peasants . . . That line is in clear opposition to the official policy of the Party" (74). Ch'en channels the Party directive of "bold in concept but gentle in execution," which prompts both the Work Team and the peasants to engage in incessant struggle meetings of group criticism and self-criticism (101). Just as Freudian theater of psychotherapy is to the capitalist West, so is political theater of public criticism to the CCP. Simply put, criticism constitutes the "talking cure" for Communist China. Hare blithely dismisses how bloody, even deadly, these struggle meetings had been, let alone the incarceration, shaming, dehumanizing, and the unspeakable physical and psychological violence leading up to them. Under the auspices of either the master psychiatrist or the wolfish Party in the People's clothing, the wayward person is reputed to have been restored to mental health in the West or to the right thinking and behavior in China. Hypothetically rejecting any authority from the divine to the imperial, the communist ideology highlights trial and error by way of the miracle of criticism to find the "true" path forward. Even the guilty, such as Yu-lai, are to be re-educated, rehabilitated, and returned to the fold, as Secretary Liu proselytizes: "We must save him. We can use him. He can be reformed" (95).

The idealism of a twentysomething Hare animates *Fanshen,* yet the playwright implicitly acknowledges the sense of futility decades later in "Obedience, Struggle & Revolt": "My desire was to use the theatre to argue for political change, and, at the start, to no other end. But early on it became obvious that the demands of what you would wish to accomplish politically cannot be so easily reconciled with what is artistically possible" (22). This appears to be a footnote to his early play *Fanshen,* or an apt inscription on its gravestone, as few remember or put on the play in the new millennium. Once cast via a host of spectral AlienAsians and the conceit of socialist ex machina, Brechtian epic theater and A-effect are largely forgotten as dramaturgical innovations. Rather, they have been co-opted by omnivorous consumerism. Addressing the viewer by looking straight into the camera, for instance, is deployed by Kevin Spacey in *House of Cards* (2013–18), reminiscent of Iago's asides to the audience, and many other actors in multiple shows.

One particular case in recent memory suggests consumerist monopoly of Brechtian AlienAsian. Of Asian descent herself, the filmmaker Roseanne Liang taps into the MeToo movement and gender equity in the sci-fi thriller *Shadow in the Cloud* (2020), pitting the heroine Chloë Grace Moretz against the villains of World War II Japanese Zero pilots and the monstrosity of the horror genre's humanoid bat. While the enemy pilots are never seen to avoid perpetuating insensitive racism, many close-ups detail the beast's maw, fangs, claws, and wings, a far safer scapegoat in the Anthropocene. In the closing shot, Moretz stares straight into the camera while breastfeeding her infant daughter after having single-handedly shot down Japanese Zeroes and beaten the monster bat to a pulp. White femininity and maternity challenge the theatergoer with her unblinking gaze, her nobility tempered, however, by the same old Brechtian AlienAsian. Rather than socialist ex machina, Liang silhouettes Moretz the white knight against the demonic other of either the unseen "Jap" pilots or the graphic, computer-generated "bat" freak, either invisible or all too visible via digitization. Good whiteness never shows without its familiar of a darker hue, a chronic condition of dependency manifested in Brecht's fixation on the female impersonator Mei Lanfang, in Hare's utopian, self-correcting yellowfaces, and in Liang's absent, faceless "Japs" displaced onto one vampiric rep.

Ask not why I conclude with the whimsical leap from Brechtian AlienAsian to Roseanne Liang, which is no more cavalier than the leap from Mei Lanfang to German A-effect, from Changchuang to Poundian Long Low, or from the communist land reform to the British agitprop. Ask, instead, why the stature of Bertolt Brecht and Sir David Hare in the first place, the esteem accorded them with their Orientalist streaks surely disturbing. But when one of them "Orientals" "does a number" on us, the same number of glib coupling of disparate things, such as German drama theory and Liang's whitewashed Hollywood, critics demur. The world remains stubbornly Brechtian in projecting its own alienation and unease onto "easy" AlienAsians.

CHAPTER 8

Love in a Falling City

David Hare's *Saigon* and the Musical *Miss Saigon*

> Chris will come to me like the phoenix
> and he'll take me off on his wings.
>
> —"This Is the Hour," *Miss Saigon,* act 1

Romance set against a city under siege or on the eve of falling into enemy hands has long been a literary trope for killing two birds with one stone, or for doubling the dramatic effect of tragic conflicts between political entities and characters. Even more so when Eros and Thanatos are pitted on the stage under the time and spatial constraints of live performing arts! Sweet Eros and bitter Thanatos sharpen each other like biting a sugar cube as one sips scalding Turkish coffee, or Vietnamese coffee in the context herein. The panorama of a falling Saigon in 1975 accentuates the lovers ripped apart. The death drive to "do in" the other political party clashes with the sex drive to "do it" with the mate. As Saigon changes overnight to Ho Chi Min City, as the last US Marine helicopter roars off the embassy roof, David Hare's BBC/PBS *Masterpiece Theatre* screenplay *Saigon: The Year of the Cat* (1983) and Claude-Michel Schönberg and Alain Boublil's musical *Miss Saigon* (1989) culminate in the paradox of the fall. Saigon falls and characters fall out of love, only to witness the rise of love as a romanticized, idealized affect. To stage the undying spirit of love amounts to a collective denial of, and at the minimum sugarcoats, the trauma of war and the mortality of human bodies, if not human love. Inspired by the Vietnam conflict, the Western playwright and, subsequently, musical composer and lyricist subconsciously kill yet another bird, the undead bird of the "yellow" race in their Orientalist representations, in addition to the two usual casualties of war—combatants and/as lovers. Whereas the socialist Hare centers Anglo-American "affairs," pun intended, at the expense of marginalizing the natives, the musical practitioners help themselves to the white male fantasy of Puccini's *Madame Butterfly* (1904).

Saigon falls in the crosshairs of East and West. On the one hand, the vertical axis runs temporally through various hostilities, armed or cultural. The geisha or China doll stereotype of white male fantasy calcifies in Pierre Loti's *Madame Chrysanthème* (1887). It resonates with, if not infects, Puccini's opera *Madame Butterfly* (1904) and Hollywood films *Love Is a Many-Splendored Thing* (1955), based on Han Suyin's novel, *The Teahouse of the August Moon* (1956), based on Vernon J. Sneider's novel, and *Sayonara* (1957), based on James A. Michener's novel. That such films are sired from previous incarnations as novels demonstrates Hollywood's karma doomed to reprise the West's id of masculine hegemony over the Orient. As though anticipating the joint forces of Asians and Pacific Islanders in the millennial formulation of APIDA (Asian Pacific Islander Desi Americans), East Asian–centric white fallacy veers off to the South Pacific in *Mutiny on the Bounty* (1962), based on Charles Nordhoff's novel. The trajectory from print to film is streamlined in David Henry Hwang's stage play and ensuing film *M. Butterfly* (1993). Whereas white males never tire of conceiving Orientalist phantasmagoria, the off-white (yellow-ish) Asian American Hwang gives the motif an ethnic, queer spin. A playwright of Asian descent comes to fulfill "racial castration" of Asian males from the effeminate Charlie Chan and Fu Manchu to clowns like Mickey Rooney's Mr. Yunioshi in *Breakfast at Tiffany's* (1961). The forbidden love of East and West continues with timely political correctness and a certain level of ethnic awareness in David Mitchell's *The Thousand Autumns of Jacob de Zoet* (2010).

Intersecting with the vertical axis is the horizontal axis, more of a spatial one where narratives are set in and around Saigon throughout the struggle, spanning from the French colonial rule of the 1950s to the full-blown Vietnam War with the US in the 1960s and '70s. Graham Greene's *The Quiet American* (1955) plays on the triangular love of a worldly, cynical, and middle-aged English journalist, a young, foolhardy CIA operative, and a kept woman, the Vietnamese Phuong, meaning phoenix. Greene's Phuong echoes *Miss Saigon*'s Kim, quoted in the epigraph, where Kim dreams of her white knight descending like a phoenix to "take me off on his wings." Phuong is the fetish with which to fly Westerners—the young America as well as the old British Empire—away from the ruins of war. The American GI Chris is believed by Kim to effect an imminent deliverance for her and their mixed-race son. Over half a century later, David Rabe's *Girl by the Road at Night* (2010) translates the violence of the battlefield into the violence in the brothel with the front, ironically, of a roadside carwash, two-in-one cleaning service for military vehicle and military personnel. Because it had come to a bad end, Vietnam is one of those ongoing stories the West has kept repeating to itself to feel better.

Saigon: The Year of the Cat

In space or in time, it matters little where and when romance comes to an abrupt halt. All alike as Orientalized stock images of symbolically castrated males and fetishized, hypersexualized females, the spread or centerfold of China dolls, Japanese geishas, or Vietnamese bargirls constitutes but variations in the white masculinist discourse. Hence, the intersection of love and war in Vietnam heightens the dramatic tension in *Saigon* and *Miss Saigon*. *Saigon: The Year of the Cat* is one of David Hare's early plays in the 1980s. A socialist in conviction, the playwright appears to have worked out the kinks, or "chinks," pardon the expression, in his psyche before settling down in the new millennium to pen Anglo-American-centric BBC/PBS political dramas and TV movies: the thrilling Johnny Worricker spy trilogy that includes *Page Eight* (2011), *Turks & Caicos* (2014), *Salting the Battlefield* (2014), and, most recently, *Roadkill* (2020). In addition, mainstream filmscripts worthy of Hollywood such as *The Hours* (2002) and *The Reader* (2008) have added "white" feathers in his cap. Replaced are the "colored" ones from exotic lands: Maoist China and communist agitprop in *Fanshen* (1975), the fall of Saigon in his 1983 screenplay, and postcolonial India in *A Map of the World* (1983). Now that Hare has "righted" himself from the leftist days of his youth, let us look back, wistfully, at the early works, *Saigon* in particular, to see how Hare managed to get the passion for revolution out of his hair. As his hair grays, the increasingly white filmic universe of the mature Hare is largely foretold by *Saigon,* its setting in Southeast Asia notwithstanding.

Taking a page out of Graham Greene's 1955 novel, *The Quiet American,* Hare's *Saigon* focuses on the blooming of love between a twenty-eight-year-old, good CIA agent, Bob Chesneau, and a good-hearted English bank official, Barbara Dean, "almost 50" (211). Barbara has had a string of "secretive" assignations ever since her first, "with a friend of my father's," once again implying a generational difference of May-December attraction (212). As *Saigon* opens *in medias res* of not only the war but also the romance, we even catch a glimpse of her one-time liaison with another bank employee, Donald Henderson, a Scot of twenty-five. The wide gap in age and cultural background of what appears to be "the couple" (231) at the heart of Hare's play augurs the eventual decoupling of Barbara and Bob in the fall of Saigon as well as the divorcing of the old Vietnam from the young America.[1] In Hare's progressive, albeit patronizing, false equivalence, Barbara with her British decency and stiff upper lip substitutes for the loss of Vietnam. Apples and oranges it seems—to be associating Barbara's flight and Vietnam's plight at all. But Eros and Thanatos are also binary opposites until Freud's shotgun marriage in *Beyond the Pleasure Principle* (1920).

As the lens through which the crumbling world is perceived, Barbara's in-betweenness impregnates the whole film, starting from the opening scene in her bedroom where she reclines in a restless siesta. This tableau sets the stage by fusing multiple strands: a lone English woman languishing in a "double bed" for a Spanish siesta in the French Indochina, as yet unaware of her American gentleman caller, Bob. Her voiceover echoes that limbo state: "Afternoons have always hit me the hardest . . . Mornings are fine, there's something to look forward to, and evenings, yes, I began to cheer up" (211). A riff on the sphinx's allegory of the life course from the morning of infancy to the noon hours of one's prime to the evening of senility, Barbara's interior monologue portrays the angst- and ennui-ridden midlife crisis, deepened by the "no-man's" land—or bed, for that matter—she inhabits in Saigon.

In that bed, the mise-en-scène is accompanied by the stage direction that "she is sweating slightly" (211), which points to the subtropical heat at high noon. Figuratively, though, she perspires under the purgatorial heat, slowly desiccating, despite a late bloom with Bob, into stage directions at the close of the play. "An old English spinster" in "a panama hat" is seen being evacuated in a helicopter, homebound to "my mother" in Bournemouth, England, "where you go . . . planning to die" (287, 282, 221). The classic plantation panama hat is worn by an ex-colonist with a golden heart in a decolonizing Vietnam. That hat would be replaced overnight by the Viet Cong's topee or pith helmet, yet another residual of colonial fashions still trending under new management of Uncle Ho, having just ousted Uncle Sam. Indeed, the two jaws of the Western vise on Vietnam—politics embodied by Bob from the CIA and the US Embassy as well as money symbolized by Barbara's bank—shatter into smithereens in the wake of the Tet Offensive, the beginning of the end.

Set in Vietnam, Hare's play betrays colonialist characters' lifestyle that mimics, recreates England in denial of local conditions. The *London Times*, particularly the sports section, is pored over religiously by the bank manager

---

1. The age difference seems a recurring motif in David Hare's plays. Even in his mainstream BBC/PBS Johnny Worricker spy trilogy of the 2010s, that gap remains between Bill Nighy's Worricker and Rachel Weisz's Nancy Pierpan in *Page Eight*, but not so much between Nighy's and Helena Bonham Carter's characters in *Salting the Battlefield*. Carter plays, after all, Nighy's wife, unlike the love interest role for Weisz.

Haliwell and other expatriates. Even Donald Henderson's outrage over English teams staffed with Scottish players on the other side of the globe seems out of place amid a Vietnamese civil and proxy war. The Cercle Sportif, a French colonial club, offers nighttime socialization where Barbara plays card games with Americans and one Vietnamese, the foreign minister Van Trang. The games of "orthodox Acol" or "two clubs" are probably familiar to few other Vietnamese (216). Tied not only professionally but also personally to foreigners and their homeland, the foreign minister regrets not being able to attend Sports Day at Cheltenham Ladies' College in Gloucestershire, England, where his daughters study.

Among Westerners and the westernized Vietnamese elite, Barbara embodies white conscience. At the poker table, she compliments the all-girl English boarding school but is soon distracted by bargirls propositioning in the adjacent main lounge. While upper-class Vietnamese women learn to be English ladies, their lower-class counterparts ply the oldest trade. Barbara's playtime also coincides with prostitutes' worktime. Colonialists feign working for the natives to advance the colonial agenda and interest; colonized prostitutes feign play and erotic pleasure for survival. Barbara thirsts for love; her doppelgangers for johns with money. Her attention to the main lounge, in fact, causes the club to evict the working girls, who proceed to solicit in the shadows of the bush outside the club premises. The conscientious Barbara asks Judd, Bob's CIA colleague, to give her money to them. In return, one woman asks: "Thank you. Number One. You wanna fuck me?" (219). As shocking as it may sound to polite society, this rhetorical question is business as usual in transactional sex. But it betrays Barbara's act of kindness. Furthermore, it problematizes the first encounter of Barbara and Bob. In the shadow of war (and) prostitutes, Bob offers Barbara a ride, since "the wheels" of the taxi "have finally fallen off" (219). Bob's ominous quip foreshadows the impending political crisis. The Ford Pinto in which Bob drives Barbara home happens to be a CIA-issued, standard "spook" vehicle. Any individual affair in Saigon is already entangled with the body politic; those involved have to be transported there by the US and British airplanes, culminating in their rendezvous in a Ford subcompact car. Barbara's almost un-English forwardness in inviting Bob for a drink and more suggests the depth of her longing in the long afternoon of her life. While her invitation goes unreciprocated initially, Bob is the one with fallen wheels, gutless with no balls, pardon my French, to move to engage emotionally.

Although lacking reserve in her approach to Bob, Barbara exemplifies the proverbial English decency elsewhere. She organizes exit papers for a Vietnamese bank clerk, entertains obtaining more for the clerk's relatives, and almost defers to others the much-coveted slot in last transports out of the falling city in order to stay with Bob. Hare's characterization of Barbara Dean countenances inconsistencies, unabashedly. Described as "definitely erotic" (211) in the opening bedroom pose, Barbara explains away her apartment's unlocked door to Bob—"No one wants a white English woman"—which contradicts both her lounging sultry debut and her gentleman caller's "wants" (226). The veteran playwright surely sees the through line of a mature, uninhibited woman opening her door and herself to sexual advance, but he chooses to mask it behind the white lie of her undesirability. Undesirable to whom? Certainly, white males—Henderson, Bob, and even Judd—crave intimacy. This leaves local Vietnamese males to be the placeholder for "no one." Instead of a Barbara devoid of sexual charm, it comes down to Asian masculine impotence, incapable of mounting any wooing or "wounding." The broadminded cosmopolitan writer lapses, perhaps subconsciously, into Orientalist racial castration.

This charge stems as much from reading between the lines cited above as reading the lines themselves, especially the protagonists' dialogue with the Indigenous characters. Quoc is a bank employee, faithful and steadfast under duress, unruffled by Henderson's outburst. Quoc's Oriental "impassive[ness]" is as much a racialized construct as Henderson's Gaelic flare-up (238). Quoc even calmly covers for the bank manager, Haliwell, who has absconded. Meticulous and perspicacious, he counsels Barbara about leaving behind her "cardigan" to avoid arousing suspicion and mass panic in her final getaway (273). To veil their departures, the seasoned playwright directs to have both Haliwell's "coat" and Barbara's sweater be left on the scene—an unwitting Freudian slip of colonialists' English attire entirely inappropriate in the tropics (274). Quoc's grace under fire reprises Haliwell's performance; he has earlier disarmed a Vietnamese gunman demanding all his savings, contrary to bank regulations. Granted, Quoc faces no barrel of a gun, except his refusal to forsake his post at the bank would subject him to unimaginable misery meted out to Western collaborators once the Viet Cong take over. Meant to provide a nativist anchor in the maelstrom on the eve of the Communist takeover, Quoc's characterization stems from the stereotype of colonial subalterns serving white masters and institutions blindly.

Hare's liberal progressiveness resembles Orientalism in bifurcating Vietnamese masculinity: the good Quoc, who so borders on the automaton that his goodness looks suspect; and the bad Nhieu, Bob's informant anxious for documents for himself and "some [of his] girls" to perhaps carry on pimping in the promised land (248). This unsentimental portrayal of a CIA asset approximates that of a depraved traitor, which is what the US turns into when Nhieu and countless other spies are left behind in Saigon, to be ferreted out

FIGURE 8.1. Bob's gifts of a six-pack of beer for Nhieu and a doll for the girl in *Saigon: The Year of the Cat*.

one by one based on rows of file cabinets with 3×5 cards, all unshredded, unburned, exposed in prolonged shots of the deserted embassy office. The BBC production, directed by Stephen Frears, follows Hare's stage directions closely, training the camera unblinkingly on those index cards: "Then we adjust to settle in the foreground on the drawer full of agents' name plates, forgotten on the desk. We hold on that" (293). But Frears recasts Nhieu, apparently no procurer of illicit sex in the TV movie, in a melodramatic scene where a young Vietnamese woman translates for the meeting. Bob, in fact, brings gifts of a six-pack of beer for Nhieu and a doll for the girl (figure 8.1). Ironically, alcohol would come into some use in one's final hours, but no doll can do time for the girl in a re-education camp.

Stereotyping Orientals coexists with caricaturing Yankees, particularly the US ambassador, played by E. G. Marshall, absent initially in the TV movie because he insists on being seen by his own dentist back in North Carolina. Upon return, the ambassador corrupts, downplays Bob's intelligence report on Nhieu's doomsday scenario for the sake of securing an aid package from Congress, just as he did throughout the war exaggerating, playing up intelligence. Even more clownishly, he refuses to have documents incinerated for fear of polluting his swimming pool or have the old tamarind tree on the embassy compound chopped down to make way for the helicopter evacuation. Figure 8.2 captures the ambassador, upon rejecting Bob's report outright, looking up in reverie of his own, oblivious to the apocalypse unfolding on the

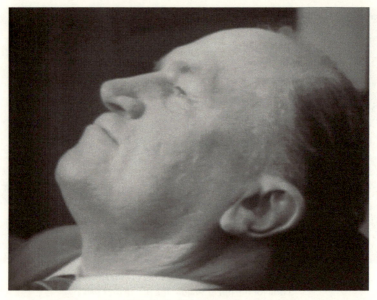

FIGURE 8.2. The US ambassador dreams of securing military aid and a satisfactory conclusion to the armed conflict in *Saigon*.

ground and his subordinates' presence in the room. With his head in the cloud, so to speak, the ambassador launches into a dreamy tangent, quite an elaborate dramatization of Hare's simple direction "off on his own tack" (251), which serves to encapsulate American naivety and wrong*head*edness. Indeed, the way the ambassador relaxes with outstretched neck reminds one of a guillotine looming over a nincompoop like Lu Xun's Ah Q.[2] The only difference is that Ah Q and the Vietnamese would be decapitated, not the ambassador. The final retreat is communicated to Saigon's Westerners via a broadcast of Bing Crosby's "White Christmas," an encrypted white lie to avoid wholesale panic and chaos among the Vietnamese population. Whites are summoned to rendezvous at assembly points for the trip home as though it were Christmas. If Crosby's song were not factual, part of the historical absurdity of the Vietnam War, this heavy-handed finale would be a flaw sinking the play. As it were, Crosby's mellifluous, heart-warming "White Christmas" culminates the abandonment of Vietnam and the severance of the lovers homeward bound, respectively.

Before mellowing into the mainstream BBC and Hollywood productions, the early socialist Hare borrows heavily from the like-minded Bertolt Brecht.

---

2. Ah Q is nobody in Lu Xun, whereas the US ambassador controls the lives of millions of people.

Brechtian epic theater's alienation-effect seeks to break the illusion of the fourth wall, disrupting empathetic identification between characters onstage and the audience. Brecht theorizes that this detachment would give rise to a thinking—not just feeling—audience, calling them into action for social change. The dramaturgy of *Fanshen,* for instance, bears more than a family resemblance to Brecht's *The Good Woman of Setzuan* (1947) in having actors assume multiple roles, in directly addressing the audience, and in didactic, bald-faced pontificating on what is good and right. *A Map of the World* likewise mixes the filming in the studio setting with performers' "real" lives, even with the intrusion of "real" people portrayed by the performers. The caveat is that such "real people" remain performers, enacting a circular metanarrative that begs the question of reality and performativity. Also (mis)shaping the presentation of the "real" is, for instance, *A Map*'s distinct continental, leftist anti-Americanism in the beautiful yet "ugly" American character Peggy, whose dissolute sexual freedom turns her into one from America "the land of the fleas" rather than "the free," to transpose "r" and "l" as *A Map*'s Bombay locals are wont to do.[3]

Although such practices transgress against the Western theater tradition, they are arguably inspired by Peking Opera conventions introduced to Brecht by the female impersonator Mei Lanfang and others in Moscow in 1935. Despite being part of the BBC programming, epic theater's fingerprint on *Saigon* is clearly visible in scene 32 that closes part 1. The stage direction specifies that Barbara Dean "*turns. Her eye catches camera*" precisely at the point when her voiceover narrates: "Donald *did* leave with comparative dignity.... Compared with some of the rest of us, I mean" (239). The violation of Stanislavsky's invisible fourth wall implicates the viewers in the coming shameful desertion of Vietnamese, as "the rest of us" includes whoever is being gazed back at by Barbara Dean, if only Stephen Frears had executed Hare's direction. A further concession to the popular *Masterpiece Theatre* on both sides of the Atlantic, Dame Judi Dench, who plays Barbara, intones the final words while looking off-frame, away from the camera, inviting not spectatorial self-reflection through her accusing eyes but the male gaze at her cleavage through the open blouse (figure 8.3). Voyeuristic sex beats the vision of mass suffering and death; ratings from televisual pleasure trumps activism on social justice.

---

3. David Hare is well aware of the pushback to his ugly American Peggy, who offers a night of intimacy to whoever wins the debate between a young British idealist and a cynical Anglo-Indian novelist. In the introduction to the collection of his *The Secret Rapture and Other Plays* (1997), Hare candidly describes to his interviewers, Faber and Faber editors, "the same hostility from the public" reported by three different actresses in Peggy's role when the play toured in Australia, England, and New York.

FIGURE 8.3. Dame Judi Dench's Barbara Dean looks off-frame instead of at the camera as she exits scene 32 in *Saigon*.

Miss Saigon

Miss Saigon picks up where Hare left off, on the eve of the fall of Saigon. Temporary continuum, however, does not guarantee stylistic kinship. Whereas *Masterpiece Theatre* director Frears forgoes some of Hare's provocateur as well as Brechtian alienation stance, not to mention sentimentalizing Vietnamese characters, *Saigon* the script and the teleplay remain scathing critiques of the US debacle in Southeast Asia. By contrast, the musical *Miss Saigon* is a modern version of Puccini's opera *Madame Butterfly* (1904) without Hare's socialist bent and with a great deal more bathos. In his exploration of Saidian Orientalism collaging Puccini's Japan and *Miss Saigon*'s Vietnam, Jeffrey A. Keith in "Producing *Miss Saigon*" argues that the West is addicted to "Southeast Asia's sexualized reputation," where Saigon is gendered, "sensual and feminine" (248, 252). Feminizing Saigon, the DVD of the musical's twenty-fifth-anniversary gala, performed live at Prince Edward Theatre, London, on September 22, 2014, is even packaged with an epigraphic photograph captioned "This photograph is the start of everything." The composer Schönberg claims that his initial inspiration lies in that photograph "from an October 1985 *France Soir* news story that pictured a Vietnamese woman bidding a sorrowful farewell to her child, who was traveling to the United States to be with her father" (Keith 269). This melodramatic opening invites theatergoers to enter into an age-old story of East-West entanglements from Italian opera to Broadway-style musicals.

As part of what Angela Pao calls the "maternal lineage" ("Eyes of the Storm" 26), Puccini's plot is faithfully preserved: the innocent Vietnamese prostitute Kim (played by the Filipina Lea Salonga in its original London run and by Eva Maria Noblezada in the 2014 performance cited herein) at the whorehouse Dreamland falls in love with her American customer Chris and bears his son Tam after Americans have evacuated from Saigon. The boy-meets-girl scenario is made possible by the pimp Engineer (played by Jonathan Pryce in London) and by Chris's colleague John, indeed one of the johns at Dreamland. Having redeemed himself as an advocate for Amerasian children, "Bui-Doi" fathered and abandoned by American GIs, John reluctantly informs Chris after locating Kim and Tam in the post-US Vietnam, now that Chris is married to Ellen, who is American and blonde. Like her Japanese "ancestor" and the photographic epigraph, Kim commits suicide to free Chris from the moral choice and to give Tam a better life with his father in the US.

The brothel Dreamland under the tutelage of the Engineer presents spectators with explicit sexuality as bargirls peddle themselves to American soldiers. After erotic dancing, background copulating, and Broadway singing and dancing, Gigi is the newly crowned "Miss Saigon." Gigi wastes no time in asking the lottery winner for the night, none other than the African American GI John, to "take me to America," which so revolts John that he shoves her off, despite her pledge to be a good wife while stroking his crotch. John reacts so vehemently because Gigi violates the whole mirage of Dreamland set up to dispel the impending doom. The johns flee from the nightmare of Vietnam by indulging themselves in the pleasures of the flesh, while Gigi and her colleagues dream of safe passage by enduring the indignity and pain inflicted on their bodies. Indeed, even the Engineer clamors for a US visa by offering his "girls" or even himself in exchange.

Rejected by John, Gigi bursts into song, one of the politically correct lyrics of "The Movie in My Mind" to counterbalance the salacious scene of transactional sex. Most significantly, Gigi sings of "Flee this life / Flee this place." Just as Gigi sets the stage of Saigon's abjection and precarity, Kim and the brothel chorus take over the song, refreshing the romantic dream. Ironically, "the Movie in [Kim's and other actor's] Mind" is less on the prostitutes' collective mental screen than in front of each theatergoer's or DVD viewer's eyes, on the stage or on the screen. Such Brechtian thinking through the song's empathetic power returns us to Gigi's key phrase on fleeing that animates the whole play.

The flight is foretold by *Miss Saigon*'s "logo" of the helicopters silhouetted by the sun, bright yellow against a wash of red. A cinematic trope made famous by *Apocalypse Now* (1979), *Platoon* (1986), and a long line of Vietnam War films, the chopper is the "weapon of choice" in the difficult terrain of the tropical jungle, ferrying American soldiers to the theater of war to hunt down the Viet Cong. Yet it also signals flight of the hunted, flying away to evacuate the wounded and to transport Americans and Vietnamese to safety, such as the infamous photograph of one of the last helicopters taking off from the US Embassy rooftop on April 30, 1975. The morphing of the hunter and the hunted crystallizes in the ambiguity of "flight"—to fly to one's prey or to fly away because one *is* the prey. The musical's helicopter logo epitomizes that paradox. Is the sun rising or setting at dawn or dusk? Is the chopper plunging into the battlefield or pulling out of one? Given the racist pidgin transposition of "r" and "l," that either-or conundrum bifurcates the operative word "flee" into its Orientalist and homophonic familiars of "free" and "flea." To flee to the land of the free is to become a flea, an unwanted refugee in America's body politic. To flee is driven by the urge to be free. Freedom, however, entails a wretched life of fleadom in a bipolarized, xenophobic, and refugee- and immigrant-averse MAGA Trumpland.

From the musical's logo to the stage, *Miss Saigon* has long capitalized on the spectacle of a descending and ascending helicopter, deus ex machina on the crane, to ferry out soldiers. Figure 8.4 captures one of these hair-raising moments when the Vietnamese with documents in hand, Kim included, are barred by the embassy gate. Crouching by the gate under the strong gale from the rotor blades and the deafening noise, the Vietnamese witness the vanishing of the promise made by the *Promised Land* as the helicopter rises, its beacon lights or headlights blinding like the Gorgon's gaze. Left to fend for herself, Kim is further burdened by the evidence of her collaboration with the imperialists—the mixed-race Tam. In her final confrontation with Thuy, her Vietnamese fiancé and a Viet Cong officer, Kim shoots Thuy, who is poised to stab Tam, making it imperative to escape from the communist soldiers with their rifles and red flags arrayed on the backstage straight out of Madame Mao or Jiang Qing's Model Revolutionary Peking Operas. The homicide sets the stage for her to flee Vietnam, not to retire from life altogether. The foreshadowing of her tragic end comes about when a tormented Chris awakening from his nightmare is seen comforted by Ellen, their bed cantilevered high up in the air, while down below Kim solos (figure 8.5). The duet would close in Kim's favor, but not the duel over Chris's choice of his lifelong companion.

Filmic split screen is utilized through spatial division of the stage vis-à-vis an upper level aloft. Brechtian alienation-effect comes into play for an empathetic dramatic theater entirely opposite to Brecht's intention in epic theater. Whereas Brecht's song and dance is designed to distance viewers emotionally,

FIGURE 8.4. The Vietnamese crouch by the embassy gate as the helicopter roars off in *Miss Saigon*.

FIGURE 8.5. Ellen comforts Chris as Kim solos downstage in *Miss Saigon*.

to prompt critical thinking and social action, West End and Broadway musicals comprise less dialogue and plot than trilling and emoting. Music seeks to move rather than to dissociate the audience. Lyricism and musicality do not digress from the plot; they constitute the plot. Filmic theme music and theme songs freeze the climax in poetry and musical notes, transcending, sublimating the prosaic dialogue and plot. By contrast, Broadway musicals strive to stay midair, so to speak, on an elevated plane of emotional intensity,

FIGURE 8.6. John sings of the misery of mixed-race Bui-Doi in *Miss Saigon*.

occasionally relaxing and lapsing into a spoken line or two, before characters break into song and dance all over again. Brecht is ill-advised to dispense of emotion, which, unequivocally, moves the audience. The seven character "e-motion," after all, is six-seventh "motion," should we do unto the English word what Ezra Pound has done in dissecting Chinese ideograms as well as what Brecht himself has done in abstracting, theorizing the female impersonator Mei Lanfang's Moscow performance in 1935.

Although characters in *Miss Saigon* are largely one-dimensional, either innocent like Kim or depraved like the Engineer, John evolves somewhat throughout the play. He debuts in Dreamland in the stereotype of a Black stud in dreadlocks, his barrel chest and torso bare under a sleeveless army vest. John procures Kim at Dreamland for Chris, who "thinks too much." Yet John returns in act 2 in a face-off of sorts, in suit and tie, hair closely cropped, presiding over a conference in the crusade on behalf of Amerasian children. Figure 8.6 shows John hitting the high note before a lectern and a screen of an apparently mixed-race Bui-Doi, "The dust of life / Conceived in Hell, / And born in strife." Even this doubling of Brechtian A-effect by means of song and the prop of a slideshow intensifies the affective power, not to steer away from it. In a self-righteous manner, John's "hymn" around a "pulpit" lives up to the spectacle that the musical is destined to be, evolved from "Gilbert and Sullivan operettas of the late 19th century" to "its current form of Oscar Hammerstein and Jerome Kern's Show Boat in 1927" (Pao 24).

Brechtian A-effect does work in a circuitous way in the cross-casting of Jonathan Pryce as the Engineer in London's run. Yoko Yoshikawa writes that

"Pryce had been acting in yellow-face, with prosthetically altered eyelids and tinted makeup" ("The Heat Is On" 43). Angela Pao confirms the actor's facial makeup, complemented by Orientalist music: "On stage, Jonathan Pryce originally played the role using eye prosthetics and make-up, the traditional applications of Western theatre and film to signify Orientalness. His entrances are marked in the score by parallel musical signifiers, auditory caricatures of the tonalities characteristic of Asian musical forms" (33). Such Orientalist representations meander through Western dramas, from Brecht to Hare to Schönberg and Boublil, from the auteurist stage to the commercial one, from the performer's body to the spectator's mind. Long after the fall of Saigon, an Orientalist afterlife in the millennial West arises still, loving and hating things Oriental simultaneously.

CHAPTER 9

Eastern Witch from the West

Xianniang in Niki Caro's *Mulan*

Reviewing Niki Caro's live-action *Mulan* (2020), film critics such as Peter Debruge in *Variety* and Brian Truitt in *USA Today* associate the witch character played by Gong Li with Hawk on account of her metamorphosis into the raptor. The IMDb film website and closed captioning simply identify her as Xianniang, which means "Immortal Woman." Remaining unnamed other than the "witch" diegetically, that is, so addressed by characters within the film, she is alluded to, extradiegetically, by reviewers and subtitlers in two diametrically opposed ways for the Anglophone global cinema. To call her by the shorthand Hawk underlines the dark animal kinship; to call her Xianniang risks alienating the non-Sinophone audience, who most likely would not have turned on closed captioning and who would have missed the deification implicit in xian (immortal) even if they had. Either name removes the character from the centrality of humanity, leaning to bestiality or to beatification. The former name resonates with the tangibility of cinematic special effects of a soaring hawk and the flock of batlike birds; the latter is largely occluded because of the unintelligibility of romanized Xianniang.[1]

---

1. This chapter is drawn from "Eastern Witch from the West: Xianniang in Niki Caro's *Mulan*," *Neo-Disneyism: Inclusivity in the Twenty-First Century of Disney's Magic Kingdom*, edited by Brenda Ayres and Sarah E. Maier, Peter Lang, 2022, pp. 115–29. Reproduced by permission of Peter Lang.

Ironically, the visible materiality of the hawk and batty birds constitutes digital mirages, technological sleight of hand; the impenetrable Xianniang encrypts two concrete Chinese ideograms, 仙娘, an abstract mess sourced from a solid mass of fifteen brushstrokes, five to form 仙, ten to form 娘. However, in a world where traditional calligraphy and penmanship have been flattened into romanization via keyboards, the five brushstrokes of 仙 are cut down to the four keystrokes of xian in pinyin, and the ten brushstrokes of 娘 to the five keystrokes of niang. Translation converts meaning or soul as much as it casts off form or body. What if the meaning rests solely in the form? What if the spirit of the character—both the fictional person and the words pointing to that person—resides in the letter of the character? Contrary to Walter Benjamin's utopian prophecy, "The Task of the Translator"—not only subtitlers but cultural translators of film reviewers and filmmakers like Niki Caro—may unwittingly amputate the source culture in exchange for the mighty prosthesis and filmic gadgetry to win over the target culture.

To proceed with the name of "least resistance" yet most fraught in English, the witch Hawk is a twenty-first-century "walk-on" (fly-in?), entirely absent in the genesis of the Mulan legend, the fifth-century "Ballad of Mulan." Nor does she exist in any previous reincarnations in the Chinese and English language, including Maxine Hong Kingston's ethnic classic *The Woman Warrior* (1976) and the Disney animation *Mulan* (1998). The closest one can find is the animation's monstrous, gorillalike Hun leader Shan Yu with his barrel chest, long arms, sharp fangs, and slant eyes. Given their shared predator attributes, Caro casts the witch as a familiar, "a slave" to her Shan Yu character, Böri Khan, complete with an umlaut over "o." The diacritical mark ousts the character from the English language and culture, while effecting no change in its pronunciation. Purely decorative, the "ö" is for looks only, aiming to rub off on the character played by Jason Scott Lee, made up to look Central Asian, almost Arabic, as do his dark-clad, masked, and turbaned cohort of shadow warriors. That the Khan's horde debut by multiplying from one Khan on horseback to many, like a mirage out of the desert, validates their Central Asian or Near Eastern association. Drawing not only from the long Chinese dynastic memory against northern nomadic "barbarians," Caro also taps into post-9/11 worldwide paranoia in pop culture, where villainy carries an odious Orientalist, Muslim tone.

The witch's same-sex look-alike is the shaman or "Great Wizard" in figure 9.1 from *Matchless Mulan,* one of a handful of Chinese media conglomerate iQIYI's rush productions during the lull of *Mulan*'s delayed global release, bumped off by COVID-19 from Wuhan. Two letters apart, albeit with identical

FIGURE 9.1. The shaman or "Great Wizard" in *Matchless Mulan*.

vowels, Wuhan and Mulan resemble Sino-ese twins: one COVID-born at the close of 2019, the other all but aborted the following year.

Given the absence of the witch before 2020, is Caro's addition to the cast a Western wolf in Eastern sheep's clothing, speaking in English to boot, swallowing whole the gullible Anglophone audience? Is Caro affixing, fixating on, a feminist, homoerotic tail to an imperial, heteronormative Chinese tale? Is Caro a Western neo-imperialist bewitching—pun intended—the world in the name of a liberal, all-Asian performance?

Mulan Who?

Before turning to the supporting actress Hawk, the spotlight ought to stay a while longer on the leading actress, Mulan. High time for a paternity test for Mulan: What is her last name? Is it the Chinese tradition's Hua, although her literary debut in "The Ballad of Mulan" does not exactly spell that out? Is it the Cantonese-inflected Fa, as in Kingston's *The Woman Warrior*? Kingston's ethnic classic introduced this cross-dressing heroine who, as Chinese legend has it, substituted for her ailing father for battle against invasions along China's northern borders. Is her surname Disney, when the 1998 animation absorbs Kingston's ethnic angle into its multicultural lineups of teenage girl power? Grounded in the whiteness of Ariel in *The Little Mermaid* (1989) and of Belle in *Beauty and the Beast* (1991), Disney adroitly expands to and whitewashes Arab Jasmine in *Aladdin* (1992), Native American Pocahontas in the eponymous 1995 animation, gypsy Esmeralda in *The Hunchback of Notre Dame* (1996), and Chinese or Asian in *Mulan*.

For decades, the Chinese performing arts and film industry have produced their own heroines. As opposed to Mulan Hollywood, China proudly presents Mulan Huallywood à la the second syllable of *zhonghua* for China, eerily punning its very own hua (flower, prosperity) with her surname. *Hua Mulan* (2009), featuring China's lead performers Wei Zhao and Kun Chen, arrives almost as a delayed response to the popular Disney animation. Under the auspices of the Magic Kingdom, Niki Caro turns Mulan Disney into a feature film with an Asian and Asian American cast in 2020. The global release of Mulan Caro, so to speak, having been postponed due to COVID-19, iQIYI cobbles together in the meantime *Matchless Mulan* and *Mulan Legend*, both streamed online in the summer months of 2020. An animation, *Kung Fu Mulan*, by Leo Liao follows on Caro's heels in being released in October 2020. Ian Shepherd directed *Hua Mulan*, a short documentary for children, which was distributed as a DVD in November 2020. American children were ill-served by opportunists like Shepherd, whose narrator pronounced Hua in two separate syllables—HU-A. This is a mistake as basic and silly as English learners whose native tongues are monosyllabic turning "Ian" into two distinct words: "I-AN." Ultimately, a paternity test may prove futile in the face of so many serial sperm donors: Hollywood, Huallywood, Disney, Caro, iQIYI, Liao, and Shepherd.

At the heart of the Mulan legend in "The Ballad of Mulan" (木蘭辭 *Mulanci* circa 400 AD) lie twin binarities of gender and race. A female pretends to be her father in a border conflict between China's majority Han people and another, unnamed race to the north. That the breach comes from an unidentified source arises from centuries-old Chinese anxiety over the amorphous umbrella term of northern nomadic "barbarians," who have made relentless incursions into China, culminating in two dynasties—Mongolians' Yuan and Manchurians' Qing—both eventually establishing their capitals in Beijing. "The Ballad of Mulan" betrays, however, the porousness of that dichotomy between Chinese and non-Chinese. Answering the imperial conscription, Mulan in "The Ballad" describes it as having been handed down from "the Khan," which segues subsequently to "the Son of Heaven," the traditional Chinese address of respect for the emperor. In her triumphant homecoming, Mulan is granted an audience with the Son of Heaven, which changes in no time to "the Khan asks what she wants." To call China's emperor "the Khan" after chieftains of northern nomads is not only bewildering but verging on blasphemy, as if one nomadic Khan bent on offense meets Beijing's Khan in defense. Arguably, the Ballad's switch stems from a fluid tribal perception of the nation's leader, one that flips between northern Khans and Chinese emperors. Mulan is likely to be a member of the northern minorities retaining residuals of tribal linguistic habits, despite having been assimilated and Sinologized. Proper nouns for concrete things, ranging from daily objects to human relationships of naming such as the Khan, are the last to go anyway in any assimilation.

The Disney animation glosses over the Ballad's racial blurring by pitting the northern Huns commanded by the apelike Shan Yu against the Han army stationed along the Great Wall. At the outset, the imperial decree mobilizes male conscripts in response to the Hun incursion. Disney identifies the villain's race as "Hun," whereas the Ballad does not. The clarity of Disney is cartoonish, given the Ballad's historical ambiguity. Not only narrowing down the umbrella term *Huns* to *Rourans*, Caro's film also takes leave of the Ballad in the setting of Mulan's village. Her family lives in the renowned tourist site of Hakka adobe roundhouses in Fujian and southern China, over a thousand miles away from the northern borderland of the Ballad. The Hakka, suffice to say, is one of the most ancient Han ethnic groups, entirely different from tribal nomads, Sinologized or not, along the Great Wall.

To a vigilant Chinese reader, the racial obfuscation would cry out from the text. Yet another obscuring concludes the Ballad. The male impersonator through twelve years of military service returns to her parents after the war, changes back to her female costume and makeup, and shocks her comrades. The last lines read: "The male rabbit's feet are kicking, the female rabbit's eyes squint, almost closed / Both rabbits running side by side, how can you tell whether I am male or female?" "Kicking" and "squint[ing], almost closed" comprise a Chinese maxim, *pushuo mili* ("kicking, hopping" and "misty, unclear"), over the confusing and mysterious state of things. In China's patriarchal, heteronormative tradition, that unsettling haze is never meant to include sexual orientation. A dozen years of gender-bending aberration in the military constitute an extreme condition with the express purpose of extolling filial piety in a family and patriotism in a nation. The female serves at the pleasure of the father or the father figure.

The racial, national division of Han and Hun has already been deconstructed by the Ballad's internal evidence. Conceivably, even the gender division is subject to debate should we take the Ballad's last word at its word. The rhetorical question at the end, "How can you tell whether I am male or female?," is literal because Mulan defies gender binarism. Rather than either-or, she is both-and as well as neither-nor. Instead of two rabbits—a female Mulan and her male colleague—running alongside each other, kicking barbarian butts, pardon the expression, the cross-dresser inhabits both rabbits, both roles, in Freudian terms. The buck's kicking of hind legs symbolizes phallic erection; the doe's squinting eyes acquire a vaginal likeness or orgiastic expression. Or the other way around at the moment of orgasm: female leg muscles spasm; male eyes swoon. Ideally, *la petite mort* culminates lovemaking of two bodies and consciousnesses into one climax, bridging Eros and Thanatos, equating Self and Other. The various Freudian scenarios circle back to Kingston, who capitalizes on androgyny when General Fa Mu Lan alters her armor to mask her pregnancy. The most masculine moment of killing happens to be the most feminine moment of gestation.

Hawk Caro

Hawk the witch materializes out of left field of the Mulan legend or, geopolitically, to the left of China all the way to the West—Europe and America and Australia, from which Niki Caro hails. Hawk performs black magic on the battlefield, courtesy of special effects and computer-generated imagery. Occidental, Hollywood media technology conjures up the ghost of a phantasmagoric Orient, except this Orient is possessed by the Anglo-European mania over sorcery. How to read Hawk's power, which includes possessing, merging, and zombiefying her victims of a Central Asian caravan merchant, an imperial soldier, and, lastly, the imperial chancellor? Taking control of these victims' body and mind resonates with Western—not Eastern—vampire lore, which ties in with the repeated mise-en-scène of swarms of batlike birds in flight cross-dissolving into the witch on foot. Vampiric possession and bats fall within Western popular culture. Hawk is empowered by Orientalism, harking back to Bram Stoker's *Dracula* (1897) from across "the most Western of splendid bridges over the Danube . . . [taking] us among the traditions of Turkish rule" (1). Turkish or Transylvanian, Dracula transports itself in a coffin to England, bringing Eastern despotism and death to individual sentience. In reverse, the Chinese witch's agency flows from the Australian Caro and the Western mythology over witchcraft.

Long before Hawk graces the screen, the stigma of the witch is already introduced by Mulan's mother, but in reference to Mulan. The mother fears that neighbors would "call her a witch" had Mulan failed to conceal her inborn *chi* (*qi* in pinyin), a supernatural power manifested in her gliding through air or letting her weapons fly. In fact, villagers do curse Mulan as a "witch" after she gives chase to a chicken, her gravity-defying prowess surpassing that of any mortal male. The two women warriors of Hawk and Mulan are inextricably intertwined through the indeterminacy of the witch and the warrior in the eye of patriarchy, one that colors women's perception right from the outset. This chi is essential for military exploits, and hence celebrated in male heirs. Misplaced in a female body like Mulan's that leaps across rooftops, this mysterious force of the chosen damns her instead. Women's sole avenue to

FIGURE 9.2. Hawk urges Mulan to join forces in Niki Caro's *Mulan*.

"bring honor to the family" is through arranged marriage, one of many places where Caro follows verbatim the animation's stilted lyrics and dated plot. Such Orientalist stereotypes span the two decades of Disney's animation and Caro's feature film. Amid the millennial maelstrom over racial and gender injustice, Caro has not disabused herself of Orientalist vocabulary and milieu. Rather, she recycles the plotline and the high points of the animation to cater to millennial audiences who had grown up on Disney animations. The live-action feature film constitutes a collage of Orientalist banalities.

One such cliché concerns Chinese families; Caro's retelling of *Mulan* hinges on a Confucian-style family. Beyond reiterating stereotypical virtues of loyal, brave, and true carved on Mulan's sword, the Hua family heirloom, a fourth inscription is added to the back of the emperor's sword bequeathed to Mulan in the closing moments after she has saved the empire. The fourth word is *xiao*, filial piety, rendered as "devotion to the family." This commends Mulan's dedication to "honor," to borrow the Orientalist buzzword again, her biological family as well as the collective family headed by the emperor.

Family becomes the point at which Hawk's and Mulan's destinies diverge. In their confrontations, Hawk sees through Mulan's disguise. "We are the same," urges Hawk at joining forces in figure 9.2, "we will take our place together." If Mulan agrees, they would become "agents fighting structural injustice and gendered oppression together," as Zhuoyi Wang notes in "From *Mulan* (1998) to *Mulan* (2020)" ([2022] 7). Yet while their chi or innate abilities housed in female bodies are similar, Hawk is practically an orphan, shunned by all except the Khan, a cruel adoptive father who exploits her talents. The Khan, in turn, rages against the Chinese emperor (played by Jet Li) as if he were a rebellious, even parricidal, son about to set aflame the bound yet composed father figure. The Khan seethes in fury in the name of avenging his own father of the same name, slain by the emperor earlier. Whereas Mulan replaces her father in battle to keep him alive, the Khan wishes to kill and replace the emperor as the master of the land. That he does so under the guise of revenge veils his desire to be the father; that Böri Khan is what both the father and the son are called suggests the identical impulse of the alpha male, always singular after displacing the biological or symbolic patriarch. Despite his grotesque scars and weathered countenance, the Khan looks almost churlish, childish as he strikes two scimitars to generate fiery sparks that alight on and burn the emperor's unruffled face, a silly child's game, a "warm-up" for the imminent burning at the stake. The Khan's lame bluster promises no paternal patronage to Hawk or any of his followers. By contrast, Mulan's loving biological family comes under the wing of the Father of China, the emperor, the Son of Heaven. By corollary, Mulan becomes the beloved granddaughter to Heaven.

Absent a family, Hawk's power seems corrupted into *maleficium* in opposition to Mulan's chi. In their skirmishes, Caro performs a shotgun marriage of Western demonology and Eastern mysticism. However, both witchery and chi remain so ambiguous and ill-defined that they are presented as not only alike but causal. Mulan's repressed chi comes to fruition on account of Hawk's "mercy killing" of the male impersonator in her to free her chi. Feeling spurned by Mulan's refusal to be true to her feminine core, Hawk flings a dart at Mulan's heart, disposing of this "toy" soldier who could have been so much more. Yet that dart is stuck in Mulan's tight, breast-flattening wrapping: Mulan is saved by her disguise. Having fainted from this near death and gradually coming around, Mulan 2.0 sheds all pretense of masculinity, including armor and helmet, her long black hair flowing in the wind, riding to the rescue of her comrades. Letting go of the masquerade clearly empowers her, but the logic escapes the viewer. If the corset-style wrapping has shielded her, then she ought to take on more—not less—protective gear, including gender. Caro romanticizes to win over the viewer's heart, not the head. The rush of a feeling of triumph, along with the crescendo of music and tracking shots, is designed to overwhelm the audience emotionally.

Hawk's demise reprises this scene of mercy killing to birth Mulan, but in reverse. Hawk dares to challenge her master the Khan, inspired by the heroine Mulan, a model for what Hawk could have been, if only she had fared in a more tolerant world, a.k.a. imperial China. Sensing a greater threat, the Khan turns his arrow aimed at Hawk toward Mulan. To save Mulan a second time, Hawk dives down to take the arrow in figure 9.3, making possible the subsequent duel between Mulan and the Khan. Nevertheless, Caro's triumphant plotline proceeds from one narrative cage to another, from racial stereotypes of nomadic and marauding Huns to those of patriarchal and compassionate Hans. Despite their seeming antagonism, both Mulan and Hawk gravitate to the same Confucian patriarchal center. Hawk's realization that "they accept

FIGURE 9.3. Hawk dives down to take the arrow in order to save Mulan.

you, but they will never accept me" pivots on "they," the world of men which adjudicates between heroism and hedonism, between the flight of the phoenix and the fall of the hawk.

Their closeness is foreshadowed by their avian avatars: hawk and phoenix. The difference rests in the fact that Mulan is blessed by the phoenix soaring well above her, an ancestral spirit watching over her. Indeed, in her showdown with the Khan on bamboo scaffoldings—yet another trite kung fu tableau going all the way back to King Hu's bamboo grove in *A Touch of Zen* (1971)—where the emperor is manacled, the phoenix rises up in the distance behind Mulan, its wings extending from Mulan's shoulders as though endowing her with aerial chi (figure 9.4). The phoenix is conjured up out of nowhere as much by Mulan's desperation after losing her sword as by the emperor's exhortation: "You are a mighty warrior. Rise up like a phoenix!" Mulan is enabled by Chinese mythology over the phoenix, the counterpart to the dragon embodied in the emperor, as well as by Western mythology over the birth of the phoenix out of the cauldron that has incinerated her sword into ashes. The phoenix's wings over Mulan's shoulders are the brief moment where the corporeal splicing occurs. In Hawk's case, either the raptor or the batlike throng metamorphoses into Hawk on foot. Whereas Mulan's humanity remains intact with a fleeting image of two-in-one high up on the bamboo scaffoldings, Hawk's identity collapses with those of animals. The divergence notwithstanding, their chi keeps them aloft. The male principle, on the other hand, seems bound to the earth. The emperor is in bondage; the only martial stunt he pulls is to catch the arrow shot by the Khan. Even the arrow returned to pierce the Khan's heart is aerially kicked and redirected by Mulan, after being flung high by the emperor. The Khan, of course, breathes his last, prone on the ground.

FIGURE 9.4. The phoenix rises with wings extending from Mulan's shoulders.

The witch and the warrior differ only in terms of social acceptance, which debunks the neoliberal notion of individual meritocracy. Hawk, rejected by all, turns to serve the Khan like a slave. By contrast, Mulan finds herself through male impersonating first, and subsequently through male rescuing, but only after the rebirth of her femininity at the hands of Hawk. Since the male she saves happens to be the Chinese emperor, Mulan is not only spared for transgressions against the military code of conduct and gender roles but is well-nigh apotheosized. The witch dies; the warrior flies high. Mulan in history fades; Mulan in Disney learns English and does a bit of queerbaiting with her fellow witch in what Caro intimates is "a love scene."

Niki Caro's addition of Gong Li as the witch culminates gender instability throughout centuries of retelling in the East and the West. In Robert Ito's *New York Times* review of September 3, 2020, Caro notes: "And there's a scene between Mulan and Gong Li's character that's literally directed like a love scene. It's all conscious, and yet the movie can also live for a general audience quite happily." Caro consciously fashions homoerotic tease that has remained repressed in textual subconsciousness owing either to the absence of other females, as in "The Ballad of Mulan," or to the dominance of heterosexual romance, as in Mulan and Shang of the Disney animation and Wei Zhao and Kun Chen of *Hua Mulan*. Nevertheless, Caro hastens to promise that the LGBTQ motif lends itself to a heteronormative co-optation by Disney's general audience. Caro's proviso suggests a balancing act between commercial interests and artistic visions. Caro visualizes what is hiding in plain sight for almost two millennia: Mulan cross-dresses not to replace her father but to be herself, a self that is both female and male.

To keep the general audience happy, Caro continues to veil Mulan's sexual orientation, favoring her femininity. The casting of Yifei Liu as Mulan has undermined any possibility of gender destabilizing. Liu has been catapulted to fame by playing lead roles in TV adaptations of Jing Yong's wuxia (swordplay) novels. Jing Yong is the pen name of Louis Cha, the pre-eminent wuxia novelist, one given to unabashed male fantasy in the proverbial *jianghu* (River and Lake), the alternate universe of swordplay akin to the lawless Wild West of Hollywood's westerns. In fact, Liu has been designated by Jing Yong as the perfect candidate for his female protagonists in *Demi-Gods and Semi-Devils* (2003), *Chinese Paladin* (2005), and *The Return of the Condor Heroes* (2006). Treasured for her willowy femininity by Jing Yong and Caro, Liu pales in comparison to a number of other choices whose physique, carriage, and elocution problematize gender divisions, such as China's Yao Chen or Taiwan's Megan Lai. (Incidentally, Yao Chen is one of the three celebrities of the spotlight squad, along with Charlize Theron and Misty Copeland, featured in the Breitling women's watches ad in the *New York Times Style Magazine*, Women's Fashion, Feb. 21, 2021, as well as online https://www.youtube.com/watch?v=9tLEI-0NFi4. Apparently, many Chinese, women and men alike, purchase this status symbol.) Truth be told, it may be Liu's teenage years in the US and English proficiency that land her this Disney role.

Thus, the question "Mulan Who?" suggests, racially and paternally, Mulan Hu, with "Hu" (胡) a double entendre for a Chinese surname as well as a term that lumps together all northern "barbarians," for she may well have been of non-Chinese descent. With regard to gender, it veils the question "Whose Mulan?," a phallic fetish into which the Chinese and the West, the male and female director and film industry, project longing for power, so long as this symbol returns to traditional femininity and commercial viability.

Gong Li, who plays the witch, rose to stardom in Zhang Yimou's *Red Sorghum* (1988) and several other films by the Chinese director. Gong Li of late has turned to international productions, ranging from the English-mangling Madame Hatsumomo in *Memoirs of a Geisha* (2005) to Lady Murasaki in *Hannibal Rising* (2007) to Isabella in *Miami Vice* (2006) to Anna Lan-Ting in *Shanghai* (2010). The first two roles are Japanese, the latter two Chinese. Hawk's white face paint serves as a mask, accentuating the character's enigmatic, otherworldly aura. The face paint brings to mind the Great Wizard's Maori-style facial tattoo in *Matchless Mulan* (figure 9.1). A true, unadorned face would show oneself plainly. Masquerading lends itself to mystification, either the supernatural Hawk who transforms into a torrent of bats or the Great Wizard who dispatches a flood of rats against the matchless Mulan's garrison. Ultimately, the Eastern witch and the Orient are shadows thrown by Niki Caro and Disney on the cave wall of, by, and for the West.

PART 4

OFF-WHITE POP-UPS

CHAPTER 10

Chinatown Comedy unto Itself

Any narrative proceeds in time and space, linearly or circuitously, like human life itself. Most surprising is when the plot not only thickens but flips, looping back on itself. In minority literature, such reversal of fortune from a minority's tragic disenfranchisement to, practically, a sitcom with a happy ending manifests psychological longing, even wish fulfillment. Insofar as such ethnic comedies recur in novels, films, radio plays, and graphic novels, they constellate into a multi-episode, multigenre, and decades-long serial drama produced and consumed jointly by white and nonwhite—particularly off-white, "yellow-ish," or Asian American in the case at hand—artists and audiences.[1] This series is deeply moving on occasion, yet functionally soap-opera-ish in killing time and in defusing racial tensions between the majority and minority cultures. The narrative switch from tragic irresolvability to comic resolution bespeaks the psychic need for an exit from an existential condition with no exits. That these imaginary exits feel good but, ultimately, fail is evident in the fact that ethnic comedy persists like a never-ending saga, a story retold time and time again for it is simply that: a good story.

This cultural addiction to nice and satisfying conclusions comes about despite such stories' structural weakness and illogic. The stories routinely

---

1. See my *Off-White: Yellowface and Chinglish by Anglo-American Culture* (2020).

reach a climax of conflicts, only to be swept away in a dramatic turn of events on the closing pages or scenes. Morphing from initial social realism, artists reach for magical thinking as the "out." A paltry tag-on turns tears into smiles, even smiling through tears, all for the bittersweet bang, trading collective racial strife for individual triumph. The white world, invisible and Godlike, looms over and interpellates Asian America penning the last lines in, what else, English to be consumed by, who else, the Anglophone public. The off-white characters' losses and wins must translate into sales in and for the white world. Hence, straitjacketed Asian American characters extricate themselves by moving between two states of being, most prominently displayed in transit, such as through the ambivalent physical space of Chinatown apartment stairs as well as Chinatown itself, the clashing of private sexuality and public sentiment, and the translingual style of Chinglish. Louis Chu's 1961 classic novel *Eat a Bowl of Tea,* Wayne Wang's 1989 film adaptation, Alice Wu's 2004 film *Saving Face,* and Lulu Wang's 2016 radio play and subsequent film adaptation *The Farewell* (2019) serve to illustrate this ethnic liminality.

From the 1960s to the new millennium, Chinatown comedies shuttling between two states of being have formed a subgenre, a semi-spinoff from the American road movie: only half because, paradoxically, they appear to go somewhere out of Chinatown, upwardly mobile, but stay frozen within it discursively, if not physically. Chinatown presupposes a site within a foreign land, a circumscribed space that had been born amid white persecution of Chinese coolies after the transcontinental railroad was completed in 1869 and their "cheap labor" judged to be a threat by nativists. The Chinese Must Go! movement on the West Coast engendered the Chinese Exclusion Act (1882–1943), forcing Chinese to congregate in coastal cities for safety. Since its inception, Chinatown spells entrapment by and within America. On the other hand, for many Americans of Chinese descent eager to embrace the future, Chinatown denotes a moribund ancestral culture and the catering to white, touristy taste. For some, Chinatown is a home away from home. For others, it is a bondage to the past. Between the two extreme forms of survival strategy, an in-and-out movement informs Chinatown comedy, ending happily via the deus ex machina. This final deliverance veils the contradiction of Chinese bodies in motion and in stasis *at once,* going places and going nowhere. America's unwanted guests turn into hosts of Chinatown exclusives narrated by Asian American artists deemed newsworthy by American readers and viewers. Characters' alleged mobility entails an M. C. Escher–esque walk up and down Chinatown apartment stairs, stopping at the staircase landing, taking the elevator or the subway train, and departing from and returning to the ethnic enclave.² The Möbius strip–style circularity spins like a hamster wheel, to the delight of Chinatown hamsters and white owners. The body stays still, more or less, while moving, just as Chinatown is locked within a mere tofu square of city blocks, yet forever vibrating, spilling over with residents and tourists. The body is never alone, invariably in pursuit of happiness by way of melodramatic romance and the prospect of a family. In its enigmatic duality, Chinatown is the synecdoche of Chineseness or Chinese diaspora: Americans of Chinese descent take leave of the ancestral language and culture yet remain "perennial aliens" in the public eye. "You can take yourself out of Chinatown," to Sinologize the misogynist American saying on the Chinatown "girl," "but you can't take Chinatown out of you."³

Ethnic Comedy out of Tragedy

A social comedy and a novel of manners, *Eat a Bowl of Tea* depicts New York's postwar Chinatown bachelor community with a scarcity of women and families, a direct result of the Chinese Exclusion Act that had barred most Chinese from entry for half a century. Passed by Congress, signed and upheld by various presidents in consonance with America's xenophobic ethos, this US law aimed to drain the Chinese communities of any lifeblood, to let the ethnic minority wither and die. They would be made to, to revise Dylan Thomas's refrain, "go gentle into that good night," as these aliens were largely muted, unseen anyway to the white world. Louis Chu's aging bachelors, many of whom had left their wives in Guangdong and lived as de facto widowers for decades, gossip endlessly about sexual liaisons within the ghetto, the only excitement available to these retirees with no families in their old age and little resources beyond sustenance of a meager living. Chattering away about individual transgressions maintains moral standards and social cohesion while perversely satisfying their repressed manhood. In crude and vulgar hometown dialect, Chu deftly chronicles bachelors' conversations in Cantonese-inflected English, a Chinglish in the best sense of the word. Linguistically, *Eat* appears to inhabit the fissure between two languages, quite a sleight of hand

---

2. I am referring specifically to Escher's 1951 *House of Stairs*, where staircases intertwine like a Möbius strip with centipedes rolling up and down, mobile yet trapped.

3. The Victor Wong character in Wayne Wang's *Dim Sum* comments on Geraldine leaving with her boyfriend yet immediately returning to her mother in Chinatown once she learns that her mother is ill: "You can take the girl out of Chinatown, but you can't take Chinatown out of the girl."

in secreting shadows of a mother tongue within an Anglophone novel through and through. The appearance of linguistic doubleness while deploying English and English only stems from spatial ambiguity: Chu's Little China unto itself, as though apart from the Big Apple or Big America. Linguistically and spatially, Chu gives the impression of the Other, yet he never ventures far from English and America.

Chu accomplishes this feat, for he knows the old world as well as the "new" world of Chinatown. In fact, the new resembles the old, especially when assimilation is well-nigh nonexistent among New York Chinese of the 1940s and 1950s: the same dialect, marriage banquet, and human relationships. Chu knows both China and America well, for he himself is an in-between figure. Emigrated at the age of nine, Chu is akin to both his protagonists: the immigrant father Wang Wah Gay, who runs the Money Come Club, a mahjong club in an apartment basement, and his son Wang Ben Loy, who emigrated at seventeen, served in the US Army during World War II, and returned to China before the Communist takeover to marry Lee Mei Oi, a life trajectory mirroring Chu's own. All but a bride in an arranged marriage, Mei Oi is the daughter of Lee Gong, Wah Gay's confidant in Chinatown. Like many an Asian American novelist, Chu favors alternating points of view to straddle the immigrant generation and second-, American-born generation. Strictly speaking, Chu and, to some extent, Ben Loy fall into the 1.5-generation. Unlike other Asian American novelists, such as Amy Tan's *The Joy Luck Club* (1989), launching the white gaze at San Francisco's Chinatown, Chu is an insider well versed in the intricacy of the ghetto's politics and sexual politics.

The story revolves around the newly wed Ben Loy and Mei Oi. Prior to his marriage and unbeknownst to his father, Ben Loy has been leading a double life with his restaurant colleague and roommate Chin Yuen, frequenting and frequented by various white prostitutes, so much so that he contracted venereal diseases. However, Ben Loy is not unique in this "active," even promiscuous, lifestyle. Absent sexual partners amid the bachelor community in the pre-civil-rights era rampant with miscegenation and discrimination, Wah Gay and other old-timers had availed themselves of similar "entertainment" during their lonely sojourns toiling in the US. While perfectly capable in bed in their Guangdong hometown right after wedding, Ben Loy develops erectile dysfunction at "All Seas Hotel" in Hong Kong en route to America, a condition that persists in New York (65). Fine on homeland, Ben Loy loses his virility at sea, so to speak. Diagnosed by doctors as a psychological rather than physiological problem, Ben Loy's symptom stems from the symbolic castration of Chinese America in white colonies of Hong Kong and New York's Chinatown. This "racial castration," in David Eng's words, explains the miraculous restoration, albeit temporarily, of Ben Loy's manhood on vacation in Washington, DC, and in the happy ending, presumably lasting into the future, by "eating a bowl of tea" prescribed by a San Francisco herbalist.[4]

Before the happy ending, though, Ben Loy's inadequacy is exploited by Ah Song, a Chinatown dandy in his forties, forcing himself on a disillusioned Mei Oi in a scandalous extramarital affair. The assignation becomes part of Chinatown lore. Wah Gay avenges the family and community honor by slicing off Ah Song's left ear on the staircase of his daughter-in-law's apartment, apparently after the lovers' tryst. Contrary to immigrant aversion to white authority, Ah Song files battery charges at the New York Police Department. The Chinatown association kicks into high gear in response, commanding Ah Song drop all charges, banishing him for a period of five years, with which Ah Song complies resentfully. Sex becomes politics, sexual politics, to be precise, where power informs what happens in bed and in the boardroom. Too ashamed to stay, Ben Loy and Mei Oi as well as their fathers, Wah Gay and Lee Gong, quit New York. The couple recommits to a family life on the West Coast. A dramatic turn in the concluding chapter has Ben Loy regain his manliness after eating a bowl of tea. In their postcoital joy, the couple muses upon the newborn's second "haircut party" to which both fathers would be invited as honored guests (250).

A family reunion over an infant who is, not to mince words, illegitimate, misbegotten by Ah Song! Chinese America hates Ah Song, a transgressive, pardon the expression, bastard, yet it loves the bastard he sires. Instinctively, the bachelor community grasps its own role as a mere extra on the American stage, eerily similar to the loner Ah Song without family and support network. Despite this subconscious acknowledgment of the bastard's bastard, the community evinces a split psyche in outlawing Ah Song. Way Gay's cousin, Wang Chuck Ting, the Wang Association leader, adroitly effects the political reality by way of a magisterial oratory. Chuck Ting identifies Wah Gay with every member potentially threatened by Ah Song. From one single criminal act, Chuck Ting shifts to communal harmony, bypassing US laws as well as individual responsibility (221). While expelling the offender surnamed Jo, a rare one in Chinatown, the Wangs and the Lees and the rest acquiesce to accepting a stray's stray into the fold. A minor happy ending for a minority which can ill-afford to be choosy.

Indeed, the chain reaction of the incident renders casting blame next to impossible, particularly when the chain reaction works both ways. A

---

4. See David Eng's *Racial Castration* for a psychoanalytical approach to the representation of Asian America.

chicken-or-egg debate lurks over the identity of the culprit and the genesis of the crime. In a tautological fashion, Wang Wah Gay wields the "razor-sharp knife" in retaliation for Ah Song's violation of Mei Oi, which makes the Wangs "lose face," shaming them publicly (183). The extramarital liaison is partially self-induced by Ben Loy, whose impotence drives Mei Oi away. Anecdotally, Ben Loy's condition is traced back to his consorting with white prostitutes, a personal chapter out of a collective history of oppression under racist laws robbing Chinese America of any hope for love and family. True to its name, the Chinese Exclusion Act excludes, legislatively keeping America's body politic white, an intact, nonporous bulb, a blue-blooded phallus, ready to bloom and inseminate unsullied. Yet the story of the phallus comes after that of the stairs, a transitional space for a person to go up or down gradationally. As a figure of speech, the stairs map out the steps a penis on that person takes to raise or lower itself.

Stare at the Stairs

Given the limbo state in which Chu's Chinatown finds itself, the recurring motif of apartment stairs merits attention. The stairs denote a work in progress, leading to the rape by Ah Song and, subsequently, turning into the crime scene against him. One ascends the stairs to one's apartment, the proverbial castle and refuge from street noise and social chaos, only to descend the stairs once again for one's livelihood. Ascend and descend pun with assent and dissent. Homecoming upstairs is ideally what the heart desires, most agreeable. In reverse, one descends into what the Chinese call "the Red Dust," a world fraught with conflict and dissension. This conventional scenario ignores, however, the cases where home traumatizes and street liberates. Beyond wordplay on ascend/descend and assent/dissent, the rise-fall rhythm by way of stairs transports us to the heart of Louis Chu's novel, where everything begins to go awry.

In chapter 20, the Cantonese bride Mei Oi tries to cool herself in the stifling July heat of crammed Chinatown apartment buildings by throwing open and sitting at the apartment door, "lift[ing] the bottom of her dress above her knees." Tactilely, the raised dress allows the breeze to stroke her calves, up her thighs, and further up. The cooling, caressing air also brings, ominously, Ah Song "coming up the stairs," whose "bobbing head" turns Mei Oi's face "crimson." "As soon as his eye level came up to the landing," Mei Oi is spied "sitting by the open door." The bobbing head with eyes peeking across the landing means staring straight up from the floor below at Mei Oi's "exposed legs" before she manages to "pull the hem of her dress down over her knees" (92–93). The eyes evoke the periscope of a submarine scouting for any opening by the Chinatown playboy Ah Song. The low-angle glance is thrown from, in a manner of speaking, the glans penis, known in Chinese as *guitou*, turtle head. Guitou comes across as an apt figure of speech for the round tip of the male member; they appear to be sp(l)itting image of each other. The turtle rears its ugly head, straightening itself, tensing up, for the "fresh meat" that blushes.

Mei Oi's face turns crimson as blood rushes into her cheeks out of embarrassment and shame. Such blood coursing through her veins is driven by the bobbing head and peeping eyes from below the landing, up into Mei Oi's dress. The rising blood reddens the innocent Mei Oi's face and hardens the philanderer Ah Song's penis about to achieve its full erection in the sexual harassment and assault. What transpires inside Mei Oi's apartment is a case of statutory rape, nonconsensual sex, but one veiled as an incremental, stairlike ravishing where Mei Oi is bound by traditional etiquette to invite Ah Song in, never thinking that he would accept. Ah Song proceeds to manipulate her, step by careful step, through cruel truth and outright lies. Chipping away Mei Oi's defense with the truth of her bridegroom Ben Loy's past dalliance "at the local whorehouses" and the deception of his family wealth in Canada and passion for the bride here and now, Ah Song touches his nose repeatedly, subconsciously acknowledging his Pinocchio itch from the facial organ that substitutes for the Freudian phallus (94). Facial features, Freud argues, displace the penis and vulva, as Ah Song's punishment also comes in the form of a symbolic castration of the sheared-off left ear, a biblical, Cain-style face branding that Ah Song bears whichever Chinatown he scurries off to.[5]

One delay tactic Ah Song resorts to requires scrutiny, for it doubles back to the novel's title: "Brew me a cup of tea and I'll leave," thirsty on a hot day, as it were. While "the trapped steam started to escape from the lid," a compliant Mei Oi "gingerly flipped open the lid, threw in a fingerful of Jasmine tea leaves, and quickly let the cover down" (97–98). Dried tea leaves soak up boiling water, spreading out from the curled-up, parched form, born again in fragrance and taste. In theory, the ritual of hospitality unfolds in this give-and-take circulation: offering a cup of tea to quench the guests' thirst, to provide a quick fix to the caffeine urge, and to lubricate *guanxi* or social networking. Such flow of goodwill in sharing fragrant liquids comes to a screeching halt. The piping hot liquid full of bloated leaves is neglected in favor of Ah Song's penis pulsing with blood, full of semen, which ultimately impregnates Mei

---

5. Scattered through his oeuvre, Freud theorizes the phallic fetishizing of facial features. Most prominent is "Fetishism" (1927), where the "shine on the nose" creates "a substitute for the penis" (198).

Oi. The newly wed Mei Oi resembles tea leaves steeped in desire for months, waiting to be savored by Ben Loy, whose impotence leaves her cold, curled, and dried up. Coerced by Ah Song to perform the ritual of brewing, Mei Oi unknowingly becomes the tea, downed forcibly by the surrogate mate Ah Song. From one supposedly serving tea, Mei Oi herself turns into the drink and then the compulsive drinker, so famished for love that she grows to welcome Ah Song's passionate kisses. Indeed, she is hooked, eagerly plotting the next rendezvous. She clings to her rapist as if addicted, a textbook case of Stockholm syndrome. The role reversal of tea brewer and tea drinker, host and guest, parallels multiple transferences in this scene. The ambiguity of stairs for homecoming and the rapist's coming—arriving and ejaculating—repeats itself in tea that doubles as social lubricant and sexual lubricant.

While the tea leaves sit and breathe, Ah Song gets up to rape in the guise of fervent passion from "a little boy wanting something—desperately begging, pleading. Like that beggar man in Sunwei," part of Mei Oi's childhood memory from Guangdong. Instead of the deflowering predator, Ah Song feigns to be the weak supplicant. Unbeknownst to Ah Song, his ploy conjures up Mei Oi's association with the hometown beggar, who used to "call out over the top of the half doors: *Good little girl, have a kind heart and give me something to eat*" (93). What a labyrinth of psychological and cinematic montages of self versus other; of the younger self versus the older self; and of the "tramp" of loose morals "knitting a green hat" for Ben Loy versus the "tramp" who is poised to trample her, her marriage, and her community! The Sunwei vagrant pleading for food over the half doors collapses subliminally with Ah Song's turtle head barely over the landing, soliciting. Half doors, by design, are not full-length, just as the landing is situated between floors. Both signal embryonic places for those neither in nor out, with ulterior motives for the "good little girl" or the good woman. The girl once imagined herself magnanimous in sharing food; the good woman "so rudely forced," in T. S. Eliot's words in *The Waste Land* (1922), now fancies a lover by offering her body as food.

Between the crime of rape and its punishment, both via the stairwell, the stairs are also the setting for interim pivotal moments. Rumors of Mei Oi and Ah Song's illicit relationship begin to surface when the rent collector Chong Loo "tiptoed down the stairs" and witnessed Ah Song descending from Mei Oi's apartment (111). Quite appropriately, the collector of debts initiates communal reckoning at the site of stairs, a public access to private spaces, a place on loan to renters no different from Chinatowns at the mercy of a landlord called America. Likewise, Ben Loy goes down the stairs not only to the Money Come Club to be apprised of the return trip for a bride, but also to the Wah Que Barber Shop, where he comes face to face with his disgrace. The

Cantonese opera blasting from the shop happens to play "Gim Peng Moy," featuring Pan Jinlian, the archetype of adulteress-murderess from the fourteenth-century novel *Outlaws of the Marsh*.[6] Ben Loy intuitively "compared Mei Oi to Gim Peng Moy." He quickly dismisses the thought since he has "no brother" like the one murdered in the classic (121); he misses the point since he *is* the brother cuckolded by his Chinatown "brother" Ah Song. These stairwell skirmishes culminate in Wah Gay's vengeance "hidden underneath the staircase," waiting. "The footsteps started coming down the stairs, walking rapidly but softly, as if tiptoeing," against whom Wah Gay "pulled out a razor-sharp knife" (183). The razor comparison calls forth all the sharp objects, good or ill, in the novel: the rape; the Chinese Exclusion Act; the barber shop where the affair is made public; and the haircut party.

Flow Courtesy of Blockage, Phallically and Politically

An erection, be it her clitoral or his penile, seems so instinctive that it is nothing short of a miracle, no different from the function of any other body part, from the brain down to the little toe. The three third-person singular pronouns—it, her, his—in the previous sentence's phrasal insertion already point to coital coordinational confusion, since, now and then, it fails to harden despite her or his willing it to do so, or it hardens despite her or his willing it not to do so. In heterosexual love, it/id, he, and she either work in cahoots to make it "come" or work just so-so, even worse. On the male side insofar as Chu's novel is concerned, to ejaculate, to let loose pent-up desire and semen, an erection first arises out of shutting off the corpora cavernosa, the sponge-like, blood-gorged penile tissues. The tunica albuginea is the fibrous envelope preventing blood from seeping through the veins that would lapse into the condition of erectile dysfunction. Blockage by the tube-shaped valve is key to the buildup and eventual release of biological and psychological overflow. Run-off is only possible by damming up during foreplay. Paradoxically, stemming the blood flow opens the "semenal" flow, seminal to the propagation of humanity and the well-being of the individual. Orgasmic "blast-off" presupposes voluntary withholding, bulking up with stimuli, until such point for the involuntary, albeit whole-hearted, abandonment. Should the wrap-around membrane leak, though, the bulge vanishes. Whatever is bottled up stays bottled up. No blockage, no flow.

---

6. Pan Jinlian (Pan Gold Lotus) from *Outlaws of the Marsh* reappears in the sixteenth-century pornographic *Jinpingmei* (*The Plum in the Gold Vase*). She yokes lust and the murderous drive.

Latinate anatomical terms such as the corpora cavernosa and the tunica albuginea are as resistant to memory as the legalese that effects the Chinese Exclusion Act: "That from and after the expiration of ninety days next after the passage of this act, and until the expiration of ten years next after the passage of this act, the coming of Chinese laborers to the United States be, and the same is hereby, suspended." Any idea who or what "the same is hereby" alludes to? Easier to cast both in plain English: the valve holding phallic blood is the legal shield keeping the political bloodline pure and white. Blockage of any "colored" flow enables the one flow of white semen; disabling circulation sets up phallic ableism. Erection is indubitably privileged by means of blockage, shut-down, close-off. "Build the Wall!," as a latter-day false prophet once proselytized.

The binaries are stark, favoring the exception of stiff shafts to the rule of softies. Sexual organs spend most of their lives idling, but only the rare moments when they rear up stand out, literally. The prejudice is indisputable given that a stigma of a medical term—erectile *dys*function—is devised based on the negativity of "dys," not to mention the "im" in impotence, while its counterpart—priapism of hours-long erection, resulting in tissue damage—is little known other than the mis-association with dogs getting stuck in a copulatory tie. At any event, animals' mating season is as brief as a female's estrus for days or weeks, but human beings manage to blow it up into a sex industry, perhaps the entire entertainment industry, like the Roman circus right after bread. We are conditioned to not see what is hiding in plain sight: a sleeping penis, an invisible whiteness. Instead, we miss the forest for the trees, mistaking a "hard-on" for the norm and the Chinatown hard-boiled crime and punishment for a comedy unto itself. The blindness to the American cultural context abets white invisibility and supremacy, the mastermind behind minority misery. Supremacy and misery unfold as though it were each group's respective fate. Chu plays into the White Maker's hand with his remarkable craftsmanship in Chinglish and his pathetic characterization of individual psychology in a novel of manners.

Chinglish and the Girl

At first blush, Chu's language may seem daunting. Whereas Amy Tan and certain other Asian American novelists cater to Anglophone readers, minimizing Chinese expressions to the extent of excising romanization altogether, Chu consciously or subconsciously writes for bilingual, bicultural insiders, never bothering to limit foreign-sounding words or even to gloss them. Granted, your "esteemed family name," my "insignificant name," and the like sound outdated and formal, but they faithfully reflect traditional Cantonese culture of the 1950s New York Chinatown and, down to this day, formulaic exchanges of names among Sinophone strangers in China and in Chinese diaspora. Even odd expressions of the "beautiful country" for America and the "green hat" for the cuckolded persist as part of common lexicons. Mei Oi calls Ben Loy "Loy Gaw" (Loy Brother); her father is known as "Lee Gong" (Lee Grandfather); a female relative is referred to as "Eng Shee" (surnamed Eng). These perplexing monosyllabic names are compounded by nonsensical titles of a brother for husband, a grandfather for father, and a surnamed something for a woman. Without belaboring the convoluted human relationships, suffice to say that the Chinese language and culture posit one's role in relation to others in a family tree as massive as one's hometown or homeland. In contrast to American culture's level playing field of hypothetical equality among all, a land of the so-called first-name basis, these Chinese addresses instantly place a person within a hierarchy. America idealizes the individual as sovereign and unique; China defines the personhood relative to the community.

The aforementioned is but the tip of Chu's uncompromising Chinglish; this style disorients Anglophone readers in the same way the Anglophone world estranges immigrants. Conceivably, Chu could have been duplicating the immigrant experience in the US through the defamiliarizing alternate universe of Chinatown for white readers. Truth be told, Chu simply does what comes naturally to him as a writer between two worlds. Any claim for Chu as a cultural iconoclast in a subversion of America's status quo self-destructs in view of the novel's linguistic slippages and psychological obfuscation.

Writing in English sprinkled with Cantonese, Chu embarks upon bifurcating his Chinglish to high and low, reminiscent of the duality of stairs, of tea, and of the genre of tragicomedy. His Chinglish is split between the high-flown and the crass, abusive rhetoric of the bachelor community. The exaggerated, euphemistic language is deployed in formal gatherings, deliberately elevating the others at the expense of self-effacement. At the wedding banquet for Ben Loy and Mei Oi, for instance, Wang Chuck Ting, president of the Wang Association, lowers his own position by introducing several vice presidents as presidents. At the other end of the spectrum, bachelors fling profanities at one another not so much to offend as to solidify close bonding and to exhibit intimacy.

At the Money Come Club prior to the falling out, mahjong players trade insults: "Many-mouthed bird, go sell your ass," "You dead boy" (16); "Shut up your mouth," "Wow your mother" (17). The awkwardness of these phrases is downright refreshing, translated from Cantonese without Anglicization, although "wow" does sanitize the f-word. "Shut up your mouth" seems redundant, but that is precisely how the Chinese silence others. It is to Chu's credit that he refrains from the Americanism of "shut your trap." Left-handed compliments undergird apparent curses as well. Ah Song swears at Wah Gay "You go to hell" while yawning, a body language that transforms the foul language into a sign of their closeness (18). "Where are you going to die?" retorts Wah Gay, who later comments in Ah Song's absence that "he is a beautiful boy" (18). "Boy" is not meant to demean; rather, it indicates endearment from elders in the big family of Chinatown bachelors. Like Jews and African Americans, an oppressed minority survives by gallows humor, layered meaning, rhetorical dualism, and talking out of both sides of the mouth.

Certain slippages do mar Chu's linguistic virtuosity. The cook known as Fat Man replies to Ah Song's query about a recent film "*Ma ma foo foo,*" the meaning of which—"so-so"—is taken for granted and not glossed for Anglophone readers. This demonstrates either a conscious dismissal of the mainstream market or an unconscious misstep that would doom the novel, out of print for decades until republication in 2020. Ah Song's comeback line to Fat Man's small tip is the slangy "cheapskate" (177). Such Americanisms proliferate among bachelors' banter of "Atta boy" and more (205), a language proficiency far above the level of old-timers immersed not in English but in Little China and the old ways. On the one hand, transliteration of the Chinese language puts off English readers. On the other, Americanisms spring from Chu's head and are shoved into his characters' mouths.

Any speech act reflects psychology or the lack thereof, which is most acute in the stock character Mei Oi. Chu's depiction of Mei Oi feels "off" right from the outset. In their initial meeting arranged by matchmakers in Guangdong, she is so brazen as to approach Ben Loy for the time of their next meeting, which Wayne Wang's film adaptation preserves. Her aggressiveness betrays the flaw of over-Americanizing in Chu's characterization. Married, she comes on strong: "Do you . . . Loy *Gaw* . . . do you want to make me very happy tonight?," where the dots simulating pauses and hesitations contradict the eagerness of her solicitation (67). Her erotic innuendo is in keeping with the stereotype of "sex crazy" Americans in Wang's film. When she learns of her pregnancy, no compunction plagues her over the identity of the father. She telephones Ah Song to warn him away from their rendezvous because of her father-in-law's surprise visit bringing her traditional foodstuff for pregnant women. No sense of guilt haunts her, apparently. When Ben Loy slaps her with his shoe for the adultery, she adeptly deflects the blame, attributing it to his impotence. The Chinese symbolism of a "broken shoe" for an adulteress, as if worn or used by multiple men, is lost in this case of domestic violence. Even after exposure and Chinatown pressure, Mei Oi never quite mends her ways, pleading for Ah Song's affection in a series of love letters. Her lover does return to her arms when they resettle in New York after a brief stint at a Connecticut restaurant arranged by Wang Chuck Ting for the sake of appearances. While in Connecticut, Ben Loy's friend Chin Yuen pays them a courtesy call. Chin Yuen and Mei Oi, contravening Chinese customs, physically touch each other at one point, poised on the verge of further flirting. Both muse about the likelihood of an assignation.

Even in the couple's final showdown after Ah Song was caught not red-handed, but red-eared, outside Mei Oi's apartment, she stammers: "I have been like a crazy woman . . . What I have done is the work of a crazy woman . . . I . . . I don't blame you if you disown me" (210). Just as the reader's "first impression" of Mei Oi back in Guangdong is one of undue Americanization, Mei Oi's self-splitting into an erstwhile "crazy woman" to account for her recidivism smacks of Western psychology over a sovereign selfhood, temporarily astray but has since righted the course. To put it in modern lingo: she was not herself; she is and owns herself now. Speaking like a true Westerner, Mei Oi countenances two selves: the owner as opposed to the owned, once split but coalesced now. The Chinese tradition would be hard pressed to suffer this explanation by way of Christian born-again redemption. A Chinese was, is, and will always be oneself, in theory if not in practice. One is compelled to not only own oneself at all times, but one owes it to others to do so—a social indebtedness integral to Chineseness. Any failing to fulfill such debt obligation would result in guilt and shame, which barely grace this tragicomedy, certainly not the last pages on the happy ending. Ethnic comedy is made possible herein by ghettoizing oneself: Mei Oi and Ben Loy's conjugal bliss in the final pages that, reputedly, lifts all sorrows, theirs and their fathers' and, of course, their faraway Chinese mothers'. Generically and collectively, ethnic comedy is made possible by ghettoizing Chinatown from the white world. Indeed, white characters only cameo at the beginning as Ben Loy and Chin Yuen's prostitutes and at the end as police officers in pursuit of the slasher Wah Gay. White temptation and white authority bookend the novel, two Freudian slips in an otherwise alternate universe of Chinatown floating in a black hole that is decidedly not white. Happy endings proliferate, courtesy of proverbial Asian hard work in not seeing whiteness in, ironically, the off-white Chinatowns of Wayne Wang, Alice Wu, and Lulu Wang.

Wayne Wang's *Eat a Bowl of Tea*

With a background similar to Louis Chu, Wayne Wang broke into the film industry by way of Hong Kong, California, and independent filmmaking. His

1989 adaptation of *Eat a Bowl of Tea* debuted on PBS's American Playhouse, featuring veteran actor Victor Wong as Wah Gay, mixed-race Russell Wong as Ben Loy, and the director's wife, Cora Miao, as Mei Oi. That a tall, mixed-race Russell Wong stands in for the representative Chinese American male conjures up the specter of Henry Golding playing the lead role of *Crazy Rich Asians* in Jon M. Chu's 2018 rom-com based on Kevin Kwan's best seller. Two Asian American filmmakers—Wang and Chu—three decades apart see fit to feature mixed-race, "whitewashed" actors for Asian male leads, an implicit kowtowing to the history of racial castration of Asian masculinity and to the white preference for shades of their own likeness onscreen. Shadows of whiteness in Wong's and Golding's faces and bodies provide grounding for mainstream identification among an almost exclusively Asian cast set in Chinatown and, in Golding's case, the Sinologized metropolises of New York, London, and Singapore, as though the world is one big Chinatown, one Sinoverse.[7]

Despite their shared tactic in casting, the shift from Wayne Wang to Jon M. Chu and Alice Wu foreshadows an ecosystem of literary and filmic output that has evolved away from Hong Kong in the latter decades of the twentieth century to an American- and Chinese-based one in the twenty-first. In Wang's film, Cora Miao, Siu-Ming Lau (Lee Gong), Eric Tseng (the dandy villain Ah Song), Lydia Shum (the new apartment resident), and many more hail from Hong Kong. The British colony's dominance in film production has been taken over by China as seamlessly as the repatriation in 1997. Jon M. Chu is, of course, a Californian and his film features Awkwafina, a New Yorker. *Saving Face* is made by Alice Wu, also a New Yorker. The Chinese expatriate artists, such as Joan Chen in *Saving Face,* also contribute to the longevity of Chinatown comedy.

Part of PBS's American Playhouse, Wang's film informs and educates the public. While Louis Chu writes to insiders acquainted with the impact of the Chinese Exclusion Act on the Chinese American community, Victor Wong's voice-over in the opening scene narrates the historical context that creates the perversity of the bachelor enclave. This background knowledge is reprised by the wedding banquet's speaker, Henry Wang, who marks the momentous occasion of a Cantonese bride joining her husband in Chinatown, something unheard of for half a century. Note that both characters' elocution unfolds in a

---

7. If the white audience prefers partially white actors for identification, then what accounts for the Asian audience exhibiting the same desire for mixed-race performers? This gnawing question betrays a postcolonial psyche idolizing whiteness, be it India's Anglophiles, Taiwan's Nipponphiles, or Asia's booming business of cosmetic surgery inscribing Caucasian features of double-lidded eyes, a straight and high-ridged nose, shaved cheekbones for slender faces on Asian faces.

native speaker's English rather than a foreign accent deployed by many actors herein, to the extent of the pidginized, almost speech-impaired stammering of Siu-Ming Lau's Lee Gong. Victor Wong's slangy delivery in effect renders the Chinese immigrant story *our* story, part of the American story. The filmmaker not only tells but also shows the bachelors' dilemma as Wah Gay—not Ben Loy—visits a Chinese prostitute—not Louis Chu's white prostitute—and leaves to find a long queue of Chinese seniors waiting their turn outside the door. This appalling ratio imbalance repeats itself at the dance hall, where young Chinese men stand three deep, listening to a songstress's "Slow Boat to China." Whereas "no boat to Chinese women" seems more accurate, it is the scarcity, the impossibility that intensifies and romanticizes the object of desire—the Orient nearly beyond reach for the songwriter Frank Loesser's intended white ears in 1948, a tune rerecorded by all-American singers from Bing Crosby to Liza Minnelli. That consuming Oriental vision turns into a real-life itch, a chronic pain, for Wah Gay and his look-alike lookers-on.

Louis Chu's over-Americanization is woefully enacted in Cora Miao's Mei Oi. In their initial arranged meeting in the countryside of Guangdong, Mei Oi makes a face by crossing her eyes, breaking the ice and eliciting Ben Loy's giggles. This prank jars against her shy, coquettish demeanor elsewhere. At the village square, against the screen showing Ronald Colman and Jane Wyatt's *Lost Horizon* (1937), the lovers, both onscreen and off, make a pledge to each other, whereby Mei Oi takes the initiative of kissing Ben Loy. Her forwardness is well-nigh anachronistic for a rural girl of the late 1940s and foreshadows a tragedy of sorts. Jane Wyatt's accelerated aging once outside the Shangri-la parallels Ben Loy's "aging" into an old man's loss of potency once outside his ancestral land as well as Mei Oi's "rotting" of her moral fiber.

Ben Loy's erectile dysfunction is attributed by the film to two causes. The first one is explicit. Kissing Mei Oi in bed, Ben Loy reaches for Wah Gay's photograph on the night table to lay it face-down. The flattened picture fails to raise his penis, which is chalked up to "too many people watching" by a frustrated Ben Loy. Indeed, mahjong players and barbershop customers bandy about, incessantly, over whether Mei Oi's belly has begun to protrude and whether Ben Loy is "No Can Do." As opposed to the first cause, the second cause is only implied. One of the rare moments when Ben Loy is "up" to it, a white woman, apparently paying her old client a visit, disrupts their conjugal plan. Disappointments and obstructions such as these lead to a teary Mei Oi, chanced upon by Ah Song at the subway stairs, serendipitously echoing Louis Chu's apartment staircase. Wayne Wang deletes the subsequent rape scene, turning it into a scared yet titillated Mei Oi half-inviting, half-submitting to the rakish Ah Song, with Eric Tseng's signature sneer of a smile.

A tragedy seems destined when the protagonists scatter in the wake of the ear-slashing. In utter disgrace, Wah Gay is bound for Havana, Lee Gong for Chicago, and the couple for San Francisco where they landed together years before, suggesting a reset and a second chance. This scenario is strengthened when Mei Oi, in practically the penultimate scene, produces a packet of herbal medicine she has special ordered from China "guaranteed" to cure Ben Loy. Wayne Wang has expedited the healing before the couple even reaches the West Coast. Nonetheless, as the two "grandfathers" bid farewell in front of a shuttered Money Come Club, this could conceivably be the finale where little is resolved. This ending with no end in sight would reflect faithfully the American chronic paranoia over the Yellow Peril, the Chinese Exclusion Act, the internment of Japanese Americans, the Trumpian "Kung Flu," the spate of anti-Asian hate crimes concurrent with COVID-19, and the next relapse sure to come in a long-running series. This American serial drama has cast Asian America as Ah Song the interloper who pays dearly with a body part. Americatown's—not Chinatown's—symbolic castration of Asian America is displaced onto ethnic self-mutilation, from youthful debauchery to marital impotence to extramarital affairs to extrajudicial revenge. Perhaps to compensate for a guilty conscience, the mainstream America of PBS, NPR, Hollywood, and popular culture welcome the "Mongoloid" aliens' American-born and/or American-trained offspring—Wayne Wang, Jon M. Chu, Alice Wu, and Lulu Wang—to tell their stories, so long as they share a nice fairy-tale closure. To stop feeling bad about what was, is, and will be done to it, Asian America tells a good story; to stop feeling bad about what it has done and is yet to do, America has a good story told.

No exception to this melodramatic formula, Wang magnifies Louis Chu's happy ending. This contrasts sharply with his earlier low-budget indie films: *Chan Is Missing* (1981) closes with Chan still missing; *Dim Sum* (1985) with Chinatown entrapment. Wayne Wang's flexibility may have landed him his next big Hollywood project, the film adaptation of Amy Tan's *The Joy Luck Club* (1993). To intimate an uplifting note despite their relocation in *Eat*, Wah Gay and Lee Gong call each other "grandpapa." The mutual address of respect heralds a familial and communal sanction of the grandchild born to Mei Oi and "that son of the bitch," as Ben Loy curses Ah Song, an expletive implicating, subconsciously, Mei Oi as the "bitch." Evidently after a lapse of many months, punctuated by Mei Oi's second pregnancy, the film concludes with the bang of the two grandfathers trimming a toddler's hair in a high chair, visually realizing the novelist's promise of a reunion at the "haircut party." In his shirt with a pronounced floral motif and riding boots, holding two Afro-Caribbean gourd maracas or rumba shakers, Wah Gay appears just arrived from a tropical vacation. This festive haircut party cleanses the shame of historical castration; it also restores the family, whereby Ah Song's lost ear is the figurative seed sowed in Moi Oi, being scissored and sculpted into the bawling toddler, giving PBS viewers an earful. Flanking the haircut are Ben Loy, busy with the all-American male pastime of barbecuing, and Mei Oi, full-bellied with Ben Loy's child this time around, bringing the birthday cake to the firstborn. Picture-perfect, the cheerful gathering has family photos snapped in the couple's backyard with white picket fences against the backdrop of the Bay Area fog, as though it were rolling in from the previous establishing shot of the Golden Gate Bridge. Out of real American serial nightmares, ethnic comedies on film reels cannot be more soothing than these freeze frames of family portraits spanning three generations, albeit sans the grandmothers, the firstborn's biological father, and unspecified missing persons, otherwise known as racial ghosts.

Alice Wu's *Saving Face*

The baton of Chinatown comedy is passed on to gay filmmaker Alice Wu. Her *Saving Face* revolves around the lesbian courtship between Wil, a surgeon about to complete her internship, and Viv, a ballerina about to turn modern dancer, both with intricate ties to the Mandarin-speaking Chinatown in Flushing, Queens, a ride away on the 7 train from Louis Chu's Cantonese-speaking lower Manhattan Chinatown. The transitional junctures of the protagonists' respective careers mirror their inchoate romance. While Viv is openly gay, Wil struggles with coming out to her traditional single mother, Hwei-Lan Gao or simply "Ma," as well as the tightly knit ethnic community. That few audiences would ever remember her foreign name mentioned just once or twice in the feature film means that she comes across as the archetypal immigrant "Ma," who has haunted Asian American culture since Maxine Hong Kingston's Brave Orchid in *The Woman Warrior* (1976), with a caricature of an afterlife in Amy Chua's *Battle Hymn of the Tiger Mother* (2011). This archetypal mother(land) is fetishized, hatefully tyrannical, unmitigatedly exasperating, yet also endearing, even mythically empowering as warrior models. From the civil-rights-era protagonist Maxine's Brave Orchid to Chua's tigress alter ego to the millennial Wil's Ma, they personify the secret ingredient of paradox that makes Asian America, that spices it up for the white clientele's palate. These alien Mas and Pas and Grandmas and Grandpas and racial ghosts give Asian America the body, literally, while breathing spirit, like well-aged wine's body of aroma and flavor, into literary and filmic ethnic comedies.

As such, the lesbian motif is ratcheted up by Ma's pregnancy without divulging the identity of her lover even under the pressure of Wil's stern grandfather, so much so that Ma is banished. When Ma lands on Wil's doorsteps, that is, the front stoops to her brownstone apartment, most likely in the adjacent borough of Brooklyn, Wil is shocked that Ma would be kicked out of the apartment Ma co-owns. The theater of the absurd finds the clown Ma in shades at night in a pathetic attempt to hide her swollen eyes, with a stuffed luggage and a supersize, eighteen-roll pack of toilet paper, squatting on the stoops. The toilet paper flung at Wil drops like the punchline for a cheap laugh. This spectacle evidently involves the grandfather, who disowns the co-owner of the property, and the "source" looming behind the father figure—the unnamed, unnameable Chineseness.

Indebtedness in lives and proprietorship of spaces in Alice Wu are as torturous as those in Louis Chu. In a series of dramatic twists, the ethnic comedy culminates in the final moments when Wil comes out of the closet by embracing and deep-kissing Viv on the Chinatown dance hall floor and when Ma finally accepts the hand of Little Yu, decades her junior. Unlike the dismemberment inflicted on the trespasser Ah Song, Alice Wu envisions a larger tent where differences in sexual orientation and age are no longer sources of shame and guilt. To be shamefaced in the community returns us to Wu's film title and to Louis Chu. Wah Gay takes drastic action because he has lost face, which he redeems by defacing Ah Song. Face, *lian* or *mianzi* in Chinese, does not immediately evoke facial features or one's look, as in "a pretty face." Rather, it amounts to the equivalent of one's reputation, dignity, even social standing. *Geimianzi* (give face) means to honor, which is how a drunken Wah Gay feels at Ben Loy's extravagant wedding banquet as Wayne Wang films it. By contrast, *diumianzi* (lose or squander face) means to be humiliated. Either flattering or discrediting, an individual is an island either lapped by social accolade or buffeted by slight in an elaborate communal guanxi or interconnectedness.

Transposed from a Chinese to an American context, Asian Americans' mianzi—their face and physique—is the racial marker to mainstream Americans, a marker they can never "lose." Nella Larsen–style passing as white is denied Asian Americans, with the possible exception of the mixed-race. Yet Chinatown comedies insulate the community as though it were an alternate universe unaffected by the larger white society. Losing of face, thus, proceeds in an entirely traditional fashion. Ma withholds her lover's identity, for revealing it would incur greater shame than the fact of her pregnancy out of wedlock. Wil dreads coming out of the closet when the closet is not so much her workplace with white and Asian American colleagues as the ethnic enclave of Flushing: she fears being flushed out in shame. Saving face, however, is hardly a translation from the Chinese language, which offers no equivalent. The provenance of the film title hails as much from Chinese mianzi as from the English expression of "face-saving." Wu coins this term that mongrelizes the positive pole of giving face and the negative pole of losing face. Yet Wu's "third wheel" of a title intimates Christian salvation, an American way out of the Chinese way, a light-hearted, humorous exit from the shadows of patriarchal authority figures and systems, either Henry Wang's pontificating speech at Ben Loy's wedding or Alice Wu's grandfather, the "Big Professor," expostulating traditional virtues at The Planet China, a club where China *is* the planet, the host, where Chineseness reigns supreme, at least within the bubble of Chinatown.

Sneaking a Christian metaphor into the Chinese-sounding title parallels Wil stealing a glance at the love interest Viv during her grandfather's long-winded, didactic public speech in Chinese. In an underhanded manner, the West is embedded in, in bed with, the East. The film's three-ringed structure is also set through that glance. At the center are the gay lovers with their young cohort, including Wil's African American "smoking buddy" Jay; immediately circumscribing and policing Wil and Viv are their families—Wil's hospital supervisor happens to be Viv's father, and Viv would soon squirm under the scrutiny of Wil's Ma; the outermost circle consists of the older immigrant generation, both Mandarin- and Shanghainese-speaking, swapping gossip and community goings-on. The great water in which the triple ripples appear and vanish is absent, however. The white host society remains imperceptible, although it penetrates the lovers' professions in Western medicine of surgery and in ballet–modern dance, not to mention their speech, behavior, and mentality. Wil is to practice in New York hospitals; Viv lands a dance contract in Paris. Even the titular Chinese face, where all the trouble began and where the comedy ultimately resides, is both denied and cherished in the brisk opening scene à la Hollywood rom-com when Wil waits impatiently to peel off her facial cleansing mask, accompanied by light, fast-tempo music of strings and accordion.

Films outstrip novels in bilingual potential, since non-English-speaking actors with the aid of subtitles are free to deliver lines in their native tongues, which can only be accomplished in Anglophone novels through strings of nonsensical, disconcerting romanization of foreign words, to be followed by glosses in English. What feels natural onscreen, once the audience is accustomed to reading subtitles while watching, presents an insurmountable obstacle on the page. In his oeuvre, Wayne Wang's *Eat a Bowl of Tea* does not stand out in its use of Cantonese. Native speakers' Mandarin, Shanghainese, and Cantonese have long graced Wang's films, complemented by non-native-speakers' mangled Chinese dialects. Hong Khaou also avails himself of bilingual performers like Pei-Pei Cheng in *Lilting* (2014). Tapping into this film tradition, Alice Wu takes full advantage in key scenes, synchronizing bilingualism with the film's movement between contraction or recoil from the foreign and relaxation or attraction to kindred souls.

In terms of reception, the immigrant generation is alienating to the English-speaking American public, who are drawn instead to the young US-born generation speaking English and behaving in the American way. While distanced from non-English-speaking immigrant "clowns" like Ma, the American audience would identify with, for instance, Wil and Viv at the vending machine on the hospital staircase landing, which Americanizes Louis Chu's foreign setting of Chinatown stairwell. Viv's nasal sounds disapproving of Wil's choice of junk food at the vending machine because "your body knows what you want" come close to orgasmic moans, intimating their mutual attraction. But what the heart desires in a lesbian love repels the ethnic community; the sugar and adrenaline high Wil's body craves is deemed bad for the body politic of Chinatown. Intuitively, American viewers grasp the irony of healthy and junk food, homoeroticism and heteronormativity. It requires more reflection when the third wheel—Ma—is added to the dialogue.

Because Viv insists on meeting Wil's Ma, the three dine together at Wil's apartment, now taken over by Ma. The bilingual code-switching at the dinner table is lopsided to privilege the one in power—Ma. To ingratiate herself with Ma, Viv tries to accommodate, whereas Ma stays well within her comfort zone of the Chinese language, which reflects the overall illusion of Chinatown comedy unto itself. Even before witnessing how Viv wipes off the grease on Wil's thigh, Ma senses their intimacy and deliberately puts down Viv's profession, *wunü*. The subtitle's translation of "a Go-go dancer" is a rung up from the original of "a taxi dancer" or even a prostitute, which Wil takes care to elide in her translation for Viv. Groping for Chinese words in response to Ma's rapid-fire queries, Viv struggles to reciprocate: "*wozai* [I at] New York City Ballet." Her body tensing, looking toward Wil for help, Viv's two labored Chinese words segue into the English proper noun too difficult to translate. Haltingly, Viv carries on the conversation in partial Chinese. She once again contorts her mouth and tongue to articulate three foreign words "*xianzai wo*" (right now I), accompanied by the unseemly, working-class gesture with her chopsticks pointing in the air. Giving up the effort, Viv lets flow the rest of the sentence in English: "taking a break *tiao* [dance] modern," with the sole verb giving the semblance of Chinese. Viv's code-switching comes at great physical and psychological costs, as if she enunciates the few Chinese words with the force of her whole being, before reverting back to the spontaneous "modern [dance]." That she skips "dance" in "modern dance" only illustrates her confidence in communicating in English. Viv's Chinese repertoire, by comparison, is woefully limited; even the repetition of *"wozai"* with a minor addition and reshuffle, *"xianzai wo,"* requires a deep breath before the relaunch. Asian Americans like Viv are caught in this awkward position: Americans view them as perennial aliens speaking alien tongues; Chinese take it for granted that they speak their heritage language. This minority condition is akin to orphanhood, misconceived by both linguistic legacies. Artists like Alice Wu, equipped with W. E. B. Du Bois's double consciousness, transform a minus into a plus by critiquing both linguistic parents in an insider-outsider, personal-clinical way that only an orphan is capable of.

Halfway through the precarious bilingual dinner, Viv's most fluent Chinese phrase *"nide* baby *haoma?"* ("Your baby fine?"), referring to Ma's unborn child, freezes all conversations, until Ma cleverly deflects to her "baby" girl Wil by touching Wil's cheek, a face-saving strategy in front of the next generation. That Viv would bring up such a taboo subject only highlights how Americanized she is. More attuned to the Chinese way, Wil represses more and magnifies each of Viv's muscle tensions, particularly when Ma seems cornered by Viv's query on her pregnancy. The-guest-turned-hostess lording over Wil's apartment and dining table, Ma embodies Chinatown comedy utterly unconcerned with the white, English-speaking host society and a "whitened" Viv. The only occasion where Ma ventures an English word, "China," to inquire after Chinese-language films at a DVD rental store lands her in the porn section. Even the one brief puncture of the Chinese bubble contributes to the comedy's laugh track. Much is sidestepped for Wu's Chinatown comedy to come to fruition. To put it bluntly, i.e., viscerally, the split-second tenseness of Viv's body groping for Chinese words or of Ma's body for English words, before easing back to their natural form, symbolizes the chronic immigrant condition with no letup, 24/7, in America, except in the dreamscape while Ma binges on Chinese soap operas.

The dinner is only one of many scenes where generations and cultures clash. Alice Wu montages East and West in a series of shots featuring the grandfather doing his morning Tai Chi at a basketball court while inner-city African American youths walk by and hail him. The Tai Chi shadow boxing looks fake, with half-hearted, truncated, out-of-balance steps and pushes that only seem authentic, worthy of hailing, to outsiders. This "airy" scene of a senior in slow motion, feigning union with the transcendent *qi* or *chi* (air, mythical energy as in kung fu and wuxia films), resonates with a subsequent scene on the rooftop, where smoking buddies Wil and Jay share the young people's recreational moment inhaling another kind of air. "Aren't you going to see Vivian off at the airport?" Jay asks, stunned by the lovers' going separate ways. In response, Wil flicks her wrist holding the cigarette and shrugs: "We broke up." As though a copycat, Jay shrugs and flicks his wrist in adolescent mannerisms: "So?" Wil once again repeats the same body language and line with slightly raised, agitated voice: "We broke up." The back-and-forth simulation looks downright rude to the Chinese audience, shrugging off the lovers' crisis and flicking off the confidant Jay's concern. But to the American audience, the mirroring pretense of nonchalance and coolness strengthens the bond, as they duplicate each other's body language and words. The minimalist American body language alienates the Chinese but looks just about right to the American. By contrast, the faked Tai Chi half-moves are kitschy, nonsensical to the Chinese but wow the American, making a great deal of paranormal sense. Cultural literacy in one means illiteracy in the other; seeing through the chicanery in one means being blind to that of the other.

The double happy ending starts when Wil discovers the love letter hidden in the packet of herbal medicine for the pregnant Ma. Wil assumes that she has chanced upon the identity of the father—the herbalist Old Yu, whose medicine his son Little Yu delivers to Wil at the subway station. Reading the unnamed missive, Wil's accented Mandarin changes to Old Yu's voice-over when the letter vehemently rejects public censure of their love. Even Wil with her own transgressive sexual orientation instinctively presumes that the age-appropriate Old Yu is the mysterious father rather than the young lover hiding in plain sight: Little Yu who handed the herbal medicine to her. The subtitle does not translate a key phrase in the letter, *banicong mingyun de jiasuoli jiefang chulai* (把你從命運的枷鎖裡解放出來 to liberate you from the shackles of fate). The first part condemns Chinese women's traditional shackles of social roles. Note that social constructs of oppression against women are displaced upon the abstraction of mingyuen or fate. What is man-made, literally, turns into heaven-made, if not self-made by having been born *The Second Sex*, as in Simone de Beauvoir's 1949 classic. The latter phrase *jiefang* calls forth the liberation of China by the Communists in 1949, yet this rhetorical origin underlines the irony that Wil's Ma finds emancipation in the land of the free, an American freedom from Chinese patriarchy embodied by her father. Both historical misogyny and the geopolitical message are lost in the subtitles.

Armed with this misidentification, Wil crashes Ma's wedding with an Old Cho under her father's direction, a face-saving tactic before the imminent birth. Just as the reverend intones *zaizhude mianqian* (在主的面前 before the Lord or, literally, before the face of the Lord), Wil stops the proceeding, pointing to Ma's supposed lover Old Yu in attendance. It climaxes when Little Yu stands up instead to declare his love. The grandfather bemoans *wodelian dougeini diuguangle* (我的臉都給你丟光了 all my face is lost for your sake).

The chaotic and hilarious energy of this ending harks back to the film title when both the Christian God's and the Chinese grandfather's faces are forsaken for true love. Neither face shows up in subtitles, which are, after all, a quixotic quest for faithful rendition.

Like Wayne Wang's coda of sorts after a lapse of months, Alice Wu's coda "three months later," as the intertitle makes clear, returns to the dance floor of The Planet China, where Wil finally braces herself to kiss Viv in public, their love a late bloom amid the waltz that takes not only paired dancers but also a "village"—the Chinese community—spinning in sync. The duality of distance-*cum*-closeness, or in-and-out in Wu's happy ending, testifies to the classic Asian American conundrum. After dismissing the communal gaze with a synchronized "f— them!," Wil and Viv embrace and kiss in a vertical, high-angle shot. The lovers' still center defies the community, but it is anchored within a frame surrounded by waltz dancers at The Planet China, all whirling around them. The lovers disowned by and disowning the Chinese heterosexual family constitute the unmoved mover of the mise-en-scène, blessed by the choreography of the same community.

The joyous kinetics of dancers extends to closing credits, interspersed with scenes of the best of all possible worlds. Hence, the grandfather intends to stop by to ensure that the newborn grandchild not be "contaminated," veiling his affection under the façade of righteous admonition. Viv's divorced parents complain about modern dance but take comfort in the fact that Viv is at least marrying a doctor, the ideal Asian American profession, gender notwithstanding. Even Ma enjoys her freedom so much that she forbids Little Yu from moving in.

From Chinatown to Sinoverse Comedy

Fairly familiar with the New York cityscape, I made an educated guess regarding Wil's Brooklyn residence based on the subway ride she takes to the City through the Manhattan Bridge parallel to the Brooklyn Bridge.[8] Fairly familiar with first-generation immigrantscape, myself being one like Wil's Ma, I have no need to guess when I call out the cultural typecast of schizoid immigrants.

---

8. Not only the subway to and from Brooklyn, but I also wager that Wil's Ma's aborted wedding takes place at East Manor Restaurant and Catering (豪庭王朝 *Haoting Wangchao*), renamed Good Fortune Restaurant, on 46–45 Kissena Blvd., Flushing, New York. While the square colophon of the Chinese logo *Haoting Wangchao* (Grand Court Dynasty) remains on the shop façade, the name has been changed from its regal-sounding avatar to fortune-cookie-style chinoiserie.

For novelists, immigrant characters' alleged psychic schism has long been a tempting and expedient trope, given the bicultural, bilingual existence. Dear Reader, has it ever occurred to you to question this prevailing conundrum of how immigrant clowns like the shamefaced Wil's Ma morph in the same breath into crowning racial pride, such as the single mom in defiance of the world? How is it possible that headless immigrants speaking pidgin no better than baby English and behaving erratically, if not idiotically, turn out in Chinatown comedies to heal Asian American racial wounds and to spearhead identity formation? These Asian immigrants are the primary wound for Asian American bildungsroman that begins by identifying with, and wishing to be, mainstream whites, and that closes, happily, with pride in ethnic differences. Wil's Ma is deployed less to represent immigrant (grand)parents' neurosis than to work out Asian America's own. Projecting onto immigrant characters its split psyche, Asian America owns itself by disowning, outgrowing Asian immigrants, if only to repossess them as materials, raw or finessed, for repurposed art. Would you willingly subject yourself to the discursive slaughterhouse of contradictory extremities? Would you take on the persona of Frankenstein (de)composed of a patchwork of dead tissues and stock traits? Yet we applaud when the same old trick is played on immigrant characters and, by corollary, on you and me.

On the other hand, in our "Chinese Century," so pronounced by President Xi Jinping, Chinatown comedy has broken out of the urban ghetto in the hands of such transnationals as Kevin Kwan and Jon M. Chu. Indeed, Chinatown is as much a site as it is an inner sight seen with the mind's eye, denoting a physical place as well as a psychic space. Both you and I would call forth, effortlessly, images and sounds of Chinatown from New York, London, Paris, Milan, Yokohama, Bangkok, and whatnot. Instead of waning in an open global village, Chinatown swells into, as it were, Chinaworld neocolonized by Kwan's crazy rich Asians, scintillating with a Sinovision of life and, as in Lulu Wang's *The Farewell,* death, among other practitioners. Liberated from Chinatown historically secreted within America, Chinaworld of the future gobbles up the fictitious universe, mutating into a Sinoverse that obviates the multiracial America and global multiverse. Discursively, Sinoverse operates unto itself, a Sinocentric cosmos as hermetically sealed as Louis Chu's and Alice Wu's New York Chinatowns, crystallized in Wu's film set of The Planet China.

From the Western perspective, though, Kwan's crazy rich is the code word for filthy rich with biblical filthy lucre. By the same token, Lulu Wang's extended Chinese family lying to a terminally ill grandmother lapses into the unflattering conceit of Oriental duplicity. Out of love, relatives from China,

America, and Japan weave an intricate web of deception to protect the matriarch from the truth of her lung cancer, which leaves her with only three months to live. The "benign shadow" on the MRI scan is somehow kept at bay three years after the diagnosis. Not knowing effects the grandmother not dying in a land so far away that ignorance is bliss, where science and shared knowledge succumb to myth-making and secrecy, a melodramatic re-enactment of Louisa Lim's *The People's Republic of Amnesia* (2014). While Lim the reporter lays out political (self-)censorship over the Tiananmen Square Massacre on June 4, 1989, Wang the raconteur retails the soft, affective power of the Sinoverse. Passed down from Chinatown's immigrants to Sinoverse's Chinese is the image of the Other, equally dichotomized, both endearing and estranging.

Lulu Wang's feature film derives from her short radio play "In Defense of Ignorance" on NPR's *This American Life*. That a long Chinese filmic adieu is originally aired on the American broadcast institution sums up the millennial Sinoverse comedy, where the storyteller Lulu Wang's ancestral and creative ties—blood-wise, money-wise, and symbolic-capital-wise—point as much to China as to America. These artists come equipped with a double vision seeing far into as well as in microscopic close-up of both lands. From the radio play's self-described "lone Westerner" narrator implicated reluctantly in a well-intentioned, life-saving Chinese lie, Wang interlaces Old China with New America, old Orientalist fallacy with new ethnic wokeness. This singular Western point of view provides the grounding for Anglophone spectatorship no less than Russell Wong's mixed-race face or Wil's and Viv's American sensibility. In the circle that revolves around exiting and revisiting Chinatown, ascending and descending stairs, eating tea and being eaten, Lulu Wang climbs up in the Anglophone world by digging to the other side of the earth through the Sinoverse rabbit hole. Wang's *The Farewell* is the latest reanimation of a series of fairy tales with predictable outcome, of which we are bound to hear more in the rise and fall of the Chinese Century contesting the American Century.

This shall be the forever war of our time waged by, not USA vs. PRC, but DSA vs. XRC. The *Dis*united States of America captures well the divided, bipolarized post-Trump America; the *X* stands for President Xi's People's Republic of China as well as the X-factor for whichever "emperor" is to succeed him. So devoid of self-reflection, so alike in their cultish fanaticism, the West's far right and the East's far left are doppelgangers. For either party, literally, either Lincoln's Party betrayed by Judases from Nixon to Trump or Marxist Messianism bedecking Mencian *yifu* (一夫 the "lone man" or autocrat in *The Works of Mencius* of the fourth century BC) from Mao to Xi, to be smeared as DSA or

XRC is tantamount to hate speech, to name-calling.⁹ The eyeball sees its favorite comedy and not itself, until gouged out, metaphorically speaking. Only a psychically detached eyeball can bear witness to its beloved mate's fixation on the Chinatown/Sinoverse comedy.

---

9. See Mencius's "King Hui of Liang" in *The Works of Mencius* (pt. 2, ch. 8), translated by James Legge in *The Chinese Classics, Volume 1 & 2*: "He who outrages the benevolence *proper to his nature,* is called a robber; he who outrages righteousness, is called a ruffian. The robber and the ruffian we call a mere fellow [*yifu*]. I have heard of the cutting off of the fellow Chau, but I have not heard of putting a sovereign to death, *in his case*" (167).

CHAPTER 11

Southern Woe, Minority Lens

Ride with Woodrell–Schamus–Ang Lee

Daniel Woodrell's *Woe to Live On* (1987) on the Civil War Missouri rebels, the bushwhackers, is adapted by Ang Lee as *Ride with the Devil* (1999), based on James Schamus's screenplay. Woodrell's South of deep woes comes to the big screen and the big world filtered through the minority lens of a Jewish American scriptwriter and a Taiwanese American filmmaker.[1] From 1991 to 2002, Schamus and Ted Hope's production company Good Machine contributed to bringing to mainstream audiences a string of "minority" tales, "minor" or marginal ones that find their way into American culture, including Ang Lee's *Pushing Hands* (1991), *The Wedding Banquet* (1993), *Eat Drink Man Woman* (1994), *The Ice Storm* (1997), and *Crouching Tiger, Hidden Dragon* (2000), plus Joan Chen's *Xiu Xiu: The Sent Down Girl* (1998). A New York Jewish sensibility, the other to Euro-American centrality, joins hands with the other "other" from across the Pacific Ocean. To conservative, "red-blooded" Americans, those of Jewish and Chinese descent are seen as hailing from afar, being part of America and apart from it. The notion of the minority lens strategically essentializes what appears to be a white Southern tale, parsing ethnic projections onto the "Dutch" and Black protagonists, despite artistic self-repression.

---

1. Daniel Woodrell's *Woe to Live On* takes for granted that its setting of Missouri is part of the South. Among other scholarly discussions, Michael Fellman's *Inside War* (1989) and Joseph M. Beilein Jr.'s *Bushwhackers* (2016) elaborate on Missouri's Southern identity during the Civil War.

As printed words alchemize into filmic dialogue, qualitative changes occur nonetheless. Take the titles for instance. The novel's title suggests a perspective from the one suffering yet also sustained by Southern woe. The narrative voice and that woe are one. The film's title, by contrast, entertains a subjectivity several times removed: Which devil? *The* Devil or the Southern devils/rebels? If the latter, then who is riding with Southern devils—the extradiegetic viewers or the two diegetic protagonists with whom viewers identify? Both scenarios? For the "Dutchy" Jake and the ex-slave Holt, perennially called by the racist n-word, riding with the devils may as well be riding along or even being ridden, being verbally abused and physically threatened by their bushwhacker comrades. The Jake-Holt minority or minoritarian viewpoint is the lens, the door to admit modern viewers with less overtly racist and possibly more progressive thinking into the other world—the South—during the Civil War. The minority lens allows the majority of the millennial audience to see through the devil's eye and empathize with, feel for, devilry.

Woodrell's novel ends with Jake and his "surrogate" family—Sue Lee, widow of his "near brother" Jack Bull Chiles and now his wife, their baby girl Grace Chiles, and his "dark comrade, Holt"—leaving the war for a "new spot for life," which "might be but a short journey as a winged creature covers it, that is often said, but, oh, Lord, as you know, I had not the wings, and it is a hot, hard ride by road" (226). It is well-nigh poetry, as the last phrase alliterates "h" in "hot, hard" and "r" in "ride by road." Taken as a whole, this concluding sentence encapsulates Woodrell's craft yoking the conversational, the oral "that is often said" and "as you know," on the one hand, and, on the other, the evocatively biblical and archaic "but, oh, Lord . . . I had not the wings." A stylistic tightrope suspended between the informal and the incantational, between bloody war and blood bond, Woodrell has indeed executed a "hot, hard ride" from the 1983 eponymous short story in the *Missouri Review* to the 1987 novel to Schamus's script for Ang Lee's western in 1999. The short story's final resting place is Woodrell's 2011 collection, *The Outlaw Album*. The long trek of sixteen years, not counting the short story's revenant in the collection, charts a course as tortu(r)ous as the Missouri River. What follows seeks to trace the three-part river: its creative genesis in the fountainhead of the short story; its convergence/conversion into the main body of a Civil War historical novel; and its emptying into the sea of public consciousness through two minority artists invisible behind the camera. If only words could slice a stream (of consciousness and textuality) and freeze it into, in the order of appearance: The Fountainhead—"Woe to Live On"; The Body—*Woe to Live On*; and The Mouth—*Ride with the Devil*! Absent that forensic clarity over a living, evolving organism, I focus on characterization and plot at the heart of the texts, the author-auteur masterminds veiled within, and the distinct language and style running through these multiple texts.

Woodrell is the one who comes up with the trope of water. "The river takes it from almost anywhere" opens the short story with the elderly protagonist Jake (Jacob) Roedel retrieving and carving the Missouri River flotsam into "tea trays" and other household items, an analogue for the writer reworking the Civil War past into art. A rare find of a "clean-shaven oak length" coincides with the passing of Jake's bushwhacker leader Coleman Younger in 1916, "the Last is Gone," as part 1's subheading notes ("Woe to Live On" 81–82). The gift from the river is put to good use in memory of Younger, who was Jake's senior and apparently died an old man. Ironically, the deceased Younger returns at the height of his power as a Southern rebel and murderer in part 2, hewn and planed as much by the river flow as by Woodrell's pen. The last is gone so that Younger and his fellow renegades can ride again, made young again.

The short story comes in three parts. After the opening that commemorates Younger's death, part 2 flashes back to Jake's bushwhacking youth when he perpetrated atrocities to avenge Southern grievances and to prove his loyalty to the Confederacy. In taking innocent lives, Jake fancied himself to have procured a new Southern family and identity in denial of his "Dutchy" background, particularly his German immigrant father, Otto, eager to keep his old ways from the old world. Ironically, by joining the rebels to preserve the Old South with its heinous economy and lifestyle based on slavery, the defiant Jake failed to break away from his father. Unwittingly, Jake walked in his father's footsteps of a bygone era. Despite its brevity, the short story has amply illustrated this family dynamics inherent in Woodrell's cocktail mix of western gun fight, buddy movie, action thriller, romance, and the self-proclaimed "country noir."[2]

Part 3 returns to the present when Jake's son Jefferson vents his resentment toward Jake's rebel past, a disavowal of the father no different from Jake's against Otto. Yet his two namesakes reveal the dubious American identity: Thomas Jefferson, the founding father of the Union, hailing from the slave-holding Monticello of Virginia, as well as Jefferson Davis, the president of the Confederate States. The son's anger stems from Jake's near parricide and betrayal. Having spared a Federal soldier, Alf Bowden, from his hometown, Jake's mercy was only rewarded by Alf's retribution against Otto—shooting and torturing Otto to death. More poignantly, Jefferson objects to Jake passing on his legacy to the adolescent grandsons reaching "what we called the killing

---

2. Although Daniel Woodrell coined "country noir" to describe his 1996 novel *Give Us a Kiss*, set in the Ozarks countryside, the term can be retroactively applied to *Woe to Live On*, with a western twist.

age" (83). Jake's rebel "we" jars with Jefferson's "we" divorced from roguish lawlessness. Loyalty and betrayal flip, destabilized by the thin line between us and them. To be loyal to the South, Jake turns traitorous to Otto, his immigrant community, and the Union. A child of immigrants "born on a cold dark wave ... somewhere between Hamburg and Baltimore," Jake as a person is so "at sea" due to his birth on the sea that he desperately wishes to land, to assimilate (71).

The novel provides a much larger canvas for Jake's assimilation and its heavy price. Granted, the extent to which an immigrant contorted himself to fit into a white xenophobic South in the mid-nineteenth century outstripped anything late twentieth-century minorities like Schamus and Ang Lee must endure. One key distinction, however, separates Ang Lee from the fictitious Jake and the fiction weaver Schamus. The latter two enjoy the luxury, however guilt-ridden, of passing for white, a category incrementally expanded in the last century or two to accommodate such non-Anglo-Saxon, non-Standard-English-speaking Caucasians as the Irish, Germans, Italians, and even Jews. That large tent remains somewhat barred to Asians, proverbially the "perennial aliens," even in the twenty-first century. In reaction to the alien stereotype, Ang Lee in a distinguished career has perfected the art of the invisible Asian, channeling English classics (*Sense and Sensibility*), the 1960s and '70s (*Taking Woodstock* and *The Ice Storm*), sci-fi (*The Hulk* and *Life of Pi*), war movies (*Billy Lynn's Long Halftime Walk*), westerns (*Brokeback Mountain*), and more. The maestro's disappearing acts rub off on his *wuxia* (swordplay) magnum opus *Crouching Tiger, Hidden Dragon* (2000), where a modern, even feminist, Asian sensibility hides behind crouching swordsmen and tigresses of yore. Indeed, both the Jewish scriptwriter and the Asian filmmaker are well versed in self-erasure, dissembling what the majority favors in mass entertainment. This is a trajectory that charted the rise of many a Jewish Hollywood mogul, expat filmmaker and scriptwriter, and even all-American star. Jointly, Lee and Schamus minimize Jake's killer image in Woodrell, resurrecting him as a sympathetic character, aided in no small measure by the casting of Tobey Maguire with his boyish, photogenic face. As minority artists, they are keen on the performativity of whiteness, the absence of color. Imbued in Jake the Southerner wannabe is the minority impulse as white wannabe. Together, they portray Jake's urge of assimilation while downplaying the hot blood Jake spills in cold blood across Woodrell's pages.

Strategically, Jake passes for a white Southerner by executing a series of crimes. Jake forms with his own hand and rope the "proper" thirteen coils to lynch a fellow German immigrant, Wilhelm Schnellenberger, a "Goddamn lop-eared St. Louis Dutchman," in front of Schnellenberger's family (4).

Southern manners and propriety in the correct number of coils and other matters arise from what Daniel J. Boorstin terms the South's "Code of Honor," which perverts supposedly right form with bad content in Jake's case (*The Americans: The National Experience* [1965] 206).[3] Doing it properly sums up the South's insistence on tradition, even one as depraved and evil as slavery. This killing is further justified by dehumanizing the victim as a "lop-eared" dog from the Sin City of St. Louis. When the immigrant's adolescent son tries to loosen the noose, Jake shoots him in the back while maintaining a "profound," i.e., nonchalantly masculinist, countenance. In Woodrell's curt, tongue-in-cheek "country noir" rhetoric, Jake "booked the boy passage with his father," a murder cushioned by the alliteration of "b" and the metaphor of a generous send-off. As his nemesis Pitt Mackeson pounces on his cowardice, Jake defends himself: "But pups make hounds. . . . And there are hounds enough" (8). The novel further elaborates on Jake's excuse: "If the boy had freed the rope, the hanging would've been scotched and required doing over" (18). A clean kill requires two kills. To whitewash Jake of such wrongdoing in the cinematic makeover of the sympathetic protagonist, Schamus and Lee excise Jake's repeat offenses. They also hold in reserve Woodrell's nice turn of phrase in the canine figure of speech until page 101 of the script. "But pups make hounds" becomes Jake's half-hearted defense of the mass atrocity in the Union town of Lawrence, Kansas, an atrocity perpetrated by the likes of Mackeson rather than Jake. Jake, in fact, draws his pistol to prevent Mackeson from butchering two townsmen.

In Woodrell, Jake's stolid, "profound" visage, "elaborately cool," and heartless words are for show, a performance of Southernness at the moment when his immigrant countrymen are being "converted," often by none other than himself (8). In keeping with propriety, Southern euphemism recasts a murder as religious conversion, supposedly from a German Protestant to a born-again Southern Baptist. Manners are always mannered, stylized ways of acting and speaking, which effect a detachment from and, purportedly, a sublimation of spontaneous human response. A gentleman woos a Southern belle, for instance, by deferring his libido in accordance with chivalry and social norms. Stylization, like art, requires layering over, distancing from, real life. The proper thirteen coils somehow make right an egregious crime; a single hanging of a "Dutchman" displaces the history of African American lynching.

---

3. Book 1 on "Community" in Daniel J. Boorstin's *The Americans* (1965) identifies only four social groups, the Southerners being one of them: the "versatile" New Englanders (to be replaced, conceivably, by Silicon Valley Californians coming after Boorstin's 1965 book); the "transient" "joiners" in perpetual mobility; the "upstart" "boosters" flourishing in cities; and "Southerners, White and Black."

Subsequently, to spare the Federal prisoner Alf Bowden, Jake mocks a fellow "Dutchman" chosen to deliver the message of prisoner swap. By calling attention to the *"Ja! Ja!"* of the lucky Dutchman who drew the short straw, Jake dooms him in that he "can't hardly talk American," let alone be a competent messenger (48). Once in safety, Alf summarily executes Jake's father Otto. The characterization of Jake by Woodrell manifests a subconscious Oedipal complex, one in revolt against his German ancestry. The steep price for Jake's Southernness comprises the deaths of immigrant males, including his own father. To be loyal to the South, Jake betrays his father and the Father of the Nation in exchange for the Southern family of the Chiles in the novel as well as the larger community of the South. Asked to translate the Schnellenberger's prehanging "mumbling" to "his god," who had "missed the boat from Hamburg," Jake replies that he is "praying to Abe Lincoln" (6). Both idolatries in Southern eyes are smashed: a god in lowercase satirized as having been stranded back there; a diminutive "Abe" and his Federal government a ways away up north, too small to intervene on the German's behalf.

Owing to its length, the short story only hints at the Southern family to which Jake yearns to belong. When Coleman Younger commends his execution of the adolescent, Jake indulges in the fallacy: "It was for this that I searched, communion and levelness with people who were not mine by birth, but mine for the taking" (18). It is far too optimistic to believe that the bond is there "for the taking" since Mackeson and his ilk never partake in that "communion," a Christian compact never given, plus having been written in someone else's blood. On the contrary, Mackeson and his gang's "friendly fire" injures and nearly kills Jake and Holt in the novel. As Holt puts it in his Southern dialect, "n——s and Dutchies is their special targets," a fratricidal deviousness antithetical to the levelness and sharing imagined by Jake (204). The short story's elders of Younger and Captain Quandrill, who lend credence to Jake's Southern identity, expand substantially in the novel to the Chiles as his symbolic family.

The novel accounts for Jake's bushwhacking through the context of his "near brother" Jack Bull Chiles and his bona fide adoptive family's tragedy. The patriarch Asa Chiles is robbed and murdered by the Yankee Captain Warren "for his watch and his boots and his horse" (98). Whereas Woodrell simply has Jack Bull retell Asa's demise, Schamus and Lee see fit for a pastoral, prelapsarian overture in which the Chiles estate stages a sumptuous Southern wedding. Deceptive in its beautiful tranquility of the wedding ceremony gathered on one side of the frame, juxtaposed by liveried house slaves with serving trays on the other side, figure 11.1 captures the "Dutchy" Jake walking in between, an outsider to the Old South and to slavery. This fragile Southern

FIGURE 11.1. A Southern wedding at the Chiles estate in *Ride with the Devil*.

paradise is soon shattered by Kansas Jayhawkers' night raid. They shoot Asa in wantonness and burn down the mansion, witnessed by Jack Bull and Jake. This massacre steels them for a career of revenge for the (near) father and the South. Similar casualties of Southern sympathizers Jackson Evans, the Willards, and more demand retribution. Even those still living bear invisible scars of bereavement as well as physical scars. The one-legged veteran Clark hides in his mother's burned-out barn. Turner Rawls mutters indistinctly owing to the shot through his cheeks. The "nubbin-fingered runt of a Dutchman" Jake presents a case in point (131).

Jake's loss of his left pinkie in a firefight culminates the recurring motif of "good coming from bad" (53). As though in cognitive slow motion amid a barrage of bullets, Jake takes note of the severance: "The little finger on my left hand, a fairly useless digit, was cleaved from me. I saw it pink and limp in the dust of the chicken pen but made no move to regain it" (23). Situating the severed finger in the chicken pen underlines its residual value as chicken feed, just as fighters on either side are being devoured by war. The film's presentation goes in opposite direction from Woodrell's machismo that makes light of, makes a joke out of, physical pain. The gallows humor over "a fairly useless" body part dissipates in Ang Lee's extreme close-up of and attentiveness to Jake's bloody hand (figure 11.2). Cinematic shock effect mellows back into Woodrell's masculine aesthetics over the nubbin. Jake muses to Jack Bull on "the good side of this amputation," spinning a macabre tale of mortality. If he were hanged and left as "dead meat, pretty well rotted to a glob," Jake quips, his remains would remain identifiable as the "nubbin-fingered Jake Roedel" (36–37). So would the postwar South bear the woes of the Civil War. The secessionist South's defeat and Jake's de-digitization nourish those who come after: the infant Grace Chiles finds in the nubbin a soothing pacifier;

FIGURE 11.2. Ang Lee's extreme close-up of Jake's bloody hand in *Ride with the Devil*.

the writer Woodrell retrieves deadwood from the river of time for its rebirth in fresh telling.

Starting with Asa's murder and repeatedly with other killings, the film resuscitates the South, at least the protagonists, as the aggrieved party. Not to mince words, *Ride with the Devil* unfolds as a revenge story, doing away with Woodrell's moral ambiguity over the perpetrator and the perpetrated.[4] The minority lens cleanses the grayness of bushwhackers and their Confederate uniforms, sharpening them into either decent, reluctant Jake or depraved, crazed Mackeson and fellow scalpers. Entirely unimaginable in Ang Lee's cherub-esque Tobey Maguire, Woodrell's Jake, not to put too fine a point on it, scalps a Dutchman to demonstrate his devotion to the rebel cause. Just as the fictitious hanging of a Dutchman elides the historical lynching of African Americans, scalping a Dutchman shifts the focus away from Buffalo Bill–style scalping of dead Indians, Native Americans. Woodrell consistently deracinates racist slayings of people of color as white-on-white, North versus South outrage. From the perspective of whiteness studies contemporaneous with the 1980s short story and novel, Woodrell presents a white-centrism to the exclusion of the diversity of Civil War actors, with the sole exception of the ex-slave Holt, whose "eyes were shaded toward the oriental in shape" (113). If Woodrell wears the blackface named Holt, such stereotypical slant eyes inscribe the perennial Oriental alien onto the black mask. The use of "oriental" comes across, even in the 1980s, as antiquated and somewhat outlawed as the n-word, quainter still in lowercase. A wordsmith like Woodrell chooses this *mot juste,* conceivably, not only to construct the style of rural, dialectal,

---

4. Boorstin agrees that "from a Southern point of view, the Civil War would avenge honor rather than resolve problems" (216). Slavery was not deemed a problem to the South; antislavery was.

and non-Standard English, but also to intimate the wide gap of misperception between Holt and Jake before they form a true brotherhood.

The slant of his Asian eyes notwithstanding, Holt occupies the eye of a discursive storm over Blackness. The controversy revolves around the deployment of the n-word throughout the novel, principally in reference to Holt. As the story is set in the South during the Civil War, Woodrell borrows the racial epithet to be faithful to the times, as hateful as it sounds to our ears. A century after Mark Twain's slur-fraught *The Adventures of Huckleberry Finn* (1884), a white Southern writer runs afoul of public sensibility in dispensing the n-word so uninhibitedly. However, Woodrell's novel fails to arouse a backlash as vehement as *William Styron's Nat Turner: Ten Black Writers Respond* (1968) in reaction to Styron's *The Confessions of Nat Turner* (1967), written in the first-person voice of the slave revolt leader.[5] Instead, *Woe to Live On* with its copious slurs is quietly forgotten, gone out of print, kept half alive by Ang Lee's afterimage on the screen.

Contrary to Woodrell's profuse sprinkling throughout the novel, the tabooed n-word, according to Randall Kennedy's 2011 eponymous book, is "the superlative racial epithet—the *most* hurtful, the *most* fearsome, the *most* dangerous, the *most* noxious" (28). But it enters the discourse of "black rappers and comedians," such as Dr. Dre, Jay-Z, DMX, Richard Pryor, Chris Rock, and many more (45). Gangsta rap flaunts it as a badge of ethnic trauma and solidarity, while Kennedy cautions against cases where it indicates "an anti-black, self-hating prejudice" (45). Recent films and TV series, however, have revived the use of the n-word, from the mouth of, for instance, the young slave narrator "Onion" and white racists in Showtime's *The Good Lord Bird* (2020).

Had he been less of a consummate stylist, Woodrell could have put the relatively safe, less offensive word "negro" in the mouth of bushwhackers. Yet that compromise in naming would have been out of character for those bent upon dehumanizing their human chattel through words and deeds. "Negro" is used but once, by Schnellenberger with the noose around his neck. Unbeknownst to him, his choice of word, negro, grants so much respect to slaves that it must have enraged his henchmen, not that they needed incentive other than their leader Black John's command: "Stretch his neck. And be sharp about it" (5). The violence of lynching is, once again, couched in Southern euphemistic rhetoric that projects agency onto the victim about to be "converted," as though Schnellenberger cranes his neck to see the new God from afar. To be

---

5. For a panoramic view of works on Nat Turner, see Jean W. Cash's "Nat Turner: Misguided, 'fragmented, disjointed' Images," which includes a large section on William Styron and the controversy.

"sharp" and spirited, like the correct number of coils, turns an evil deed into a job well done.

As the historical novel readied itself for the nationwide market, it purged some transgressive episodes as well as horrible language from the short story regionally published in the *Missouri Review*. For instance, Younger's sadistic play with his Enfield rifle to find out how many Federal prisoners he can fell with a single shot results in multiple casualties, including two whose "moans sounded like man and wife in a feather bed," the messiness prompting Younger to wisecrack "Not exactly a Sharps, is it?" (88). Such devilish delight in the suffering of others constitutes the height of black humor, death throes spliced with coital vocalizations. Wicked genius often yokes these diametrically opposed metaphors of Thanatos and Eros. Beyond Freud's *Beyond the Pleasure Principle* (1920), Korean auteur Park Chan-wook's *Sympathy for Mr. Vengeance* (2002) springs to mind, particularly the scene where single males masturbate while eavesdropping on a woman's moans next door due not to lovemaking but to the agony of her failing kidneys. Younger's disappointment in his rifle less effective than those designed and named after Christian Sharps harks back to Jake's retying the noose properly.

Ultimately, Woodrell–Schamus–Ang Lee debunk Southern propriety, at least the old kind, to herald the new. Landowning, a.k.a. slaveholding, Jack Bull Chiles and George Clyde are Southern gentlemen and dandies with "riverboat manner" in the presence of ladies (85). Their idyllic Eden destroyed, both plunge into bushwhacking, drawing their respective confidants since childhood, Jake and Holt, into the maelstrom. When the widow Sue Lee graces their winter hideout, Jack Bull takes an immediate interest, just as George makes himself scarce in courting a Southern belle, Juanita Willard, living nearby. In their absence, the two outsiders Jake and Holt begin to bond, so much so that George turns jealous, a psychic deterioration accompanied by an increasing physical disheveled-ness, heavy drinking, darkening around the sunken eyes with a glazed look, and shooting an unarmed man in the Lawrence massacre. Worse still, George flees to safety under the pretense of kidnapping a "sawbone" from the town of Kingsville to attend to Jack Bull's gunshot wound, indirectly causing his death. This betrayal is a natural corollary in Woodrell when George appears more concerned with his own wellbeing. After Jack Bull is shot, "only Clyde was rested well," going "about his daily habits almost as usual," telltale signs of George's imminent desertion (138). Seeing through his lifelong friend's abandonment, Holt confides in Jake that the arm with growing gangrene should be amputated without delay. This moment is one of many where the two outcasts, originally suspicious of each other, cement a camaraderie much stronger than that with their childhood confidants, both of whom soon die, along with their Old South. This ability to see the humanity in the other is shared by Sue Lee, who was initially offended by the presence of Holt in the winter hideout, preferring the ex-slave to be "ploughing" outside. Despite her earlier imperiousness toward Holt, she mellows, getting "friendlier and more sisterly to Holt and me," and, eventually, wifely to Jake, a surrogate for Jack Bull (105).

Across the divide of race and class, Jake and Holt grow close to each other. When Jake contrives to spare his townsman Alf Bowden, Holt detects his scheme: "I am on to you, Roedel," less a threat than a good-natured, even friendly, warning, for "even in the night I could see it—he actually smiled" (49). Holt's vague smile is so rare a fissure in the ex-slave's protective shield of reticence and expressionlessness that it signals a kinship with a doppelganger, a fellow "performer" of Southernness. Holt sees Jake's true motive behind the charade of an English-speaking messenger just as Jake sees Holt's grin, the equivalent of a modern wink, under the cover of night. Reaching out to the other's humanity had started ever since Jake was prevailed upon, by bushwhackers around the campfire, to read from Northern soldiers' mailbag, which he refused at first out of decency. The illiterate Holt was so taken by the magic of reading and accessing the North's alternate universe that he had carried along the mailbag in secret, asking Jake to read more in their spare time through the winter seclusion.

Holt is not the only one captivated by these letters from Yankee soldiers' loved ones. Quite a few bushwhackers come to see their enemies as human beings through these letters.[6] Jake's reading casts a spell on the vengeful killers. Even readers and viewers are mesmerized by Woodrell's well-wrought language at once rustic and archaic as well as by Tobey Maguire's elocution in Southern drawl. From her farm in Wisconsin, a mother writes to her sons serving in the Union army: "No word of you in so long. Right past first frost of the year past." A Southern riff on the Dickensian poetic coinage of "ghost of yesteryear," Woodrell repeats two sentences with brisk monosyllabic words, plus alliterations, deceptively simple like a peasant's speech. Yet the word "past" doubles itself, as though the two sons' passing coincided with their silence since the dead of winter last year. "The year past" rings of regional dialect, but the inversion sounds lyrical, elegiac. She proceeds to describe the family farm's soil "black-rich and feels good in the hand. You boys know how it is" (67), followed by one of the rapt listeners'—Riley's—rejoinder: "My daddy was up there . . . the dirt was so rich you could eat it like porridge" (67).

---

6. It goes without saying that Ken Burns in his famed *The Civil War* TV series deploys soldiers' and their families' letters to create an affective aura for the PBS documentary.

Riley's hyperbole on the heels of the mother's address to "you boys" renders him and other bushwhackers her boys; the Wisconsin mother becomes Riley's mother.

Southern mother, like her Northern counterpart, delivers memorable lines as well. Convinced of the bushwhackers' identity as Southern men, the one-legged Clark's mother invites them into her house: "Come on and eat as what we have" (10). A strange turn of phrase, "eat as what we have," along with other quirky word choice in dialogue and narrative description, deviates from Standard English, on occasion simply by an extra, extraneous preposition, such as "as" in "eat as what we have." The novel abounds with phraseologies slightly off-kilter, bringing not only local color but also the sense that the secessionist South has already done so linguistically. With the bushwhackers' terse, often euphemized, dialogue blending civility and brutality, romance and gun fights, Woodrell creates his own brand of western, so impressive that Schamus's script and Ang Lee's film transcribe these lines verbatim onscreen while smoothing over the novel's sharp edges for the millennial sensibility.

Major revisions do occur in the paradisal opening and the conclusion when "Jacob Roedel" and "Daniel Holt" bid farewell with nothing but each other's Christian name. Coming after Holt's reminder that the wedding vows Jake took with Sue Lee are not mere words but "oaths," their parting words cement the bond of Black and white Americans, both from elsewhere—Africa, Deutschland, or other places of the Old World (133). Both biblical names, Jacob usurps his brother Esau and wrestles throughout the night, ending with a disjointed hip or a nubbin of a finger. Millennia later, the immigrant son Jake would inherit the earth of the Old South after burying his near brother. Daniel, on the other hand, emerges from the lion's den of slavery relatively unscathed. Jake's afterlife out of the long shadow cast by Jack Bull and the South resonates with Holt's spiritual liberation in the wake of George's death: "Being his friend was no diff'rent from being his n——" (125). The shadows' indebtedness to the bodies ends once the bodies vanish, affixed, instead, with their own shadows of a new family and, in Holt's case, a new mission to find his "Mama," the hidden longing confided to Jake. Whereas the innocent, apparently white Dutchy boy gets the girl, whose breastfeeding he has long enjoyed as a spectator, the free Black man poses no threat as the stereotypical stud, since he is already infantilized like Grace Chiles in rooting for "Mama."

As opposed to the novel's close that points to the "hot, hard ride" ahead, the film's finale witnesses Holt off to Texas to which his mother had been sold, a quixotic quest no different from the South's secession or the American dream as the promised land. Daniel J. Boorstin puts it in his signature witticism: "The nation would long profit from having been born without ever having been conceived" (219). This conceptual ambiguity inherent in the promised land is most productive in luring waves of immigrants, since it never bothers to spell out who has made the promise to whom, nor promising precisely what. To the "huddled masses" huddled at the feet of the Statue of Liberty, the amorphous oath is taken to be a pledge of everything for everyone, which flips dialectically into nothing for no one. As Jake and Holt, North and South, are most alike despite the color of the skin and the difference of culture and politics, the South ceases to be a regional construct. The South is us, spelled the "U.S." Writing in *The American South* (2021), Charles Reagan Wilson agrees: "the South exemplifies, sometimes in the extreme, American experiences" (2). To translate the national experience in extremis into contemporary statistics, nearly half of the US voters in the 2020 presidential and congressional elections are overwhelmingly Trumpian in defiance of election results, in denial of democratic reality. Trump, his enablers, and his followers—many in Southern red states—wage a civil war still with ballots rather than bullets, heavily armed with election lies, vote recounts and audits, court litigations, alternate realities, and conspiracy theories.

CHAPTER 12

Bipolar America

The Anti-Asian versus *Minari*

In this new millennium, America suffers from what resembles a bipolar syndrome toward Asia, hating and loving it at the same time. This psychotic split within America manifests itself in media and popular culture with respect to Asia or putative Asianness. Media representations become the window to America's soul, projecting conservative, xenophobic loathing spearheaded by Trump as well as liberal, progressive love radiating from Hollywood. The far right and the far left, however, are mirror images of each other in their extremities. Trumpian loathing stems from self-loathing; Hollywood smooches from self-cuddling.[1]

Goaded by Trumpian populism and nativism, half of America scapegoats Asians, among other peoples of color, on account of the paranoia of white replacement. This fear of dispossession is intensified by the ascent of China in the "Chinese Century," which challenges American exceptionalism and supremacy in what has been the "American Century," particularly during the Cold War and beyond. With its presumed origin in Wuhan, China, the global pandemic of COVID-19 has only exacerbated the tension. China's lack of transparency in sharing data and assisting the WHO investigators in locating the source or even the index patient has increased suspicion and

---

1. This chapter is drawn from "Bipolar America: Anti-Asian versus Hollywood's *Minari*," *Media in Asia*, edited by Youna Kim, Routledge, 2022, pp. 293–303. Reproduced by permission of Taylor & Francis Group.

resentment against China. The list of patients and the course of their illness should have been published for the sake of humanity in preventing another global outbreak.

Against Trump's America, the other half of this bipolar collective psyche overcompensates by valorizing things Oriental. The liberal forces, encapsulated by Hollywood, pick this hate-filled moment to bestow praise and awards upon Lee Isaac Chung's *Minari* (2021), as though the Korean immigrant family drama counterbalances anti-Asian hate crimes and sentiments. That *Minari* is a softball of an understated melodrama fits the bill for a feel-good breather to escape from the anti-Asian reality. Which is the real and which the dreamscape? Which is a real/reel dream and which a fake reality? The crimes committed by the Atlanta shooter Robert Aaron Long and the New York "kicker" Brandon Elliot and the unidentified anti-masker-*cum*-hammerer (Ebony Jackson, as it was later revealed) and the San Francisco stabber Patrick Thompson, just to name the most recent and most atrocious, are the reality both Asians in America and Americans of Asian descent are forced to inhabit, a reality born out of twisted minds and crazed delusions. Asians live and die in accordance with Americans' sick hallucination. The exact number of these Americans remains to be determined.

On the other hand, *Minari* purports to be largely autobiographical, where immigrant (grand)parents' life experiences are, nevertheless, adapted for the genre of family melodrama from the perspective of the filmmaker Chung's alter ego, an American-born Korean boy growing up in rural Arkansas. Where is the immigrant's shared American nightmare of being the perennial alien? Is the Ozarks the promised land sans bigotry and racism? This argument follows the trajectory of American bipolarization, swinging from hate at one end of the spectrum, manifested by AAA or Anti-Asian Anonymous to, at the other end, love showered on *Minari,* named after water celery or Chinese celery, which is practically an invasive species to conservationists of native plants, reminiscent of the nativist rhetoric against the racial other.[2]

---

2. Two other invasive species come to mind, both considered delicacies in parts of China. Asian carp has long troubled the Great Lakes region of the Midwest. Each midwestern state calls for allocation of funds to combat the spread of Asian carp through interconnected waterways. The other is watercress. Andrea Wang's eponymous children's book details her shame of being made by her Chinese immigrant parents to collect "food from a muddy roadside ditch" in Ohio ("Note from the Author"). Wang's reaction is evident from her caption to one of the paintings: "A car passes by / and I duck my head / hoping it's no one I knew." The source of her shame—her parents—become the ones to whom the children's book is dedicated: "In memory of my parents . . . immigrants and inspirations." Ironically, watercress is known in the Chinese province of Guangdong as *Xiyang Cai* (Western/Foreign Vegetable), yet Americans or Westerners in general recoil from it as a filthy weed grown near streams, swamps, and sewage run-offs.

AAA: Anti-Asian Anonymous of Atlanta and America

COVID-19 has so sickened America's body politic that the latent frailty of its composition exposes itself, triggered by Trump's racist "Chinese virus" and "kung flu" to shirk the commander-in-chief's pandemic-fighting responsibility. Amid Trump's flurry of activities casting blame for America's death tolls on the Chinese, the *Washington Post* published on March 19, 2020, Anne Gearan's reporting with a close-up photograph by Jabin Botsford. The picture is a blowup of Trump's briefing notes, where "corona" in coronavirus was crossed out and replaced by "CHINESE" in caps with the infamous sharpie.[3] An extension of Trumpian discursive and political violence, on March 16, 2021, the Atlanta shooter Robert Aaron Long took eight lives, six of whom were Asian immigrant women, at three massage parlors. In the press conference at police department headquarters in Atlanta the following day, "backed" by Mayor Keisha Lance Bottoms and two other African American police officers arrayed behind him, spokesperson Jay Baker described Long's "sex addiction." To rid himself of such temptations on a particularly "bad day," Baker alleged, Long committed mass murder. By parroting Long, Baker damned, in one fell swoop, the six deceased, ranging in age from thirty-three to seventy-four, as sex workers. A case of a mindless blabbermouth or Freudian slips of an evil tongue, evil heart? Subsequent evidence intimated that it might as well be the other way around: Long executed what lay hidden in Baker's heart or Facebook page.

Baker was later revealed to have uploaded on his website a Sinophobic T-shirt brandishing "Covid 19 / IMPORTED VIRUS FROM CHY-NA" under a biological warfare logo (figure 12.1). As deafeningly silent as the military colors raised at a battlefield, the logo accuses "CHY-NA" of waging a biological war linked to the yet-to-be-proven theory of leaked virus from Wuhan Institute of Virology in the Chinese city. The Gothic, Germanic script for "Covid 19" comprises dagger-like strokes with sharp, jagged points and hooks, as though hailing from menacing dark forces, if not straight from hell, the Third Reich. The apparel's fascist rhetoric borrowed from Nazi Blackletter to portend peril. The T-shirt designer also captured well Trump's compulsive butchering of "China" into a misshapen "CHY-NA," its first diminutive syllable associated subliminally with "Chink," followed by the hyphen for a space, a chink. Traumatic enough it is to learn once again of an active shooter from AAA, not Alcoholics Anonymous but Anti-Asian Anonymous of Atlanta, America! Furthermore, secondary trauma was afflicted by the criminal justice system, the Atlanta

---

3. See my "Kung Flu" in *America Unfiltered* (2020), or chapter 1, "Sinophobia/Sinophilia," in *The Tao of S* (2022).

FIGURE 12.1. Jay Baker's Facebook post with the image of a Sinophobic T-shirt brandishing "Covid 19 / IMPORTED VIRUS FROM CHY-NA" under a biological warfare logo.

authority of the police backed by the mayor, giving voice to the reprehensible killer. If Long spoke with his gun, he was seconded by Baker and other anti-Asian incidents.

One of which was Brandon Elliot's March 29 assault of a petite sixty-five-year-old Filipino American woman at the front door of Midtown luxury apartments at 360 West 43rd Street, a few blocks from Times Square, while shouting racial slurs and "You don't belong here!" (see CCTV footage released by NYPD: https://www.youtube.com/watch?v=Xswt73F9gUY). Throughout the kicking and stomping in plain view of the apartment staff, a security guard walked over to shut the front door, and at least two apartment personnel and one delivery man stood by, watching the street show. The assault was captured by the security camera of the apartments. The spectators' indifference added a new wrinkle to the good ol' USA's AAA: Anti-Asian Accomplice.

Long's "sex addiction" stems from the even longer Orientalist addiction of Anglo-America that stigmatizes Asian males as racially castrated and Asian females as hypersexualized.[4] A long tradition lies at the heart of white masculinity silhouetted against Asian femininity from popular culture of Hollywood and Broadway, including *Madame Chrysanthème, Madame Butterfly,*

---

4. See David Eng's *Racial Castration* (2001) and Celine Parreñas Shimizu's *The Hypersexuality of Race* (2007).

M. Butterfly, Love Is a Many-Splendored Thing, The World of Suzie Wong, The Teahouse of the August Moon, Sayonara, The Quiet American, Miss Saigon, Girl by the Road at Night, and more. To occupy the centrality of humanity, white maleness bumps other races to the opposite ends of the gender spectrum: Blackness is made to gravitate to aggressive, primitive masculinity; Asianness to passive, decadent femininity. Hence, Asian man turns effeminate, Asian woman superfeminine. Very much a white game, the US entertainment industry realizes this masturbatory fallacy with yellowface in the vein of Blackface. To rephrase Frantz Fanon's *Black Skin, White Masks,* the yellow mask was worn by white skin, including mixed-race actors. The aforementioned films feature, for instance, Jennifer Jones in *Love Is a Many-Splendored Thing* and Nancy Kwan—half Chinese and half English—in *The World of Suzie Wong.* The Japanese geishas and Vietnamese bargirls of the other films suggest the eroticized stereotypes and roles into which Asian performers must have contorted themselves to fit. It goes without saying that Asian, mixed-race, and white female leads comprise the love interest to white male leads, often ending in tragic deaths, from Madame Butterfly to Miss Saigon onscreen to Atlanta massage parlor off-screen.

Also in real life outside the celluloid frame, fetishization of Asian women prompted a predator like the University of Southern California gynecologist George Tyndall to specifically prey upon Asian and Asian American female students from 1989 to 2016. Plenty to pick from: USC, after all, is facetiously dubbed the University of Southern Chinese. It matters little that these films and sexual assaults have been set across the globe, in Japan, "CHY-NA," erstwhile Saigon, Atlanta, or Los Angeles, for Asian women everywhere are, as they like to say, "all alike" in reputedly dedicated as a body, pun intended, to white male pleasure.

Beyond white supremacy on the back of Asian gender roles, what does it say about Asian American citizenship when we use derogatory terms like "Chink" in public, while shunning the n-word, as Randall Kennedy expostulates in his 2002 book? Name-calling Asians is but being "factual," more acceptable than name-calling African Americans. Whereas the n-word has been tabooed as the unsayable, other racial epithets remain as part of the public discourse. Racism comes in gradations, depending on the political clout of the group being discriminated against. That we are saying "Asians" but never "Africans" for "African Americans" suggests grouping Asians, i.e., Asian Asians, with Asian Americans. The American Self, white or Black, defines itself vis-à-vis the Asian Other. As such, America continues to be addicted to an externalized AlieNation, a.k.a. AlienAsian or Alien Asians. The "Southern redneck" incarnate Long and the "motha killa" on lifetime parole Elliot displace their self-alienation onto the perennial alien, their sense of victimization onto the scapegoat deemed not from these parts.

This psychic transference is America's repetition compulsion. We have, alas, seen this horror movie many times before. Déjà vu all over again, as it replays the Chinese Exclusion Act (1882–1943), the only time when a race was barred from entering the United States, until it metastasized into Trump's Muslim ban from 2017 to 2021. Allied with China against Japan during World War II, the US interned Japanese Americans in the wake of Pearl Harbor. Because the US was unable to avenge itself against the stealth attack, President Roosevelt, Congress, and the American people decided to round up the usual suspects, including US-born Americans of Japanese descent, and put them in concentration camps en masse across the West Coast. Ironically, to prove their patriotism, Japanese American volunteers from these camps bid farewell to their families and joined the 442nd Infantry Regiment, the most decorated unit for its size in US military history. These soldiers strove to prove their allegiance, which was cast in doubt, but they might have also wished to ensure, at least subconsciously, the safety of their family still held "hostage" by the US government. The 442nd Infantry Regiment was sent to fight Nazis in Italy rather than Japan's Imperial Army in the Asian theater, conceivably, for suspicion of mixed loyalty. Did the Pentagon have the same concern over sending German or Italian Americans to fight the Axis?

Fast forward to Vincent Chin, who was bludgeoned to death in Highland Park, Detroit, in 1982 by two white unemployed automobile workers mistaking him for Japanese. Rendered "out of work" by what they called "Japanese imports [import cars]," Ronald Ebens and his stepson Michael Nitz got into a brawl with Chin at Fancy Pants, a nude bar, where Chin was celebrating his upcoming wedding in a stag party with three friends, one of whom, Jimmy Choi, was also Asian American. The erotic dancer Racine Colwell testified that Ebens blamed the "little mother fucker" for having made them "lose their jobs." This pointed to one of the ceaseless waves of Asia-bashing, this one directed against Japan in the 1980s, to be continued with the present wave against "CHY-NA" orchestrated by Trump. That Chin at five years old had been adopted from Guangzhou, China, by white parents and was apparently so Americanized that he hosted his stag party at a nude bar did not mitigate white resentment. On the contrary, the Asian-looking man enjoying himself with sex workers might have incensed the disgruntled ex-workers.

At the bar, Ebens was cited as calling Chin a "Chink," a "Nip," a "Boy." While driving around the block to stalk Chin and his friend Jimmy Choi, the father and the stepson picked up a Jimmy Perry, to whom US$20 was offered to solicit his assistance in "catching a 'Chinese guy' and 'busting his head.'"

In his own testimony, Ebens admitted that he told Perry that he "was looking for two orientals [sic]." Incontrovertibly, race contributed to, if not caused, the deadly clash. Likewise, race played a role in the two dancers' testimonies: the prosecution witness Racine Colwell, a white woman, pitted against the defense witness Starlene, a Black woman. Defense attorneys raised doubt about Colwell, who had known Chin from another establishment; Starlene appeared unreliable as well. Starlene claimed to have been such a rookie that she shied away from Chin's largesse of inserting bills into her wardrobe while allowing Ebens to "go down" on her to perform fellatio.

The legal wrangling resulted in Ebens's acquittal in 1987. No public outrage or riot broke out afterwards like what happened on the heels of the Rodney King acquittal in 1992. Although it was white police officers who stood trial, Korean-owned businesses bore the brunt of Black and Brown rage in South Central LA. The similarity of how race and gender intersected is striking in these violent crimes perpetrated by, in the order of appearance, Ronald Ebens along with Michael Nitz, Robert Aaron Long, Brandon Elliot, and more. Men preyed upon women in a Detroit bar, Atlanta spas, and New York City. Femininity was either sexploited to gratify male desire in the first two cases or stomped on for its undesirability, for not "belong[ing] here," in the Elliot case. Desirability is a will-o'-the-wisp, shining bright if possessed with youth and glamor, darkening if without. "Possessed" is the modus operandi: males are obsessed with possessing female bodies, even if it means dispossessing them of dignity and life. Such male drivenness is driven by biological impulses out of control, or the will to power unleashed by alcohol, delusions of grandeur, and sheer hate.

The exception appeared to be Vincent Chin. Vincent Chin availed himself of an extreme form of masculine pastime at Fancy Pants, only to find himself becoming the hunted due to race, his head bashed in by Ebens's baseball bat, the other pastime of American males.[5] Marked by their Asianness or alienness, Vincent Chin and his fellow victims in Atlanta, New York, and elsewhere arise as the New Jew. The historical scapegoat in Christendom is joined by Asians in this "Chinese Century." The ascent of China in the twenty-first century elicits jealousy and fear, sentiments most unbecoming to American exceptionalism. With China breathing down America's neck in the race for supremacy, the US reaction would only intensify. Trump's inflammatory "Chinese virus" had lit the fire of Sinophobia. As WHO investigators were thwarted in their probe into the source of COVID-19, as the viral wildfire continued to spread with

---

5. Two decades ago, I published a piece linking Vincent Chin and baseball, "Vincent Chin and Baseball: Law, Racial Violence, and Masculinity," chapter 4 of *The Deathly Embrace* (2000). That chapter is one instance, and a literal one at that, out of many such "deathly embrace[s]."

no end in sight, we shall witness more anti–Asian Anonymous flare-ups across America, a bit swampier after the stoking by Trump.

Any intersection of race and gender must not forget the third rail of socioeconomic class, which returns us to New York, where the haves and the have-nots coinhabit uneasily. Brandon Elliot and the upscale apartment staff who stood idly by at 360 West 43rd Street seemed to be all Black. Ebony Jackson, the New Yorker who took a hammer to two Asian women with masks on May 2, 2021, was also Black. These belonged to the string of Black-on-Asian violence, whereby homeless or economically deprived African Americans assaulted Asian passersby. Should a Black elderly person be attacked by Elliot, would the security guard and others simply shut the front door and turn their backs? Would an upper-class white, Black, and even Asian elderly person dressed to the nines inflame Elliot as much, yet also intimidate and inhibit him? Should an Asian resident of the luxury apartments be the victim, would the staff feel duty-bound to intervene and lend a hand? There were at least four of them against one Elliot, for goodness' sake. Was the Filipino woman picked out on account of her physical frailty as well as plain, unremarkable clothing? Or was she simply in the wrong place at the wrong time, a self-comforting excuse we have all used to explain away killings and crimes? Should one blame this on the depraved Sin City of New York, on its lower-rung Black citizenry, or simply on those individual culprits and accomplices with no larger significance whatsoever?

Let us disabuse ourselves of the last scenario of wishful thinking and self-delusion ill-fitting our time of #MeToo, racial reckoning, and socioeconomic equity. A bottom feeder in an affluent New York, Elliot apparently blamed whatever he was experiencing on an Asian stranger weaker and more powerless than himself. Elliot's taking it out on an alien was acquiesced to by the complicit apartment staff entrusted with maintaining order inside and around the building, surely including its "storefront." Cowards they all were—men with guns and fists, in uniforms with badges and no guts! But let us not prejudge and put words into their mouths. The ongoing investigation may yet reveal the truth behind the action of Elliot and the inaction of the security guard and bystanders, behind Long's bullets and Baker's official and unofficial, public and Facebook, statements. Satiated with Asian blood, bipolar America turns to water and life.

Minari, an Invasive Species?

Receiving six Oscar nominations and awarded Best Supporting Actress for Youn Yuh-Jung's role as the grandmother, *Minari* tells the story of a Korean immigrant family in 1980s Arkansas. The parents Jacob Yi and Monica, along with their children Anne and David, relocated from California where they had eked out a living as chicken sexers. David suffers from a heart condition that prevents him from overexerting himself. A normal child's activities such as running and capering are forbidden. David's weakened heart circles back to immigrants' warped lives. What used to be the immigrant's assets and capabilities—the Korean language, cultural literacy, and much of their professional skills—become moot, irrelevant in a new place as though they now lapse into liabilities and disabilities, robbing the immigrant of the power of speech, of comprehension, and of action. Typical of immigrants from a farming background, Jacob dreams of owning and harvesting his own land instead of scrutinizing "chicken butts" for the past ten years. Upward mobility from the bottom of society and from chicken's bottoms drives Jacob.

What Jacob plans to plant, however, reflects the immigrant paradox: one leaves home to replicate the lost home. Jacob grows Korean vegetables in Arkansas' fertile yet parched soil for California's massive immigrant population. The supplier and the consumer engage in a transaction of Koreanness outside of Korea: growing, partaking of Koreanness because they have parted from it. A local religious fanatic, Paul, is Jacob's trusted help. Paul, on occasion, bursts out praising the Lord. Every Sunday without fail, Paul slogs along the country road, carrying Christ's wooden cross on his shoulder. Although Monica is a devout Christian, Paul, unlike his apostolic namesake who proselytized in Asia Minor, does not seem to have any effect on Jacob. Much to Jacob's dismay, Korean wholesalers back out of their deal at the last minute. A furious Jacob is left with a whole shed of vegetables and fruits wilting under the southern sun. Class resentment erupts as Jacob curses sly, untrustworthy Korean compatriots in the cities. This remains, however, the formula to minority success in businesses: milking one's own kind for cheap labor to stay competitive in the majority market. Filmmaker Chung chooses to feature intraracial antagonism, and only briefly for that matter, rather than interracial tension. Local Ozark residents appear to accept the immigrant family; no significant racial rancor and conflict arise between the poor country folks and the new arrivals. Playing safe in his melodrama, Chung refrains from ruffling white self-image and mainstream sensibility.

No Ozark bigotry rears its ugly head, except an innocent enough remark from a white boy, Johnnie—"How come your face is so flat?"—countered by David's matter-of-fact "It's not." David and Johnnie later become fast friends. Unfavorable first impressions give way to harmony and bonding. What troubles David more, akin to Jacob's troubles with metropolitan Koreans, is the coming of his grandmother, foul-mouthed, ill-behaved, a downright stereotypical alien that is an *idée fixe* out of white representations of Asians. David's narrative perspective is key to the relative success with mainstream media. In between white and Korean cultures, speaking predominantly in English with the feel of an American bildusroman, David is the perfect conduit for the alien universe and, particularly, the alien grandmother to reach the screen without ever alienating white sensibility. David's exasperation over a grandmother who shares his room, eats disgusting food, and blasphemes approximates how an American would react to an unknown transplant. From the centrality of the Americanized Korean boy, the grandmother is polarized into the hated intruder and the mythical savior. Savior indeed; even David's heart is strengthened as the grandmother urges him to run wild outdoors, contrary to the parents' warning. While the first, immigrant generation, such as Jacob and Monica, struggles to raise a family, the second or third generation, such as David, enjoys the luxury of romanticizing ancestral heritage, albeit in a problematic, self-contradictory way.

David's pivotal role is beyond dispute. On the one hand, white resistance resonates with the boy's frustration over the grandmother's bizarre and incomprehensible behavior. On the other, the white audience identifies with David, including his affiliation and "blood" ties with the grandmother, a familial, spiritual succor in life's struggle. That the grandmother is, simultaneously, the destroyer and the savior comes through most vividly in the wake of Jacob's grocery debacle. Incapacitated by a stroke, the grandmother seeks to help the family but accidentally torches the shed stacked with vegetables. After the grandmother passes, the bereft father and son revisit the riverbank where she had sowed minari seeds brought from Korea, seeds that would be deemed contraband smuggled in nowadays, if not in the 1980s. Jacob and David squat, a Korean body language considered uncouth in the West, to gather minari flourishing in patches near the water, the sole surviving vegetables, the gift of life from the dead, after a fire caused by the grandmother (figure 12.2). The grandmother is the fire that incinerates and the water that inspirits. A loop of familial and cultural ecosystem, she drinks the grandson's urine by accident and gives herself back in water celery from Korea by design, the filmmaker's design, that is.

Rather than a simple, feel-good happy ending, this finale reveals an unwitting irony. For Asian Americans, just like their fellow Americans, the alien grandmother is mythologized only in death. She is redeemed as a redeemer *after* she is killed narratologically. No good alive, she is worth a million in death. Such is the course of life for this nation's minorities. Early settlers' "The only good Indian is a dead Indian" alchemizes into the "noble savage" for settlers' children, through a Midas White Touch that transubstantiates a genocide

FIGURE 12.2. David and his father, Jacob, squat to gather water celery planted by David's late grandmother in *Minari*.

into golden memory. Beyond retiring the grandmother from life, Chung retires, likewise, the stereotype of the raging immigrant patriarch taking it out on his family for a lifetime of disillusionment, a stock character prevalent in Asian American literature and film. Jacob, fortunately, never rises to the occasion, so to speak. David's nasty trick of having the grandmother drink a coke bottle of his urine infuriates Jacob, not only morally but subconsciously. What the grandson does to the grandmother with his urine echoes what society has done to Jacob the chicken sexer, whose profession hinges on the cloaca, the posterior orifice for feces and reproduction. The immigrant family eat because Jacob and Monica have been "eating (chicken) shit."

In his towering rage, Jacob follows, supposedly, the Korean tradition, dispatching David to fetch a switch for his own punishment, possibly a lashing on the calves. This is already a "downgrade" from the weapon of choice in Korean historical dramas, which favor wooden clubs in the shape of police truncheons. The protagonist Chunhyang in Im Kwon-Taek's *Chunhyang* (2000), for example, is treated to a savage beating after she rejects the advances of the lecherous local magistrate, the father figure for villagers. By having the camera pan up, away from the "crime scene," to the tune of Chunhyang's nonstop *pansori* singing amid smacking of flesh and cracking of shin bones, Im aestheticizes and insulates the beating that would cripple anyone tied to the chair. In place of Im's shift to the musical to avert violence, Chung elects a pseudo-realistic twist. The father's fury dissipates when David returns with a single blade of Arkansas long grass to stroke gently, lovingly the grandmother's cheeks. A family trauma is forestalled with David's stroke of genius in using what is practically a light feather to move and remove Jacob's mountain of wrath, a fusion of Korean flaming sword of forbiddance and American prairie grass of forgiveness. A melodramatic wish fulfillment for the boy to flee from the shadow cast by the father! For the boyish Hollywood, *Minari* exits the shadow of anti-Asian hate crimes perpetrated by the bottom of America—Atlanta crazies and New York homeless and more—under the command from the very top of Trump's White House and the Trumpian horde in Congress, in states, and in localities.

Minari concludes with a local Arkansas diviner locating underground water with a forked divining rod, the spot subsequently marked by the heavy black rock Jacob carries, a tradition from Korea with its rocky landscape and rock art. The coming together of the local and the exotic portends life, as water is, one hopes, to ooze from below that rock. Bipolar America evinces a contrast: half of it sheds Asian blood in assaults; the other half lets flow the secret of life, all the way from Asia, subterraneously, symbolically. Half of it sacrifices Asian bodies; the other half sacralizes Asian ghosts.

CODA

Refugees with Guns, *Laobing* with Phallus

Ghost of Taiwan circa 1949

Approximately one million Nationalist (Kuomintang) mainland Chinese and their families under Generalissimo Chiang Kai-shek retreated to Taiwan in 1949, having lost China to the Communist troops under Chairman Mao Zedong.[1] Taiwan had recently emerged from the Japanese colonization of 1895–1945 with a population mostly of Fujian, Guangdong, and Hakka descent, whose ancestors had migrated across the Taiwan Strait during the Ming and Qing dynasties (1368–1911), subduing the Indigenous Austronesian peoples.[2] The historical conundrum of Taiwan, thus, culminates in 1949 when Nationalist soldiers arrived with their weapons and young families. Was this flood of military personnel and civilians an occupation force, taking over control from the Japanese Empire and from southern China's settler-colonizers of aboriginal lands? Were they war refugees? Were they both or something else altogether, awaiting half a century later their proper name?

The conundrum of their historical identity crystallizes in my late mother's memory when she, always reluctantly, shared snatches—themselves stylized—from her saga of *taonan*, the well-worn phrase of "fleeing disaster" deployed by her generation of mainland Chinese to describe their escape from

---

1. Situated in the Midwest of the US with a paucity of Chinese-language materials, I sought help to jump-start the project from Drs. Antonia Chao at Donghai University, Fu-chang Wang at Academia Sinica, and Youhua Wang at National United University, who generously shared their expertise. My argument and any errors herein are solely mine.

2. See Fu-chang Wang's *Ethnic Imagination in Contemporary Taiwan*, 147.

the Japanese first and then the Chinese Communists of the 1930s and 1940s. Taonan is a lexicon seared in the Chinese consciousness because it recurs throughout millennia of dynastic history with endless wars and waves of refugees. A young mother of a toddler, whose second child perished months after birth for reasons unknown, she and my father jostled with the masses at the Guangzhou dock, trying to board any ship bound for Taiwan before the communist attack. I recall her frenzied eyes and hands and voice, as though shaking still after all those years, when she described how the crowd fought on the gangplanks to the ship, many falling into the sea. In total despair, they suddenly spotted my father's Huangpu Military Academy classmate Zhu Jinfeng (Zhu Gold Peak), an army officer commanding his squad of *qiangbing* (槍兵 armed soldiers, literally "gun soldiers"). Zhu ordered his soldiers to commandeer a boat, ferrying my parents and eldest brother to the far side of the ship for boarding.

Without Zhu and his "gunmen," I would not have been born, at least not in Taiwan. Had I been born and come of age in China to an ex-Nationalist family during the Cultural Revolution, I would not be writing this in English as a foreign-born American academic. Every Lunar New Year when I was growing up in Taiwan, Zhu was our honored guest since he stayed a bachelor for years, a factory foreman in the remote town of Tucheng, "Dirt City," which suggested to a child's imagination how far he had fallen, from his namesake tiptop to the ground. The child also came to see "foreman" as possibly the parents' euphemism for doorman. Throughout my childhood, I had difficulty deciphering his heavy accent, nor the patience to follow his slow, labored speech. (How could Taiwanese-speaking workers on the factory floor understand their foreman's instructions?) He lost all his pensions and assets in a failed marriage to a young Taiwanese or Indigenous wife, plus his jaw due to a botched surgery. So heavily bandaged was he one Lunar New Year that he could hardly eat. Our "savior" Uncle Zhu soon vanished; his "gun soldiers" might have fared even worse in Taiwan, had they made it across.

By reading doorman into foreman, do I restore or distort the truth? Do I disrespect the dead and, in Susan Sontag's words, "the pain of others"? If Zhu were my father's classmate, why did my father not command his own "gunmen"? To seize a boat in front of a horde of panicked refugees by the dock, how many guns with bayonets had Zhu arrayed to prevent the melee of scrambling onboard? If Zhu had at his disposal such an overwhelming force, what was his military rank and why did he fall so precipitously in Taiwan? Had my parents ever shared their escape on Zhu's boat in Zhu's company? If so, did details vary? If not, why did they not retell the story, since gratitude seemed due for the Ma family's redeemer on his annual visit? Conceivably, Zhu's marital debacle had never been the subject around the Lunar New Year dinner table in Zhu's presence. How did the family lore of Zhu's coming to the rescue in Guangzhou devolve into his tragic end in Taiwan? How did the narrative of Zhu's fall relate to the Mas' generational exodus from China to Taiwan and to America? The Ma family embarked on a journey to Taiwan, only to disembark decades later in America in an endless flight of the Taiwanese Other or *waishengren* (foreign province people or mainlander) morphing into white America's "perennial aliens." Like a long shot into family and collective history, my focus is decidedly off, the details blurred. The truth may never be known, only questions surrounding my late parents' reluctant and perhaps unreliable memory and my own postmemory of trauma twice removed. The occluded vision herein rather befits Taiwan, a ghost island in history and in collective unconscious specializing in spectrality.

Dubbed by Wu Zhuoliu as the *Orphan of Asia* (1945), Taiwan has long been a convenient waystation for the Portuguese, Dutch, Spanish, British, Japanese, and even dynastic Chinese colonizers to stop and replenish, or even to settle, ever since the sixteenth century. Taiwan has been the "founding foundling" fathered and abandoned by these foreign masters, the last one in 1949 claiming to be Taiwan's biological father.[3] This essay focuses on novels and short stories, personal and historical accounts, and films of that fraught moment when refugees, some with guns, fled to Taiwan for dear life, crushing other lives in their wake. Their settling-in unsettled those who had already settled there, a karmic cycle entirely man-made. Specifically, I explore the shared literary and filmic motif of *laobing* (老兵 old soldiers or Nationalist veterans, in the plural or the singular) as pedophiles, perverts, and phantoms. Represented largely by second-generation waishengren or mainlander writers, many of these old soldiers or veterans—armed no longer with guns, but fetishized as phantasmagoric phalluses—had relocated to Taiwan without much education and life skills, some of whom were even drafted at gunpoint in China, the so-called snatched soldiers. One of the most wretched groups in postwar Taiwan without money and family, laobing–*cum*–sexual predators displace the ambivalent subconsciousness of Nationalist refugees with guns and that of their children, both of whom project their collective trauma and sin onto the scapegoat in their midst. Also transferred onto laobing, precisely because of their disempowerment, is waishengren's awareness of their own increasing irrelevance to Taiwan(ese)-centric politics and culture. So goes the historical irony of host/age. Like any foreign body multiplying itself in a host body, one becomes the host by taking hostage the natives and their land. The uroboros of time in the form of rise and fall, death and rebirth, would eventually

---

3. The trope of "founding foundling" for Taiwan is used in my chapter 1, "Trauma and Taiwan's Melodrama: Seven Orphans of *Cape No. 7*," in *The Last Isle* (2015).

loop back, as it has for waishengren, devouring that which used to devour. Although deemed strangers ill-adapted to the island, laobing, serendipitously, embody Taiwan, the orphan ghosts that come in handy as tropes since they can be unhanded anon. Waishengren and Taiwanese writers do unto laobing—the sacrificial lamb straitjacketed in wolf's clothing—what China and the international community have done unto Taiwan.

Taiwanese writer Li Ang has long ago availed herself of gothic metaphors for Taiwanese women under patriarchal oppression, attested to in her preface to *Kandejian degui* (Visible Ghosts [2004]): "Such a ghost island is borderless and not a country, and its voices are outside the center of the grand national body and can be taken as extraterritorial ghost talks and indiscernible ghost sounds" (8, qtd. in Chia-rong Wu's *Remapping the Contested Sinosphere* [2020] 35). Li Ang in effect splices Taiwan's body politic with the female body. To call oneself a ghost beyond humanity smacks of the posture of self-abasing and self-caricaturing, reminiscent of Freudian psychologizing of jokes in *The Joke and Its Relation to the Unconscious* (1905). Rather than Freudian subconsciousness, Taiwan is explicitly treated as a political pariah by the international community, not quite a nation, the Taiwanese not quite a people, as the twenty-three million Taiwanese are de facto stateless, if not homeless, in the eye of all but thirteen countries, plus the Holy See, last I checked. The collective disenfranchisement rubs off even more on Li Ang's five female ghosts at the mercy of "a patriarchal, Han-dominated society" in *Visible Ghosts* (34, translations herein mine unless otherwise noted). Magical disabilities, however, animate Li Ang's ghostly tropes. In her 2011 novel *Fushen* (Possessed), she likens Taiwan's repeated colonization to spiritual possessions with supernatural affinities, albeit implied. By giving voice to specters, *Visible Ghosts* further capitalizes on spectrality, Li Ang's and Taiwan's area of specialization. This heritage extends to the Taiwanese Australian scholar Chia-rong Wu. In citing Li Ang's *Visible Ghosts* in his *Remapping*, Wu borrows from Li Ang in seeing Taiwan as a "ghost island," an apt term for the nation's increasingly beleaguered and precarious "half-life" under the long shadow cast by Beijing's "Chinese Century." The voices emitted from the not so "grand national body" are indeed "ghost sounds," not excepting those sounds shoved into rather than generated from the mouths of apparitional laobing.

Laobing and Their Makers

If laobing were the pedophiliac, perverted, and phantasmagoric Frankenstein's monsters, then the mad scientist Frankenstein, or the rapacious Republican China and Nationalist Taiwan, had made them, particularly early Nationalist policies in Taiwan forbidding soldiers from marrying. Taiwanese sociologist Antonia Chao lays out the crux of the issue:

> It was towards the end of the Chinese Civil War of 1946–49 that the Nationalist (KMT) government attempted to counteract its military failures by means of recruiting involuntarily people from the rural areas of the Mainland. . . . Throughout the 50s, marriages to these "snatched soldiers" was legally forbidden by the KMT's Taiwan-based government-in-exile for the purpose of maintaining national security. The result of this enforced provision was that for the next fifty years thereafter the majority of this cadre of "snatched soldiers" (now officially singled out as "glorious citizens"), remained unmarried. ("Modern State" [2004] 2)

"Recruiting involuntarily" means to coerce joining up, often at gunpoint. "Glorious citizens" may well be translated as "honored citizens." Sexual problems, however, come to taint and dishonor their images. Chao has detailed such sexual abjection in a series of sociological articles, touching on all three organizing motifs herein.

Chao in her abstract to "Nationalistic Language as an Open Secret" (2002) cites interviews of the "first-generation of Mainlanders" to analyze the "Open Secret" of their sex life, one labeled "magic realism" (46). These laobing interviews preserve their voices, albeit in a piecemeal fashion. The keyword "Materiality" in her article's subtitle refers to economic transactions that are the basis for marriages and families. The title's "Open Secret" describes rampant cheating in the miserable life of laobing eking out a living by duping one another. Chao records a Ms. Sun who finds laobing, including the subject Uncle Dai, "physically perverse, and psychologically perverse" (70). Another interviewee, "Uncle Dai," has devoted his retirement to appease "laobing's hungry ghosts" (72). Conceivably, helping these ghosts find peace can be interpreted as Uncle Dai trying to find peace himself. What is perversion in the eye of Ms. Sun is but Uncle Dai's sense of urgency for his fellow comrades, all the late laobing.

In "The Modern State," Chao studies "Taiwan's Glorious Citizens and their Mainland Wives." Twice in her field study, Chao was invited by two "Medicinal Liquor Uncles" to partake of liquor spiked with proverbial aphrodisiacs "good for men and women" (4). A college researcher collecting primary materials is mistaken for a sex worker by these lonely, aging bachelors. An Uncle Zhang even solicited explicitly: "My bed is not so small, we'll manage, no problem!" (6). Yet another laobing, Uncle Jiang, enjoys multiple partners, practically his "four wives" (17), reflected in one of Chao's subheadings in quotation marks: "All honored citizens are perverts" (20). This negative public perception seems to justify treating laobing's private sex life as fair game. By way of materialist and socioeconomic analyses, Chao seeks to dismantle the assumption of laobing aberration. The alleged perversion reaches into the ghostly realm in "Intimate Relationships and Ethical Practice." Recalling the forced march near Hankou, China, in 1948, an Uncle Wei mocks himself: "I was between man and ghost that time anyway. If I die, I become a ghost. If I survive, I wouldn't be all that different from being a ghost" (538). Uncle Wei belittles his younger self to satirize his present, frail and phantomlike, left to waste away at an "Honored Citizens' Home," an assisted-living facility in Taiwan. Self-pity and self-mockery are designed to shame the society that has deprived him of dignity.

Chao's realistic portrayal of laobing's lifelong dilemma parallels literary representations of laobing by waishengren writers, mostly second-generation Taiwanese writers of mainland Chinese descent. Many were born and raised in Taiwan, quite a few in *juancun,* military dependents' villages dotted across Taiwan to accommodate the flood of mainlanders. The moniker waishengren aims to distinguish the subjects from *benshengren* (this province people), Taiwanese residents whose ancestors arrived from Fujian, Guangdong, and other mainland provinces long before 1949, some as early as the eighteenth and nineteenth century. Waishengren or second-generation writers coalesced around a re-envisioning of laobing at the turn of the century as a collective root-searching to counteract, even if subconsciously, benshengren or Taiwanese writers' home-soil or nativist movement.[4] As benshengren formed their ethnic identity and took over governance through democratic elections, waishengren, approximately 10 percent of the twenty-three million Taiwanese, felt compelled to claim their own heritage. In a modernizing, majority-ruled Taiwan, the disappearance of obsolete, housing-project-style juancun and other waishengren symbols, most of all the Nationalist-dominated government, came to inspire second-generation writers to launch nostalgic backward glances. That the literary and artistic glance converges around laobing as pedophiles, perverts, and phantoms is already foreshadowed by Chao's sociological treatises unwittingly skirting all three p's, to be read in Mandarin's fourth tone *pi*'s (屁) for "farts" in the plural—unseemly, malodorous, undesirable, yet recurring outbursts from the bottom, pun intended, of Taiwan's humanity. At a minimum, laobing are symptomatic of Taiwan's digestive problems, a case of constipation, so to speak, after having consumed snatched soldiers

---

4. See Sung-sheng Yvonne Chang's *Modernism and the Nativist Resistance* (1993) for the tension between the island's modernist and nativist movements.

and extracted their sweet youth. More broadly, laobing stand as a clue to the endemic malaise of the ghost island's traumatic history and culture.

Given the fact that laobing live on largely through waishengren writers and artists, i.e., children of "refugees with guns," my opening's "project[ing] their collective trauma and sin onto the scapegoat" ought to be revised as "posttrauma and original sin." After all, few of these chroniclers of laobing have experienced the cross-strait flight themselves, nor were they grown up enough to enact Nationalist discriminatory policies to personally, systematically sin against the Taiwanese population, schoolyard bullies excepted. Yet faced with the aging of the first-generation mainlanders, the dissipation of juancun, and the erosion of other Nationalist icons, they reconstruct the past through a race to the bottom, as it were. The abominable laobing existence signals waishengren's elegy for themselves, mourning the demise yet, paradoxically, sounding like the mea culpa for past sins, or transgressions against the deceased as well as the living, against mainlanders as well as Taiwanese. Although narrated often from the laobing perspective and set in their lives, these laobing stories have less to do with laobing than with second-generation waishengren writers themselves, less to do with laobing memory than with waishengren's perversion of postmemory, as Marianne Hirsch defines it.[5]

This dynamic is antithetical to the prototype of trauma studies—Holocaust narratives. Hirsch maintains in *Family Frames* (1997) that "postmemory is distinguished from memory by generational distance, and from history by deep personal connection." Postmemory is deemed "a powerful and very particular form of memory precisely because its connection to its object or source is mediated not through recollection but through an imaginative investment and creation. . . . Postmemory characterizes the experience of those who grow up dominated by narratives that preceded their birth, whose own belated stories are evacuated by the stories of the previous generation shaped by traumatic events that can be neither understood nor recreated." Hirsch concludes on a lyrical note: "[Postmemory] is as full and as empty, certainly as constructed, as memory itself" (22). Indeed, memory floods the mind's eye, even fills one's eyes with tears, when it has no corporeal existence other than a surge of synaptic, electromagnetic signals, fleeting and intangible.

Squarely taking on the subject of the Holocaust in *The Generation of Postmemory* (2012), Hirsch reiterates the heft of Holocaust family lore that has

---

5. What Marianne Hirsch terms postmemory is variously named "'absent memory' (Ellen Fine), 'inherited memory,' 'belated memory,' 'prosthetic memory' (Celia Lury, Alison Landsberg), 'mémoire trouvée' (Henri Raczymow), 'mémoire des cendres' (Nadine Fresco), 'vicarious witnessing' (Froma Zeitlin), 'received history' (James Young), 'haunting legacy' (Gabriele Schwab)" (*The Generation of Postmemory* [2012] 3).

been weighing on her since 1997, so much so that she pronounces: "the magnitude of my parents' recollections and the ways in which I felt crowded out by them" (4). Opposite to Hirsch's felt inadequacy, laobing are largely "bumped off" in narratives purportedly dedicated to them; they are replaced by waishengren writers' preoccupation with the here and now. Literally, laobing denote "old soldiers," where veterans and bachelors are rolled into one, without family and children. No waishengren writer claims Hirschean family lineage, or bloodline, to laobing; none of them professes an "evacuat[ing]" of his or her creative self by laobing memory. The inextricability of Hirsch's postmemory and her Holocaust-survivor parents' memory does not disturb waishengren, who are at liberty to project fallacies onto laobing. Take, for instance, Taiwan's celebrity writer, Long Yingtai.

Long served as Taipei's director of culture from 1999 to 2003 under Mayor Ma Ying-jeou, and subsequently as Taiwan's minister of culture from 2012 to 2014 under President Ma Ying-jeou. In 2009, during the lull between her two government tenures, Long published *Dajiang Dahai 1949* (大江大海 1949, or *Big River Big Ocean 1949*) in the *CommonWealth Magazine* (天下 雜誌). The afterword pays tribute to Professor Kong Liangling, "who created an unprecedented 'Distinguished Humanities Scholar' Chair" at the University of Hong Kong, allowing Long "a yearlong retreat devoted solely to writing," apparently this book (281). Long likens Kong's academic maneuvering in Hong Kong to the Sanskrit-Buddhist blessing *jiachi* (加持, adhiṣṭhāna or blessing). Thus blessed by political figures in Taiwan as well as academic figures in Hong Kong, Long endows us with a loose, messy collage of interviews, reminiscences, historical facts, imaginary reconstructions, and personal reveries in the name of the Nationalist exodus from China to Taiwan in 1949. Long's personal, narcissistic proclivity is sprung on the reader right from the outset when an unidentified photograph of a possibly mixed-race young man graces the epigraph, who turns out to be Philip, Long's son educated in Germany. The book thus opens with Philip's interview of Long, who was born in Kaohsiung, Taiwan, in 1952, an overture that is tangentially related to the exodus of 1949 and a preview of Long's power of association spanning not just "Big River Big Ocean" in the title but also, far more expansively, continents, histories, and whatnot. This metanarrative of interviews within interviews sets the stage for the palimpsests of the book. The epigraph of sorts identifies the *waishengren* as "losers" in China's Civil War, concluding with "I, proud of being the next generation of 'losers.'"

Although Long's very first interviewee, Guan Guan, a Taiwanese modernist poet, is a typical laobing, one of the snatched soldiers "kidnapped" by the Nationalists (108), Long proceeds to focus on an array of Taiwan's Who's Who, renowned figures of politicians, entrepreneurs, scientists, and military generals, all from the upper crust of society in China and in Taiwan, far removed from "snatched soldiers" who are the "bottom feeders." For example, Guan Guan's interview is immediately followed by that of Ya Xuan, an even more celebrated modernist poet, but a *liuwang xuesheng,* or a refugee student who fled the Japanese and the Communists in groups constituted by the school principal, teachers, and schoolmates. Both poets cry during the interviews at the point of their departure from home (52, 65), comforted by Long, an affective reaching out.

But even Guan Guan himself stands as a counterexample to laobing desolation, for he has developed into a wordsmith and climbed up the social ladder. By featuring Guan Guan as a premier "model laobing," de facto the only case of laobing, Long borders on repudiating laobing en masse who have failed to, as Americans love to boast, "pull themselves up by their own bootstraps," as though never having exploited Native Americans, Black slaves, Chinese coolies, and Hispanic labor. Long's choice of Guan Guan and only Guan Guan rings of the nomenclature of Asian "model minority" deployed by mainstream white people in the US to castigate, underhandedly, Blacks, Latinx, and Native Americans. If Long intends a tribute to the refugee generation in *Big River Big Ocean,* the bottom rung of the exodus is "drowned out," or, as Hirsch puts it, "crowded out."

Long branches into a remapping of Taipei via China's geography, since most urban streets are indexed and coordinated with China's provinces and cities in four directions. In a brilliant touch, Long, however, chooses to flaneur across not only the coalesced maps of Taipei's city streets and China's cities but also numerous armed conflicts, ranging as far as Germany during World War II, courtesy of Philip's German ancestry. Superficial skimming of collective memory and warfare signals a flight of fancy away from the cross-strait exodus of 1949, a flight long presaged by Long's overture with Philip. Long's vast dabbling closes in the last one hundred pages or so on postwar resettlement of the Japanese, the Nationalist troops, and the Aborigines drafted by the Japanese. Rather than her titular 1949, "circa 1949" befits her rambling across wartime Leningrad, postwar Germany, Southeast Asia, Japan, China, the US, and Taiwan.

Long is not the only waishengren writer who proffers counterexamples to laobing degeneration into the three p's. Laobing are downright virile, if not the alpha males and ladies' men, in Zhang Fang, Ma Xiu, and, to a lesser extent, the film *Lao Mo's Second Spring* (1984). Despite their shared theme of laobing protagonists as manhood incarnate, Zhang and Ma are in fact diametrically opposed writers. Born in 1932 in Shandong and part of Taiwan's Nationalist literary establishment, Zhang Fang in *Zhangchaoshi* (When the Tide Rises [2001]) pens a counternarrative to the second-generation mainlander authors, mostly born and raised in Taiwan. Instead of an aging, disenfranchised laobing, the protagonist Zhao Tieyuan (Zhao Iron Origin) epitomizes masculinity, giving tremendous sexual pleasure to his Indigenous wife twenty years his junior as well as a lovelorn widow across the street, not to mention a teenage sweetheart in Shandong.

Zhao makes a living by selling *jiaozi* and other foodstuffs along the highway in Eastern Taiwan. His wife sees Zhao as both her "husband and father" (17). The title suggests the high tide as though Zhao climaxes in midlife or Zhao's sexual partners invariably achieve multiple orgasms, courtesy of his sexual prowess. Postcoitally, Zhao is commended by the widow as suitable for "Taipei's midnight cowboy or Ximen Qing in *Jinpingmei*" (63). *Jinpingmei*, also translated as *The Plum in the Gold Vase*, is a graphic, even pornographic, novel in 1610. Ximen embodies, of course, the quintessential lecher in China, who is turbocharged by a legendary surgical intervention of grafting strips of a dog penis onto his male member. Parallel to Zhao Tieyuan, Zhang Fang develops a parallel plot where another laobing singer, Gao Shu, Zhao's acquaintance, is wooed by a daughterlike singer, whose father is two years younger than Gao Shu. A reiteration of the Electra complex rampant in laobing fantasies, Gao winds up marrying a local Pescadores Islands widow. A happy ending ensues when the Zhao and Gao families, along with lovers, converge on the Pescadores Islands, forming a ménage à quatre, or even larger. Financial prosperity hinges on sexual prowess across the land mass of China and the islands of Taiwan and the Pescadores.

According to the author's note to *Zhongshan Beilu Pintie 1964* (*Collage along Zhongshan North Road 1964* [2002]), Ma Xiu was born in 1964, over three decades after Zhang Fang. Ma describes himself as "an unemployed drifter, graduated from Shilin Elementary School [in Taipei], with no other commencement ceremony" in his life. "Having languished in the city, he strolls along the streets still at the age of thirty-eight" (11), the exact age when he published his novel in 2002. The author's proximity of age to the saxophone-playing, forty-two-year-old protagonist Lao Shu encourages a reading of Lao Shu as the author's alter ego, a masturbatory self-transference onto someone adored by three females young enough to be his daughters: twenty-four-year-old Georgie, daughter to the "fallen royalty" of a mainland military general, a Zhongshan North Road bar singer entertaining Vietnam War American GIs on R&R; nineteen-year-old Yuanyuan, a first-year economics student at Taiwan's premier university, daughter to a Taiwanese city councilman and power broker; and Xiao Lian, a runaway from southern Taiwan's juancun. All three young women find in the middle-aged saxophone player a dependable lover. While Georgie and Lao Shu indulge themselves in passionate sex to the tune of live performance by the Glenn Miller Band at Taipei's Zhongshan Hall, Yuanyuan peeps from outside the bar window. The voyeur is as much Yuanyuan as it is the reader. Thus inspired by the thrill of a Peeping Tom, Yuanyuan prevails upon Lao Shu to accompany her to the Children's Amusement Park. Riding the merry-go-round hobby horse, Yuanyuan "leans her whole youthful body into his aging, slouched back" (87). This pedophiliac fantasy blossoms in Yuanyuan's handjob in public: "He senses her hand reaching into his suit pants pocket, gentling stroking. He is surprised and embarrassed. His whole body thrills to it, and not just the male member" (88). Ma Xiu's idealized masculinity, Lao Shu, is beloved by young women of both mainlander and Taiwanese descent, notwithstanding the age difference, the social class divide, and his physical handicap—a limp from having the tendon of his left leg severed during the Kinmen (Quemoy) Islands heavy shelling in the August 23, 1958, Taiwan Strait Crisis (37). Impregnated by her sugar daddy, Xiao Lian also seeks Lao Shu's help in an illegal abortion, with Lao Shu signing as her husband at the underground clinic.

Narratologically, Ma Xiu switches among the three females as if they were like-minded concubines serving their benevolent master Lao Shu. His lower social class stems from his veteran, laobing background. Having grown up in Harbin, China, he joined the Communist Party's People's Liberation Army before switching to the Nationalist Army, retiring only after the 1958 shelling. Such nostalgia waxing over the past in China of the 1930s and 1940s and on Zhongshan North Road in Taipei in 1964 are filaments of imagination from an author born in 1964. Ma Xiu graces his novel with occasional reflections of Taiwan's multilingual universe when Georgie visits her elementary school classmate's grocery stand in Shilin, and across the bar counter between the Mandarin-speaking Georgie and the bilingual Yuanyuan.

The February 28 Incident in 1947 and the ensuing White Terror set the stage for the latter half of the novel, when Yuanyuan and Georgie reminisce about their childhood growing up on different sides of the White Terror.[6] In addition to switching between the two women, the latter half does so against the backdrop of February 28, complemented by Lao Shu's wartime experience with the two rivaling armies. More gratuitous sex between Lao Shu and the virgin Yuanyuan enlivens the latter half on political struggles. This novel was a finalist of the fourth Crown Popular Novel competition in 2002, a contest sup-

---

6. For Taiwan's White Terror, see Sylvia Li-chun Lin's *Representing Atrocity in Taiwan* (2007).

posedly based on reader votes. Taiwan's long-standing mass-market publisher Crown specializes in such soft porn to appeal to the general readership under the Nationalist puritanical, paternalistic apparatus, with a nod to political correctness now that the mainlander-majority Nationalist government had been replaced by the Hoklo-majority Democratic Progressive Party. Crown's novels, be it erstwhile Qiong Yao's self-indulgent romances or Ma Xiu's twenty-first-century soft porn in the name of nostalgia, serve as a release valve for sexual repression and political discontent. That Ma Xiu's protagonist happens to be a laobing bespeaks the author's and his reader's identification with this relic of history fast disappearing in their midst.

Whereas Long Ying-tai, Zhang Fang, and Ma Xiu idolize laobing, the far more prevalent approach among waishengren writers appears to be to distance themselves while lamenting laobing as objects of pity, even of abomination in extreme cases. Liu Daren's *Plankton Tribe* (1990) crystallizes the second-generation's duality. Set around 1965, the novel revolves around a group of college bohemians devoted to modernism, editing journals, and critiquing politics. The opening is ominous as a Taiwanese intellectual is arrested. Idealistic and rebellious, the novel concludes tragically as the protagonist Xiao Tao falls out of love and studies abroad, some native Marxist rebels are betrayed and arrested during the White Terror, and some others flourish in combining modern westernization with commercial enterprise. Xiao Tao's rebellion against his stern mainland Chinese father represents the generational divide, deepened by the Taiwan Strait wedged between the China-born, first-generation waishengren and the Taiwan-born second-generation. A case in point: Xiao Tao "relinquishes them [his parents]. Their entire generation, the cautious, discreet generation. He has folded them into history, a failure, inglorious, a history of flight with neither beginning nor end" (127). Ironically, Liu Daren revisits the parents' generation in *Plankton Tribe*, discursively resurrecting them even as his protagonist consigns them to the dustbin of history.

Laobing as Pedophiles

Seminal to laobing (mis)representations, Zhu Tianxin's autobiographical essay "Thinking of My *Juancun* Brothers" (1992) unfolds in a stop-and-go fashion for twenty-three pages, three of which are devoted to Lao X (Old X, so named with an English letter in the Chinese original), a veteran of the Nationalist Army and an alleged pedophile. Guilty until proven innocent, Zhu condemns these laobing codenamed Old X with anecdotal evidence. Undoubtedly, some of these old soldiers were unscrupulous, even malevolent; bad apples exist in every corner of society. Yet to stigmatize all old soldiers in such a broad stroke betrays psychological scapegoating, which exorcizes Zhu's and the second-generation waishengren's own fear, guilt, and shame. The naming of "Old X" joins the negativity of aging with the placeholder "X" for the unknown, thus for every single laobing. Zhu's naming is "name-calling": laobing from China, languishing among the Taiwanese population, are xenophobically Othered, and Anglicized in such a way that it denotes mystery in English, doubly so for non-English-speakers.

Zhu imagines that on the wedding night of an imaginary juancun woman, on the verge of conjugal intimacy, she would suddenly recall not only her childhood crush Brother Bao in "her father's military undershirt" but also Lao X from her childhood juancun (76). One impending watershed moment that turns a young woman into a married woman triggers a long-buried traumatic memory of sexual knowledge involving two father figures, especially the latter: the "bad" laobing-father. Zhu nicknames this woman, "Let's call her Xiao Ling," whose childhood shame emerged when several daredevil juancun boys, in Zhu's narration, peeked from Lao X's window:

> They usually see Lao X and Xiao Ling doing strange things. Either he strips or he strips off Xiao Ling's clothes and pants. Because of impotence or caution, these Lao X-s won't go so far as to make Xiao Ling bleed or to be found out by the mother at the evening bath. . . . While listening to the story or playing Chinese chess, [these boys] would be dazed, staring at Lao X's crotch, recalling his big cock. Without passing any judgment, they just feel: Fuck! What a King of the Beasts! (78)

Naming the molester "Lao" (Old) and the molested "Xiao" (Little) sets the stage for pedophilia. Yet self-contradiction remains: Lao X's alleged impotence and colossal penis, which stems from fetishizing laobing as an ambivalent phallic symbol that is there and not there, that is larger-than-life and symbolically castrated. Zhu's essay, alas, becomes one of the two sources—more anecdotal than factual, more literary than historical—for the historian Dominic Meng-Hsuan Yang to damn all old soldiers as sexual predators: "Many of the young, the mentally handicapped, and the impoverished became targets of the old soldiers' sexual advances and molestation" (*The Great Exodus from China* [2021] 246). Such a monumental historic project on the forgotten genesis of mainlanders in Taiwan, such slapdash reliance on Zhu's hearsay, such cavalier conviction of laobing en masse!

Zhu's "Thinking of My *Juancun* Brothers" in 1992 is a thinly veiled revision of two characters in an otherwise identical chapter title of eight characters in Ku Ling's *Foreign Province Hometown* (*Waisheng Guxiang* [1988]). Zhu's "Brothers," "*Dixiong*," reverses the word order of Ku Ling's "*Xiongdi*" while preserving the meaning. Zhu's unacknowledged borrowing tantamount to plagiarism is comparable to, to use an analogy in English, a shortening of Ku Ling's "Brothers" to "Bros" and calling the title her own. Akin to the rebelliousness of Liu Daren and other waishengren writings, Ku Ling's characters also manifest the urge to "get out" of mainlanders' juancun.[7] In utter loneliness, the narrator of Ku Ling's autobiographical "Thinking of My *Juancun* Brothers" confesses: "I stare at the tiny source of light [in the skylight], my heart filled with the impulse to break out of this little house." Under duress, a young girl, Maotou, also vociferates: "I only want to leave home, the farther the better!" (178). As the narrator moves away, his "brothers" and "sisters" see him off. Yet the symbiosis of leaving and returning haunts the narrator: "They are probably like me, wishing to get out of that place as early as possible. But so many years after having left, my urge to return grows stronger. I'd very much like to go back to see our village" (190). Waishengren wish to return precisely because there is nowhere to return to; what has been lost remains lost forever.

Ku Ling's preface "Ancestral Origin" demonstrates part of the reason behind his collection. A child of a Mandarin-speaking father and a Hakkanese-speaking mother, Ku Ling grows up polylingual, mastering Mandarin, Taiwanese, and Hakkanese, an admirable achievement in and of itself. Growing up among these dominant tongues in Taiwan gives him a unique perspective on the notion of ancestral origin, one closely tied to one's language(s). In the preface, Ku Ling offers a fleeting glimpse of sexual molestation perpetrated by a retired laobing working at the government unit where Ku Ling's father served. The laobing "often offered her [Ku Ling's precocious classmate] money to molest her" (12). For that reason, the young Ku Ling was tasked with escorting the female student back home. How to comfort these nameless victims? How to atone for our sins? A sense of futility and resignation may have contributed to rounding up the usual suspects of laobing pedophiles in Zhu Tianxin. Ku Ling's short story "Zhang Dragon Zhao Tiger" (張龍趙虎) succinctly chronicles how the two comrades from China's anti-Japanese and Civil War to the present share the bride price as well as the marital bliss with a fifteen- or sixteen-year-old mentally unstable girl. The two protagonists' names—Zhang Dragon and Zhao Tiger—are so random that they have

---

7. See my "Get Out of the Village" not only for the contradiction of "get out" versus "get back in" but also for the double entendre of "departing" and "learning/acquiring from."

served as placeholders for actual names and, in this case, for everyman, i.e., every old soldier.

Beyond hints of pedophilia, Ku Ling gives other deviant images of laobing, such as outlaw criminals bordering on the heroic swordsman in wuxia fiction and film, thus resonating with Zhang Fang and Ma Xiu's alpha males and dialectical opposites to laobing representations. The name of the title character in Ku Ling's "Uncle Ke Sili" (柯思里伯伯) anagrams the word order of Li Shike (李師科), an old soldier who committed the first armed bank robbery in Taiwan's history.[8] Beyond northern China, the hissing sound of "si" and the retroflex "shi" are not as sharply differentiated anyway as they are for the Beijingnese. After having purchased a color TV, the bank robber Li Shike entrusted a fellow veteran with the remainder of the money to help with the education of the veteran's child. Li was turned in to the police, put on trial, sentenced to death on May 21, 1982, and executed five days later. The lightning speed with which the case was closed sought to erase the miscarriage of justice of the earlier coercion of another suspect as the bank robber, who, according to the police, jumped to his death on May 7, 1982.

The ambiguous distancing from and identifying with laobing surfaces in the relationship of Uncle Ke Sili and Ku Ling's narrator, the fellow veteran's teenage son. The robber was "thin and slight, his size just like mine" in the TV footage, the adolescent recalls (39). The adolescent is the one who, in the presence of Uncle Ke earlier, scoffs at three young robbers of a jewelry store. The teen boasts that he would rather rob a bank, which would be the first of its kind, like acing a "first choice school" in Taiwan's annual college entrance exam. That Uncle Ke actually did it and stashed the cash with the teenager's father suggests that Ke did it in a peaked cap and mask to prevent the teenager from such notoriety. The magic in switching Li Shike into Ke Sili reprises Zhu's wordplay on her titular "Dixiong," or "Brothers." Both waishengren writers breathe life into a dead or dying organism of the mainlander identity. Waishengren's vanishing, albeit aesthetically resuscitated in short stories and essays, seems all but certain, given that they are collapsed into the bottom feeders, laobing. Symptomatic of waishengren's vacillation, the teen narrator's affinity to Uncle Ke morphs into the father-son hostility in another of Ku Ling's story, "Father and Son" (父與子), which minces no words in curses lobbed across the generational chasm: the father calls the son "Rebel! Subversive! Damn!," which is countered by the son's "Rigid! Backwards! Idiotic loyalty!" (72).

---

8. See Chuang Wen Fu's "Exploring the Subject of Old Soldiers in the Book *Wai-shen-gu-shan* [sic] Written by Ku-lin."

Laobing as Perverts

The shock of laobing pedophiles culminates long-standing representations of laobing as perverts. These nightmarish figures double, uncannily, as having initiated waishengren writers' dreamscape of storytelling. The duality goes back a long way to Taiwan's modernist pioneer Bai Xianyong, whose afterword to *Lonely Seventeen* (1976) offers a cameo of Lao Yang. That this laobing graces the afterword rather than the preface doubles back to the fetish of laobing: the alpha fallen to the omega, one that continues to haunt the alpha. The army cook, Lao Yang, used to serve Bai's eminent father, Bai Chongxi, the military general who presided over China's southwestern theater of war. Lao Yang became the family cook at the Bai estate in Taiwan, now that Bai Chongxi was relieved of his command after having retreated to the island. From their hometown, Guilin, China, Bai's father must have retained Lao Yang's service in part because of ancestral ties. Lao Yang is hailed by Bai Xianyong as "the teacher who initiated me" through his stories of the Tang dynasty folk heroes and heroines, launching Bai into a career of imaginative storytelling (329). This tribute resembles Zhu Tianxin's Lao X, elevated as juancun children's "initiating master" with endless tales of the "Extermination War against the Communists, *Romance of the Three Kingdoms* and *Outlaws of the Marsh*, or countryside ghost and monster stories" (77).

Although soon forgotten in the rise of such a precocious novelist as Bai Xianyong, immersed as much in Chinese classics as in Western modernism, this laobing of a cook entertained the seven-year-old Bai, bedridden with tuberculosis, with stories of the Tang dynasty. In his "greasy, coal-dusted military cotton coat, with dirty fingernails," Lao Yang regaled the young master with "Eastern Expeditions [to Korea] of Xue Rengui" and "Western Expeditions" of Fan Lihua (330). Like the mother's womb, Lao Yang played the role of a progenitor of Bai's imaginative life, only to receive a nod that is too little too late. Lao Yang is laobing writ small in Bai Xianyong, the pioneer of second-generation mainlander Taiwanese writers. Bai's belated, minimalist tribute to Lao Yang echoes Zhu Tianxin crediting laobing in general for the power of storytelling in "Thinking of My *Juancun* Brothers." The irony lies in the fact that although laobing appear to tell stories to the child Bai and Zhu's juancun brothers, it is the other way around: Bai and Zhu are telling stories about laobing. Given that the stories are far from complimentary, with the odious ring of stereotypical Othering and scapegoating, the telling amounts to telling on them.

In Bai's magnum opus *Wandering in the Garden, Waking from a Dream* (1971), the Lao Yang–esque Wang Xiong has already charted the lowest hell into which laobing characters are prone to fall. Despite its original Chinese title, *Taipei People,* Bai's collection of short stories focuses on the mainlanders stranded between nostalgia for China and their youth, on the one hand, and, on the other, aging and decay in Taipei. From the home-soil perspective, Bai's characters are non-Taipei people, their hearts lying elsewhere, their bodies poisoned cups of memory and melancholia. Wang Xiong in "A Sea of Bloodred Azaleas," translated by Bai Xianyong and Patia Yasin, embodies not only laobing but spans all three p's under discussion, an early prototype of the controversial representations by the second generation, as Bai was born in 1937, fled to Hong Kong in 1948, and then the family settled in Taiwan. Wang Xiong is a forty-year-old family servant obsessed with his six-year-old young master, who bears resemblance to his spoiled child bride back in China. Wang Xiong was "originally . . . a peasant boy from the Hunan countryside . . . trotting off to town to sell the two baskets of grains on his carrying pole; the minute he stepped outside his village he was taken away" (69–70). This snatched soldier winds up serving the narrator's relatives in Taipei. Owing to the class difference, this obsession has never had the opportunity to fester into pedophilia, for the willful young master mocks and dismisses him in English, which Wang could not possibly understand: "*You are a dog!*" (73). The young master then switches to Chinese, which Wang does understand: "He looks like a big gorilla!," a put-down resonating with his namesake Xiong for "bear" (73). Such slights turn Wang Xiong into a morose pervert of sorts, silently watering "bloodred azaleas" that used to be the young master's favorite.

In the wake of the family maid taking up the taunt "Big Gorilla—Big Gorilla—" (75), Wang assaults her, leaving her unconscious, "her skirt ripped to shreds, naked to the waist, her breasts covered with bruises and scratches, a ring of finger-marks around her neck," as though mauled by a beast (76). After Wang Xiong's bloated, fish-nibbled body is retrieved from the Keelong seashore, the young master's mother believes "every night . . . someone water[s] the garden," resulting in azaleas "exploding in riotous bloom as if a chestful of fresh blood suddenly had shot forth from an unstanchable wound and sprayed the whole garden, leaving marks and stains everywhere, bloodred" (77). The representation of Wang Xiong spans the fall of a masochistic, pseudo-pedophiliac slave into a perverted beast savaging a maid and finally into a ghost watering azaleas that his beloved used to love. Reminiscent of Zhu Tianxin's and Ku Ling's sleights of hand over their essay and short story titles, Bai's aesthetic ending sublimates laobing's spilled blood into beauty, a precursor to the problematic aesthetics of violent psychosis in Hao Yuxiang's *Nilü* (*Travel in Reverse* 2010).

Travel in Reverse is set in a dysfunctional family with a mainlander father who is irresponsible and sexually promiscuous, fraternizing with different women at the expense of his own family. The three p's incontrovertibly rub off on Hao's father figure. Hao's afterword concludes with her indebtedness to "my father and mother. All because of them, I am able to read the big book of life" (190). Nonetheless, this acknowledgment jars with the thinly veiled autobiographical fiction beset by a deadbeat dad, caring little for the young daughters he left behind as he flirted with his hospital staff and marrying various mainland wives, reminiscent of Antonia Chao's "Medicinal Liquor Uncles." More ironically, the book opens with the author accompanying her father in the return to his ancestral home in Shandong after half a century of separation. Her father becomes helpless and disoriented, to be babied by the daughter. In keeping with his lifelong shirking of responsibility, the father takes off for a nearby city, abandoning the author to a family of strangers. Part of waishengren writers' pathologizing of laobing-style characters, Hao rebels against the father figure and the mainland heritage while loving them obsessively. Hao's ambivalence is evidenced by Chen Jianzhong's commentary appended to the final pages of *Travel in Reverse,* as though Hao wishes the critic to reveal what she could not bring herself to confess. Chen dubs the protagonist's psychological complex "a daughter passing judgment on her father and her Electra obsession" (192).

The author recalls her junior high school trauma of witnessing an exhibitionist's "smooth black testicles, weighed down, on the verge of breaking and dropping" (47). The school discipline director reprimanded the class, all of whom clamored to peek at the exhibitionist, so much so that the schoolgirls continued to "immerse themselves in the scene of the fattened sausage, the joy of the sizzling meat lingering still as they smack their lips" (47). The narrator's reverie is externalized in her classmates at large, a fig leaf for the incestuous metaphor of oral sex. Hao's first-person narrative voice simultaneously pushes off and highlights the Electra complex: "I was the only one who felt ashamed because this man didn't look like my father at all. But what led me to such an absurd notion?" (47–48). Like the laobing fetish, Hao's father figure overlaps with an exhibitionist bearing scant physical resemblance to the father yet evoking him nonetheless. The sighting of the patriarchal testicles also comes dismembered from the penis, yet the "sausage" in absentia is viscerally savored in the smacking and licking of lips. Paradoxically, the phallic father is eaten, a castration that sires the father in girlish fantasies. In primitive fantasies of *Totem and Taboo* (1913), Sigmund Freud theorizes that the cannibalizing of the father by usurping sons allows the sons to acquire the patriarchal power. Hao enacts a female, Electra version of uniting with the father orally, incestuously.

Such convoluted neurosis parallels the narrator's memory of her father mistaking a girl at a stationery store to be herself, although "I don't wear glasses, nor have any hair braid" (48). Her father's incredulous mistake is a projection of the daughter's own subconscious desire to cease being herself in order to bypass the incest taboo. The forbidding psychosis climaxes in "He is no longer my father. He is more like a son whom I gave birth to and raised." Eventually, the daughter character's abortion realizes the incestuous drive. The bald doctor performing the abortion comes to montage with her father: "I climb up from the operating table to caress my father's hair. His hair is as soft and golden as a baby. Out of my vagina flows pearly green blood. He stretches his tongue to lick it. The soft tongue gently strokes my vulva back and forth" (169). The symbolic fetus secreted within "pearly green blood" is her morally bound self, making way for the desired consummation with the father. That the fetus is invisible reprises the exhibitionist's missing penis that should have fronted his "smooth black testicles." In her idiosyncratic style, Hao exemplifies how the second generation's portrayals of the first generation have much more to do with the children themselves than with the parents.

Laobing as Phantoms

The physical presence of laobing as pedophiles and/or perverts in literature of the late twentieth century and early twenty-first century enjoys a digital and cinematic afterlife, virtual and phantomlike, in Taiwan's video game *Detention*, launched in 2017, and the subsequent eponymous film in 2019. The franchise of *Detention* does not cancel out literary representations of laobing as phantoms in Zhang Dachun's "The General's Gravestone," Zhen Xin's "Old Soldier," and other writings. Not only does Zhang Dachun's general suffer from dementia in his last days, but his spirit wanders the land and advises what to carve on his gravestone, apparently falling on the living's deaf ear. Zhen Xin's web story is set at one of Taiwan's sea defense outposts, where the master sergeant Old Deng is an old soldier who fought the Communists before retreating to Taiwan. To survive on the battlefield, Old Deng and his comrades resorted to cannibalizing enemies' corpses. This transgression against fundamental human taboos has forever marked Old Deng as a grotesque, branded by the likeness of disfigured faces on his back. "On his back is a large uneven pustule of a deep brown color. It looks revolting, the pustule as though moving, squirming. Upon a closer look, it resembles several twisted faces." While the military doctor calls it "cadaver poison" for those who have consumed human flesh, Old Deng believes that it is but a "human face tumor . . . cackling

FIGURE 13.1. The *laobing* janitor Uncle Gao's facial disfigurement in the horror film *Detention*.

whenever I can't bear the pain." Owing to his evil past and mark, Old Deng is assigned to the outpost to fend off ghosts, ranging from the "water ghosts" of the Communist frogmen in night raids, to anti-Japanese resistance fighters' souls, and to multiplying specters with unknown origins.

Outstripping thousands of words, however, is a single image from the film *Detention*. Meet Uncle Gao in figure 13.1, the laobing and high school janitor with one eye gouged out and front teeth pulled by the White Terror police interrogators for his alleged treason and communist sabotage in sharing the school storeroom keys with a reading group in its secret, prohibited night gatherings. Out of a film unfolding in a female ghost's repetition compulsion fraught with trite conceits of the horror genre, only one character shocks and repels viewers via frontal facial mutilation. No other character—neither the student protagonist-*cum*-female ghost Fang, nor her love interest Teacher Zhang, nor Teacher Wei in the love triangle, nor any member of the reading group—countenances such distortion, from which viewers would instinctively recoil. Before turning around for public viewing in figure 13.1, Uncle Gao, his back to the camera, drinks and throws dice in a big rice or noodle bowl, mumbling to himself. Sins such as alcohol and gambling are endemic among the have-nots in an attempt to anesthetize the pain of living and to dream of striking it rich. In a Shandong accent sprinkled with the constant refrain of "*An*" (俺) for "I," Uncle Gao grumbles under his breath that he had fought with the troops in China and loves the [Nationalist] Party, only to be relegated to the abjection of janitorial duties, trading access to the storeroom for a few cigarettes. The reference to cigarettes is not accidental, since the Nationalist policemen's roughing up of an illegal cigarette vender at Taipei's railway station on February 28, 1947, caused the chain reaction of the White Terror.

For this alleged crime, viewers witness in the next shot that Gao's eye was hollowed out, half his face in a bloody pulp, and several front teeth extracted. The horror is foreshadowed by a close-up of the bowl containing not dice, but bloody teeth. As though cloned from *The Lord of the Rings*' Treebeard, a mammoth Tree Man in the high school teacher-officer Bai's uniform and cap would soon strangle Gao to death.[9] Whereas members of the reading group would all be suspected of communist sabotage, arrested and tortured in prison, bloodied and waterboarded, none of them manifests Gao's frontal defacement. Younger characters, students and teachers alike, are afforded cinematic decency, some bloodstains and bruises notwithstanding. By contrast, stomach-churning, nauseating abomination is reserved for the most unbecoming character from the lowest rung of the society: laobing.

Whereas film reviews and scholarly analyses converge upon the White Terror, encapsulated in the cold, violent teacher-officer Bai, whose surname means "White," no attention has been paid to Uncle Gao, a marginal character befitting laobing as the fetish, flashing just once for the shock value, doomed to recede into oblivion. Plenty of ink has been spilled over the teacher-officer Bai instead, who mutates into the looming Tree Man. In the video game, this monstrosity used to be in a Taiwanese peasant's tunic and high-water pants with a conical hat.[10] In contrast to the local, traditional costume of the specter, the face of the video game's teacher-officer Bai resembles, according to Chia-rong Wu in "Spectralizing the White Terror," the former president Ma Ying-jeou (81).

Detention's Chinese title *Fanxiao* (返校) alludes to the custom of designated dates during the summer vacation whereby students report back to school for checkup of their summer homework and for school grounds cleaning. However, *fan* puns with subversion or insurrection against the school, which is the synecdoche of the Nationalist Taiwan. The Chinese title appeals to young video-game players more attuned to a student life. Yet would high school students be so fixated on the banned books of Tagore and Turgenev that they engage in underground meetings to discuss *Fathers and Sons* and the like? Would not students in puberty be more drawn to the other sex than to an Indian and a Russian writer? On the other hand, would not Marxist treatises be more pertinent to the implied subversiveness? To place the reading group in universities seems more credible, which may put off young consumers of video games and horror movies. The White Terror, the martial law era, the

---

9. For an explanation of the system of teacher-officers in Taiwan's educational system, see my "Forgotten Taiwanese Veteran's Memory of Compulsory Service."

10. Chia-rong Wu in "Spectralizing the White Terror" describes this monster as "the long-haired Lantern Specter (*guichai* 鬼差) that wears a Tang suit and a bamboo hat with a lantern in his hand" (77). Evidently, the film transposes a native ghost in video games into a symbol of Nationalist teacher-officer. Wu calls the school storeroom in which the reading group holds secret meetings a "bunker" (80).

first-generation waishengren, including my late parents, and, in particular, laobing are all fading memories to Taiwan's youth, who may dismiss them as a bad dream. Second-generation waishengren writers have failed to pre-emptively preserve laobing as round, three-dimensional, and evolving individual characters with their own agency. Instead, waishengren writers project onto the most disenfranchised in their midst, laobing, their own sense of marginalization and precarity in Taiwan's political and cultural life. Over time, laobing imagery has petrified into the triptych of pedophiles, perverts, and phantoms on the altar to Taiwan's collective unconscious.

WORKS CITED

Absurd Accident (提著心吊著膽). Directed by Li Yuhe, performances by Gao Ye, Ren Suxi, Heyi Pictures, 2017.

Améry, Jean. *At the Mind's Limits.* Translated by Sidney Rosenfeld and Stella Rosenfeld. Indiana UP, 1980.

Amrohi, Kamal, director. *Mahal.* Performances by Ashok Kumar, Madhubala, M. Kumar, The Bombay Talkies, 1949.

Ba Jin. *Reunion* (团圆). https://ishare.iask.sina.com.cn/f/15968575.html. Accessed 1 Mar. 2021.

Bai, Ronnie. "Dances with Mei Lanfang: Brecht and the Alienation Effect." *Comparative Drama,* vol. 32, no. 3, fall 1998, pp. 389–433.

Bai Xianyong. Afterword. *Lonely Seventeen,* by Bai Xianyong, Vista, 1976, pp. 329–40.

———. "A Sea of Bloodred Azaleas." Bai Xianyong's *Wandering in the Garden, Waking from a Dream: Tales of Taipei Characters,* translated by Bai Xianyong and Patia Yasin, Indiana UP, 1982.

"The Ballad of Mulan." 386–535 AD. http://www.tsoidug.org/literary_comp.php.

Bataille, Georges. "The Big Toe." *Visions of Excess: Selected Writings, 1927–1939.* Translated by Allan Stoekl, U of Minnesota P, 1985, pp. 20–23.

Beilein, Joseph M., Jr. *Bushwhackers: Guerrilla Warfare, Manhood, and the Household in Civil War Missouri.* Kent State UP, 2016.

Benjamin, Walter. *Illuminations.* 1955. Translated by Harry Zohn. Shocken, 1969.

———. "The Task of the Translator." *Illuminations.* 1955. Translated by Harry Zohn, Shocken, 1969, pp. 11–25.

Berg-Pan, Renata. *Bertolt Brecht and China.* Bouvier Verlag Herbert Grundmann, 1979.

The Best Partner (精英律師). Performances by Jin Dong, Lyric Lan, Zhu Zhu, 42-episode TV series broadcast by Dragon Televison (东方卫视), 21 Dec. 2019–12 Jan. 2020. https://dramasq.biz/xj/cn191220/1.html.

Black & White Episode 1: The Dawn of Assault (痞子英雄). Directed by Cai Yuexun, performances by Zhao Youting, Huang Bo, Angelababy, Hero Pictures Co., 2012.

Black & White: The Dawn of Justice (痞子英雄二部曲：黎明再起). Directed by Cai Yuexun, performances by Zhao Youting, Huang Bo, Zhang Junning, China Film Group Corporation, 2014.

Blade Runner. Directed by Ridley Scott, performances by Harrison Ford, Rutger Hauer, Daryl Hannah, Warner Bros, 1982.

The Blue Kite. Directed by Zhuangzhuang Tian, performances by Xuejian Li, Fengyi Zhang, Beijing Film Studio, 1993. https://www.youtube.com/watch?v=qigWopqAhTc.

Bodek, Richard. *Proletarian Performance in Weimar Berlin: Agitprop, Chorus, and Brecht.* Camden House, 1997.

Boorstin, Daniel J. *The Americans: The National Experience.* Vintage, 1965.

Brecht, Bertolt. *The Good Woman of Setzuan.* 1947. Translated by Eric Bentley. U of Minnesota P, 1999.

———. "*Verfremdung* [Alienation] Effects in Chinese Acting." *Brecht on Theatre,* edited by Marc Silberman, Steve Giles, and Tom Kuhn, translated by Jack Davis, Romy Fursland, Steve Giles, Victoria Hill, Kristopher Imbrigotta, Marc Silberman, and John Willett, Bloomsbury Academic, 2019, pp. 176–85.

Breitling Women's Watches Ad. *New York Times Style Magazine,* Women's Fashion, 21 Feb. 2021, p. 69. https://www.youtube.com/watch?v=9tLEI-0NFi4.

Broe, Dennis. *Birth of the Binge: Serial TV and the End of Leisure.* Wayne State UP, 2019.

Burke, Edmund. *A Philosophical Enquiry into the Origin of Our Ideas of the Sublime and Beautiful.* 1757. Routledge, 2008.

Burns, Ken, director. *The Civil War.* 9-episode TV series, PBS, 1990.

Cao Xueqin (Tsao Hsueh-chin). *Dream of the Red Chamber.* Translated and adapted by Chi-chen Wang. Doubleday, 1989.

Capra, Frank, director. *Lost Horizon.* Performances by Ronald Colman and Jane Wyatt, Columbia, 1937.

Cargas, Harry James. *Harry James Cargas in Conversation with Elie Wiesel.* Paulist Press, 1976.

Cash, Jean W. "Nat Turner: Misguided, 'fragmented, disjointed' Images." *Mississippi Quarterly,* vol. 72, no. 1, 2019, pp. 117–45.

Castelli, Alberto. "Perspectives on Asia: Is China Kitsch?" *International Journal of Asian Studies,* vol. 18, no. 1, 2020, pp. 87–102. https://doi.org/10.1017/S147959142000042X.

Chang, Sung-sheng Yvonne. *Modernism and the Nativist Resistance: Contemporary Chinese Fiction from Taiwan.* Duke UP, 1993.

The Chang'an Youth (长安少年行). Performances by Wang Yuwen, Caesar Wu. 24-episode TV drama broadcast on Tencent, 20 Apr. 2020–4 May 2020. https://dramasq.me/cn200420/2.html#3.

Chao, Antonia. "Intimate Relationships and Ethical Practice." *War and Society* (戰爭與社會：理論、歷史、主體經驗). Taipei: Lianjing (聯經), 2014, pp. 517–72.

———. "The Modern State, Citizenship, and the Intimate Life: A Case Study of Taiwan's Glorious Citizens and Their Mainland Wives." *Taiwan Sociology,* no. 8, 2004, pp. 1–41. *Airiti Library,* https://doi.org/10.6676/TS.2004.8.1.

———. "Nationalistic Language as an Open Secret: Diaspora, Cultural Citizenship, and the Materiality of Mainlanders' Self-Narratives." *Taiwan: A Radical Quarterly in Social Sciences*, no. 46, 2002, pp. 45–85. Airiti Library, https://doi.org/10.29816/TARQSS.200206.0002.

Chen Kaige, director. *The Emperor and the Assassin*. Performances by Li Xuejian, Zhang Fangyi, Chen Kaige, Shin Corporation, 1998.

———, director. *Farewell My Concubine*. Performances by Leslie Cheung, Fengyi Zhang, Gong Li, Beijing Film Studio, 1993.

———, director. *The Promise*. Performances by Cecilia Cheung, Dong-Gun Jang, Hiroyuki Sanada, 21 Century Shengkai Film, 2005.

———, director. *Yellow Earth*. Performances by Xueqi Wang, Bai Xue, Qiang Liu, Xi'an Film Studio, 1984.

Chen, Lingchei Letty. *The Great Leap Backward: Forgetting and Representing the Mao Years*. Cambria, 2020.

Children of a Lesser God. Directed by Randa Haines, performances by William Hurt, Marlee Matlin, Paramount Pictures, 1986.

Chinese Box. Directed by Wayne Wang, performances by Jeremy Irons, Gong Li, Maggie Cheung, Canal+, 1997.

Chronicles of the Ghostly Tribe (九层妖塔). Directed by Lu Chuan, performances by Mark Chao, Jin Chen, Li Feng, Chuan Films, 2015.

Chu, Jon M., director. *Crazy Rich Asians*. Performances by Constance Wu, Henry Golding, and Michelle Yeoh, Warner Bros., 2018.

Chu, Louis. *Eat a Bowl of Tea*. 1961. Lyle Stuart, 1990.

Chua, Amy. *Battle Hymn of the Tiger Mother*. Penguin, 2011.

Chuang, Wen Fu 莊文福. "Ku Ling *Waisheng Guxiang* Zhong De Laobing Yiti Tanxi" (苦苓《外省故鄉》中的老兵議題探析) ["Exploring the Subject of Old Soldiers in the Book *Wai-shen-gu-shan* Written by Ku-lin"]. (大葉大學通識教育學報) *Da-Yeh Journal of General Education*, vol. 3, May 2009, pp. 9-22. NCL Taiwan Periodical Literature, tpl.ncl.edu.tw/NclService/JournalContentDetail?SysId= A09054798. Accessed 25 Aug. 2021.

Chunhyang. Directed by Im Kwon-Taek, performances by Hyo-jeong Lee, Cho Seung-woo, Seong-nyeo Kim, CJ Entertainment, 2000.

Clarke, John Henrik, editor. *William Styron's Nat Turner: Ten Black Writers Respond*. Beacon, 1968.

Coming Home (歸來). Directed by Zhang Yimou, performances by Chen Daoming, Gong Li, Huiwen Zhang, Le Vision Pictures, 2014.

Conrad, Joseph. *The Heart of Darkness*. 1899. https://www.gutenberg.org/files/219/219-h/219-h.htm. Accessed 10 Oct. 2020.

Crow, Charles L. *American Gothic*. U of Wales P, 2009.

De Witte, Melissa. "China's Cultural Revolution Was a Power Grab from within the Government." *Stanford News*, 29 Oct. 2019. https://news.stanford.edu/2019/10/29/violence-unfolded-chinas-cultural-revolution/.

Debruge, Peter. "Review of *Mulan*." *Variety*, 3 Sept. 2020. https://variety.com/2020/film/reviews/mulan-review-live-action-adaptation-1234758090/.

DeLillo, Don. *Mao II*. Viking, 1991.

Den Tandt, Christophe. *The Urban Sublime in American Literary Naturalism*. U of Illinois P, 1998.

Detective Chinatown (唐人街探案). Directed by Sam Quah, Mo Dai, Wenyi Yao, and Mukuan Lai, performances by Ze Qiu, Janine Chun-Ning Chang. 12-episode TV series broadcast on iQiyi, first aired 1 Jan. 2020. https://www.iq.com/play/19rrhxy5t9.

Detention. Directed by John Hsu (徐漢強), performances by Gingle Wang, Meng-Po Fu, Jing-Hua Tseng, 1 Production Film, 2019.

The Elephant Man. Directed by David Lynch, performances by John Hurt, Anthony Hopkins, Brooksfilms, 1980.

Eliot, T. S. "The Love Song of J. Alfred Prufrock." 1915. https://www.poetryfoundation.org/poetrymagazine/poems/44212/the-love-song-of-j-alfred-prufrock.

———. *The Waste Land.* 1922. https://www.poetryfoundation.org/poems/47311/the-waste-land. Accessed 1 July 2020.

Empresses in the Palace (後宮甄嬛传). 76-episode TV series broadcast on 17 Nov. 2011 on YouKu. https://dramasq.biz/xj/zhenhuan/1.html.

Eng, David L. *Racial Castration: Managing Masculinity in Asian America.* Duke UP, 2001.

The Eye of the Storm (*Baofeng Yan* 暴風眼). Performances by Yang Mi, Zhang Bingbing. 40-episode TV series broadcast on iQIYI, first aired 23 Feb. 2021. https://dramasq.biz/cn210223/1.html#4.

Fanon, Frantz. *Black Skin, White Masks.* 1952. Translated by Charles Lam Markmann. Grove Weidenfeld, 1967.

Fellman, Michael. *Inside War: The Guerrilla Conflict in Missouri during the American Civil War.* Oxford UP, 1989.

Feng Jicai. *Chrysanthemums and Other Stories.* Translated by Susan Wilf Chen. Harcourt Brace Jovanovich, 1985.

Flores, Helen. "Duterte Apologizes for Death of 4 Chinese in Drug Ops." *Philippine Star,* 9 Sept. 2021. https://www.philstar.com/nation/2021/09/09/2125791/duterte-apologizes-death-4-chinese-drug-ops.

Folsom, James K. "Gothicism in the Western Novel." *Frontier Gothic: Terror and Wonder at the Frontier in American Literature,* edited by David Mogen, Scott P. Sanders, and Joanne B. Karpinski, Fairleigh Dickinson UP, 1993, pp. 28–41.

Forster, E. M. *Howards End.* 1910. Knopf, 1943.

French, Howard. *China's Second Continent: How a Million Migrants Are Building a New Empire in Africa.* Knopf, 2014.

Freud, Sigmund. *Beyond the Pleasure Principle.* 1920. Translated by James Strachey. Norton, 1989.

———. "Fetishism." *Miscellaneous Papers, 1888–1938,* vol. 5 of *Collected Papers.* Hogarth and Institute of Psycho-Analysis, 1927, 198–204.

———. *The Joke and Its Relation to the Unconscious.* 1905. Translated by Joyce Crick. Penguin Classics, 2003.

———. *Totem and Taboo: Some Points of Agreement between the Mental Lives of Savages and Neurotics.* Translated by James Strachey. Norton, 1950.

Fuegi, John. *Bertolt Brecht: Chaos, According to Plan.* Cambridge UP, 1987.

———. *The Essential Brecht.* Hennessey and Ingalls, 1972.

———. *The Life and Lies of Bertolt Brecht.* Flamingo, 1995.

Galvez, Daphne. "Duterte 'Sorry' for Deaths of Chinese Suspects in Zambales Drug Sting." INQUIRER.net, 8 Sept. 2021. https://newsinfo.inquirer.net/1485021/duterte-sorry-for-deaths-of-chinese-suspects-in-zambales-drug-sting#ixzz75xlnYvUA.

Gearan, Anne. "Trump Takes Direct Aim at China as Known U.S. Infections Double and Criticism Mounts." *Washington Post*, 19 Mar. 2020. https://www.washingtonpost.com/politics/trump-takes-direct-aim-at-china-as-known-us-infections-double-and-criticism-mounts/2020/03/19/6df10828-6a06-11ea-abef-020f086a3fab_story.html.

Go Ahead (以家人之名 In the Name of the Family). Performances by Songyun Tan, Xincheng Zhang, 46-episode TV series broadcast on Hunan Television, first aired 10 Aug. 2020. https://qdramas.biz/cn200810c/.

The Good Lord Bird. 7-episode TV series created by Ethan Hawke, performances by Ethan Hawke, Hubert Point-Du Jour, Beau Knapp, Showtime, 2020.

Greenspan, Anna. *Shanghai Future: Modernity Remade*. Hurst & Company, 2014.

Gross, David S. "No Place to Hide: Gothic Naturalism in O. E. Rolvaag's *Giants in the Earth*." *Frontier Gothic: Terror and Wonder at the Frontier in American Literature*, edited by David Mogen, Scott P. Sanders, and Joanne B. Karpinski, Fairleigh Dickinson UP, 1993, pp. 42–54.

Guo, Shaohua. *The Evolution of the Chinese Internet: Creative Visibility in the Digital Public*. Stanford UP, 2021.

Hannibal Rising. Directed by Peter Webber, performances by Gaspard Ulliel, Rhys Ifans, Li Gong, Dino De Laurentiis Co., 2007.

Hao Yuxiang (郝譽翔). *Nilü* (逆旅 *Travel in Reverse*). Unitas, 2010.

Hare, David. *Fanshen*. *The Secret Rapture and Other Plays*. Grove Press, 1998, pp. 1–104.

———. "Obedience, Struggle & Revolt." *Obedience, Struggle & Revolt: Lectures on Theatre*. Faber and Faber, 2005, pp. 9–32.

———. *Saigon: The Year of the Cat*. *The Secret Rapture and Other Plays*. Grove Press, 1998, pp. 205–96.

Hayot, Eric. *Chinese Dreams: Pound, Brecht, Tel Quel*. U of Michigan P, 2004.

Hearn, Lafcadio. *Kwaidan: Stories and Studies of Strange Things*. 1904. Houghton Mifflin, 1930.

Heroic Sons and Daughters (英雄兒女). Directed by Zhaodi Wu, performances by Chu Dazhang, Tian Fang, Zhenqing Guo, Changchun Film Studio, 1964.

Hill, Matthew, David Campanale, and Joel Gunter. "'Their Goal Is to Destroy Everyone': Uighur Camp Detainees Allege Systematic Rape." *BBC News*, 3 Feb. 2021. https://www.bbc.com/news/world-asia-china-55794071.

Hinton, William. *Fanshen: A Documentary of Revolution in a Chinese Village*. Vintage, 1966.

Hirsch, Marianne. *Family Frames: Photography, Narrative, and Postmemory*. Harvard UP, 1997.

———. *The Generation of Postmemory: Writing and Visual Culture after the Holocaust*. Columbia UP, 2012.

The Horse Thief (*Daoma zei* 盜马贼). Directed by Tian Zhuangzhuang, performances by Rigzin Tseshang, Jiji Dan, Daiba, Xi'an Film Studio, 1986.

House of Cards. Season 2. Performances by Kevin Spacey, Robin Wright, and Kate Mara, Netflix, 2014.

Hua Mulan. Codirected by Jingle Ma and Wei Dong, performances by Wei Zhao and Kun Chen, Starlight International Media Group, 2009.

Hua Mulan. Directed by Ian Shepherd. Children's documentary film. 2020.

Hunter (獵狼者). Performances by Qin Hao, Yin Fang. 8-episode TV series broadcast on Hunan TV, 24 May 2021–1 June 2021. https://dramasq.biz/cn210524/3.html#1.

The Ideal City (理想之城). Performances by Sun Li, Zhao Youting, Gao Ye. 40-episode TV series broadcast on CCTV, 12 Aug. 2021–31 Aug. 2021. https://dramasq.biz/cn210812/1.html#9 or https://www.youtube.com/watch?v=nJHnqpmnUzk.

If There Is No Tomorrow (我是余歡水). Performances by Jinfei Guo, Miaomiao. 12-episode TV drama broadcast on iQIYI, first aired 6 Apr. 2020. https://dramasq.biz/xj/cn200406/1.html#8.

The Imperial Doctress (女医・明妃传). Performances by Cecilia Liu, Wallace Huo, Huang Xuan. 50-episode TV drama broadcast on Dragon TV, 13 Feb.–9 Mar. 2016. https://www.youtube.com/watch?v=kdZsNXuhrKM.

Ito, Robert. "Mulan, a Most Adaptable Heroine: There's a Version for Every Era." *New York Times*, 3. Sept. 2020. https://www.nytimes.com/2020/09/03/movies/mulan-history.html.

Jameson, Fredric. *The Prison-House of Language: A Critical Account of Structuralism and Russian Formalism*. Princeton UP, 1975.

Keith, Jeffrey A. "Producing *Miss Saigon*: Imaginings, Realities, and the Sensual Geography of Saigon." *Journal of American-East Asian Relations*, vol. 22, no. 3, Oct. 2015, pp. 243–72.

Kennedy, Randall. *N——: The Strange Career of a Troublesome Word*. Pantheon, 2002.

Khaou, Hong, director. *Lilting*. Performances by Pei-Pei Cheng, Ben Whishaw, London Film Productions, 2014.

Kim Ki-duk, director. *Time*. Performances by Jung-woo Ha, Ji-Yeon Park, Jun-yeong Jang, Kim Ki-Duk Film, 2006.

Kingston, Maxine Hong. *The Woman Warrior: Memoirs of a Girlhood among Ghosts*. Knopf, 1976.

Kobayashi, Masaki, director. *Kwaidan*. 1965. Performances by Michiyo Aratama, Misako Watanabe, Rentarō Mikuni, Criterion, 2000.

Koolhaas, Rem. *Delirious New York: A Retroactive Manifesto for New York*. Monacelli Press, 1997.

Ku Ling (苦苓). *Foreign Province Hometown* (外省故鄉 Waisheng Guxiang). Xidai, 1988.

Kung Fu Mulan. Directed by Leo Liao, performances by Danny Fehsenfeld, Vivian Lu, Gold Valley Films, 2020.

Kwan, Kevin. *Crazy Rich Asians*. Penguin, 2013.

Lao Mo's Second Spring (老莫的第二個春天). Directed by You-ning Lee, performances by Sun Yueh, Chun-fang Chang, Chin Hua Motion Picture Company, 1984.

Larsen, Nella. *Quicksand* and *Passing*. Rutgers UP, 1986.

Lee, Ang, director. *Ride with the Devil*. Performances by Tobey Maguire, Skeet Ulrich, Jewel Kilcher, Jeffrey Wright, and Jonathan Rhys Meyers, Good Machine, 1999.

Levi, Primo. *Survival in Auschwitz*. Translated by Stuart Woolf. Collier Macmillan, 1961.

Li Ang. *Fushen* (Possessed). Jiuge, 2011.

———. *Kan de jian de gui* (Visible Ghosts). Lianhe wenxue (Unitas, 2004). http://cloudwriting.campus-studio.com/workspace/index.php?bookID=327.

Lim, Louisa. *The People's Republic of Amnesia*. Oxford UP, 2014.

Lin, Sylvia Li-chun. *Representing Atrocity in Taiwan: The 2/28 Incident and White Terror in Fiction and Film*. Columbia UP, 2007.

Link, Eric Carl. *The Vast and Terrible Drama: American Literary Naturalism in the Late Nineteenth Century*. U of Alabama P, 2004.

Link, Perry. "China: The Anaconda in the Chandelier." *New York Review of Books*, 22 Apr. 2002. https://www.chinafile.com/library/nyrb-china-archive/china-anaconda-chandelier.

A Little Reunion (小歡喜). Performances by Huang Lei, Hai Qing, Gengxi Li. 49-episode TV series based on Yingong Lu's web novel and broadcast by Dragon Television (东方卫视), 31 July 2019–27 Aug. 2019. https://dramasq.biz/xj/cn190731b/1.html.

Liu Binyan. *People or Monster?: And Other Stories and Reportage from China after Mao*. 1979. Edited by Perry Link. Indiana UP, 1983.

Liu Daren. (劉大任). *Plankton Tribe* (浮游群落). Yuanliu, 1990.

Liu, Jin. "Ambivalent Laughter: Comic Sketches in CCTV's Spring Festival Eve Gala." *Journal of Modern Literature in Chinese* 現代中文文學學報, vol. 10, no. 1, summer 2010, pp. 103–21.

Long Ying-tai (龍應台). *Dajiang Dahai 1949* (大江大海 1949, River and Ocean 1949). *The CommonWealth Magazine* (天下雜誌, www.cw.com.tw), 2009.

The Longest Day in Chang'an (長安十二時辰). Performances by Lei Jiayin, Jackson Yee, Rayzha Alimjan. 48-episode TV drama broadcast on Youku, first aired 27 June 2019. https://dramasq.biz/xj/cn190627b/1.html#5.

Loti, Pierre. *Madame Chrysanthème*. Calmann Lévy, 1895.

Lovell, Julia. *Maoism: A Global History*. Knopf, 2019.

Lu Xixing and Xu Zhonglin. *Creation of the Gods*. Translated by Gu Zhizhong. Foreign Languages Press, 2000.

Lu Xun. "A Madman's Diary." 1918. *Selected Stories of Lu Hsun*. Translated by Yang Hsien-yi and Gladys Yang. Foreign Languages Press, 1978, pp. 7–18.

Luo Guanzhong. *Romance of the Three Kingdoms*. Translated by C. H. Brewitt-Taylor, edited by Khang Nguyen, and commentary by Rafe de Crespigny. https://www.threekingdoms.com/. Accessed 10 Oct. 2020.

Ma, Sheng-mei. *Asian Diaspora and East-West Modernity*. Purdue UP, 2012.

———. "Contrasting Two Survival Literatures: On the Jewish Holocaust and the Chinese Cultural Revolution." *Holocaust and Genocide Studies,* 2, 1987, pp. 81–93.

———. "Forgotten Taiwanese Veteran's Memory of Compulsory Service." *Journal of Veteran Studies*, vol. 6, no. 3, 2020, pp. 23–29. Virginia Tech Publishing, https://doi.org/10.21061/jvs.v6i3.210.

———. "Get Out of the Village: Watching *The Prisoner* with Chinese Subtitles in *Juancun*." *Taiwan Lit*, vol. 2, no. 1, spring 2021. http://taiwanlit.org/essays/get-out-of-the-village-watching-the-prisoner-with-chinese-subtitles-in-juancun-1.

———. *The Holocaust in Anglo-American Literature: Particularism and Universalism in Relation to Documentary and Fictional Genres*. 1990. Indiana University, PhD dissertation.

———. "Kung Flu." *America Unfiltered,* 8 May 2020. https://www.ucdclinton.ie/commentary-content/kung-flu.

———. *The Last Isle: Contemporary Film, Culture and Trauma in Global Taiwan*. Rowman & Littlefield International, 2015.

———. *Off-White: Yellowface and Chinglish by Anglo-American Culture*. Bloomsbury Academic, 2020.

———. *The Tao of S: America's Chinee & the Chinese Century in Literature and Film*. U of South Carolina P and National Taiwan UP, 2022.

———. "Vincent Chin and Baseball: Law, Racial Violence, and Masculinity." *The Deathly Embrace: Orientalism and Asian American Ethnicity*. U of Minnesota P, 2000.

Ma Xiu (馬修). *Zhongshan Beilu Pintie 1964* (1964 中山北路拼貼 Collage along Zhongshan North Road). Crown, 2002.

Mao Zedong. *Quotations from Chairman Mao Zedong* (*The Little Red Book*). Foreign Languages Press, 1966.

———. "Quotations from Mao Tse Tung." *Mao Tse Tung Internet Archive,* https://www.marxists.org/reference/archive/mao/works/red-book/index.htm. Accessed 15 Jan. 2021.

———. "Talks at the Yan'an Conference on Literature and Art." 1942. https://library.oapen.org/bitstream/handle/20.500.12657/41559/9780472901333.pdf?sequence=1. Accessed 15 Jan. 2021.

Matchless Mulan (無雙花木蘭). Directed by Chen Cheng, performances by Xue'er Hu, Wei Wei, Jarvis Wu, New Studio Media, 2020. https://www.iq.com/play/19rykyxerk.

McDougall, Bonnie S., translator. "Talks at the Yan'an Conference on Literature and Art." By Mao Zedong. U of Michigan P, 1980.

McTell, Ralph. "Streets of London." 1969. https://www.youtube.com/watch?v=DiWomXklfv8.

Mei Lanfang. *Wutai shenghuo sishi nian* (*Forty Years on Stage*). Zhongguo Xiju Chibanshe, 1987.

Memoirs of a Geisha. Directed by Rob Marshall, performances by Ziyi Zhang, Ken Watanabe, Michelle Yeoh, Gong Li, Columbia Pictures, 2005.

Mencius. *The Works of Mencius*. Translated by James Legge. *The Chinese Classics, Volume 1 & 2*. Wenshizhe (文史哲) Publisher, 1972.

Minari. Directed by Lee Isaac Chung, performances by Steven Yeun, Yeri Han, Alan S. Kim, Yuh-Jung Youn, Plan B Entertainment, 2020.

Minning Town (閩寧鎮, changed in Chinese to *Shanhai Qing* 山海情 2021). Performances by Huang Xuan and Rayzha Alimjan. 23-episode TV drama broadcast on Youku, first aired 7 Mar. 2020. https://dramasq.biz/cn210112b/1.html#3.

Miss Saigon. Music by Claude-Michel Schönberg, lyrics by Alain Boublil and Richard Maltby Jr. 1989. H. Leonard Pub. Corp., 1991.

Miss Saigon. 25th Anniversary Gala, performed live by Eva Maria Noblezada, Alistair Brammer, and Jon Jon Briones at Prince Edward Theatre, London, UK, 22 Sept. 2014. https://www.dailymotion.com/video/x77vk1x.

Miss Truth (大唐女法醫). Performances by Zhou Jieqiong and Toby Lee. 36-episode TV drama broadcast on Youku, from 14 Feb. 2020. https://dramasq.biz/xj/cn200214/1.html#8.

Mitchell, David. *The Thousand Autumns of Jacob de Zoet*. Random House, 2010.

Mizumura, Minae. *The Fall of Language in the Age of English*. Translated by Mari Yoshihara and Juliet Winters Carpenter. Columbia UP, 2015.

Mogen, David, Scott P. Sanders, and Joanne B. Karpinski. Introduction. *Frontier Gothic: Terror and Wonder at the Frontier in American Literature,* edited by David Mogen, Scott P. Sanders, and Joanne B. Karpinski, Fairleigh Dickinson UP, 1993, pp. 13–27.

Mountain Patrol (*Kekexili*). Directed by Lu Chuan, performances by Duo Bujie, Zhang Lei, Huayi Brothers, 2004.

Mr. Donkey (驴得水). Codirected by Lu Liu and Shen Zhou, performances by Suxi Ren, Li Da, Shuailiang Liu, Beijing Fun Age Pictures, 2016.

Mulan. Directed by Niki Caro, performances by Yifei Liu, Donnie Yen, Li Gong, Disney, 2020.

Mulan. Directed by Tony Bancroft and Barry Cook, performances by Ming-Na Wen, Eddie Murphy, BD Wong, Disney, 1998.

Mulan. Directed by Yuxi Li, performances by Chuxuan Liu, Mo Li, iQIYI, 2020. https://www.iq.com/play/owds1dsqvg.

Mulan Legend. Directed by He Jia Nan, performances by Zhang Dong, iQIYI, 2020. https://www.iq.com/play/1d39j9ta5ik.

Mutiny on the Bounty. Written and directed by Lewis Milestone and Carol Reed, performances by Marlon Brando, Trevor Howard, Richard Harris, Arcola Pictures, 1962.

Never Say Goodbye (不說再見). Performances by Ren Jialun, Zhang Junning. 47-episode TV series broadcast on iQIYI, 22 June–July 27, 2021. https://dramasq.biz/cn210622/1.html#3.

Nothing but Thirty (三十而已, literally Thirty Only). Performances by Shuying Jiang, Yao Tong, and Xiaotong Mao. 43-episode TV series on Tencent, first aired 17 July 2020. https://dramasq.biz/cn200717/1.html.

Novoland: Eagle Flag (*Jiuzhou piaomiao lu* 九州縹緲錄). Performances by Fengyi Zhang, Haoran Liu, Zuer Song. 56-episode TV series based on Jiang Nan's web novel and broadcast by Tencent Video (腾讯视频), 16 July–2 Sept. 2019. https://dramasq.com/cn190716b/1.html#3.

Ocean Heaven. Directed by Xiaolu Xue, performances by Jet Li, Wen Zhang, BDI Films Inc., 2010.

One Second. Directed by Zhang Yimou, performances by Zhang Yi, Fan Wei, Liu Haocun, Huanxi Media Group, 2020.

The Outlaws of the Marsh (*Shui Hu Zhuan*). Written by Shi Nai'an and Luo Guanzhong, translated by Sidney Shapiro. Classic Literature Collection (WorldLibrary.org).

Page Eight. Written and directed by David Hare, performances by Bill Nighy and Rachel Weisz, BBC/PBS *Masterpiece Theatre,* 2011.

Painted Skin (畫皮). Codirected by Gordon Chan and Andy Wing-Keung Chin, performances by Donnie Yen, Xun Zhou, Kun Chen, Mediacorp Raintree, 2008.

Painted Skin (畫皮之陰陽法王). Directed by King Hu, performances by Li-hua Chang, Adam Cheng, Ting Chou, New Treasurer Films Company, 1992.

Painted Skin: The Resurrection (畫皮 II). Directed by Wuershan, performances by Xun Zhou, Wei Zhao, Kun Chen, Kylin Pictures, 2012.

Pao, Angela. "The Eyes of the Storm: Gender, Genre and Cross-Casting in *Miss Saigon.*" *Text and Performance Quarterly,* vol. 12, no. 1, pp. 21–39. https://doi.org/10.1080/10462939209359631.

Park Chan-wook, director. *Sympathy for Mr. Vengeance.* Performances by Song Kang-ho, Shin Ha-kyun, Tartan Video USA, 2002.

Park, Patricia. *Re Jane.* Viking, 2015.

Pu Songling. *Strange Tales from a Chinese Studio.* 1766. Translated and edited by John Minford. Penguin, 2006.

Rattan (*Siteng* 司藤). Performances by Jing Tian, Zhang Bingbing. 30-episode TV series broadcast by KuYou, first aired 8 Mar. 2021. https://dramasq.biz/cn210308/1.html#3.

Rattan (*Banyao Siteng* 半妖司藤). Written by Wei Yu. 2014. https://www.sto.cx/book-126909-1.html.

Reborn (*Chongsheng* 重生 2020). Performances by Zhang Yi, Zhao Jinmai. 28-episode TV drama broadcast on Youku, first aired 7 Mar. 2020. https://www.ondemandchina.com/zh-Hans/program/reborn.

The Red Lantern—A Modern Revolutionary Peking Opera. Foreign Languages Press, 1972.

Resnais, Alain, director. *Night and Fog.* Argos Films, 1956.

Ringu. Directed by Hideo Nakata, performances by Nanako Matsushima and Hiroyuki Sanada, Toho Company, 1998.

Rowlandson, Mary. *Narrative of the Captivity and Restoration of Mrs. Mary Rowlandson.* 1682. https://www.gutenberg.org/files/851/851-h/851-h.htm.

Ruohua Ranran (若花燃燃). *Su Xiao's War.* Jiangsu: Phoenix, 2021. https://weread.qq.com/web/reader/0ba3262072639d980babfbekecc32f3013eccbc87e4b62e?.

Rural Love Story (鄉村愛情). Performances by Jianjun Tang, Zhao Benshan, Shufeng He, Xiaoli Wang. 13-series broadcast on CCTV, Tencent, Youku, and other media platforms, 2006–21.

Sacrifice (金剛川). Directed by Guan Hu, Frant Gwo, and Lu Yang, performances by Zhang Yi, Wu Jing, Huayi Brothers, 2020.

Saigon: The Year of the Cat. Directed by Stephen Frears, performances by Judi Dench, Chic Murray, Yim Hoontrakul. Thames Television, 1983. https://www.youtube.com/watch?v=DP20AJXbTXc.

Salting the Battlefield. Written and directed by David Hare, performances by Bill Nighy and Helena Bonham Carter, BBC/PBS *Masterpiece Theatre*, 2014.

Schamus, James. *Ride with the Devil.* Faber and Faber, 1999.

Schwarcz, Vera. *Bridge across Broken Time: Chinese and Jewish Cultural Memory.* Yale UP, 1998.

Shadow in the Cloud. Directed by Roseanne Liang, performances by Chloë Grace Moretz and Nick Robinson, Four Knights Film, 2020.

Shen Fu. *Six Records of a Floating Life.* 1877. Translated by Leonard Pratt and Chiang Su-hui. Yilin Press, 1983.

Shi Nai'an and Luo Guanzhong. *The Outlaws of the Marsh.* Translated by Sidney Shapiro. Indiana UP, 1981. http://uploads.worldlibrary.net/uploads/pdf/20130423230739the_outlaws_of_the_marsh_pdf. Accessed 3 June 2017.

Shimizu, Celine Parreñas. *The Hypersexuality of Race: Performing Asian/American Women on Screen and Scene.* Duke UP, 2007.

Shower. Directed by Zhang Yang, performances by Pu Cunxin, Zhu Xu, and Jiang Wu, Xi'an Film Studio, 1999.

Snow, Edgar. *Red Star over China.* Random House, 1937.

Sontag, Susan. *Regarding the Pain of Others.* Farrar, Straus and Giroux, 2003.

Sorensen, David R. Introduction. *On Heroes, Hero-Worship, and the Heroic in History.* 1841. Edited by David R. Sorensen and Brent E. Kinser, Yale UP, 2013, pp. 1–16.

Stevens, Wallace. "Anecdote of a Jar." 1919. https://poets.org/poem/anecdote-jar.

Stoker, Bram. *Dracula.* 1897. Penguin, 2013.

Strange, Susan. *Casino Capitalism.* Blackwell, 1986.

Strittmatter, Kai. *We Have Been Harmonized: Life in China's Surveillance State.* Translated by Ruth Martin. Custom House, 2018.

Styron, William. *The Confessions of Nat Turner.* Random House, 1967.

Sundquist, Eric J. "The Country of the Blue." *American Realism, New Essays,* edited by Eric J. Sundquist, Johns Hopkins UP, 1982, pp. 3–24.

Suzuki, Koji. *Ring.* 1991. Translated by Robert B. Rohmer and Glynne Walley. Vertical, 2003.

Sweet Life (甜蜜). Performances by Hai Qing, Ren Zhong. 38-episode TV series broadcast on Tencent, first aired 28 Feb. 2021.

Taking Tiger Mountain by Strategy—A Modern Revolutionary Peking Opera. Foreign Languages Press, 1971.

Tan, Amy. *The Joy Luck Club.* Putnam, 1989.

Tatlow, Antony. *The Mask of Evil: Brecht's Response to the Poetry, Theatre and Thought of China and Japan: A Comparative and Critical Evaluation.* Peter Lang, 1977.

Thomas, Dylan. "Do Not Go Gentle into That Good Night." *The Poems of Dylan Thomas.* New Directions, 1952. https://poets.org/poem/do-not-go-gentle-good-night.

Tian, Min. *Mei Lanfang and the Twentieth-Century International Stage: Chinese Theatre Placed and Displaced.* Palgrave Macmillan, 2012.

To Be with You (約定 2021). Performances by Li Xuejian, Xu Fan, Pu Guanjin. 36-episode TV drama broadcast on iQIYI, 8 Feb. 2021–24 Feb. 2021. https://dramasq.biz/cn210208b/1.html#4.

Todorov, Tzvetan. *The Fantastic: A Structural Approach to a Literary Genre*. Case Western Reserve Library, 1973.

Trident (三叉戟). 42-episode TV docudramas broadcast from 23 June 2020 on China Jiangsu TV and online across China. https://dramasq.biz/cn200531/1.html. Accessed July 2020.

Truitt, Brian. "Review of *Mulan*." *USA Today*, 3 Sept. 2020. https://www.usatoday.com/story/entertainment/movies/2020/09/03/mulan-review-disney-live-action-remake-improves-upon-animated-original/3451042001/.

Turks and Caicos. Written and directed by David Hare, performances by Bill Nighy and Winona Ryder, BBC/PBS *Masterpiece Theatre*, 2014.

Twenty Your Life On (二十不惑, literally Twenty No Temptation). Performances by Xiaotong Guan, Guanjin Pu, Gengxi Li, and Siyi Dong. 42-episode TV series on iQIYI, first aired 14 July 2020. https://dramasq.biz/cn200714/1.html.

Vacation of Love (假日暖洋洋). Performances by Yao Chen, Johnny Bai. 35-episode TV series broadcast on iQIYI, 25 Jan. 2021–8 Feb. 2021. https://dramasq.biz/xj/cn210125/1.html#8.

Wang, Andrea. *Watercress*. Pictures by Jason Chin. Neal Porter Books, 2021.

Wang, Fu-chang. *Ethnic Imagination in Contemporary Taiwan*. Socio Publishing, 2003.

Wang, Lulu. "In Defense of Ignorance." *This American Life*. Radio play broadcast 22 Apr. 2016.

———, director. *The Farewell*. Performances by Awkwafina, Shuzhen Zhao, Tzi Ma, Big Beach Films, 2019.

Wang Ruowang. *Hunger Trilogy*. 1980. Translated by Kyna Rubin. M. E. Sharpe, 1992.

Wang, Wayne, director. *Chan Is Missing*. New Yorker Films, 1981.

———, director. *Dim Sum: A Little Bit of Heart*. CIM Productions, Orion Classics, 1985.

———, director. *Eat a Bowl of Tea*. Performances by Cora Miao, Russell Wong, Victor Wong, Eric Tsang, American Playhouse, 1989.

———, director. *The Joy Luck Club*. Based on the novel by Amy Tan. Hollywood Pictures, 1993.

Wang, Zhuoyi. "From *Mulan* (1998) to *Mulan* (2020): Disney Conventions, Cross-Cultural Feminist Intervention, and a Compromised Progress." *Arts*, vol. 11, no. 5, 2022. https://doi.org/10.3390/arts11010005.

Warhol, Andy. *Mao Series, 1972–1974*. Metropolitan Museum of Art, New York City.

Watching It Again and Again (Can't Take My Eyes Off You). 273-episode South Korea TV series, MBC, 1998. Subsequently dubbed and broadcast in China, CCTV, 2003.

Weaving a Tale of Love (风起霓裳). Performances by Gülnezer Bextiyar, Tommy Xu. 40-episode TV drama broadcast on Youku, 27 Jan. 2021–22 Feb. 2021. https://dramaqq.com/cn210127/1.html#4.

Wiesel, Elie. *Legends of Our Time*. Holt, Rinehart and Winston, 1968.

———. *Night*. Translated by Stella Rodway. Avon, 1960.

Wiles, Timothy J. *The Theater Event: Modern Theories of Performance*. U of Chicago P, 1980.

Wilson, Charles Reagan. *The American South: A Very Short Introduction*. Oxford UP, 2021.

Woodrell, Daniel. *Give Us a Kiss*. Henry Holt & Company, 1996.

———. *The Outlaw Album*. Little, Brown and Company, 2011.

———. *Woe to Live On*. Little, Brown and Company, 1987.

———. "Woe to Live On." *Missouri Review*, vol. 7, no. 1, fall 1983, 79–93.

Wu, Alice, director. *Saving Face*. Performances by Joan Chen, Michelle Krusiec, Lynn Chen, Destination Films, 2004.

Wu Cheng'en. *Xiyouji* (*Journey to the West* or *Monkey*). Translated by Arthur Waley. Grove, 1943.

Wu, Chia-rong. *Remapping the Contested Sinosphere: The Cross-Cultural Landscape and Ethnoscape of Taiwan*. Cambria, 2020.

———. "Spectralizing the White Terror: Horror, Trauma, and the Ghost-Island Narrative in *Detention*." *Journal of Chinese Cinemas*, vol. 15, no. 1, 2021, pp. 73–86.

Wu, Zhuoliu. *Orphan of Asia*. 1945. Translated by Ioannis Mentzas. Columbia UP, 2006.

Yan Geling. *Prisoner Lu Yanshi* (陸犯焉識). Writer's Publisher, 2011. https://www.99csw.com/book/3654/index.htm.

Yang, Dominic Meng-Hsuan. *The Great Exodus from China: Trauma, Memory, and Identity in Modern Taiwan*. Cambridge UP, 2021.

Yang Jiang. *Six Chapters from My Life "Downunder"* (*Cadre School Six Records*). Translated by Howard Goldblatt. U of Washington P, 1981.

———. *Taking a Bath* (洗澡 *Xizao*). Sanlian, 1988.

———. *Us Three* (我們仨 *Women Sa*). Xinrenjian, 2003.

Yeats, William Butler. "The Circus Animals' Desertion." *The Collected Poems of W. B. Yeats*, Macmillan, 1959, pp. 335–36.

———. "The Second Coming." *The Collected Poems of W. B. Yeats*, Macmillan, 1959, pp. 184–85.

Yoshikawa, Yoko. "The Heat Is On Miss Saigon Coalition: Organizing across Race and Sexuality." *Loss: The Politics of Mourning*, edited by David L. Eng and David Kazanjian, U of California P, 2003, pp. 41–56.

Yu Hua. *China in Ten Words*. Translated by Allan H. Barr. Anchor, 2011.

———. *Chronicle of a Blood Merchant*. 1995. Translated by Andrew F. Jones. Anchor, 2004.

———. *Huozhe* (活著 *To Live*). 1993. Writer's Publisher, 2008.

———. *To Live*. 1993. Translated by Michael Berry. Anchor, 2003.

Zamperini, Paola. "Untamed Hearts: Eros and Suicide in Late Imperial Chinese Fiction." *Nan Nü*, vol. 3, no. 1, June 2001, pp. 77–104.

Zeitlin, Judith. *Historian of the Strange: Pu Songling and the Chinese Classical Tale*. Stanford UP, 1993.

———. *The Phantom Heroine: Ghosts and Gender in Seventeenth-Century Chinese Literature*. U of Hawai'i P, 2007.

Zhang Dachun. "The General's Gravestone" (將軍碑). *Sixi Worries About the Nation* (四喜憂國). Reading Times, pp. 1–23.

Zhang Fang. *Zhangchaoshi* (漲潮時 *When the Tide Rises*). Zhaoming, 2001.

Zhang, Wei. *Chinese Adaptations of Brecht: Appropriation and Intertextuality*. Palgrave Macmillan, 2020.

Zhang Yimou, director. *Coming Home*. Performances by Gong Li, Chen Daoming, Le Vision Pictures, 2014.

———, director. *The Great Wall*. Performances by Matt Damon, Tian Jing, Willem Dafoe, Legendary East, 2016.

———, director. *Ju Dou*. Performances by Gong Li, Li Baotian, China Film Co-Production Corporation, 1990.

———, director. *One Second*. Performances by Zhang Yi, Fan Wei, Liu Haocun, Huanxi Media Group, 2020.

———, director. *Raise the Red Lantern*. Performances by Gong Li, Jingwu Ma, Saifei He, China Film Co-Production Corporation, 1991.

———, director. *Red Sorghum*. Performances by Gong Li, Jiang Wen, Xi'an Film Studio, 1988.

———, director. *To Live*. Performances by Gong Li, You Ge, Shanghai Film Studio, 1994.

Zhen Xin (振鑫). "Old Soldier: Floating Corpse I and II." https://mirrorfiction.com/zh-Hant/book/10335/89158. Accessed 15 Aug. 2021.

Zhu Tianxin. "Thinking of My *Juancun* Brothers." *Thinking of My* Juancun *Brothers* (想我眷村的兄弟們). Maitian, 1998, pp. 67–90. https://book.qq.com/book-chapter/25456123.

INDEX

Absurd Accident (TV series), 39
Adventures of Huckleberry Finn, The (Twain), 199
Ah Q, 144, 144n2
AIDS villages (China), 115
Aladdin (film), 154
AlienAsian, 119–36, 208
alienation-effect (A-effect), 3, 19, 19n7, 119–36
alt-right, 89
American Century, 189, 204
American exceptionalism, 4, 43, 204, 210
Améry, Jean, 102, 102n1
Amrohi, Kamal, 54
anlian (secret crush), 66
Apocalypse Now (film), 148
Aristotelian, 30, 119–24, 131, 133
Awkwafina, 178

Ba Jin, 99–100
ba-zha (hegemon/tyrant vis-à-vis trash/loser), 65–70
Bai, Ronnie, 120n2, 122

Bai Fumei (White Rich Beautiful), 60–63
Bai Xianyong, 231–32
Baker, Jay, 206–7, 211
Bakhtin, Mikhail, 20
"Ballad of Mulan, The" (legend), 153–57
Barr, Allen H., 95
Bataille, Georges, 18
Battle Hymn of the Tiger Mother (Chua), 181
Beauty and the Beast (film), 154
Beauvoir, Simone de, 186
Beilein, Joseph M., Jr., 191n1
Belt and Road Initiative, 33
Benjamin, Walter, 96, 153
benshengren (this province people or Taiwanese), 221
Bentley, Eric, 131
Berg-Pan, Renata, 122, 128
Berry, Michael, 107–8
Best Partner, The (TV series), 39
Beyond the Pleasure Principle (Freud), 140, 200
Big Lie, 112

bildungsroman (Asian American), 188, 213
Billy Lynn's Long Halftime Walk (film), 194
bipolar America, 204–15
Black & White: The Dawn of Justice (film), 38
Black & White Episode 1: The Dawn of Assault (film), 38
Blade Runner (film), 98
Blue Kite, The (film), 103, 107, 116
Bluest Eye, The (Morrison), 60
Bodek, Richard, 121
Bollywood, 54
Boorstin, Daniel J., 195, 195n3, 198n4, 202
Botsford, Jabin, 206
Boublil, Alain, 137, 146–51
bound feet, 18n6
Breakfast at Tiffany's (film), 138
Brecht, Bertolt, 3, 19, 19n7, 119–36, 144–45, 148–49
Bride with White Hair, The (film), 46
Bridge across Broken Time (Schwarcz), 77
Broe, Dennis, 32n3
Brokeback Mountain (film), 194
bromance, 52
buddy movie, 49–50
Bui-Doi (mixed-race children fathered by American GIs), 147, 150
Bund (Shanghai), 41
bunraku (Japan's puppet theater), 58–59
Burke, Edmund, 30, 40
Burns, Ken, 201n6

cadre schools, (China), 87, 90–93
Cao Xueqin, 56
Cape No. 7 (film), 218n3
Carlyle, Thomas, 65
Caro, Niki, 152–62
Carter, Helena Bonham, 140n1
Cash, Jean W., 199n5
"casino capitalism," 30
Castelli, Alberto, 60n3
Chan Is Missing (film), 180
Chaney, Lon, 41
Chang, Sung-sheng Yvonne, 221n4

Chang'an Youth, The (TV series), 12
Chao, Antonia, 220–21, 233
Charlie Chan, 138
Chen, Joan, 178, 191
Chen, Lingchei Letty, 111
Chen Daoming, 103
Chen Kaige, 22, 68, 101, 103, 107, 115
Cheung, Maggie, 98
Chiang Kai-shek (Jiang Jieshi), 11, 110, 216
Children of a Lesser God (film), 22
Chin, Vincent, 209–10, 210n5
"China Dream," 43, 53
China in Ten Words (Yu), 36, 95, 115
Chinatown, 3, 59
Chinatown comedy, 165–90
Chinese Box (film), 98
Chinese Century, 2, 4, 10, 21, 27, 31, 49, 93, 188–89, 204, 210, 219
Chinese Communist Party (CCP), 9–28
Chinese Exclusion Act, 166–67, 170, 173–74, 178, 180, 209
Chinese Must Go! movement, 166
Chinese Paladin (TV series), 162
"Chinese virus," 206–7, 210
Chinglish, 166–67, 174–77
chinoiserie, 4, 127, 187n8
Chronicle of a Blood Merchant (Yu), 115
Chronicles of the Ghostly Tribe (film), 33, 38
Chu, Jon M., 178, 180, 188
Chu, Louis, 3, 167–81
Chua, Amy, 181
chuanyuewen (Chinese literature of temporal and spatial crossing), 44–45
Chung, Lee Isaac, 205, 212, 214
Chunhyang (film), 214
"CHY-NA" (Trump), 206–9
Close, Glenn, 70
Coleridge, Samuel Taylor, 122
Coming Home (film), 12, 95, 102–7, 116
commedia dell'arte, 100
Confessions of Nat Turner, The (Styron), 199
Confucius, 23, 31, 53, 158–59
cosmetic surgery, 60, 67, 178n7

INDEX • 255

"country noir," 193, 193n2, 195
COVID-19, 2, 153–55, 180, 204, 206–7, 210
Crazy Rich Asians (Kwan), 178, 188
Creation of the Gods (Lu and Xu), 11
Crosby, Bing, 144, 179
Crouching Tiger, Hidden Dragon (film), 128, 191, 194
Crow, Charles L., 43
Cultural Revolution, 2, 6, 9, 12, 14, 77–94, 97–100, 101–16, 132–33, 217
cyberbullying, 69

De Witte, Melissa, 78n1
DeLillo, Don, 131
Delirious New York (Koolhaas), 42n7
Demi-Gods and Semi-Devils (TV series), 162
Den Tandt, Christophe, 29–30, 40, 43
Dench, Judi, 145–46
Deng Xiaoping, 9, 23, 64–65, 101
Detective Chinatown (TV series), 39
Detention (film), 234–37
Dim Sum (film), 167n3, 180
Doctor Faustus (play), 54
doppelgangers, 31, 46, 129, 141, 189
Double Suicide (film), 58–59
Douglas, Kirk, 49
Dracula (Stoker), 157
Dream of the Red Chamber (Cao), 56, 59
Du Bois, W. E. B., 185

Eat a Bowl of Tea (Chu), 168–81
Eat Drink Man Woman (film), 191
Electra complex, 14, 225, 233
Elephant Man, The (film), 22
Eliot, T. S., 18, 172
Emperor and the Assassin, The (film), 22
Empresses in the Palace (TV series), 32
Eng, David, 138, 142, 168, 169n4, 178, 207n4
erectile dysfunction, 168, 173–74, 179. *See also* racial castration
Eros and Thanatos, 15, 20, 137, 140, 157, 200
Escher, M. C., 166, 167n2
Eye of the Storm, The (TV series), 31

Fanon, Frantz, 208
fanshen (flipping around from the prostrate position), 52–53
Fanshen (Hare), 131, 133–36
Farewell, The (film), 187–90
Farewell My Concubine (film), 103, 107, 115
Fatal Attraction (film), 70
Faulkner, William, 62
February 28 Incident in 1947, 226, 235
Fellman, Michael, 191n1
female impersonator, 3, 115, 119, 125, 145
Feng Jicai, 78
fifth-generation filmmakers, 2, 101, 107, 116
Flores, Helen, 51n10
Folsom, James K., 43
Forster, E. M., 32
Frankenstein, 219
Frears, Stephen, 143, 145–46
Freud, Sigmund, 15, 18, 56, 88, 121, 135, 140, 142, 156–57, 171, 171n5, 177, 200, 219, 233
Frontier Gothic (Mogen et al.), 31
Fu Manchu, 138
Fuegi, John, 119, 122, 127, 130

Galvez, Daphne, 51n10
Gao Fushuai (Tall Rich Handsome), 60–63
Gao Ye, 39–42
gao zhishang (high IQ), 66
gaoleng (tall and cold/cool), 66
Gearan, Anne, 206
Ghost Island (Taiwan), 6, 218–19, 222
Gilbert and Sullivan operettas, 150
Girl by the Road at Night, 138–39, 208
Go Ahead (or *Family*, TV series), 52
Golden Bracelet (maid character), 56
Golding, Henry, 178
Gong Li, 103, 152, 161–62
gong'an (Public Security or the Police), 13, 19
Good Lord Bird, The (TV series), 199
Good Woman of Setzuan, The, 119–27, 129–31
gothic supernaturalism, 2
Great Leap Forward, 107, 110–11, 133

Great Replacement (conspiracy theory), 49, 204
Great Wall, The (film), 12
Greene, Graham, 138–39
Greenspan, Anna, 36
Gross, David S., 43
Guan Guan, 223–24
guanxi (human relationship), 36, 89, 171, 182
guimi (boudoir confidantes), 2, 52–73
Gunfight at the O.K. Corral (film), 49
Guo, Shaohua, 30n2
Gülnezer Bextiyar, 12, 24

Hammerstein, Oscar, 150
Han Suyin, 138
Hannah, Daryl, 98
Hannibal Rising (film), 162
Hao Yuxiang, 232–34
Hare, David, 3, 119–21, 127–36, 137–46
Harte, Bret, 43, 43n8, 126n4
Hayot, Eric, 127, 129
Hearn, Lafcadio, 55
Heart of Darkness, The (Conrad), 63
Heroic Sons and Daughters (film), 97–100, 105
hero-worship, 65
Hinton, William, 127–28
Hirsch, Marianne, 103, 103n2, 222–24, 222n5
Holocaust in Anglo-American Literature, The (Ma), 77
Holocaust literature, 2
Horse Thief, The (film), 49
Hours, The (film), 139
House of Cards (TV series), 135
Hu, King, 160
Hua Mulan (film), 155, 161
Huallywood, 155
Hulk, The (film), 194
Hunchback of Notre Dame, The (film), 154
Hundred Flowers Campaign, 107
Hunter (TV series), 31, 42–51
Hurt, John, 22
Hwang, David Henry, 138

Iago, 31, 135
Ice Storm, The (film), 191, 194
Ideal City, The (TV series), 29, 31–42
If There Is No Tomorrow (TV series), 39
Ilha Formosa (Beautiful Island), 28
Im Kwon-Taek, 214
Imperial Doctress, The (TV series), 11
iQIYI (China), 66, 153, 155
Ito, Robert, 161

Jameson, Fredric, 47
Jia Baoyu, 56, 59
Jiang Wu, 22n8, 112n4
Jing Tian, 44, 47–48
Jing Yong (Louis Cha), 162
Journey to the West (Wu), 4, 11, 36
Ju Dou (film), 12
juancun (housing projects for mainland Chinese refugees), 221–22, 226–29, 231

Kaddish (prayer for the dead), 82
Kafka, Franz, 88, 88n4, 131
Keats, John, 61
Keith, Jeffrey A., 146
Kennedy, Randall, 199, 208
Khaou, Hong, 183–84
Kim Ki-duk, 64
Kingston, Maxine Hong, 58–60, 153–54, 181
knight-errantry. See *wuxia*
Koan, 19
Kobayashi, Masaki, 54–55
Koolhaas, Rem, 42n7
Korean Wave, 22
Ku Ling, 229–30, 232
"Kung Flu," 180, 206, 206n3
Kwaidan (film), 54–55
Kwaidan (Hearn), 55
Kwan, Kevin, 178, 188

Lang, Fritz, 104
Lao Mo's Second Spring (film), 224
laobing (old soldiers or veterans), 6, 216–37

laosanjie (old three years), 2, 101–16
Larsen, Nella, 182
Last of the Mohicans, The (film), 50
Lee, Ang, 3, 191–203
Lee, Jason Scott, 153
Levi, Primo, 78
Li, Jet, 22n8, 158
Li Ang, 219
Li Gengxi, 67
Li Xuejian, 22
Liang, Roseanne, 135–36
Life of Pi (film), 194
Lilting (film), 184
Lim, Louisa, 78, 94, 189
Lin, Brigitte, 46
Lin, Sylvia Li-chun, 226n6
Link, Eric Carl, 43
Literature of the Wounded (Scar Literature), 107
Little Mermaid, The (film), 154
Little Red Book, The, 9
Little Reunion, A (TV series), 67
Liu, Jin, 20
Liu, Yifei, 161–62
Liu Bei, 56–58
Liu Binyan, 104n3
Liu Daren, 227, 229
Liu Haocun, 96, 98
Long Yingtai, 223–24
Longest Day in Chang'an, The (TV series), 25
Lord of the Rings, The (film), 236
Lost Horizon (film), 179
Loti, Pierre, 138
Love Is a Many-Splendored Thing (film), 138, 208
"Love Song of J. Alfred Prufrock, The" (Eliot), 18
Lovell, Julia, 11
Lu Chuan, 49
Lu Xun, 10, 10n2, 133, 133n5, 144
lushe (loser), 69

M. Butterfly (play), 138, 208

Ma Xiu, 224–27, 230
Ma Ying-jeou, 223, 236
"Macao Suncity [Sun City] VIP Club," 25
Madame Butterfly (opera), 138, 146–47, 207
Madame Chrysanthème (Loti), 138, 207
Madame Mao (Jiang Qing), 102, 112, 132, 148
"Madman's Diary, A" (Lu), 10, 10n2
Maguire, Tobey, 196, 198, 201
Mahal (film), 54
"man-eat-man," 10
Mao Zedong (Mao Tse-tung or Chairman Mao), 9, 35, 86, 88, 92, 94, 112, 114, 134, 216
Map of the World, A (play), 139, 145
Marlow, Christopher, 54
Marshall, E. G., 143
Marxism, 3, 10, 12, 15, 29–30, 35–36, 63–65, 119n1, 120, 120n2, 127, 130–33, 189, 227, 236
Matchless Mulan (film), 153–55, 162
Matlin, Marlee, 22
McTell, Ralph, 27
Mei Lanfang, 19n7, 119, 121, 145, 150
Meidao (Beautiful Blade, US dollar), 23
Memoirs of a Geisha (film), 162
Mencius, 189, 190n9
Mengele (Nazi doctor), 85
Metropolis (film), 104
Miami Vice (film), 162
Miao, Cora, 178–79
Michener, James A., 138
Minari (film), 4, 204–15
Mining Town (TV series), 12–14, 19–21, 23–28
Minnelli, Liza, 179
Miss Saigon (musical), 137, 146–51, 208
Miss Truth (TV series), 12
Mitchell, David, 138
Mizumura, Minae, 62
Möbius strip, 167
Mogen, David, 31, 44
Moretz, Chloë Grace, 135–36
Morpheus (*Matrix* character), 1
Morrison, Toni, 60

Mountain Patrol (or *Kekexili*, film), 49
Mr. *Donkey* (film), 68
Mulan (Disney film), 3, 152–62
Murakami, Haruki, 59
Mutiny on the Bounty (film), 138

Nakata, Hideo, 55–56
Nationalist (Taiwan's Guomintang), 11
Neo (*Matrix* character), 1
Never Say Goodbye (TV series), 31, 50
Nezha, 11
Nietzschean, 90
Night (Wiesel), 79–86, 92–93
Night and Fog (film), 80
Nighy, Bill, 140n1
Noblezada, Eva Maria, 147
nongtang (Shanghai traditional housing), 39–43
Nordhoff, Charles, 138
Nothing but Thirty (or *Thirty*, TV series), 52
Novoland (TV series), 72
nuelian (abusive, sadomasochistic obsession), 66

Ocean Heaven (film), 22n8
off-white (yellow-ish), 3–4
1.5-generation, 168
One Second (film), 12, 14, 94–100, 105, 116
Oriental Pearl Tower, 31, 41
Orientalism, 3–4
Orphan of Asia (Wu), 218
Othello, 31
Outlaws of the Marsh, The (Shi and Luo), 11, 52, 134, 173

Page Eight (TV series), 139
Painted Skin (film), 46, 63
Pan Jinlian, 39, 173, 173n6
Pao, Angela, 147, 150–51
Park, Patricia, 60
Park Chan-wook, 200
Peking Opera (Beijing Opera), 3, 19n7, 115, 119, 125

People's Republic of Amnesia, The (Lim), 78, 94
"perennial aliens," 43, 167, 185, 192, 194, 198, 205, 209, 218
Phantom Heroine, The (Zeitlin), 54
Pigsy, 4
Platoon (film), 148
Plum in the Gold Vase, The (Lanling Xiaoxiao Sheng), 225
Pocahontas (film), 154
Pope, Alexander, 61
postmemory, 103, 103n2, 218, 222–23, 222n5
Pound, Ezra, 127, 150
Prisoner Lu Yanshi (Yan), 95, 102
Prison-House of Language, The (Jameson), 47
Promise, The (film), 68
Pryce, Jonathan, 147, 150–51
Pu Guanjin, 67–68
Pu Songling, 63
Puccini, Giacomo, 138, 146–47
Pushing Hands (film), 191

Qian Zhongshu, 79, 86–91, 112
Qin Hao, 44
Qiong Yao, 227
queerbaiting, 161
Quiet American, The (Greene), 138–39, 208

Rabe, David, 138–39
racial castration, 138, 142, 168, 169n4, 178, 207n4
Rainer, Louise, 130
Raise the Red Lantern (film), 12, 58–59
Rattan (TV series), 31, 42–51
Rayzha Alimjan, 24–25
Re Jane (Park), 60
Reader, The (film), 139
Reborn (TV series), 12–19
Red Detachment of Women, The (opera), 105
Red Lantern, The (opera), 132
Red Sorghum (film), 12, 25, 162
Red Star over China (Snow), 11
Resnais, Alain, 80

Return of the Condor Heroes, The (TV series), 162
Revolutionary Model Dramas, 46, 132, 148
Ride with the Devil (film), 191–203
Ringu (film), 46, 55–56, 59
Roadkill (TV series), 139
Romance of the Three Kingdoms (Luo), 52, 56–58
Rooney, Mickey, 138
Rowlandson, Mary, 49
Ruohua Ranran, 32
Rural Love Story (TV series), 19

Saigon (Hare), 137–46
Salonga, Lea, 147
Salting the Battlefield (TV series), 139
Saving Face (film), 181–88
Sayonara (film), 138, 208
Schamus, James, 191–202
Schönberg, Claude-Michel, 137, 146–51
Schwarcz, Vera, 77, 86, 90n6, 92n7
Sense and Sensibility (film), 194
Seong, Hyeon-a, 64
"Serve the People," 9
Shadow in the Cloud (film), 135–36
shadow puppets, 109–12
Shakespeare, William, 54
Shanghai (film), 162
Shanghai Future (Greenspan), 36
shanzhai (counterfeits), 10–12, 27, 95
Shen Fu, 79, 86
Shi Nai'an, 11
Shklovski, Viktor, 122
Shower (film), 22n8, 42n7, 112n4
shuenkouliu (a mellifluous doggerel), 61
Sida lienü (Four Fierce/Fiery/Righteous Women), 56
Sino-fi, 45, 45n9
Siteng (Control/Govern Rattan). See *Rattan*
Six Chapters from My Life "Downunder" (Yang), 79, 86–93
Six Records of a Floating Life (Shen), 79, 86
Sneider, Vernon J., 138

Snow, Edgar, 11, 131
social Darwinism (China), 2, 10, 12, 22n8, 29, 33, 43, 48–49, 63, 65
socialist ex machina, 119–21, 127, 131, 135–36, 148, 166
Sontag, Susan, 217
Sorensen, David R., 65n5
Spacey, Kevin, 135
split screen (China), 12, 14n4, 25
split screen (Taiwan), 28n9
Stanislavsky, Konstantin, 119–24, 128, 131, 133, 145
Steffin, Margarete, 130
Stevens, Wallace, 87
Stoker, Bram, 157
Strange, Susan, 30
Strange Tales from a Chinese Studio (Pu), 63
Strittmatter, Kai, 78
Styron, William, 199, 199n5
Su Tong, 58–59
Su Xiao's War (Ruohua Ranran), 32
Sun Li, 32
Suzuki, Koji, 59
Sweet Life (TV series), 31
Sympathy for Mr. Vengeance (film), 200

Taiwan Strait, 28, 32, 216, 226–27
Taking a Bath (Yang), 89n5
Taking Tiger Mountain by Strategy (opera), 132
Taking Woodstock (film), 194
Tan, Amy, 168, 174, 180
Tao of S, The (Ma), 43n8, 45n9, 126n4, 206n3
taonan (fleeing disaster), 216–18
Tatlow, Antony, 122, 129
Teahouse of the August Moon, The (film), 138, 208
Tennyson, Alfred Lord, 4
"Ten-Year Holocaust," 2, 77–93, 96, 102
Tet Offensive, 140
Theater Event, The (Wiles), 119, 119n1, 120n2, 129
"Thinking of My *Juancun* Brothers" (Zhu), 227–29

This American Life (radio show), 189
Thomas, Dylan, 167
Thousand Autumns of Jacob de Zoet, The (Mitchell), 138
Tian, Min, 122, 125–26, 129
Tian Zhuangzhuang, 49, 101, 103, 107
Tiananmen Square Massacre, 9–10, 78, 189
Tianyan (Sky Eye), 104
To Be with You (TV series), 12–13, 20–23
To Live (film), 102, 107–16
Todorov, Tzvetan, 46, 59–60, 60n2, 63
Torrents Trilogy, The (Ba), 100
Touch of Zen, A (film), 160
Trident (TV series), 31
Trump, Donald, 43n8, 49, 88–89, 112, 148, 180, 189, 203–6, 209–11, 215
Tseng, Eric, 178–79
Turks & Caicos (TV series), 139
Twain, Mark, 199
Twenty Your Life On (or *Twenty*, TV series), 52

Uighurs, 10, 12, 24, 86
Urban Sublime in American Literary Naturalism, The (Den Tandt), 29–30, 43
Us Three (Yang), 79, 87–89

Vacation of Love (TV series), 31, 39
vampire, 55, 157

waishengren (Taiwan's foreign province people or mainlander), 218–37
Wang, Andrea, 205n2
Wang, Lulu, 3, 187–90
Wang, Wayne, 3, 167n3, 168–81
Wang, Zhuoyi, 158
Wang Ruowang, 104n3
Warhol, Andy, 131
Waste Land, The (Eliot), 172
Watching It Again and Again (TV series), 64
Watts, Naomi, 59
Weaving a Tale of Love (TV series), 12
Wedding Banquet, The (film), 191

Wei Yu, 44
Weisz, Rachel, 140n1
well-being/s (human beings who have died in wells), 53–59
Wen Zhang, 22n8
White-Haired Girl, The (opera), 46
White Terror (Taiwan), 226–27, 226n6, 235–36, 236n10
Wiesel, Elie, 2, 78–86, 90, 92–93
Wiesel, Marion, 87
Wiles, Timothy J., 119, 119n1, 120n2, 129
Wilson, Charles Reagan, 203
Wolf Totem (Jiang), 31
Wolf Warrior (film), 31, 50
Woman Warrior, The (Kingston), 58–60, 153–54, 181
womance, 2, 52
Wong, Russell, 178, 189
Wong, Victor, 178–79
Woodrell, Daniel, 191–203
Wordsworth, William, 122
World of Suzie Wong, The (film), 208
Worricker, Johnny, 139, 140n1
Wu, Alice, 3, 166, 178, 181–88
Wu, Chia-rong, 219, 236, 236n10
Wu Cheng'en, 11
Wu Zhuoliu, 218
wuxia (swordsman), 50

Xi Jinping, 10, 13, 23, 29–31, 51, 53, 86, 106, 188–90
Xianniang (immortal woman), 152–62
Xiu Xiu (film), 191

Yan Geling, 95, 102
Yang, Dominic Meng-Hsuan, 228
Yang Jiang, 2, 78, 86–93, 89n5
Yeats, W. B., 96, 116, 116n5
Yellow Earth (film), 107
Yellow Peril, 3, 180
Yoshikawa, Yoko, 150–51
Youn Yuh-Jung, 211
Yu Hua, 36, 95, 107–8, 115

Zamperini, Paola, 58
Zeitlin, Judith, 54, 54n1, 63
Zhang, Wei, 125–26, 130
Zhang Dachun, 234
Zhang Fang, 224–25, 230
Zhang Yang, 42n7, 112n4
Zhang Yi, 14, 95
Zhang Yimou, 2, 12, 25, 58–59, 95–100, 101–16, 162
Zhang Ziyi, 70, 128
Zhao Benshan, 19–20
Zhao Jinmai, 16
Zhao Lijian, 31
Zhao Youting (Mark Chao), 32, 38
Zhen Xin, 234–35
Zhu Jinfeng, 217
Zhu Tianxin, 227–29, 231–32